PERSPECTIVES ON WRITING

Series Editor, Susan H. McLeod

PERSPECTIVES ON WRITING
Series Editors: Susan H. McLeod and Rich Rice

The Perspectives on Writing series addresses writing studies in a broad sense. Consistent with the wide ranging approaches characteristic of teaching and scholarship in writing across the curriculum, the series presents works that take divergent perspectives on working as a writer, teaching writing, administering writing programs, and studying writing in its various forms.

The WAC Clearinghouse and Parlor Press are collaborating so that these books will be widely available through free digital distribution and low-cost print editions. The publishers and the Series editor are teachers and researchers of writing, committed to the principle that knowledge should freely circulate. We see the opportunities that new technologies have for further democratizing knowledge. And we see that to share the power of writing is to share the means for all to articulate their needs, interest, and learning into the great experiment of literacy.

Recent Books in the Series

Beth L. Hewett and Kevin Eric DePew (Eds.), *Foundational Practices of Online Writing Instruction* (2015)

Christy I. Wenger, *Yoga Minds, Writing Bodies: Contemplative Writing Pedagogy* (2015)

Sarah Allen, *Beyond Argument: Essaying as a Practice of (Ex)Change* (2015)

Steven J. Corbett, *Beyond Dichotomy: Synergizing Writing Center and Classroom Pedagogies* (2015)

Tara Roeder and Roseanne Gatto (Eds.), *Critical Expressivism: Theory and Practice in the Composition Classroom* (2014)

Terry Myers Zawacki and Michelle Cox (Eds), *WAC and Second-Language Writers: Research Towards Linguistically and Culturally Inclusive Programs and Practices*, (2014)

Charles Bazerman, *A Rhetoric of Literate Action: Literate Action Volume 1* (2013)

Charles Bazerman, *A Theory of Literate Action: Literate Action Volume 2* (2013)

Katherine V. Wills and Rich Rice (Eds.), *ePortfolio Performance Support Systems: Constructing, Presenting, and Assessing Portfolios* (2013)

Mike Duncan and Star Medzerian Vanguri (Eds.), *The Centrality of Style* (2013)

Chris Thaiss, Gerd Bräuer, Paula Carlino, Lisa Ganobcsik-Williams, and Aparna Sinha (Eds.), *Writing Programs Worldwide: Profiles of Academic Writing in Many Places* (2012)

ANTIRACIST WRITING ASSESSMENT ECOLOGIES: TEACHING AND ASSESSING WRITING FOR A SOCIALLY JUST FUTURE

Asao B. Inoue

The WAC Clearinghouse
wac.colostate.edu
Fort Collins, Colorado

Parlor Press
www.parlorpress.com
Anderson, South Carolina

The WAC Clearinghouse, Fort Collins, Colorado 80523-1052

Parlor Press, 3015 Brackenberry Drive, Anderson, South Carolina 29621

Printed in the United States of America

Library of Congress Cataloging-in-Publication Data

Names: Inoue, Asao B., author.
Title: Antiracist writing assessment ecologies : teaching and assessing
  writing for a socially just future / Asao B. Inoue.
Description: Fort Collins, Colorado : The WAC Clearinghouse, [2015] | Series:
  Perspectives on writing | Includes bibliographical references and index.
Identifiers: LCCN 2015037961 | ISBN 9781602357730 (pbk. : acid-free paper)
Subjects: LCSH: English language--Rhetoric--Study and teaching
  (Higher)--United States--Evaluation. | English language--Rhetoric--Study
  and teaching (Higher)--Social aspects--United States. | Discrimination in
  higher education--United States. | Anti-racism--Study and teaching.
Classification: LCC PE1404 .I47 2015 | DDC 808/.0420711--dc23
LC record available at http://lccn.loc.gov/2015037961

Copyeditor: Don Donahue
Designer: Mike Palmquist
Series Editor: Susan H. McLeod

This book is printed on acid-free paper.

The WAC Clearinghouse supports teachers of writing across the disciplines. Hosted by Colorado State University, it brings together scholarly journals and book series as well as resources for teachers who use writing in their courses. This book is available in digital format for free download at http://wac.colostate.edu.

Parlor Press, LLC is an independent publisher of scholarly and trade titles in print and multimedia formats. This book is available in print and digital formats from Parlor Press at http://www.parlorpress.com. For submission information or to find out about Parlor Press publications, write to Parlor Press, 3015 Brackenberry Drive, Anderson, South Carolina 29621, or email editor@parlorpress.com.

CONTENTS

ACKNOWLEDGMENTS

This book, like all others, is the culmination of more than my efforts. In many ways, I'm simply the messenger, shouting the news to others. Over the last five years, I've had lots of help thinking, rethinking, conceiving, discussing, and reading drafts of what would become what you hold in your hands. First, I thank my wife, Kelly Inoue, without whom I cannot do what I do every day. She makes me a better teacher, father, husband, scholar, and person just by living her example of compassionate service. I live in her long shadow and am grateful for her patience and love. I thank Victor Villanueva, my mentor and friend, who read parts of Chapter 1, and has been a constant encouragement to me. I learned much from him and his work about race and racism, and about being cheerful in the face of so much wrong in the academy. Victor is my surrogate academic father. I thank Bill Condon, my other mentor, who introduced me to the field of writing assessment. He was often on my shoulder as I wrote and revised drafts of this book. His broad smile and his gentle deep voice is always guiding me. I thank Norbert Elliot, who in subtle ways always gives me things to learn, some of which ended up in this book. I thank Mya Poe, my PIC, my friend, and from whom I've learned so much. I feel so fortunate to work with her, even though we are usually on two different coasts. I thank Chris Anderson, my first mentor, friend, and colleague from Oregon State University, whom I asked to read an earlier version of the book and who gave me valuable and important ideas. His kind and careful feedback was instrumental in making this book what it is. He was also one of my first teacher models in college, one who taught me that cultivating a compassionate ear is always the best pedagogical stance to take. I also wish to thank the incredible folks at Parlor Press and the WAC Clearinghouse, Mike Palmquist and his editorial team who made this manuscript sparkle; Sue McLeod, my editor, who was wonderful, encouraging and helpful.

Thank you to my twin brother, Tadayoshi L. Inoue, who has supported, loved, helped, and challenged me my entire life. I am always and ever-mindful of how deeply blessed and fortunate every minute of my life has been (I was born four minutes after my brother) to be a twin, and know twin-love. He has been the rock I have always had the privilege and good fortune to stand on and next to.

And then there are a number of folks who helped me along the way through conversations and emails: Tom Fox, who read the entire manuscript, gave me thoughtful and insightful ideas that made the book better in tangible ways; Carmen Kynard, who always has good things to say and encouragement to offer;

Vershawn A. Young, my dear friend whom I can count on to push me and question everything; and Chris Gallagher, who offered crucial ideas to the guiding metaphor of the book (ecology) in a 45-minute meeting we had at Cs in Las Vegas. That meeting was the tipping point for me in thinking about the book and what it should ultimately be.

I offer a very special thanks to my graduate students at Fresno State, who were a constant source of inspiration, ideas, critiques, and joy while I was there. They taught and gave me more than I feel I ever offered them. And finally, I thank my undergraduate students at Fresno State, especially the students in my Fall 2012, English 160W course that make up much of Chapter 4, who often needed to have a lot of faith in me and what I asked of them. I am grateful for the labor and trust that each year my students give me and our classes. They are why I do what I do, and what makes my career, research, and life possible. I learn how to learn from them every year.

ANTIRACIST WRITING ASSESSMENT ECOLOGIES: TEACHING AND ASSESSING WRITING FOR A SOCIALLY JUST FUTURE

INTRODUCTION: WRITING ASSESSMENT ECOLOGIES AS ANTIRACIST PROJECTS

How does a college writing instructor investigate racism in his classroom writing assessment practices, then design writing assessments so that racism is not only avoided but antiracism is promoted? What I mean is how does a teacher not only do no harm through his writing assessments, but promote social justice and equality? In the broadest sense, this is what this book is about. It's about theorizing and practicing antiracist writing assessments in classrooms.

My assumption is that writing teachers should carefully construct the writing assessment ecology of their classrooms both theoretically and materially. In fact, we should continuously theorize and practice writing assessment simultaneously. So this book is about antiracist classroom writing assessment as theory and a set of practices that are productive for all students and teachers. I realize that thinking about race or racism in one's pedagogy and assessment practices will rub some readers wrong. They will say we need to move past race. It's not real, so we shouldn't use it theoretically or otherwise in our assessment practices. I do not deny that race is not real, that there is no biological basis for it, but biology is not the only criterion for considering something as real, or important, or worth discussing and addressing in our assessments. Because of this important concern by many who might read this book, I dedicate the first three chapters to addressing it in several ways. I think all would agree that we want classroom writing assessments to be antiracist, regardless of how we individually feel this project can be accomplished. This book is my attempt at finding a way toward this worthy end.

My main audience for this book are graduate students, writing teachers, and writing program administrators (WPAs) who wish to find ways to address racism in their classroom writing assessment practices, even those who may not be sure if such phenomena exist. In other words, I have in mind writing teachers who wish to cultivate antiracist writing assessments in their writing classrooms. Thus there are two strands in this book of interest to writing teachers: one concerns defining holistically classroom writing assessment for any writing teacher, which can lead to better designed and implemented writing assessments in classrooms; and one is about theorizing writing assessment in ways that can help teachers cultivate antiracist agendas in their writing assessment practices. In my mind, these are really the same goals. We cannot do one without the other. If we are to enact helpful, educative, and fair writing assessments with our students, given the history of whiteness and all dominant academic discourses promoted in schools and disciplines, we must understand our writing assessments as antiracist projects, which means they are ecological projects, ones about sustainability and fairness, about antiracist practices and effects.

Thus all writing teachers need some kind of explicit language about writing assessment in order to create classroom writing assessments that do all the things we ask of them in writing courses, and have the ability to continually (re)theorize and practice them better. Additionally, I see an audience in teachers who are looking to understand how to assess fairly the writing of their diverse student populations, which include multilingual populations, working class students, disabled students, etc. More specifically, I am interested in offering a usable theory of writing assessment that helps teachers design and implement writing assessments that are socially just for everyone. My focus, however, will be racism. I realize that race and racism are different things. Race is a construct. It's not real. But there are structures in our society and educational institutions that are racial. These structures help construct racial formations in the ways that Omi and Winant (1994) explain, which I'll discuss in Chapter 1.

Racism, on the other hand, is real. It is experienced daily, often in unseen ways, but always felt. We may call the racism we see something else, like the product of laziness, or just the way things are, or the result of personal choices, or economics, but it is racism. There are social patterns that can be detected. Thus, I do not use racism as a term that references personal prejudice or bigotry. I'm not concerned with that kind of racism in this book. I'm concerned with structural racism, the institutional kind, the kind that makes many students of color like me when I was younger believe that their failures in school were purely due to their own lacking in ability, desire, or work ethic. Racism seen and understood as structural, instead, reveals the ways that systems, like the ecology of the classroom, already work to create failure in particular places and associate it with particular bodies. While this book could focus on any number of dimensions that construct diversity in our classrooms, I have chosen race (and antiracism as a goal) because it has salience for me as a teacher, past student, and scholar. I am a teacher of color, a former working class student of color, who attended mostly or all-white classrooms in state universities. Racism was a part of the scene of teaching and learning for me, a part of my day-to-day life. I know it still exists, even in writing classrooms where good, conscientious teachers work.

But this could be my own demon, my own perceptions of things. Why articulate a theory of writing assessment around antiracism and suggest others use it? Why not let the second half of the book's title, teaching and assessing for a socially just future, be the main subject of the book? Beyond the ethical need to eradicate racism in our classrooms, racism is a phenomenon easily translatable to other social phenomena that come from other kinds of diversity in our classrooms (e.g., gender, sexual orientation, religious affiliation, linguistic differences, ethnic differences, disability, etc.). The dynamics are similar even though the histories of oppression are different. These other dimensions, of course, intersect and create what we often think of when we think of race, because race isn't real. It's fluid and broad. It's a construct we see into the system, which at this point the system (re)constructs through these other structures, like economics and linguistic differences (from a dominant norm). So the ways race and racism function in writing assessment, in my mind, epitomize larger questions around fairness and justice. Furthermore in the U.S., the default setting on most conversations, even about justice and fairness, is to avoid the racial, avoid speaking of racism. So I choose not to. The conversation needs to happen. It hasn't in writing assessment circles.

I'm mindful of Stephanie Kerschbaum's (2014) work on the rhetoric of difference in the academy. I realize I could be engaging in what she calls "taxonomizing difference," a theorizing that often "refuses to treat racial and ethnic categories as monolithic or governed by stereotypes by recognizing the variation within categories," but the categories offered tend to be "relatively static referents" (p. 8). This denies the individual ways that students exist and interact in language and in classrooms. Or I could be engaging in what Kerschbaum calls "categorical redefinition," which "focuses on producing more refined and careful interpretations within a specific category"(2014, p. 10), for example, my insistence throughout this book on seeing the Asian Pacific American students at Fresno State as primarily Hmong students. Both rhetorics of difference, according to Kerschbaum, can allow the researcher or teacher to place identifications and associate cultural and linguistic attributes to students instead of allowing any differences, and their nuances within supposed racial or ethnic categories, to emerge through actual interactions (2014, p. 9). So one dance I attempt in this book is to talk about race and racism in writing assessments without forgetting that every individual embodies their racial identity in unique linguistic and other ways. But there are patterns. We must not lose them in our attempt to acknowledge individuality.

More important, if you can see the way racism is one product of all writing assessments, then you can see the way biases against non-heterosexual orientations might be, or certain religious affiliations, or gender bias, or economic bias. The dynamics are similar. They are all dynamics of power, but they are not historically the same, and they are not just about bias or attitudes toward people. I'm not, however, suggesting that these dimensions of difference are equal in social weight or consequences, that the oppression experienced and felt by students who proclaim a Christian identity is on par with the issues that male African-American students on the same campus face, nor am I suggesting that any of these dimensions are separable. Of course, we cannot simply think of a student as one-dimensional, as her race, or her gender, or her sexual orientation, or her class upbringing. All these dimensions intersect and influence each other, creating individuals within groups who are as unique and different from each other within a racial formation as they are from those of other social groups. Kimberle Williams Crenshaw (1991) explains this phenomenon as "intersectionality," a dynamic of oppression in which multiple structures intersect, such as issues of class, economics, culture, and race. So when I speak of race in this book, I'm thinking in localized terms, ones that assume local racial formations' economic and other patterns as much as I'm thinking of racial structures. So while this creates diversity within locally diverse populations, we can still find patterns in those populations, as well as a few exceptions. The patterns come mostly from the structures people work in, and particular racial formations tend to be affected and moved by particular structures. This creates the racialized patterns. So I'm not interested in the exceptions, only the patterns. As a culture, we (the U.S.) focus too much on exceptions, often fooling ourselves into believing that because there are exceptions, the rule no longer exists or that it's easily broken by anyone with enough willpower or hutzpah.

In popular culture and talk, race is often a synecdoche for a person's physiognomy, heritage, culture, and language, even though these things cannot be known by knowing someone's self-identified racial designation, or by their physical appearance, or some other marker of race. Race is also easily seen by most people as a construct that should not be held against a student, nor should it be used to judge the merits of their labors, yet few deny that most large-scale writing assessments are racist, or at least reveal different performance patterns that are detected when results are disaggregated by racial formation. Many have already discussed the negative effects of various writing assessments on students of color (Fox, 1999; Inoue & Poe, 2012a, 2012b; Soliday, 2002; Sternglass, 1997; White & Thomas, 1981). Others have investigated the effects of a variety of large-scale tests on students of color (Hong & Youngs, 2008; Jencks & Phillips, 1998; Madaus & Clarke, 2001; Orfield & Kornhaber, 2001; Plata, 1995). We can find racist effects in just about every writing program in the country. We live in a racist society, one that recreates well-known, well-understood, racial hierarchies in populations based on things like judgments of student writing that use a local Standardized Edited American English (SEAE)[1] with populations of people who do not use that discourse on a daily basis— judging apples by the standards of oranges. Racism has always been a part of writing assessment at all levels.

Some may argue that I'm painting this picture of racism in writing assessments, in writing classroom assessments particularly, too broadly. I'm lumping the accurate judgment of performance of say some Blacks who do not perform well into the same category of writing assessments as those assessments that may exhibit cultural, linguistic, or racial bias in the judgments or decisions made. To put it bluntly, the argument is that sometimes students do not write well, and they should be evaluated accordingly, and sometimes those who do not write well will be Black or Latino or multilingual. Just because a writing assessment produces patterns of failure or low performance by students of color who participate in it doesn't mean the assessment is racist. This is an important argument. I do not argue to let students slide academically because they happen to be by luck of birth a student of color.

On the other hand, I see a problem with this argument. Why do more Blacks, Latinos, and multilingual students relatively speaking perform worse on writing assessments than their white peers in writing classrooms? At Fresno State, for instance, between 2009-2012, the average failure rate for Blacks in the first-year writing program was 17.46%, while the average failure rate for whites for the same years was 7.3% (Inoue, 2014b, p. 339). Whites have the lowest failure rates of all racial formations, and this is after the program revised itself completely in part to address such issues. That is, these are better numbers than in the years before. I realize that there are many ways to fail a writing class beyond being judged to write poorly, but these internally consistently higher numbers that are consistent with other writing programs suggest more, suggest that we cannot let such numbers pass us by just because we can assume that teachers are not biased.

I'm not saying we assume bias or prejudice. I'm saying let's assume there is no bias, no prejudice. Now, how do we read those numbers? What plausible assumptions can we make that help us make sense of these data, what rival hypotheses can be made? Do we assume that more Blacks, Latinos/as, and Asians at Fresno State are lazier or worse writers than their white peers? Is it the case that on average Blacks, Latinos/as, and Asians at Fresno State simply do not write as well as their white peers, that there is some inherent or cultural problem with the way these racial formations write? Or could it be that the judgments made on all writing are biased toward a discourse that privileges whites consistently because it is a discourse of whiteness? Could the writing assessment ecologies be racist?

I am mindful of the concern in the psychometric literature that mean scores (like those I cite above) do not necessarily constitute test bias (Jensen 1976; Reynolds, 1982a, 1982b; Thorndike, 1971). I'm not concerned, however, with test bias in the psychometric sense, which amounts either to intentional bias on the part of teachers, or a disregard for actual differences that do or do not exist among populations of people (Inoue & Poe, 2012b, p. 352; Reynolds, 1982a, p. 213). In one sense, I'm concerned with writing assessment as a much larger thing, as an ecology that is more than a test or an essay or a portfolio or a grade or a rubric. I'm concerned with what might broadly be called fairness in the ecology , which is a measure of its sustainability. In an important article on how legal definitions of disparate impact can be used to understand assessment consequences, Poe, Elliot, Cogan, & Nurudeen explain fairness: "the *Standards for Educational and Psychological Testing* provide four principal ways in which the term fairness is used: lack of bias; equitable treatment in the testing process; equality in testing outcomes; and the opportunity to learn" (2014, p. 592). I'm most concerned with the second, third, and fourth items, but the first is also a concern, only not in terms of individuals but bias in the ecology. For Poe and her colleagues, they see much of fairness in assessments hinging on whether an assessment has disparate impact, which can be understood through an assessment's methods. They explain:

> the *unintended racial differences in outcomes resulting from facially neutral policies or practices* that on the surface seem neutral. Because discrimination flows from the test design, process, or use of test scores, rather than from the intent of the test giver, disparate impact analysis focuses on the consequences of specific testing practices. (2014, p. 593)

In the end, Poe et al. see that "good decisions about our writing assessment practices for all students means attending to the various ways that we understand the impact of assessment on our students" (2014, p. 605). Yes. This is the impetus for antiracist writing assessment ecologies, fairness.

But wait, aren't we talking about the academic discourse that we've all agreed students must come to approximate if they are to be successful in college and elsewhere. This is what Bartholomae (1985) has discussed, and that perhaps more students of color have a harder time approximating than their white peers. If we are beyond the old-fashion bigotry and bias, then what we are saying is that there is something wrong with the academic discourse itself, something wrong with judging everyone against an academic discourse that clearly privileges middle class white students. In fact, there's something wrong with judgment itself in writing classrooms. Is this racism though? Is promoting a local SEAE or a dominant discourse that clearly benefits those who can use it properly, a racist practice?[2] When you're born into a society that has such histories of racism as we have, no matter what you think, what you do personally, you will participate in racist structures if you are a part of larger institutions like education, like the discipline of composition studies, or the teaching of writing in college. This doesn't make us bad people, but it does mean we must rethink how we assess writing, if we want to address the racism.

What should be clear at this beginning point is that racism is still here with us in our classrooms. You don't have to actively try to be racist for your writing assessments to be racist. As Victor Villanueva (2006) explains in an article about writing centers, we don't live in a post-racial society. We live in one that has a "new racism," one that uses different terms to accomplish the same old racial hierarchies and pathways of oppression and opportunity. We cannot eradicate racism in our writing classrooms until we actually address it first in our writing assessments, and our theories about what makes up our writing assessments. Baring a few exceptions, composition studies and writing assessment as fields of study have not focused enough attention on racism in classroom writing assessment. In the following pages, I attempt to make racism a more central concern in thinking about and designing classroom writing assessment.

MY PURPOSE AND SCOPE

This book attempts to theorize and illustrate an antiracist writing assessment theory for the college writing classroom by theorizing writing assessment as an ecology, a complex system made up of several interconnected elements. I ask: how can a conscientious writing teacher understand and engage in her classroom writing assessments as an antiracist project with her locally diverse students? My answer is to see classroom writing assessment as an ecology with explicit features, namely a quality of *more than*, interconnectedness among everything and everyone in the ecology, and an explicit racial politics that students must engage with. Additionally, this antiracist assessment ecology contains seven elements that can be reflected upon and manipulated. This means that when we design our writing courses, we must think first about how writing assessment will exist and function in the course, how it constructs the ecology that students and teachers work and live in, how it is sustainable and fair. In fact, I assume that all writing pedagogy is driven by the writing assessment ecology of the classroom, no matter what a teacher has done or how she thinks about her pedagogy, no matter what readings are discussed. Classroom writing assessment is more important than pedagogy because it always trumps what you say or what you attempt to do with your students. And students know this. They feel it. Additionally, writing assessment drives learning and the outcomes of a course. What students take from a writing course may not be solely because of the assessments in the course, but assessment always plays a central role, and good assessment, assessment that is healthy, fair, equitable, and sustainable for all students, determines the most important learning around writing and reading in a course.

In Chapters 1 and 2, I lay some groundwork for a theory of antiracist classroom writing assessment ecologies that addresses diversity and racial formations, and explain the metaphor of ecology. In Chapter 1, I discuss the importance of the concept of race as a nexus of power relations and the significance of racial formations in the U.S., defining racial *habitus* in the process. I identify specifically the hegemonic, the white racial *habitus* that is pervasive in writing classrooms and their dominant discourses. Additionally, I define racism, since it figures importantly in antiracist writing assessment ecologies. The focus on a white racial *habitus*, however, is important in understanding how writing assessment ecologies can be antiracist projects because it focuses attention on dispositions in writing and reading that are separate from the white body, structures that reproduce themselves in a variety of ways, yet historically these dispositions are associated with the white body. I end the chapter by defining local diversities, since diversity itself is a term fraught with problems, one of which is that it means such a broad range of things depending on what school or classroom one is referring to. I focus on racial diversity and give examples of locally diverse student populations at Fresno State in order to demonstrate the usefulness of the term. If classroom writing assessment ecologies are a way to conceive of antiracist assessment projects, then a clearly understood notion of local racial diversity is needed.

In Chapter 2, I theorize antiracist classroom writing assessment using Freire's problem-posing pedagogy, post-process theory, Buddhist theory, and Marxian theory. The chapter defines antiracist classroom writing assessment ecologies in three ways, as "more than" their parts, as productive, even limitless in what students can do and learn; as a system that is characterized by the interconnectedness of all that makes up assessment; and as a Marxian historic bloc, which uses Gramsci's famous articulation of the concept. Ultimately, I show how antiracist writing assessment ecologies provide for sustainable and fair ways to assess locally diverse students and writing, ways that focus on asking students to problematize their existential writing assessment situations by investigating the nature of judgment. These investigations compare a white racial *habitus* to those found in the classroom among students.

In Chapters 3, 4, and 5, I detail the elements that make up classroom writing assessment ecologies, use the theory to explicate my own classroom writing assessment practices, and offer a heuristic based on the ecological elements that can help teachers reflect upon and design their own antiracist classroom writing assessment ecologies. In Chapter 3, I explain the elements of a classroom writing assessment ecology. These elements can be used to explain, parse, and design any ecology. These seven elements are power, parts, purposes, people, processes, products, and places. Understood in particular ways, these elements offer richly explanatory potential for teachers. Among them are relationships that can also be explored in a similar way that Kenneth Burke (1969) describes ratios between elements in his dramatistic pentad. Seeing the relationships between elements in a writing assessment ecology can help students and teachers consider local consequences of the assessment ecology they co-construct. My discussion of these ecological elements is not meant to replace terms like validity or reliability, but enhance them, particularly for the writing classroom. I do not, however, attempt to make these connections or elaborations, as I believe writing teachers do not need such elaborations to design good, antiracist writing assessment ecologies, nor do their students need such language to participate and shape those ecologies.

In Chapter 4, I illustrate my theory of writing assessment as ecology by using it to describe and explain my own classroom, a writing course I taught in the fall of 2012 at Fresno State. I look most closely at several students' movement through the ecology from initial weeks to exiting the course, showing the way they reacted to the ecology and its unique writing assessment elements. I show how an antiracist ecological theory of writing assessment informs my class design, and helps me see what students understand and experience as more fully human beings, and what products they leave the ecology with. While I do not argue that my course was able to create an antiracist classroom writing assessment ecology, it comes close and offers insights into one. Ultimately, I argue that much can be gained by teachers and students when they think of their classrooms as antiracist writing assessment ecologies more explicitly, and I suggest ways that my classroom begins to do the antiracist work I encourage in this book.

In the final chapter, I offer a heuristic for antiracist writing assessment ecologies that I hope will be generative for writing teachers. The heuristic distills the previous chapters' ideas into a usable set of questions that may help teachers design and test their own antiracist classroom writing assessment ecologies. The heuristic is based on the discussion from Chapter 2 and the seven elements from Chapter 3. While I offer an extensive set of questions, they are only meant to be generative, not exhaustive. This closing discussion offers ways to think about the heuristic and what it offers and what critique the heuristic may provide to conventional writing assessment ecologies. I close the book with a few stories of writing assessment ecologies from my own past as a child and young adult in hopes that they reveal why racism and whiteness are important to consider in any classroom writing assessment ecology.

My project in this book, then, is to think holistically about what classroom writing assessment is or could be for teachers and students. It's about seeing classroom writing assessment in its entirety, not just parts of it, which we often do when discussing it. While I'll suggest here and there ways to think about writing assessment in large-scale settings, even use a few large-scale writing assessment examples, such as placement decisions or high stakes tests, large-scale writing assessment design, implementation, or validation are not the focus of this book. I do believe that an ecological theory of classroom writing assessment offers ideas toward large-scale writing assessment and its validation, but I am not engaging with discussions of large-scale writing assessment or its validity in the way that others have concerning cultural validity (e.g., Huot, 2002; Inoue, 2007, 2009c; Messick, 1989; Moss et al., 2008; Murphy, 2007; Ruth & Murphy, 1988).

In one sense, I am gathering together in one place vocabulary that writing assessment folks have used in various ways for years. We just haven't put it down in one place, assembled everything together to show what the entire ecology looks like and how it is experienced by students and writing teachers. We certainly haven't named it as an ecology, or considered it as an antiracist project. The closest we come is Ed White's *Teaching and Assessing Writing* (1994), but his account avoids a detailed discussion of race, cultural diversity, or multilingualism. And his discussion isn't about theorizing classroom writing assessment as a whole, or as an antiracist project. White is more practical. This is just as true for White's *Assigning, Responding, Evaluating: A Writing Teacher's Guide* (2007). Both are important introductions for teachers and WPAs when designing classroom writing assessments, or program assessments, but they don't attempt to theorize classroom writing assessment holistically and as an antiracist project in the way I do in this book. They don't draw on any literature outside of writing assessment or composition studies to make sense of race, racism, or whiteness, as I do.

One might argue that my project does not create new theory or understandings about writing assessment or its validation, classroom or otherwise. It simply repackages the same theory already adequately described by others applying yet another set of terms, ecological ones that are unnecessary. This is not true. By recasting writing assessment as an antiracist classroom ecology, I offer insights into writing assessments as complex systems that must be thought of as such, revealing them as more than what they seem, and suggesting what we might do better tomorrow, especially if we want to promote antiracist agendas. Understanding classroom writing assessment as an ecology that can be designed and cultivated shows that the assessment of writing is not simply a decision about whether to use a portfolio or not, or what rubric to used. It is about cultivating and nurturing complex systems that are centrally about sustaining fairness and diverse complexity.

While a teacher could use a theory of writing assessment as ecology without having an antiracist agenda for her classroom, I have couched my discussion in these terms because an antiracist agenda in the writing classroom is important and salient to me and many others. Some writing assessment theorists would speak of this goal in terms of designing a classroom writing assessment that is valid enough for the decisions a classroom teacher intends to make, say to determine a course grade and a student's readiness for the next course. They might speak of bias or disparate impact. I have purposefully stayed away from such language, although I have engaged in that theorizing in other places by discussing the way writing assessment can be theorized as a rhetorical act that can be mapped to the ancient Hellenic discussions of *nomos-physis* (Inoue, 2007), and by discussing writing assessment as a technology that helps us see racial validity (Inoue, 2009c).

However, I have found that many writing teachers are turned off by the language of psychometrics, and it doesn't make any clearer what we need to do in the classroom, nor does it help students understand their roles and responsibilities in the ecology without a lot of reading into the literature of educational measurement and psychometrics. Additionally, these discussions are more concerned with program assessment, not classroom writing assessment, the main difference being that the latter is conducted exclusively by teachers and students for their purposes, purposes of learning. So using the language of psychometrics and educational measurement is not directly helpful for classroom writing assessment, even though it could be. A different set of accessible terms are needed for teachers and students. In fact, the old psychometric terms can be a barrier for many teachers to thinking carefully about classroom writing assessment because most are not familiar with them and many see them connected to positivistic world views about language and judgment.

I have been tempted to use the language that Patricia Lynne (2004) uses to help redefine the psychometric terms used in writing assessment, which agree better with the common social constructivist assumptions that most in literacy studies, English studies, and composition studies hold about language and meaning. Lynne's terms are "meaningfulness" and "ethicalness," which she uses to replace the psychometric concepts of validity and reliability. Lynne explains that meaningfulness references the "significance of the assessment" and "structures the relationships among the object(s) of writing assessment, the purposes of that assessment and the circumstances in which the assessment takes place" (2004, p. 117). Meaningfulness urges two questions for teachers to ask: "why is the assessment productive or necessary or appropriate?" and "what [do] assessors want to know and what [do] they need to do to satisfy their defined purposes?" (Lynne, 2004, p. 124, 125).

Ethicalness, on the other hand, "addresses the broad political and social is-

13

sues surrounding assessment," and "organizes and provides principles for understanding the conduct of the participants and the procedures for evaluation" (Lynne, 2004, p. 118). It can urge writing teachers to ask: "who is involved in the decision-making?" and "what procedures will the assessment requir[e]?" (Lynne, 2004, p. 138). Lynne's terms are perhaps more usable and friendly to writing teachers generally, but they don't explicitly account for all of the elements that move in and constitute any ecology, elements that writing teachers should be aware of since they are part of the ecology's design. These terms also do not account for the relationships among elements in an assessment that make it more fittingly an ecology. As Lynne's questions suggest, her terms account for an assessment's purposes, people, power (politics), and processes (procedures), but not explicitly or systematically, not in interconnected ways, and it could be easy to ignore or take for granted the parts, products, and places within classroom writing assessment ecologies. Most important, Lynne's terms do not account for whiteness, or the ways local diversities complicate the judging of writing by a single standard, even though her terms could.

If there is one ecological element that may be the best synecdoche for the entire ecology, it is place. Antiracist writing assessment ecologies, at their core, (re)create places for sustainable learning and living. This is their primary function, to create places, and I think we would do well to cultivate such assessment ecologies that self-consciously do this. Ultimately, I hope to show less conventional ways of understanding and enacting classroom writing assessment, since conventional ways have not worked well in reducing the racial hierarchies and inequalities we continue to see in schools and writing classrooms. Conventional writing assessment practices rarely if ever dismantle the racism in our classrooms and schools because they do not address whiteness in the dominant discourse as hegemonic and students' relationship to it.

Let me be very clear. Racism in schools and college writing courses is still pervasive because most if not all writing courses, including my own in the past, promote or value first a local SEAE and a dominant white discourse, even when they make moves to value and honor the discourses of all students, as the Conference on College Composition and Communication's statement of Students' Right to Their Own Language asserts (CCCC, 1974; reaffirmed in 2003). I will discuss in Chapter 1 why this is still the case, although given what we can easily see in SAT scores, college admissions, and failure rates in writing programs, the case is made by the racialized results we live with today, where students of color do worse than their white peers. And unlike many teachers who see critical pedagogies alone as the way toward liberation and social justice for students of color and multilingual students, I see things differently. The problems of racism in writing classrooms are not primarily pedagogical problems to solve alone. *Rac-*

ism is an assessment problem, which can only be fully solved by changing the system of assessment, by changing the classroom writing assessment ecology. Thus assessment must be reconceived as an antiracist ecology.

But when I say "writing assessment," what exactly am I talking about in this book? For writing teachers, I've found no better way to describe the range of judging that teachers do than Stephen Tchudi's (1997) description in his introduction to *Alternatives to Grading Student Writing*. Tchudi characterizes the degrees of freedom in various acts of judging student writing, which move from a high degree of freedom and low degree of institutional pressure in acts of responding to a limited degree of freedom and high degree of institutional pressure in grading. He offers four basic acts of judging, which I refer to generally in this book as "writing assessment":

- **Response.** "naturalistic, multidimensional, audience-centered, individualized, richly descriptive, uncalculated";
- **Assessment.** "multidimensional, descriptive/analytic, authentic, problem solving, here-and-now, contextualized criteria, formative/process-oriented";
- **Evaluation.** "semi-deminsional, judgmental, external criteria, descriptive/analytic, rank ordering, future directed, standardized, summative";
- **Grading.** "one-dimensional, rewards/punishments, rank ordering, not descriptive, a priori criteria, future directed, one-symbol summative" (Tchudi, 1997, p. xiii)

Thus when I refer to activities, processes, judgments, or decisions of assessment, I'm speaking mainly of the above known kinds of judgment, which all begin with processes and acts of reading. As you can see from Tchudi's descriptions, response is freer and more open than assessment, which offers an analytic aspect to judgments on writing but less freedom than responses. Meanwhile, evaluation is even more restrictive by being more judgmental and summative than assessment, while grading is the most limited of them all, since it is one-dimensional and not descriptive.

We must be careful with using such distinctions, however. Thinking about classroom writing assessment as essentially a kind of judgment or decision whose nature is different depending on how much freedom or institutional pressure exists in the judgment misses an important aspect of all classroom writing assessment that my ecological theory reveals. All of the above kinds of judgments are based on processes of reading student texts. Assessment as an act is at its core an act of reading. It is a particular kind of labor that teachers and students do in particular material places, among particular people. This means that the nature of any kind of judgment and the institutional pressure present is contingent on

15

the ecology that produces it and the ecologies that surround that ecology. So while these distinctions are useful, they become fuzzier in actual practice.

WHY ECOLOGY AND AN ANTIRACISM AGENDA?

You may be wondering, what am I adding to the good work of writing assessment folks like Brian Huot, Peggy O'Neill, Bob Broad, Ed White, Bill Condon, Kathleen Yancey, and others who have written about writing assessment in the classroom? While very good, very conscientious scholars and teachers who have much to teach us about validity, reliability, the nature of judgment, portfolios, and reflection (self-assessment), none of these scholars use any race theory, postcolonial theory, whiteness theory, or Marxian theory to address racism in writing assessments of any kind, but especially writing assessments in the classroom. To date, I have seen nothing in the literature that incorporates a robust racial theory, Marxian theory, postcolonial theory, or a theory of whiteness to a theorizing or practical treatment of classroom writing assessment. My ecological theory of writing assessment incorporates such theories because such theories offer a way to understand the ecology of people, environments, their relationships, and the politics involved.

Thus what I address is the fact that students of color, which includes multilingual students, are often hurt by conventional writing assessment that uncritically uses a dominant discourse, which is informed by an unnamed white racial *habitus*, which we see better when we use analytical tools like postcolonial theory, whiteness studies, and Marxian theory. A theory of writing assessment as ecology adds these theories to our thinking about classroom writing assessments. Thus it doesn't matter if teachers or readers see or read student writing with prejudice or with a preference for whiteness in their classrooms. It doesn't matter at all. What matters is that the assessment ecology produces particular results, determines (in the Marxian sense) particular products, reinforcing particular outcomes, which make racist cause and effect difficult (even impossible) to discern. What matters is that writing teachers and students not only have a vocabulary for thinking about writing assessment in its most complete way, but that that vocabulary be informed by other pertinent theories. Having such a vocabulary offers explicit and self-conscious ways to problematize students' writing assessment situations, a central activity in antiracist writing assessment ecologies.

I've made a bold claim above about some very fine writing assessment scholars, so let me illustrate how racism in writing assessment often gets treated (or avoided) by scholars and researchers by considering one very good writing assessment scholar, Brian Huot, one we would all do well to listen to carefully. My goal is not to demean the fine work of Huot. In fact, I am inspired by his trailblazing, by his articulation of key connections between writing assessment and student learning, and his advocacy for composition studies as a field to know more about the literature of writing assessment (mostly the psychometric and educational measurement literature) in order to do our work better, but I argue that we must now cut a broader trail, one that offers us additional theories that help us explicitly understand racism in writing assessment.

In his important work *(Re)Articulating Writing Assessment for Teaching and Learning*, Brian Huot (2002) discusses writing assessment as a field and a set of classroom practices. In Chapters 3 and 5, he focuses explicitly on classroom writing assessment. In Chapter 3, he argues convincingly that writing teachers need to teach students how to assess writing themselves in order to help students become better writers. He says, "[a] crucial missing element in most writing pedagogy is any experience or instruction in ascertaining the value of one's own work" (2002, p. 67). In short, we must teach assessment to students, so that they can understand the nature of judgment and value, which in return makes them more critical and effective writers. To do this, he promotes what he calls "instructive evaluation," which "involves the student in the process of evaluation … in all phases of the assessment of her work" (2002, p. 69). Instructive evaluation focuses attention on how judgments are made through the processes of reading student texts. In many important ways, I have tried to take up Huot's call by engaging students in the full cycle of writing assessment through a cycle of rubric creating, drafting, judging, revising, and reflecting on the ways students read and make judgments on peer's texts (Inoue, 2004). I call it "community-based assessment pedagogy," and I still use a version of it today, which I show in Chapter 4. I extended this pedagogy by arguing for writing teachers to teach the rhetoric of writing assessment (Inoue, 2010), which offers students ways to understand the nature of valuing and judgment, which provides them with ways to write from more critical and informed stances. So Huot—and particularly *(Re)Articulating*—has helped me to understand a long-term pedagogical and scholarly project, of which the present book is a continuation.

But in his discussion of teaching assessment to students, or involving them in the full cycle of assessment, there is no mention of the ways that the judgments possible or the dominant discourse that informs those judgments are already constructed by racial structures, for instance, a white racial *habitus*, or a dominant white discourse, which we might for now understand as a set of linguistic codes and textual markers that are often not a part of the discourses of many students of color, working class students, and multilingual students, but is a part of many white, middle-class students' discourses.

To illustrate, imagine that we are Olympic-level sprinters, and we've been tasked to bring together all the athletes from the Olympic games in order to determine how good of an athlete everyone is by measuring how fast everyone runs a 400-meter sprint. We use this measure because it seems a good measure to us. We are conscientious and caring. We really are trying to be fair-minded to all so we judge everyone by the same standard, but we only know how to judge a 400-meter sprint. It's what we know. Sure, we will do fine. Sprinters will be judged highly, but what of those curlers, or the snowboarders, or the swimmers, or the archers, or the skiers, or the tennis players, or the water polo players, or the wrestlers? You get the idea. In the name of finding a consistent (i.e., fair) way to judge everyone by the same standard, we have made an unfair assessment of athletic prowess by narrowing our definition of what it means to be an athlete, by ignoring the diversity of athleticism. Racism in the writing classroom often works in similar ways. We define "good" writing in standard ways that have historically been informed by a white discourse, even though we are working from a premise that attempts fairness.

In fact, when writing classroom assessments do not account for whiteness or the dominant discourse's relation to various racial formations in the class, and that discourse is used to make judgments on writing and writers, racism is bound to happen. It is systemic that way. Consider Huot's closing words on using assessment to teach writing:

> Using assessment to teach requires the additional steps of having students apply discussions of writing quality to their individual texts or compile criteria for individual papers that they can discuss with a teacher or peer group. Students can only learn the power of assessment as they can other important features of learning to write—within the context of their own work. Learning how to assess entails more than applying stock phrases like *unity, details, development,* or *organization* to a chart or scoring guideline. Students and teachers can use these ideas to talk about the rhetorical demands of an emergent text, so that students could learn how to develop their own critical judgments about writing. This creation of a classroom pedagogy for assessment should provide students with a clearer idea about how text is evaluated, and it should work against often nebulous, underdeveloped, and unarticulated ideas they have about why they like a certain piece of writing or make certain revisions. (2002, p. 78)

Certainly, this is a good way to understand writing assessment in the classroom as pedagogical in very tangible ways, important ways, ways that as I've mentioned above I've been inspired by. I'm invested in this kind of pedagogy of assessment. I do not knock this aspect of Huot's ideas: that we teach students how to understand the nature of judgment in informed ways, ways that begin with their own writing, but the above articulation avoids discussing race as an important part of the student's subjectivity as a reader and writer, and thus as an important part of the inquiry into the nature of judgment.

Given this, I pose a question: when students discuss writing quality or compile criteria for a rubric, when they use ideas like "unity, details, development, or organization" to "talk about the rhetorical demands of an emergent text" as more than "stock phrases" —all excellent things to do—how will they negotiate the ways that any "text is evaluated" against a dominant white discourse? How will they confront the fact that most of the time evaluation, whether it's a teacher's or students', in a writing course means a set of hegemonic dispositions toward texts? How will they understand past or present evaluations of texts, of their own texts, as more than an individual's failure to meet expectations or goals, but also as a confluence of many other structures in language, school, and society, forming expectations they (and their teacher) have little control over?

While I do not think Huot means for this to happen, I can see how a class that engages in such a pedagogy can easily turn into a class that asks students to approximate the academic dispositions of the academy (whatever that may mean for that class) without any explicit way of interrogating the system that asks for such texts, or such evaluation of texts. I can see the course missing important opportunities to interrogate the dominant discourse as normative, or interrogating the hegemonic ways of evaluating texts in classrooms, some of which are rhetorical in nature. It is one thing to investigate how a judgment is made and how to articulate one's judgments in order that they may help writers in some way, but it is an entirely different reflective process to investigate the ways judgments on our writing, and the judgments we make, participate in larger normative discourses that have uneven effects on various groups of people, that privilege some students over others. And it is yet another thing to link these ways of judging to the historically reproduced dispositions of whiteness.

Huot's good theorizing misses these opportunities, which leaves open the chance for racist effects in the writing assessment. He seems to be more concerned with students' inability to articulate their judgments of texts in ways that are rhetorical (again, a good thing to focus on in a classroom), but this is at the expense of seeing those rhetorical ways of judging as hegemonic, as historically connected to broader dispositions toward texts that are not necessarily universal but rather are part of dominant white academic discourses, which sets up a hierarchical system of privileging through the valuing of texts. The hierarchy, while not intended to be, turns out often to be racist.

To his credit, Huot does not ignore racism in writing assessment altogether.

In Chapter 5, Huot centers on the most important process of any classroom writing assessment, reading and forming feedback to students about their writing or themselves as writers. Through a look at the literature on response, he notes that the field has no formal theory of response. What we have are various accounts, as good as they are, of how to respond to student writing, such as Straub's important work (1996a; 1996b; 1997; 2000). He concludes about the literature of the field: "the focus is once again only on practice, with little attempt to see response within a theoretical, pedagogical, or communicative context" (p. 111). In his move toward a theory of reading and response, a start at filling this theoretical gap in the literature, Huot discusses Arnetha Ball's (1997) very good study on the reading practices of African-American and European-American teachers, which turns out to be different along racial lines. He admits that at least in this case, "teachers with different cultural orientations saw very different things in student writing" (2002, p. 117). This, however, is the end of his comment. He moves from summarizing Ball's study of race in a writing assessment, which he reads as culture, to talking about Sarah Freedman's (1984) work, which talks about the culture of schools generally, how they construct roles and expectations for students and teachers. After Freedman, he discusses Faigley's (1989) important essay, "Judging Writers, Judging Selves," which helps him identify the ways that readers are situated historically and so have historically changing tastes that affect the way we read and judge student writing.

Huot's transition from Ball to Freedman is telling in the way he treats race, and by implication racism. He says, "[i]t's important in talking about the influence of culture in teacher response that we not forget that school itself is a cultural system bound by specific beliefs and attitudes" (2002, p. 117). True enough. No argument here. But what about racism, isn't that an historical set of beliefs, tastes, and practices too? There is no connection to race or racist practices. Ball's findings do not come up again. It is important to note again, however, that race is not real, but racism is. And it's racism that must be considered first.

This avoidance of any deep treatment of racism in his discussion becomes more problematic near the end of this otherwise fine chapter. Huot builds to a very intriguing model for teachers and students for "moving toward a theory of response" (2002, p. 132). There are five elements to the model, but there is no explicit way to interrogate or understand racism in practices in the model. The model offers as its most important term, "context," which is informed surely by the work of Ball and his earlier discussion. Not surprisingly, context is the center of the visual model, and the other four elements revolve around it, influencing it. Context is described as: "Particular writer, particular moment of a particular work in a particular curriculum, particular institution, particular issues, and particular audiences" (Huot, 2002, p. 132). With all these particulars, one might think that teachers shouldn't ever think in terms of larger social patterns or effects, or should treat every reading and response scene as one in which we cannot judge it next to others. This means that every judgment, every assessment of every student is unique. In this way, the model attempts to resist being racist by using the abstract liberal tenant of individualism (e.g., we are all unique). It theorizes that the particulars of any context determine what we do, how we read, why we read, what meaning or judgments we can make, etc. But it resists acknowledging in any way race or racism as a phenomenon, resists noticing or acting on larger patterns. By referencing individualism, by referring to all students as individuals, the model loses the ability to see broader patterns by any number of social dimensions. It resists seeing and acting against racism as structural. To many, this model would amount to not seeing racism, ignoring it, then saying that it doesn't matter. It may not matter, but you cannot know that until you investigate it.

There are many good things about Huot's theorizing of context for reading and response; however, treating every student as a unique student, as a particular student, isn't in contradiction to seeing racism as affecting our students of color, seeing larger, broader patterns that reveal the uneven relations to the dominant discourse and the judgments it promotes as unevenly tilted in favor of white students. But this nuance, even in a very nuanced and complex model for reading and responding, is lost because of the way Huot does not treat racism in his discussion. In part, this is because those in the field of writing assessment do not have vocabularies to help them discuss racism.

Most important, Huot's avoidance of considering racism in his discussion is the larger cause of this theory of reading and responding to lack a necessary attention to an antiracist agenda, which I know he would want to promote. Through it all, Huot, like most others, never attempts to understand context or historically changing values in reading, for instance, through other theoretical lenses that could help reveal racism, such as those of postcolonialism, whiteness studies, and Marxian theories, which could reveal ways that historically changing tastes and values may be influenced by historically changing racial formations in various schools, or the particular manifestation of whiteness in an assessment, or the historical structures of racism that affect who goes to school when and where at what times in U.S. history. This lack of treating racism makes it invisible in this otherwise very good theory of reading and response, which is the thrust of Huot's chapter.[3]

ABOUT THE RESISTANCE TO RACISM

I get a lot of resistance to explicitly thinking about race and racism in discussions of writing assessment, or I get silence, which I take as one form of resistance. This probably is an unfair assessment of some, I realize, but these discussions in hallways, classrooms, conferences, and over email are a part of why I write this book. And I feel it necessary to address these resistances in this introduction as a way to conclude it.

What troubles me are people who look at racial inequalities, look at racism in writing classrooms and programs, like the numbers and statistics I show later in this book and say, "how do we know that is racism?" My mind often whirls at such questions. Forget for a moment how it happened, inequalities are here. No African-Americans in your classes, few in your school. Where are the Native Americans? Most who are there, do not do well. They fail. Why? Isn't it enough to see such patterns? Does it really matter whether readers envisioned Latino or Black writers when they judge blindly the writing on the SAT writing exam or the English Placement Test (EPT) in California, which I discuss later in this book, or the writing of African-American students in first-year courses at Fresno State, the ones with a higher failure rate than any other racial formation? Here's what matters to me. White students uniformly and historically do better on most if not all writing assessments, large-scale or classroom. It may not be intentional, but it is racism, and it is a product of the writing assessment ecologies we create. Do not get me wrong. I do not blame white students or teachers. I blame writing assessments.

Richard Haswell disagrees with me to a degree, but he voices an important critique of the use of racism as a concept and goals in writing assessments. In his review of *Race and Writing Assessment* (Inoue & Poe, 2012a), Haswell's (2013) central critique of the book is that there is a contradiction in any investigation of racism in writing assessments. He says, "People cannot go about eliminating racism without constructing the notion of race, and the construction of race can only further racism" (Haswell, 2013). A little later, he makes an even more direct claim, which can be read as a criticism of the present book and its antiracist project: "any writing assessment shaped by anti-racism will still be racism or, if that term affronts, will be stuck in racial contradictions" (2013). What follows are a discussion of four "racial aporias" that we live with because we live with the contradiction of race.

The fourth aporia that Haswell identifies is one about the subject position of the researcher or teacher in an antiracist writing assessment project, such as the one this book attempts to articulate. He states it this way: "Writing scholars position themselves outside institutional racism to understand it but their understanding concludes that there is no outside" (2013). The point that Haswell is making is that no one can escape their own racial subjectivity or the structural influences in society and school that make up what we call race and racism. We taint our own efforts at antiracist writing assessments. Of the contributors of the collection, Haswell claims, "None of them voice the possibility that this pervasiveness of racial formations might include their own relations, conceptions, and identities," and he concludes, "the editors note that their book, which repeatedly castigates the stylistic criterion of high academic English as a racial formation, is entirely written in high academic English" (2013).

I do not deny these observations at all, but they do not make an antiracist project of any kind, including an antiracist writing assessment theory, impossible to do or wrong-headed. On the contrary, because we are all implicated in racism in our classrooms and in society, because race is already constructed for us historically, because racism already exists, because we already live in racial contradictions, we should be engaging in antiracist projects. The use, for instance, of a Standardized Edited American English (SEAE), a hegemonic discourse, is not an indicator of racism on my part because of what and why I say what I do. No, my discourse is an indicator of my subversive success at making a local SEAE and dominant discourse my own, making that discourse less white and more universal by diversifying it, and pushing us all to interrogate our uses of it in our classrooms. I've worked hard to have the voice I have in the academy, made some linguistic sacrifices, changed my ways with words and my dispositions toward texts, but I'd argue my voice and what it says changes the academy too, just as others' voices have.[4] SEAE, of course, is often a racial marker, a marker of whiteness, but not a marker of one's racial formation, nor a marker of racism unless it is used against students in a writing assessment as the standard. Its use by a researcher or teacher isn't necessarily a racist act, neither is identifying those standardized structures as racialized, and people who historically have been racialized by them. The point isn't to get rid of race. Race is one way we mark diversity and complexity, difference. The point is to get rid of racism, unfair racialzied hierarchies. Haswell would have me avoid race completely in hopes that it withers and dies for lack of attention, which then creates a nonracist world. But to deny race is just another way to deny diversity, which is natural and needed in all systems. So it is how writing assessments deploy discourses and judgments that make them racist not our references to difference.

As Haswell notes, there are contradictions, aporias. SEAE is learned, but not always by choice. I will be the first to admit that I lost my ghetto English a long time ago (but not the swearing) for the wrong reasons, for racist reasons. I cannot help that. I was young and didn't understand racism or language. I just felt and experienced racism, and some of it was due to how I talked and wrote in school. I was captivated by the kind of English I read in the first few books of my literary life, *White Fang, Lord of the Flies, To Kill a Mockingbird*. It sounded smart and clever, even magical, magical in the ways that Gorgias speaks of language in his famous fragment, *Encomium of Helen*. Language bewitched me quite literally. Part of that spell had racist components. Since then, I've come to see that language as a hegemonic discourse that, like all others, can be helpful and harmful depending on how it is used and what it communicates.

I don't expect everyone to see my project as the best beginning to antiracist writing assessments, but don't tell me there isn't racism in writing classrooms. Don't tell me we can ignore it and that doing so will make it go away. Don't tell me we shouldn't see race and that's the answer to racism. Doing so tells me that my experiences of racism in school and out are just figments of my imagination, that they must have been something else, that we just cannot know if there is racism anymore, that we just have to ignore it and all will be well, that we just wait a little while longer. As a middle-aged man, I know better. Waiting is complicity in disguise. I've seen and experienced too much. It ain't my imagination. Any denial of racism in our writing assessments is a white illusion. It upholds a white hegemonic set of power relations that is the status quo. It is in the imagination of those too invested in a white racial *habitus*, regardless of their racial affiliation. Hell, I denied it when I was younger. I had to. It would have eaten me alive, and I likely would not be able to do what I do today if I hadn't. More aporias around racism.

CHAPTER 1: THE FUNCTION OF RACE IN WRITING ASSESSMENTS

In order to understand why an antiracist project is so important to any classroom writing assessment ecology, even before I define that ecology, the concepts of race, racial formation, and racism need to be discussed and defined. Therefore in this chapter, I argue for a term, "racial *habitus*," as a way to understand the function of race in writing assessment ecologies, making all writing assessment ecologies racial projects of some kind.[5] I distinguish racial *habitus* from Omi and Winant's (1994) term, "racial formations," which I use to refer to the actual people that populate schools and writing classrooms. I discuss the term "racism," which might initially be understood as a larger set of historical structures, assumptions, and effects (or consequences) of any racial project. Through my discussions of racial *habitus* and racism, I address several criticisms or resistances by those who may feel that a focus on racism in classroom writing assessment ecologies may be misguided or wrong. What I hope to make clear is that we have no choice in thinking about racism in our writing assessments. And if we care about antiracist or social justice projects in the writing classroom, we need to care about and address explicitly the way race functions in our classroom writing assessments. Thus, I ask in this chapter: how might we define race and understand its function in classroom writing assessments so that we can articulate antiracist writing assessments?

THE IMPORTANCE OF RACE

Race is an important social dimension, a lived dimension of everyone's life despite its socially constructed nature (Ferrante & Brown, 1998; Gossett, 1963). No one can avoid the way race is structured in our lives, even those who do not wish to see it, and even though it isn't real in the same way someone has black hair or brown eyes. Our social, economic, and political histories in the U.S. are underwritten by the construct of race, as many have discussed already, particularly by looking at whiteness and the creation of white bodies and people (Hannaford, 1996; Ignatiev, 1995; Lipsitz, 1998; Mills, 1997; Roediger, 1999). The influence of the concept of race is in the coded ways we talk about each other, the words we use for race and to avoid its reference (Bonilla-Silva, 2003a, 2003b; Villanueva, 2006). It is in the way we behave and perform our identities (Inda, 2000; Young, 2004, 2007), which can also be seen in discussions of gender performativity (Butler, 1990; Salih, 2002). Many in composition studies

have argued that race is an important social dimension that we must pay attention to if we are to teach better, assess better, and build a more socially just future (hooks, 1994; Hurlbert, 2012; Prendergast, 1998; Villanueva, 1993, 1997;
Young, 2007).

Even those who promote multilingual and translingual pedagogies (Horner
& Trimbur, 2002; Horner et al., 2011; Jordan, 2012), which are not focused
on race but linguistic difference from the dominant academic discourse, often
assume racial structures that support and are associated with the linguistic and
language competencies of all students. In other words, even if we wish to avoid
talking about race and just talk about linguistic difference, which appears to be
about a *real* difference in groups of people in the writing classroom, appears to
be a dimension without prejudice, appears safer to notice and judge because
we're judging writing, not race, the people who most often form multilingual
English students or linguistic difference from the dominant academic discourse
are racialized in conventional ways, as are their languages and writing. In fact,
our discursive performances are some of the ways race is produced as a social
dimension that distinguishes people (Inda, 2000). Race is often marked through
language. In short, those who identify primarily as African-American, or Lati-
no/a, or Asian-Pacific American often are the multilingual students or the linguistically different in schools.

As a social construction, race is complex, often composed of multiple factors
that intersect in one's life despite the fact that it is a fabrication by people over
time. We made up race, then it became something real. But it is not real, just as
gender isn't real. I'm reminded of Stephen J. Gould's (1981) discussion of the
reification of the construct of IQ. In his well-known book, *The Mismeasure of
Man*, Gould (1981) draws out historically the ways that IQ tests and the testing
of intelligence through the nineteenth and twentieth centuries led to clear racist
consequences by creating the construct of IQ and using it against non-white
populations to show their inferiority to whites. Gould shows how easy it is for
people to "convert abstract concepts into entities" (1981, p. 24), meaning once
a test becomes accepted, its results, like an IQ number or an SAT or EPT score,
are "reified," which then allows the reification to be deployed in a number of
ways in society. While we act as if the signifier of an IQ or EPT or SAT score
is something real, the test itself created this thing. We forget that the construct
that the scores allegedly measure are created by the tests and do not actually exist
before those tests.

In his compelling sociological account, F. Allan Hanson (1993) comes to this
same conclusion, showing historically how various tests and examinations create
the very attributes and competencies they purport to measure. Thus there is no
IQ before IQ tests, no remedial status before the EPT. One might say (although

it isn't completely true), in the case of Fresno, there is no racial hierarchy until the EPT produces it. While the EPT is not testing race, per se, race is a complex set of material and discursive factors that create groups of students with similar competencies and literacies in the test. Race functions through the EPT because the test does not account for the multiple literacies, the multilingual capacities, of all the students currently taking the test. It uncritically and unknowingly accounts for one kind of literacy, a dominant one, a hegemonic one, a white, middle class discourse (I'll offer evidence of this claim later in this chapter).

It is no coincidence, then, that race was used to understand the results of intelligence tests early in the 20th century. One example should do. As Norbert Elliot (2005) explains, the army alpha and beta tests that determined intelligence, thus opportunities for taking positions in the military, were given to recruits in the second decade of the twentieth century (pp. 59-60). A part of the concerns that the test makers had once they began testing recruits was the high frequency of illiteracy in southern Black and immigrant recruits, which they associated with mental deficiency or lack of intelligence (Elliot, 2005, pp. 64-66). It didn't occur to the test makers that perhaps the construct of intelligence in their tests was not universal, and required particular experiences and cultural references that Blacks from the south and immigrants just didn't have access to (for different reasons). Instead, Robert Yerkes, the man in charge of the tests, concluded that the illiteracy of any group of recruits was dependent on the number of Black recruits in the group. Additionally, he concluded that most immigrants from Italy, Poland, and Greece were illiterate (and thus less intelligent), than their English, Scottish, and Irish immigrant counterparts (Elliot, 2005, p. 66). Race functioned to make sense of the test results, validating their findings.

In these obvious ways, race has had a strong connection to assessment generally since assessment tends to confer social and economic privileges. Tests like the army alpha and beta, the SAT and EPT, often are gateways to educational and economic access, privilege, and jobs. Many have shown the ways that U.S. society in general has been designed to protect such privileges and access for whites and kept them at arm's distance to racialized others (Ignatiev, 1995; Lipsitz, 1998; Mills, 1997; Roediger, 1999). Many of these structures still exist, even if only as lingering, familial economic privileges (or lack of privileges) gained by past generations and available to the present generation. Many of these structures exist in everyday reading and judging activities that teachers do with student writing, as Lester Faigley (1992) convincingly shows. In his discussion of Coles and Vopat's collection, *What Makes Writing Good*, Faigley demonstrates that particular class—and I argue racial—dispositions function to produce judgments of student writing, particularly dispositions concerning perceived "authenticity" and "honesty" (1992, p. 121). The examples of authentic and honest writing from the collection not only reveal a middle class set of tastes but a clear white racial set of experiences and perspectives. Faigley's conclusions are ones about the ways that such reading practices by teachers are an exercise of Foucauldian power, power that is difficult to see thus more potent and pervasive (1992, p. 131). I would add to Faigley's critique that it is race that functions in such daily classroom writing assessment practices, hiding behind power relationships set up by the judgment of student writing by teachers who use a dominant discourse. To put this another way, power is hidden more effectively because a set of white racial dispositions are already hidden in the assessment in various places, assumed as the standard.

Thus it is imperative that writing teachers consider explicitly and robustly the function of race in their classroom writing assessments, which often are a response to large-scale assessments, such as the ACT, SAT, AP, and EPT. The assessment community calls this relationship "washback" (Weigle, 2002, p. 54) when a test influences school and classroom curricula, but it might also be called "whitewashing." If we think that these large-scale tests are racist, or could be, and we know they washback into our classrooms, or are supposed to, then it seems reasonable to assume that our classrooms are constituted by racist institutional structures, and race is a factor in our classrooms. In his chapter on the neoliberal narratives of whiteness that structures racism in the U.S., George Lipsitz offers a reading of the film *Lean on Me* (1989), but begins it with a fitting way to close this section:

> My sister and mother both taught at Eastside at different times during the 1960s and 1970s and established reputations as the kind of demanding and dedicated instructor students remember long after their school years have been completed. Over the years, I have learned a great deal about what it means to try to offer a quality education in an inner-city school from them. My father, my mother, my sister, and many of their colleagues and friends have devoted much of their lives to that effort. I know how hard a job they have, how much patience and love it takes to try to neutralize the effects of poverty and racism even temporarily. I know as well that no amount of good intentions, no mastery of teaching techniques, and no degree of effort by individual educators can alter meaningfully the fundamentally unequal distribution of resources and opportunities in this society. (1998, p. 141)

If as teachers, we cannot alter such pervasive unequal distributions of resources and opportunities in our students' lives, which affects who they are and what they bring to our writing classrooms, then I think our best strategy as antiracist educators is to change the way we understand and do writing assessment, while simultaneously building arguments and movements to change the larger structural racism in our society and schools. But this antiracist project begins in our classrooms because it is the only place we, as writing teachers, can begin.

LANGUAGE'S ASSOCIATION WITH RACE

Racial formations—material bodies that are racialized—are connected closely to language use and our attitudes toward language. Laura Greenfield (2011) makes this point in a number of ways. She argues that in U.S. society and schools, most people, including writing teachers, tend to ignore or overlook the "linguistic facts of life" that linguist Rosina Lippi-Green (1997) identifies and that reveal the structural racism in society and language preference. These facts of life are long-established linguistic agreements in the field:

- All spoken language changes over time.
- All spoken languages are equal in linguistic terms.
- Grammaticality and communicative *effectiveness* are distinct and inter-dependent issues.
- Written language and spoken language are historically, structurally, and functionally fundamentally different creatures.
- Variation is intrinsic to all spoken language at every level. (as quoted in Greenfield, 2011, p. 33; Lippi-Green, 1997, p. 10)

These agreements essentially say that all language varieties, from Hawaiian Creole English to Black English Vernacular to Spanglish are legitimate, rule-governed, and communicative. They are not degenerate versions of English or "bad English," yet they are often seen in a lower position of power and prestige than the local variety of SEAE. It isn't because SEAE is inherently better, more logical, more effective, or more efficient.[6] It is because whiteness and white racial formations historically are closely associated with SEAEs and dominant discourses. Greenfield concludes, explicitly connecting SEAEs with the white body:

> The language varieties deemed inferior in the United States
> (so much so that they are often dismissed not simply as infe-
> rior varieties but not varieties at all—just conglomerations of
> slang, street talk, or poor English) tend to be the languages
> whose origins can be traced to periods in American history
> when communities of racially oppressed people used these
> languages to enact agency. It is no coincidence that the lan-

> guages spoken by racially oppressed people are considered to
> be inferior in every respect to the languages spoken predom-
> inantly by those who wield systemic power: namely, middle-
> and upper-class white people. (2011, p. 36)

Thus so-called proper English or dominant discourses are historically connected to the white body. This makes sense intuitively. We speak with and through our bodies. We write with and through our bodies. As teachers when we read and evaluate our students' writing, we do so through and with our bodies, and we have in our minds a vision of our students as bodies, as much as we have their language in front of us. Who historically has had the privilege to speak and write the most in civic life and in the academy? Whose words have been validated as history, truth, knowledge, story, the most throughout history? White people. Additionally, the material conditions that our students come from and live in affect and shape their bodies, making them who they are, making us who we are as teachers. The material conditions of the classroom, of our students' lives, as we'll see in later chapters, greatly determine their languaging and the writing assessment ecology of the classroom. I argue that in most cases writing teachers tend to have very different local histories and material conditions than their students of color and multilingual students, often the common thread is race.

Allow a few crude examples to help me make the point that race is connected to the judging of English. In the seven years I helped run the first-year writing program at Fresno State, an historically Hispanic Serving Institution where white students are the numerical minority, there have been to my count seven teachers of color teaching in the program total. Every year, we bring in around ten to twelve new teachers, sometimes more. We usually have around 25-30 working teachers at any given time. This means that on average there has been one teacher of color teaching first year writing at any given time. The rest are, for the most part, white, middle class, and female. Given my experiences at three other state universities and a two-year college, these conditions seem to be the norm. A report by the Center for American Progress on "Increasing Teacher Diversity" in public schools in the U.S. cites equally alarming statistics from the National Center for Education Statistics. Racial minority students make up over 40% of students in all schools in the U.S., but only 14.6% of all teachers are Black or Latino/a, and in 40% of public schools there is no teacher of color, not one (Bireda & Chait, 2011, p. 1).

If the dominant discourse of the academy is taught almost exclusively by white, middle class teachers, then is it possible that such conditions will affect the discourse valued in writing assessments? Is it possible that those who achieve such positions, such credentials, might have achieved them because they can use and favor the dominant discourses? If so, it is no wonder that dominant discourses in schools are closely associated with the white body and whiteness, which makes them associated with race.

Some might argue that the picture Greenfield and I paint for why any local dominant discourse is valued is inaccurate. My paradigm seems to say that teachers think about race when they judge students' writing. In one sense, yes. Greenfield and I are saying this. We cannot help it. Gender and race are the first things people identify (or try to) about a person when they meet them. We look, often implicitly and unconsciously, for markers that tell us something about the person so that we can interact with them appropriately. Why would teachers be any different? But at a more fundamental level, Greenfield argues that teachers are simply a part of systemic racism, a structural racism in schools and society that we don't control, and may not even be fully aware of. The fact that most if not all college writing programs demand that their students produce some dominant discourse, then judge them on their abilities to approximate it, according to Greenfield, is racist, since all dominant discourses are associated closely with white middle- and upper-class racial formations in the U.S.

But wait, some may argue further that even if this is true, even if structural racism does form the context of any writing course, it doesn't change the fact that there is a dominant discourse that is the lingua franca of schools, the workplace, and civic society. If you can approximate it, you have more power in those circles. You, in effect, negate the structural racism that may hold you back, keep power and privilege from your grasp. And so, in good writing classrooms, goes the argument, one can honor and respect the languages that all students bring to the classroom, then teach and promote a local SEAE so that those students have a chance at future success. This pedagogy is posed as antiracist, or at least one whose goal is social justice. This kind of argument and pedagogy, says Greenfield, is based on two false assumptions. The first is that these other language varieties, say BEV, are somehow less communicative and cannot do the job needed in the academy or civic life (Greenfield, 2011, p. 49). A simple example will show the flaw in the pedagogy's logic. Hip hop and rap are mainstream musical genres now, have been for years. Most of the lyrics are based on BEV, yet the music is listen to by people from a wide range of socioeconomic strata and by all racial formations in the U.S. and worldwide. If BEV isn't as effective in communicating in civic life, how is it that it is so popular, so mainstream? How is it that it connects to so many different kinds of people? How is it that it can tell such compelling stories? Is it that we don't mind Black people entertaining *us* (a white mainstream audience), but we don't want *their* language tainting the so-called important areas of *our* life, academics, knowledge making, civic life, law, politics, etc.? Are we just slumming in Harlem when we celebrate the relatively few Black entertainers and sports figures, the few who make it economically, the exceptions, so that we can ignore the multitudes who do not?

The second false assumption that Greenfield says supports the above pedagogical decisions is that "[p]eople believe falsely that by changing the way people of color speak ... others' racist preconceptions will disappear and the communicative act will be successful" (2011, p. 49). So teach Blacks or Latinos/as to speak and write a dominant discourse and they will have more power and opportunity. They'll be more communicatively successful. The logic here says that today people aren't racist toward people, but they may be toward the languages people use. Consider again the hip hop example. If we really did believe that changing the language of people of color would gain them power and opportunity, make them more communicative, then again I ask why are Hip Hop and rap so popular? It's mainly performed by Blacks in the U.S., although it has become a global genre. Could it be so popular if it wasn't effectively communicating ideas and narratives?

We are talking about the exceptions really. The rule is that African-Americans who speak and write BEV are not usually successful in school or civic life. But is it because they are not able to communicate effectively and clearly? According to Greenfield, the answer is no. Referencing several studies that prove the fact, she argues that people really are racist toward people because of the way racialized white bodies historically have been and are closely wedded to local SEAEs. She says:

> Black people are not discriminated against because some
> speak a variety of Ebonics—rather, I argue, Ebonics is stig-
> matized because it is spoken primarily by Black people. It is
> its association with a particular people and history that has
> compelled people to stigmatize it. Our attitudes toward lan-
> guage, it appears, are often steeped in our assumptions about
> the bodies of the speakers. We assume an essential connec-
> tion—language as inherently tied to the body. In other words,
> language varieties—like people—are subject to racialization.
> (2011, p. 50)

What does it mean that Ebonics or Spanglish or some other variety of English is stigmatized already in writing classrooms? The word's root is "stigma," which the OED defines as " a mark made upon the skin by burning with a hot iron (rarely, by cutting or pricking), as a token of infamy or subjection" (Stigmata, 2015). Thus something stigmatized is something already judged, something already in subjection, something lesser. No matter what antiracist motives a teacher may have, including my own motives, we all work within conditions and systems that have branded some languages as less communicative, less articulate, less than the dominant discourse. No matter who we are, we always struggle against antiracist systems in the academy.

We shouldn't pretend, however, that any local dominant discourse, BEV, Spanglish, or any variety of multilingual English is monolithic or self-contained, therefore these stigmas are also not categorical. What I mean is that everyone speaks and writes a brand of English that has its nuances, its deviations. For instance, not every African-American student will speak BEV, and not everyone who uses it will use BEV in the same ways that others will use it. V. N. Volosinov (1986) makes this point clear about language generally, arguing that there is no *langue*, only *parole*, only language that is in a constant state of flux and change. Vershawn A. Young's (2004; 2007; 2011) arguments for "code-meshing" agrees and helps us see the nuance, helps us see why it's difficult to speak of BEV or a dominant white discourse alone. In fact, none of us speak or write solely some brand of English alone. We use variations of English that we encounter around us. Young (2007) argues that we all have hybrid Englishes. We speak in codes that are meshed with other codes, and we should account for this in the classroom. Additionally, because the dominant discourse is a white racial discourse, associated with white bodies historically, Young explains that "[w]hen we ask Black students to give up one set of codes in favor of another, their BEV for something we call more standard, we're not asking them to make choices about language, we're asking them to choose different ways to perform their racial identities through language" (2007, p. 142). However, just because we can see the hybridity of any brand of English, it doesn't mean the stigmas go away. The question is: how do we not let the stigmas determine how we assess writing in our classrooms?

The bottom line is we cannot separate race, our feelings about the concept or particular racial formations, which includes historical associations with particular racialized bodies in time and space, from languages, especially varieties of English in the U.S. This makes language, like the dominant discourse, racialized as white (I'll say more about this later in this chapter). More important, as judges of English in college writing classrooms, we cannot avoid this racializing of language when we judge writing, nor can we avoid the influence of race in how we read and value the words and ideas of others. Lisa Delpit offers a poetic way to understand language and its connection to the body, which I read with racial undertones: "[o]ur home language is as viscerally tied to our beings as existence itself—as the sweet sounds of love accompany our first milk" (2002, p. xvii). Freire has another way of pointing out the power of language in our lives, the power it has in making our lives and ourselves. He says, "reading the world always precedes reading the word, and reading the word implies continually reading the world" (1987,

p. 23). When we read the words that come from the bodies of our students, we read those bodies as well, and by reading those bodies we also read the words they present to us, some may bare stigmata, some may not.

THE FUNCTION OF RACE IN THE EPT WRITING ASSESSMENT

I've just made the argument that race generally speaking is important to English as a language that we teach and assess in writing classrooms. But how is race implicated in writing assessments? How does race function or what does it produce in writing assessments?

One way to consider the function of race in writing assessment is to consider the consequences of writing assessments. Breland et al. (2004) found differences in mean scores on the SAT essay among Asian-American, African-American, Hispanic, and white racial formations, with African-Americans rated lowest (more than a full point on an 8 point scale) and Hispanic students rated slightly higher (p. 5), yet when looking for differences in mean SAT essay scores of "English first" (native speakers) or "English not first" (multilingual) students, they found no statistically significant differences (p. 6) —the mean scores were virtually identical in these two groups. I don't know how Breland and his colleagues determined native speaking proficiency, but my guess is that it may fall roughly along racial lines. These findings have been replicated by others (Gerald & Haycock, 2006; Soares, 2007), who found that SAT scores correlate strongly to parental income, education, and test-takers' race. Similarly, in Great Brittan, Steve Strand (2010) found that Black Caribbean British students between ages 7 and 11 made less progress on national tests than their white British peers because of systemic problems in schools and their assessments. These patterns among racial formations do not change at Fresno State, in which African-American, Latino/a, and Hmong students are assessed lower on the EPT (see Inoue & Poe, 2012, for historical EPT scores by racial formation) than their white peers and attain lower final portfolio scores in the First Year Writing (FYW) program readings conducted each summer for program assessment purposes (Inoue, 2009a; 2012, p. 88). Race appears to be functioning in each assessment, producing similar racialized consequences, always benefiting a white middle class racial formation.

Between 2011 and 2014, I directed the Early Start English and Summer Bridge programs at Fresno State. All students who were designated by the English Placement Test (EPT), a state-wide, standardized test with a timed writing component, as remedial must take an Early Start or Bridge course in order to begin their studies on any California State University campus. Even a casual look into the classrooms and over the roster of all students in these programs shows a stunning racial picture. These courses are ostensibly organized and filled by a test of language competency, however, each summer it is the same. The classes are filled with almost exclusively students of color. Of all the 2013 Bridge students, there were only four who were designated as white by their school records—that's 2% of the Bridge population. And the Early Start English program is almost identical. So at least in this one local example of a writing assessment (the EPT), when we talk about linguistic difference, or remediation (these are synonymous in many cases), we are talking about race in conventional ways.[7]

The remediation numbers that the EPT produces through blind readings by California State University (CSU) faculty readers also support my claims. In fall of 2013, as shown in Table 1, all students of color—it doesn't matter what racial formation or ethnic group we choose—are designated by the EPT as remedial at dramatically higher rates than white students. The Asian-American category, which at Fresno State is mostly Hmong students, are the most vulnerable to this test, with 43.9% more of the Asian-American formation being designated as remedial in English than the white formation.[8] How is it that these racially uneven test results are possible, and possible at such consistent rates? How is it that the EPT can draw English remediation lines along racial lines so well?

Table 1. At Fresno State, students of color are deemed remedial at consistently higher rates than white students by the EPT (California State University Analytic Studies, 2014)

Race	No. of First-Year Students	No. of Proficient in English	% of Designated as Remedial
African- American	119	61	48.7%
Mexican- American	1,298	593	54.3%
Asian- American	495	161	67.5%
White Non-Latino	601	459	23.6%
Total	2,965	1,548	47.8%

While my main focus in this book is on classroom writing assessment, the way judgments are formed in large-scale ratings of timed essays are not much different from a single teacher reading and judging her own students. In fact, they show how language is connected to the racialized body. The processes, contexts, feedback, and consequences in a classroom may be different in each case, but how race functions in key places in classroom writing assessment, such as the reading and judgment of the teacher, or the writing construct used as a standard by which all performances are measured, I argue, are very similar. And race is central to this similarity because it is central to our notions of language use and its value.

To be fair, there are more things going on that produce the above numbers. There are educational, disciplinary, and economic structures at work that prepare many students of color in and around Fresno in uneven ways from their white peers. Most Blacks in Fresno, for example, are poor, go to poorer schools because of the way schools are supported by taxes, which are low in those parts of Fresno. Same goes for many Asian-American students. But why would the Mexican-American students have twice as frequent remediation rates as white students? There is more going on than economics and uneven conditions at local schools.

Within the test, there are other structures causing certain discourses to be rated lower. Could the languages used by students of color be stigmatized, causing them to be rated lower, even though raters do not know who is writing individual essays when they read for the EPT? Consider the guide provided to schools and teachers in order to help them prepare their high school students to take the EPT. The guide, produced by the CSU Chancellor's Office, gives the rubric used to judge the written portion of the test. Each written test can receive from 1 to 6, with 6 being "superior" quality, 4 being "adequate," 3 being "marginal," and 1 being "incompetent" (2009, pp. 14-16). The rubric has six familiar elements:

a. response to the topic
b. understanding and use of the passage
c. quality and clarity of thought
d. organization, development, and support
e. syntax and command of language
f. grammar, usage, and mechanics (CSU Office of the Chancellor, 2009, p. 14)

At least items e and f correspond to a locally dominant SEAE, while a, b, c, and d correspond to some conventions and dispositions that are a part of a dominant discourse. The guide offers this description of a 4-essay, which is "adequate," that is, not remedial:

a. addresses the topic, but may slight some aspects of the task
b. demonstrates a generally accurate understanding of the passage in developing a sensible response
c. may treat the topic simplistically or repetitively
d. is adequately organized and developed, generally supporting ideas with

reasons and examples

e. demonstrates adequate use of syntax and language

f. may have some errors, but generally demonstrates control of grammar, usage, and mechanics (CSU Office of the Chancellor, 2009, p. 15)

I cannot help but recognize this rubric. It's very familiar. In Chapter 13, "Evaluation," of William Irmscher's (1979) helpful book, *Teaching Expository Writing*, he provides a very similar rubric, one I've used in the past in writing classrooms:

- Content
- Organization/structure/form
- Diction/language/style
- Punctuation/mechanics
- Grammar/style (1979, pp. 157-159)

Irmscher's dimensions are a variation of the five factors that Paul Diederich (1974) and his colleagues, John French and Sydell Carlton, found in their factor analysis of fifty-three judges' readings of 300 student papers in a 1961 ETS study. The five factors they found most important to academic and professional readers' judgments of student essays were (in order of importance/most frequently used):

- Ideas
- Usage, sentence structure, punctuation, and spelling
- Organization and analysis
- Wording and phrasing
- Style (Diederich, 1974, pp. 7-8)

Diederich explains that these five factors that most of his readers used to read and grade essays only accounted for 43% of all the variance in the grades given to the set of papers in his study. He says, "the remaining 57 percent was unexplained" (1974, p. 10). Most likely, the unexplained variance in grades was due to "unique ideas about grading that are not shared by any other reader, and random variations in judgment, which may be regarded as errors in judgment" (Diederich, 1974, p. 10). In other words, most of what produced evaluations and grades of student writing simply couldn't be accounted for in the study, and could be unique or idiosyncratic. Each reader has his or her own unique, tacit dimensions that do not easily agree with the tacit dimensions that other readers may have. But what does this have to do with the EPT's use of a very similar rubric and how does it help us see race in the assessments of writing made on the EPT?

Diederich and his colleagues show us that reading student writing, like the impromptu essays written for the EPT, will be judged by other factors as well as those explicitly expressed. Even with careful norming, which I'm sure occurs in the EPT readings, there will still be variance. Readers will read from their biases. They have to. That's reading. But the question I'm wondering is: What stigmata do they see? Is this what is affecting the racialized remediation rates? The guide, to its credit, explains that readers will not "penalize ESL writers excessively for slight shifts in idiom, problems with articles, confusion over prepositions, and *occasional* misuse of verb tense and verb forms, so long as such features do not obscure meaning" (emphasis in original, CSU Office of the Chancellor, 2009, p. 16). It's the qualifier I wonder about. Isn't it possible that many readers will read confusion over prepositions or misuse of verb tense and forms, as obscuring meaning? Is it possible that multilingual students, like Fresno State Hmong students, will usually have more than "occasional" slips in the above linguistic features of their texts? Without doing a detailed linguistic analysis of samples, it seems plausible that such features of texts are associated with many students of color's discourses. For sure, multilingual students, like most Hmong and many Latino/a students at Fresno State, use discourses that are characterized by "misuse of verb tense and verb forms," as well as the other items listed. Are these markers read as stigmata though? Does seeing such linguistic markers compel a lower judgment by a reader who is most likely white, female, and middle class? It would seem that the instructions allow for this interpretation.

All EPT writing prompts direct students to read a short paragraph from a published argument, then explain it and make an argument agreeing or disagreeing with it. In one of the examples in the guide, the passage is from Sue Jozui, which argues against advertisers' use of celebrities' testimonials or endorsements to sell products. Here's the excerpt from Jozui:

> Advertisers frequently use the testimony of a celebrity to support a claim: a football star touts a deodorant soap, an actress starts every day with Brand A coffee, a tennis pro gets stamina from Brand X cereal, a talk-show host drives a certain kind of car. The audience is expected to transfer approval of the celebrity to approval of the product. This kind of marketing is misleading and insults the intelligence of the audience. Am I going to buy the newest SUV because an attractive talk-show host gets paid to pretend he drives one? I don't think so. We should boycott this kind of advertising and legislate rules and guidelines for advertisers. (CSU Office of the Chancellor, 2009, p. 17)

The prompt then states: "explain the argument that Jozui makes and discuss the ways in which you agree or disagree with her analysis and conclusion. Support your position by providing reasons and examples from your own experience, observations, or reading" (CSU Office of the Chancellor, 2009, p. 17).

Often the most instructive examples of student writing are the ones that reveal the borderlands, the margins that define the mainstream. The 2-essay, the "very weak" essay is a four-paragraph essay, one that does not reiterate Jozui's argument, but attempts to argue both sides of the issue. It has many more errors in local SEAE usage than any of the other sample essays rated higher, but in some ways, it does try to offer an academic approach by considering opposing points of view. It appears, however, to lack focus and a conventional organizational pattern. The 2-essay reads:

> If a football star touts a deodorant soap, an actress starts everyday with brand. A coffee, a tennis pro get stamina from Brand X cereal and if a talk show host drives a certain car it does not mean that your going to do that. I agree with Jozui if an atractive talk-show host gets paid to pretend to drive a car, it does not mean that your going to go buy one.

> It would be good boycotting this kind of advertisement but theres always a positive & negative side to the advertisements. Boycotting this advertisement will be good so it wont be misleading or insulting anyones intelligence. If a celebraty want to be advertised with a product or something at their own I think they have the right to. On my positive side of it I see it that its okay to be advertised, one thing is to be advertised & get known or get the product known, and another thing is buying the product.

> Some examples are for May 1st theres been a law trying to pass people, news reporters, and radio stitons were saying that on May first no one should go out & boycott by not buying anything that day, and not even going to work. That was getting known, so that point was to do a lot of peoples ears but not everyone did it about sixty to seventy percent of people I bet did not listen to them, if they were not going to work who was going to pay them for those hours lost no one, but, the other thirty to forty person of people did do the boycott. They did no care about it they want the law to pass.

> Everyone has the right to advertise. But its not like your going to go buy something just because come one else did. You

have to follow your thought do what you wanna do not do what you see other people do. (CSU Office of the Chancellor, 2009, p. 22)

The guide offers these judgments on the "serious flaws" of the 2-essay:

- The writer begins by responding to the topic of celebrity advertising and the proposal to boycott it, but then goes off topic and writes about another kind of boycott entirely.
- The essay reflects a lack of understanding of Jozui's arguments and seems instead to be discussing the right of celebrities to be in advertisements and the consequences for people who participate in boycotts.
- The essay has no apparent focus or organization. After agreeing with Jozui, the writer tries to mount a pro and con argument, and by the third paragraph resorts simply to a stream of consciousness.
- The lack of command of language makes it difficult to understand what the writer is saying: "If a celebraty want to be advertised with a product or something of their own I think they have the right to."
- A variety of serious errors occur throughout the essay. The third paragraph is composed almost entirely of a single run-on sentence. (CSU Office of the Chancellor, 2009, pp. 22-23)

If we assume that the prompt, a familiar kind of argumentative prompt, was free of structural racism—that is, we assume that such tasks are typical in the curricula of schools where this student comes from and are typical of the discourses that this student uses—and we assume that the expectations around the first four items on the rubric are not culturally or racially biased (we can more easily assume that the last two items are racially biased), then we can conclude that the above judgments are "serious flaws" in the essay, and perhaps the essay deserves a score of 2. But what if we assumed that the prompt itself is already biased toward a dominant discourse that is associated closely to a white body and a white discourse?

Putting aside for the moment the many errors and miscues in the essay (some of which can be accounted for by the impromptu nature of the test), this essay might be one that engages in a rhetoric that could be a product of some other discourse(s), a discourse other than the dominant white one promoted in the EPT test prompt, rubric, and explanations of judgments that are assumed to be normative. Take the most problematic, third paragraph, which is judged as "off topic" and "stream of consciousness." This paragraph surely contributes to the assessment that the essay lacks focus and organization. But the paragraph does offer a material perspective on the discussion. It takes the abstract discussion of boycotting advertisements that use celebrities and juxtaposes a discussion of something that allegedly occurred on May 1 in California, an actual boycott. There is a clear connection, but it's labeled by the guide as off topic. While there could be explicit connections to the current discussion about celebrities in ads, this discursive strategy might be associative or working from a logic of juxtaposition. These are logics that usually do not expect explicit connection to be made by the writer. But is the guide's assessment of the essay racist because it refused to value this paragraph in this way?

While this is purely speculative, since I don't know when this essay was written exactly, only that it was written before 2009, the publication date of the guide. The paragraph could be referring to the "Great American Boycott" of 2006 and 2007 (Associated Press, 2007), in which millions of Latino/a immigrants boycotted schools and businesses for one day in order to show the degree to which the U.S. depends on them financially. It is a decisively racial reference, which likely most EPT readers at the time would have been aware of, since Los Angeles was one of the cities with the largest turnout in 2006, estimated at 400,000 (Gorman, 2006). In fact, it is reported that in L.A., the protesters chanted, "Si, se puede" ("Yes, it can be done") (Glaister & MacAskill, 2006), which was the motto of the United Farm Workers organization, headed in part by César Chavez.[9] While the writer of the 2-essay doesn't mention any of these details, one could read them underneath the text. The references to "not even going to work," "hours lost" from work, and the sense that many "did not care" that they lost some money but wanted social and economic change seems to be sentiments felt or experienced by those in the student's community.

These changes are not simply about labor, but about Latino/a labor in California, about immigration policies, and racially defined immigrants and their material struggles with participating in social justice projects, like a boycott. They are about the experience of Latino/a immigrants engaging in a boycott that is meant to affect advertising and consumer consumption. These references are only off topic if you don't find such Latino/a cultural references valid in a discussion about the marketing of consumer products. If a reader's primary relation to such advertisements is that of a buyer, and not the laborer or retail worker working in the department store stocking and selling the soap or cereal, then this paragraph may seem off topic. But what if a reader imagined that her primary relation to the production and distribution of such advertisements was as a laborer who made such items available to customers? Then, I think, this paragraph, with its reference to the Great American Boycott, is far from off topic and racialized as Latino/a in a California context. It calls upon the common relations of Latinos/as in California to Capitalist consumption.

Yes, I read a lot into the essay, maybe too much, but that is the point. White discourses and dispositions tend to lean on abstraction, and avoid such racially politicized readings of texts. I don't think the writers of the prompt or the guide intended for such an assessment to be valid of this essay because it racializes it. Does this mean that the essay should get more than a rating of 2? I think so. In the above ways, it addresses material concerns in a pretty unique way, in a way that matters to many in California, in a way that stretches the prompt to be more applicable than simply about an abstract idea like celebrities in ads, in a way that may very well matter to the student writer.

I cannot argue definitively that the guide or any judge would consciously see the markers of this text as racialized stigmata, but it doesn't matter. What the guide does promote is a particular ideal text, one that values only abstract ideas, with no sensitivity to the way particular racial formations might respond differently, respond from their own social conditions. This ideal text, I argue, is informed by a dominant white discourse, seen in the rubric and the way it asks readers to judge from it. The assessment that the guide promotes seems to ignore the possibility that what is "off topic" is culturally and socially constructed by a dominant, white discourse, and that any response will be constructed by one's material relations to the ideas around advertising and consumer economies in a racially divided California. Judging essays in the way the guide asks teachers to do produces the uneven and racist consequences that we see in Fresno State's remediation rates and its Early Start and Bridge programs. One cannot know who this writer is, but that's not the point. The point is what gets read and stigmatized in the text while not explicitly about race ends up having racist consequences.

RACIAL *HABITUS*

Up to this point, my use of the term race has been imprecise. At the same time, race as an abstraction or as a social dimension in which people are grouped or group themselves is tricky to define too finely. It encapsulates an historically organizing set of structures that structure social interactions and society, to draw on Pierre Bourdieu's phrase for *habitus* (Bourdieu, 1977, p. 72). The term *habitus* gives us a way to think about race as socially constructed in at least three ways:

- *discursively or linguistically*, that is, through discourse and language practices;
- *materially and bodily*, or through people's material conditions and the bodily and material markers that our environments leave on us; and
- *performatively*, or through the ways we perform, behave, and act, which includes what we consume in conspicuous ways.

Bourdieu defines *habitus* as "not only a structuring structure, which organizes practices and the perception of practices, but also a structured structure: the principles of division into logical classes which organizes the perception of the social world itself the product of internalization of the division into social classes" (1984, p. 170). That is, race as *habitus* structures and is structured into our lives, bodies, languages, actions, behaviors, expectations for writing, reading practices that judge writing, etc. Quoting Pierre Bourdieu, E. San Juan uses this definition of *habitus*:

> Bourdieu means "the conditionings associated with a par-
> ticular class of conditions of existence that produce *habitus*,
> systems of durable, transposable dispositions, structured
> structures predisposed to function as structuring structures,
> that is, as principles which generate and organize practices
> and representations that can be objectively adapted to their
> outcomes without presupposing a conscious aiming at ends
> or an express mastery of the operations necessary in order to
> attain them." (2002, p. 52)

For Bourdieu, *habitus* is multiple, historically situated structures composed of and conditioned by practices, material conditions, and discourses, that iterate into new structures (i.e., structuring structures), all the while these structures are durable and transposable, even when history and conditions alter them superficially. Racial *habitus*, then, is one way one might think of race as a set of structuring structures, some marked on the body, some in language practices, some in the ways we interact or work, write, and read, some in the way we behave or dress, some in the processes and differential opportunities we have to live where we do (or get to live where we can), or where we hang out, work, go to school, etc. Thus, racial *habitus* places an emphasis on the continual (re)construction of race as structures, as sets of dispositions that are discursive, material, and performative in nature. We speak, embody (are marked materially), and perform our racial designations and identities, whether those designations are self-designated or designated by others. Another way to say this is that racial *habitus* explains the way race is made up of discursive, material, and performative structuring structures.

To complicate further the concept of race as a social dimension, race has two ways of being experienced and referenced in the world that make it slippery and ambiguous in any given situation beyond the historically changing nature of it.[10] It is a dimension that can organize one's own subjectivity in the world, the way one acts, speaks, relates to others, and behaves. This is its *subjective* dimension. Everyone experiences race subjectively, or from a particular subject position and set of experiences, which intersect with other dimensions of experience (e.g., class, gender, sexuality, disability, etc.). One might consciously or unconsciously reproduce particular racial structures in language, dress, behavior, appearance, etc. that structure one's own sense of one's racial subjectivity. In this sense, race is consciously a set of discursive, material, and performance choices.

Race is also commonly seen or understood by others through physical, linguistic, social, and cultural markers, structuring structures themselves that have uneven and various meanings to others. This second dimension is race's *projective* dimension, or one of others' perceptions and expectations placed upon the person or persons in question. It is the dimension of race that people or institutions use in order to know people and organize them either privately or institutionally. Even though we may not publically act on or voice assumptions about racial formations or individuals in our midst, we all have such assumptions. It's hard not to given the way our minds work to help us make sense of things, people, and experiences, particularly the unknown. In this sense, race is projected onto individuals and groups for a variety of purposes, often institutional.

Allow me to offer an example that illustrates how racial projection affects assessments (sets of judgments and decisions about people), despite a contradictory racial subjectivity. Growing up in Las Vegas, I was at least five or six shades darker than I am today. I was short, skinny, with jet black hair and brown eyes. In that context, among the working class whites at school and in our neighborhood, I was a "beaner," a "dirty Mexican," a "trouble-maker." In that context, where local Mexican-American communities were vying for working class jobs against whites, any brown-skinned, brown-eyed boy was a Mexican. It didn't matter that my name is as Japanese as you can get, very obviously non-Anglo, but that marker itself was read as a marker of the racial other that was most at odds with working class whites in my neighborhood and school. Unlike ethnicity, race is usually a broad brush stroke, not a fine penciled line. All my actions, all that I did, walking past a fence or a neighbor's trailer, knocking on a door to see if a friend could play, or trying to get a soda from a vending machine at the trailer park's office, all were seen as suspicious activities, ones that suggested I was surely up to no good.

I'm not making up this feeling of being suspect everywhere, every day, by everyone. The stigma was real, so real that a group of white trailer park tenants and the manager (also white) got together, wrote a letter to my family, listing all the activities my twin brother and I had done in the last year. One more misstep and we were evicted, kicked out. Interestingly, there were a list of activities and wrong-doings attributed to my brother and me during the previous summer, a summer we had spent with our grandmother in Oregon. We were not even in the state, yet all bad things were attributed to us, the Mexicans in the trailer park. To my white, working class neighbors, it seemed obvious and clear that all wrong-doing in the trailer park were markers that my brother and I had been there. Our skin tone, eyes and hair were judged to be Mexican, which told them about our natures as boys.

I have always been proud to be Japanese-American, to be Asian-American, despite the racial and ethnic ambiguity that has often followed me. This is why I've placed extra effort and labor in my racial subjectivity, even back then, even as a pre-teen and teenager. It didn't matter what I said, or what I claimed to be. My performance, my physical and material appearance, even my discourse, which was quiet around adults, especially men (having almost no contact with men until deep into high school), was assessed as Mexican, as trouble-maker, as racial other. No matter what I did or said, it was seen as suspicious or bad. And because I was raised by a single-parent, my mom, who didn't have a college education, worked several low-paying jobs just to keep the lights on, our clothes were not the newest or nicest. They were clean and cared for, but there were several years in which we had to make do with last year's school clothes, last year's shoes. These economic constraints only reinforced the other material markers that constructed me as Mexican in the eyes of the whites around me.

I believe writing teachers, as good-hearted and conscientious as most are, use racial projection in the same ways that I experienced as a boy. Perhaps they do not make the same exact assessments when working with students of color, but we do racially project our notions and expectations onto others we meet, others we read, others we evaluate and grade in the writing classroom. If we didn't, it would be difficult to teach, to interact with any group of students, to understand the language offered us in writing by our students. We have to have assumptions, otherwise nothing makes sense. Now, I realize that some may find my conclusion about racial projection difficult to accept. They might say that they don't have to see race or assume and project some set of racial attributes in order to get along and work with others who appear different from them. Fair enough. Yet, I too find the typical alternative conclusion, that we can escape such racial projections in our interactions with our writing students when reading their writing, including multilingual writing, equally unacceptable and unrealistic. This practice of ignoring racial *habitus* in our lives, in reading and writing practices, and in our dispositions for judging, is essentially an attempt to negate much of what makes all of us who we are and how we communicate. It means that a teacher who tries not to see race is forced to assume a non-racial set of dispositions, which amounts to a white racial *habitus* (discussed below). But I understand that likely those who do not accept my conclusion likely have not experienced constant racial projections that contradict their own racial subjectivity. And this is likely because they fit into a white racial *habitus* that often doesn't have such contradictions in school.

Thus these two dimensions of race, subjective and projective, may not match up in any given particular person, but they operate simultaneously. Our writing assessments should struggle with these two ways of experiencing race, race as subjectivity and race as projection by others. Although tangled and flawed, race as discursive, material, and performative are good ways to organize inquiries into what happens in writing assessments, since our life experiences, whether we acknowledge them or not as racialized, are often organized by racial subjectivity and projection to some degree, just as gendered *habitus* organize our experiences. Racial *habitus* offers language that calls attention to the dynamic, (re)productive structuring structures of discourse, materiality, and performance that are central to judging student writing. The term helps us talk about race as sets of structures—as parts in and of systems—structures that are not categorical, nor static.

To think of race as racial *habitus* has been approached by Edwardo Bonilla-Silva (2003) in his sociological work on racism and whiteness, only he focuses on a white *habitus* that produces particular language about race. In his study, Bonilla-Silva examines the ways that students from various U.S. universities use certain discursive "frames" (e.g., abstract liberalism, naturalization, cultural racism, and minimization of racism) to articulate their racial ideology and cloak it in linguistic "styles" (e.g., "I'm not prejudiced, but ..." (p. 57), "I'm not Black, so I don't know" (p. 58), "anything but race" (p. 62), "they are the racist ones ..." (p. 63)).[11] This color-blind racist discourse used primarily by white students attempts to ignore, erase, or minimize the structuring structures in language that construct racial difference and racism. He explains that "social and spatial segregation" in different communities creates a "'white *habitus*,' a racialized, uninterrupted socialization process that conditions and creates whites' racial taste, perceptions, feelings, and emotions and their views on racial matters" (2003, p. 104). Thus whites have structuring structures that construct local white racial formations, just as Hmong and Mexican-Americans do in Fresno.

Arguing that writing teachers and writing assessment theorists need to "interrogate and refashion our racial politics of assessment," Nicholas Behm and Keith Miller (2012, p. 125) provide a detailed account of Bonilla-Silva's (2006) study of color-blind racism, and explain his concept of a white *habitus* in which whites are socialized. Behm and Miller explain that a white *habitus* is a set of "historically and culturally constructed dispositions, feelings, and discourses, which '*conditions* and *creates* whites' racial taste, perceptions, feelings, and emotions and their views on racial matters'" (2012, p. 129, emphasis in original). But *habitus* may be more complex than this. Sometimes it is unconscious, so it may be more accurate to say that we participate in already existing racial *habitus*, participating in structures that are to some degree outside or beyond individuals, making *habitus* structuring structures we make our own, nuancing them in the ways that Young (2007) discusses code-meshing. Furthermore, when I speak of white racial *habitus* below, it is not necessarily linked to a racialized body, a white body, as it appears to be in Bonilla-Silva's study. Instead, the structuring structures of a local white racial *habitus* make white students, or ideal students, in writing assessment ecologies of the classroom. A white racial *habitus* exists beyond or outside of bodies, in discourse, in methods of judging, in dispositions toward texts, etc.

And so using a term like racial *habitus* can keep us from thinking of these structuring structures as simply dwelling in individuals, as inherent characteristics of individuals – since I'm rarely taking about individuals when I discuss issues of race and racism in classroom writing assessments. Instead, racial *habitus* foregrounds the macro-level phenomena, foregrounds the structures and social structuring, foregrounds the patterns among many people who associate or find themselves geographically and historically in the same places and circumstances, without forgetting that these patterns exist in individuals who augment them.

WHITE RACIAL *HABITUS*

Important to seeing racial *habitus* as a determining aspect of any classroom writing assessment project is seeing a white racial *habitus* as fundamental to all classroom writing assessment, whether we promote it, critique it, or actively promote something else. Many have discussed how to define whiteness as a construct that affects writing pedagogy (Frankenberg, 1993; hooks, 1994; Keating, 1995), which has bearing on how writing is judged in classrooms by teachers using a local SEAE or other academic expectations for writing.[12] Timothy Barnett (2000) synthesizes five statements about whiteness that the scholarship on whiteness overwhelmingly confirms, and is a good way to begin to understand whiteness as a racial *habitus* in classroom writing assessment ecologies, or as a set of structuring structures that are performed or projected onto student writing:

- Whiteness is a "coded discourse of race," that "seems *invisible*, objective, and neutral";
- Whiteness maintains its power and presents itself as "*unraced individually*" and "opposed to a racialized subjectivity that is communally and politically interested";
- Whiteness is presented as a *non-political* relational concept, defined against Others, whose interests are defined as "anti-individual" and political in nature;
- Whiteness "is not tied essentially to skin color, but is nevertheless

related in complex and powerful ways to the perceived phenomenon of race";

- Whiteness maintains power by *defining (and denying) difference* "on its own terms and to its own advantage" (my emphasis, p. 10)

As a *habitus* that is practiced in language, expected in classroom behaviors, and marked on the bodies of students and teachers, whiteness, then, is a set of structuring structures, durable, transposable, and flexible. As Barnett summarizes, these structures construct whiteness as invisible and appealing to fairness through objectivity. The structures are unraced (even beyond race), unconnected to the bodies and histories that create them. They are set up as apolitical, and often deny difference by focusing on the individual or making larger claims to abstract liberal principles, such as the principle of meritocracy. These structures create dispositions that form reading and judging practices, dispositions for values and expectations for writing and behavior. Echoing Lippi-Green and Greenfield's arguments that connect race to language, Barnett offers a succinct way to see whiteness as a racial project in the classroom, which can easily be a way we might describe any classroom writing assessment as a default white racial project:

> "Whiteness," accordingly, represents a political and relational activity disguised as an essential quality of humanity that is, paradoxically, *fully* accessible only by a few. It maintains a distance from knowledge that depends on the power of authorities, rules, tradition, and the written word, all of which supposedly guarantee objectivity and non-racial ways of knowing, but have, not incidentally, been established and maintained primarily by the white majority. (2000, 13, emphasis in original)

In her discussion of the pervasiveness of whiteness in bioethics in the U.S., Catherine Myser defines whiteness as a marker and position of power that is situated in a racial hierarchy (2002, p. 2). She asks us to problematize the centrality of whiteness in bioethics as a field of study and industry, which I argue we should do in the writing classroom too. By looking at several studies of whiteness, Myser provides a rather succinct set of discursive and performative dispositions that could be called a white racial *habitus* that writing teachers often enact:

- [A focus on] Individualism, hyperindividualism, self-determination, autonomy, and self-reliance, self-control;
- The person is conceived in purely individual terms, as a

rational and self-conscious being (the Cartesian "I" or *cogito ergo sum*), making failure an individual weakness and not a product of larger structural issues;

- Relationships are understood as being between informed, consenting individuals, but individual rights are primary, placing an emphasis on contracts, laws, and abstract principles for governing relationships;

- Cognitive capacity is the ability to think rationally, logically, and objectively, with rigor, clarity and consistency valued most;

- All problems are defined as those situations or conditions that are out of control, that disrupt autonomous functioning. (Myser, 2002, pp. 6-7)

Whiteness as a discourse and set of expectations in writing, then, like the dispositions distilled from Barnett's summary, can be boiled down to a focus on individualism and self-determination, Descartes *cogito*, individuals as the primary subject position, abstract principles, rationality and logic, clarity and consistency, and on seeing failure as individual weakness, not a product of larger structural issues.

These dispositions are very similar to Brookhiser's (1997) six traits of WASP whiteness in the U.S.[13] The important thing about whiteness, as Barnet and many others have identified about whiteness generally, is that it's invisible, often denied as being whiteness. This is the nature of whiteness as a *habitus*. Ross Chambers (1997) explains that whiteness remains unexamined through the "pluralization of the *other* and the homogenization of *others*" (p. 192). He says that whiteness has been "unexaminable" (or rather, "examinable, yet unexamined") because it is not only the yardstick by which difference (like quality of writing) is judged and identified in the classroom and out of it, but whiteness is bound to "the category of the individual" first through "atomizing whiteness" by homogenizing others, which allows it to be invisible (p. 192). This invisible and universalizing nature of the above dispositions gives some reason for why the first two items are the most telling, and perhaps contentious. These two dispositions (hyperindividualism and the primacy of the *cogito*) alone make up much of Faigley's (1992) discussion of tastes in the ways teachers described the best student writing in their courses found in Coles and Vopat's collection, *What Makes Writing Good* (1985). What did most teachers say was good writing? Writing that exhibited a strong, authentic, honest voice. And what does strength, authenticity, and honesty look like as textual markers? It is a self-reliant voice that is focused on itself as a cool, rational, thinking self in the writing and in its reading of writer's own experiences or ideas. This isn't to say these are bad qualities in writing, only that they are linked to whiteness and this link often has uneven racist consequences in classroom writing assessments.

To put it more bluntly, a white racial *habitus* often has racist effects in the classroom, even though it is not racist in and of itself. Citing Mills (1997) and his own studies of whiteness (2001), Bonilla-Silva argues that "whiteness is the foundational category of 'white supremacy' .... *Whiteness, then, in all of its manifestations, is embodied racial power*" (2003a, p. 271; emphasis in original). The maintenance of whiteness and white supremacy, even if tacit as in the "new racism" that Bonilla-Silva and Villanueva (2006) describe, is vital to maintaining the status quo of society's social, economic, and racial hierarchies, the structuring structures that (re)produce a white racial *habitus*. Bonilla-Silva (2003a) explains that the new racism isn't just "racism lite," but manifests through five key structures that I argue destroy many healthy writing assessment ecologies:

- racial language practices that are "increasingly covert," as with those who argue that using a local SEAE as the privileged discourse in a writing classroom is not racist because the course is about the appropriate language use for college students, without questioning why that brand of English is deemed most appropriate or providing ways in the class to examine the dominant discourse as a set of conventions that have been "standardized" by the hegemonic;

- racial terminology that is explicitly avoided (or a universalizing and abstracting of experience and capacities), causing an increasing frequency of claims that whites themselves are experiencing "reverse racism";

- racial inequality that is reproduced invisibly through multiple mechanisms, reproduced structurally, as in my critique of the EPT or others' findings in the SAT;

- "safe minorities" (singular examples or exceptions, often named) that are used to prove that racism no longer exists, despite the larger patterns and statistics that prove the contrary, such as the Fresno State Hmong and African-American student racial formations;

- racial practices reminiscent of the Jim Crow period (e.g., separate but equal) that are rearticulated in new, non-racial terms, such as the new use of the EPT as a *de facto* entrance exam that by result attempts to stem the tide of students of color in California universities without ever being explicitly about race. (p. 272)

In many ways, the new racism discussed by Bonilla-Silva and Villanueva occurs more frequently in our classroom writing assessments because we uncritically promote (often out of necessity) a dominant academic discourse that is associated with a local SEAE. While these discourses and sets of linguistic conventions are not bad in and of themselves, they do need interrogating with students as structuring structures that give us certain tastes in language and thought. But writing classrooms cannot leave white racial *habitus* at that, at just critical discussions of language and texts, without also using those discussions in some way to change the writing assessment ecology of the classroom. This isn't easy work, but I hope to show ways I've attempted to do this in Chapter 6.

RACIAL FORMATION, RACIAL PROJECTS, AND RACISM

To conceive of and use an antiracist classroom writing assessment theory, we need concepts like racial *habitus* and white racial *habitus*, but while these concepts reference racialized bodies and suggest a definition of racism, the terms do not inherently explain racism as a phenomenon. They also do not explain how to reference actual bodies in the classroom. As I've reiterated above, racial *habitus* is not a term that directly references students' material bodies, and racism affects real people, real bodies, not *habitus*. Thus I use the term racial formation to do this referencing. Racism then affects racial formations.

Omi and Winant define "racial formation" "as the sociohistorical process by which racial categories are created, inhabited, transformed, and destroyed" (1994, p. 55). Any racial formation, then, is a part of a dynamic, historical process, constantly changing. These changes occur because of numerous "racial projects" that create, represent, and organize human bodies in particular times and places. These racial projects "simultaneously ... interpre[t], represen[t], or explai[n] ... racial dynamics," and "reorganize and redistribute resources along particular lines" (Omi & Winant, 1994, pp. 55-56). In short, all notions of race are (re)created by various racial projects in society and schools. Individual racial formations, such as the Hmong of Fresno, are constructed subjectively and projectively through racial projects in schools, society, in the EPT, in the university, etc.

Thus racism, Omi and Winant say, isn't simply a consequence of bigotry or prejudice. Historically in the U.S. it has been an "unavoidable outcome of patterns of socialization which were 'bred in the bone,' affecting not only whites but even minorities themselves." They explain that discrimination, inequality, and injustice have been "a structural feature of the U.S. society, the product of centuries of systematic exclusion, exploitation, and disregard of racially defined minorities" (1994, p. 69). Thus today, a racial project is racist "if and only if it creates or reproduces structures of domination based on essentialist categories of race" (Omi & Winant, 1994, p. 71). In the introduction to their collection, *Race and Writing Assessment*, Inoue and Poe (2012a) provide this way of understanding the concept of racism in light of Omi and Winant's racial formation theory:

> If racial formations are about the historical and structural
> forces that organize and represent bodies and their lived expe-
> riences, then racism is not about prejudice, personal biases, or
> intent. Racism is not about blaming or shaming white people.
> It is about understanding how unequal or unfair outcomes
> may be structured into our assessment technologies and the
> interpretations that we make from their outcomes. (p. 6)

If it's not clear already, just like large-scale assessment ecologies, classroom writing assessment ecologies are racial projects, regardless of their purposes, our intentions, or their designs. These racial projects may produce fair, good, and equitable outcomes or something else. I'm sure the EPT is not intended to be racist, nor to exclude, nor to create educational barriers for Hmong students, but that is exactly what it does as a racial project, making it a racist project. The EPT as a racial project directly affects the students in writing classrooms, and affects those classrooms' writing assessment ecologies as well, because it affects how students get there, how they see themselves, and what the curriculum offers them. Despite the best antiracist intentions, any classroom writing assessment ecology can easily be racist if it doesn't explicitly account for how students get there and how they are constituted subjectively and projectively by writing assessments.

To give you an example, consider Fresno State's writing program. The conventional grading systems used in the writing program before we redesigned the curriculum, installed a grading contract, and implemented the Directed Self-Placement[14] (DSP) process, produced racialized failure rates and grade distributions among our four main racial formations, which can be seen in the first row of Table 2 (listed as "2005-06 (Engl 1)").[15] Without any ill intentions on the part of writing teachers, many of whom were and are very conscientious about issues of fairness and racism in their classrooms, almost all writing classrooms reproduced higher levels of course failure in Hmong, Latino/a, and Black racial formations, with white students having the least amount of course failure.

The changes made to the program were almost all assessment-based, reconfiguring all the classroom writing assessments, from how students get into courses (DSP), to how most courses calculated final course grades (the grading contract), to the curriculum and pedagogies available (a program portfolio). As can be seen in Table 2, the failure rates in 2009-10 for the new end course, Engl

5B (equivalent to the old Engl 1) dropped by about half in all formations, except the Black racial formation, and the failure rates generally became more even across all racial formations.

Table 2. Students of color fail writing courses at consistently higher rates than their white peers in Fresno State's First-Year Writing Program (reproduced from Inoue, 2014b, p. 338)

Academic Year	African-American			Asian-American (Hmong)		
	n	No. failed	% failed	n	No. failed	% failed
2005–06 (Engl 1)	198	45	22.7%	454	90	19.8%
2009–10 (Engl 5B)	130	25	19.2%	158	16	10.1%
2010–11 (Engl 5B)	109	18	16.5%	195	19	9.7%
2011–12 (Engl 5B)	66	11	16.7%	160	16	10.0%

Academic Year	Latino/Latina			White		
	n	No. failed	% failed	n	No. failed	% failed
2005–06 (Engl 1)	843	188	22.3%	788	121	15.4%
2009–10 (Engl 5B)	682	75	11.0%	292	21	7.2%
2010–11 (Engl 5B)	685	65	9.5%	273	23	8.4%
2011–12 (Engl 5B)	553	78	14.1%	158	10	6.3%

In this very limited way, classroom writing assessment ecologies in the program can be seen as racial projects, as projects that produced particular kinds of racial formations associated closely with failure and success. No one is trying to be racist, but it is happening systemically and consistently, or structurally through the various classroom writing assessment ecologies. What should be clear is that racism isn't something that is always a "conscious aiming at ends," rather it is often a product of overlapping racial structures in writing assessments that are subjective and projective. Racism is not usually produced by conscious intentions, purposes, or biases of people against others not like them. Racism is a product of racialized structures that themselves tend to produce unequal, unfair, or uneven social distributions, be they grades, or access to education, or the expectations for judging writing. Conversely, antiracist projects must be consciously engaged in producing structures that themselves produce fair results for all racial formations involved.

Some may argue that the above failure rates may not be showing some form of racism, rather they only demonstrate that racial formations of color have performed worse than the white racial formation, so there is no clear racist project occurring here since the cause of the above effects cannot be determined to be racial in nature. How do we know racism in writing assessments is the cause of the course failure and not something else? This critique comes from a discourse of whiteness, from a white racial *habitus* that demands that such racialized conclusions reveal in a logical fashion racist intent by teachers, disregarding effect or results, as those are typically attributed to the individual (e.g., failure). The white racial *habitus* informing this question also assumes that there be a clear cause and effect relationship demonstrated in such conclusions about racism, conclusions from observations that make no assumptions about race. But as the literature on whiteness explains over and over, there is no getting around race in our epistemologies. The assumptions around needing clear racist causes that then lead to racist effects stems from a white disposition, a rationality that is calm and cool, for such things when we discuss racism (racism is hardly a calm and cool discussion in the U.S.). What seems clear to me in the above figures is that whites perform better regardless of the assessment ecology, but some ecologies mitigate the racist effects better than others. The uneven effects of these same ecologies demonstrates a problem. But if you still need a racist cause, there is a common cause for all the course grades: the courses' writing assessment ecologies that produced the grades.

Part of my argument for racism in classroom writing assessments, like those mentioned above, is that there are larger societal structures that are racist that create and influence the classroom. As my discussion of white racial *habitus* suggests, the structures of our writing assessments come from our society, our academic disciplines, and educational institutions, which have been organized to keep whites and whiteness dominant. In Charles Mills' (1997) award-winning book, *The Racial Contract*, he argues that Western civilization historically has cultivated and maintained a "racial contract" for the purposes of maintaining such white racial dominance in society at large. In one sense, Mills' could be arguing that there is an over-arching racial project that Western societies have participated in historically. We can hear how the racialized consequences of the racial contract are easily translatable to the consequences of college writing assessments in Mills explanation of the racial contract:

> set of formal or informal agreements or meta-agreements (higher-level contracts *about* contracts, which set the limits of the contracts' validity) between the members of one subset of humans, henceforth designated by (shifting) "racial" (phenotypical/genealogical/cultural) criteria C_1, C_2, C_3 ... as "white," and coextensive (making due allowance for gender differentiation) with the class of full persons, to categorize the remaining subset of humans as "nonwhite" and of a different and inferior

> moral status, subpersons, so that they have a subordinate civil standing in the white or white-ruled politics ... the general purpose of the Contract is always the differential privileging of the whites as a group with respect to the nonwhites as a group, the exploitation of their bodies, land, and resources, and the denial of equal socioeconomic opportunities to them. All whites are *beneficiaries* of the Contract, though some whites are not *signatories* to it. (1997, p. 11)

One good way to subordinate nonwhite groups in California generally would be to maintain the EPT as a placement and entrance writing assessment, since doing so would in effect keep more students of color out of college and allow more (relatively speaking) white students in. A good way to validate its uses so as to maintain white racial supremacy is to do so abstractly, using disciplinary meta-agreements about what constitutes validity and bias, despite the contradictions those agreements create when applied to the literacy competencies of locally diverse students in, say, Fresno. This racial contract flows into, is then assumed in, all writing classrooms.

Furthermore, a part of the racial contract is the categorizing of other things that lead to racial hierarchies, such as an uncritical privileging of a local SEAE in college writing courses, or an unreflective expectation of the fictional, monolingual English speaker and writer that many have critiqued (Horner & Trimbur, 2002; Horner et al., 2011; Jordan, 2012; Lu, 1994). Before writing teachers can breach the racial contract, we have to recognize it as such, and see it as informing our past and present classroom writing assessment ecologies because it has informed the U.S. history and Western society.

There is one adjustment, however, to the language of Mills' racial contract theory that I make for use in classroom writing assessment. His language suggests that the purposes, perhaps even intent, of the racial contract's sets of agreements are to privilege whites, but I think, at least in the realm of classroom writing assessment, it should be emphasized that the *purpose* of the racial contract might be more accurately identified as its *function*, which is beyond or despite intentions or purposes. The racial contract involved in any writing assessment ecology cannot be said to regulate explicitly the assessment's purposes. Purposes are connected tightly to people, and have particular associations with writing assessments. It would be extremely rare, in my opinion, to find a writing assessment whose purposes are explicitly to subordinate students of color or deny them opportunities in a writing classroom. However, I emphasize that the racial contract for these same writing assessments *functions* in the same way that Mills describes, but not from an expressed purpose to do so, instead the racial contract of writing assessments usually functions in these ways despite our antiracist intentions or good purposes because the racial contract is structural in nature and privileges a white racial *habitus.*

To put it bluntly, when the function of a writing assessment is primarily to promote a local SEAE or dominant discourse, without regard to the literacies that various racial formations bring to the classroom, or the various ways that particular racialized linguistic structures are judged by the teacher, then many students may be treated unfairly. The writing assessment may be racist, and all in the name of an abstract liberal principle: to teach all students the same English, the dominant one, to maintain the tacit whiteness associated with the local SEAE and the writing assessment itself. My implicit argument is that this project (to assess everyone by standards of the same discourse, the same English) is an inherently racist project.

Often writing teachers claim to assess everyone by the same standards or expectations because this practice is inherently fair. If only we could stop being so fair, we might have a chance at making serious antiracist change. Fairness is often articulated as a white liberal value, but it often protects white interests by maintaining racist practices and effects by appealing to an abstract liberal principle, such as, "everyone should be treated the same." This value makes no sense when we try to transplant the abstract principle of fairness to, say, fruit. Is an orange better than an apple because it is juicier? Of course not, they are just different. And their differences are acknowledged and accepted. But when we deny racialized difference in the writing classroom, we tend to judge apples by their orangeness. I realize the metaphor breaks down, but my point is: it is not fairness that we need in antiracist writing assessment ecologies, or any antiracist project—it is not judgment by the exact same standard that we need—it is revolutionary change, radically different methods, structures, and assumptions about the way things are now and how to distribute privileges.

As I've argued similarly elsewhere (Inoue, 2007), fairness in any writing assessment ecology is not an inherent quality, practice, or trait that then allows us to claim an assessment is fair for everyone. Judging everyone by the same standard is not an inherently fair practice in a writing classroom. Fairness is a construction of the ecology itself. It is contingent, and its primary constituents are agreement and participation by those in the ecology. When you don't have enough agreement (not consensus), participation, and an acknowledgement of fairness as a dynamic and shifting construct of the ecology, it is difficult to have a fair writing assessment.

CRITICISMS OF RACE AS AN ORGANIZING PRINCIPLE

Some may argue that the problems we see, for example in the Hmong student populations and their lower performance on the EPT or the failure rates in the writing program I showed above, are mostly economic in nature, or a product of different cultural values about school or language practices, or a result of some social dimension that has nothing to do with race, that there is no need to think in terms of race because race doesn't really exist. It just confuses and muddies the waters. In short, some may argue that it is not race but other non-racial, more fundamental factors that affect any writing assessment's results.

I do not deny that such factors as economics are involved. African-Americans and Hmong in Fresno are often some of the poorest in the community, with very high poverty rates, higher than those of whites—and this intersection of economics and race is not a coincidence so we shouldn't treat it as such. These kinds of factors intersect and make up racialized experiences as political, as relations of power. In the U.S., power usually is organized around three nodes of difference: gender, race, and economics. These non-racial factors are the structuring structures that racial *habitus* references. These structures become racialized when they pool or gather into patterns in groups in society, creating distinctions from the white hegemonic group. These structures then are used as markers of difference that then justify the denial of privilege, power, and access to opportunities, such as education. Using a local SEAE as a way to determine the merit of a student, her fitness for college, or the value of her literacies in college are clear cases of societal structures that become racialized when they are used to maintain white privilege. Just because we don't call our valuing of a dominant discourse racist doesn't make it not racist. So could we deal with the above assessment issues in classrooms as economic ones and not racial ones? We could, but we'd be denying the way economics constructs racialized experiences and subjectivities in the U.S. and in our classrooms.

Furthermore in the U.S., we just do not uniformly act or behave based on fine-tuned, ethnic or cultural distinctions because the tensions among various groups have always been about maintaining or gaining power, privilege, property, or rights. Culture, language, and ethnic differences to a hegemonic whiteness are used to construct power relations, but they tend to be used to create broader racial differences. It's much easier to use a broader category like race, than distinguish between ethnic Chinese, Japanese, Korean, Vietnamese, Hmong, etc. It's easier just to say Asian. Because the bottom line is, historically the main reasons to identify the differences in any group in the U.S. has been to subordinate that group to white power and deny privileges. And even though the motives may not be what they used to be, the effects of the structures that remain are the same.

Education and literacy, the keys to the kingdom, are a part of these power relations because they tend to be seen as a way to confer privileges and jobs. Consider the discussions of literacy in the U.S. as white property, particularly around the decisions of Brown v. Board of Education (Bell, 2004; Prendergast, 2003). Or more broadly, consider the ways whiteness has been used as a way to claim and hold onto jobs and property by whites (Lipsitz, 1998; Roediger, 1999). Perhaps the most powerful term that explains how race often is used to maintain power, property, and privilege is in Pierre L. van den Berghe's term, "herrenvolk democracy" (; Roediger, 1999, p. 59; van den Berghe, 1967, pp. 17-18). Herrenvolk democracy explains the way a society, through laws and norms, creates a democratic system for a dominant group, but simultaneously offers a considerably less democratic one for subordinate groups. Race is a convenient and well-used way to construct subordinate groups, ones with less access to property, jobs, literacy, and education. Today, we use language to do this subordinating, which racializes all writing assessment.

It isn't hard to see the denial or dramatically less access to education, jobs, privilege, and social power to people of color, particularly African-Americans, Latinos/as, and Native Americans (Asians are a set of complex racial formations, uneven in their access to power). While no one is denying college entrance to, for instance, Black students because they are Black, almost all colleges use SAT and ACT scores to help determine candidacy. As mentioned earlier, Breland et al. (2004) found that SAT scores are hierarchical by race, with whites performing the best and Blacks the worst. Furthermore, GPAs and other extra-curricular activities are used by colleges in their application processes also. This means if you are poor, you likely will have gone to a high school that couldn't prepare you well for college. According to the National Center for Law and Economic Justice, Blacks and non-white Hispanics live in poverty at the highest rates of all racial groups, with just over a quarter of non-white Hispanics and 27.2% of Blacks living in poverty (National Center for Law and Economic Justice, n.d.).[16] Many more Blacks and Latinos/as live in poverty than whites, thus they are more likely to go to schools that do not prepare them for college in traditional ways, and any application they may submit likely will be viewed as weaker than their white counterparts. Economics, tax laws that fund schools unequally, and the like are some of the structuring structures that seem not to be about race but are racialized, and they structure the racial *habitus* of students. A herrenvolk democracy in schools, from elementary to college, itself structures inequality into just about all writing assessments by working from laws and norms that racially privilege a white racial *habitus* that is nurtured in some places and starved in others.

It is important to remember, though, as Bourdieu's *habitus* makes clear, that there is no "conscious aiming at ends." There are no racists, just structural and systemic racism. The herrenvolk democracy of a classroom writing assessment happens through a variety of means, such as valuing a local SEAE, but it produces a two-track system of privilege that rewards a white *habitus* exclusively. This is why translingual approaches (Horner et al., 2011), world Englishes, and code meshing pedagogies (Canagarajah, 2006; Young, 2004, 2007, 2011; Young & Martinez, 2011) are important to develop; however, I have yet to see a serious attempt at developing classroom writing assessments from such approaches. Understanding racial *habitus* as a set of historically generated discursive, material, and performative structuring structures that are both subjective and projective in nature seems a good place to begin thinking about how writing assessments might understand the Englishes they attempt to judge and make decisions on.

RACE AS PART OF A GLOBAL IMAGINARY OF WRITING ASSESSMENT

But if teachers are not consciously trying to be racist, and usually attempting to do exactly the opposite in their classroom writing assessments, which I think is the case, then what is happening? How can race affect a teacher's practices if she isn't thinking in terms of race, or if she is trying not to let race be a factor in the way she reads or judges student writing? How can my classroom writing assessments be racist if I'm not racist and I try to treat everyone fairly, try not to punish multilingual students or Black students or Latino/a students for the languages they bring with them into the classroom? In fact, I try to celebrate those languages. In short, the answer to these question has to do with larger, global imaginaries about education and race that started long before any of us were teaching our first writing courses.

Again, the Fresno Hmong are instructive in addressing these questions. There are only two ethnic formations in Fresno that can be called refugees, the Hmong and Armenians. The experiences of Hmong in Fresno are racialized. Hmong are the newest, having arrived in three waves, between 1975 and 1991, 1992 and 1999, 2000 and the present (Yang, 2009, p. 79). The Hmong originally came to Fresno not by choice but because it was the only way out of persecution and the eroding conditions in the refugee camps of Laos and Thailand (Chan, 1994; Dao, 1982; Lieb, 1996, pp. 17-20). Coming in three distinct periods and under very similar conditions makes the Hmong racial formation quite consistent in regards to living conditions, cultural ties and practices, employment, languages spoken, and educational experiences. However because they share Asian physical traits and come from Asia as refugees after the Vietnam war, Hmong tend to be seen and treated as foreigners, as the racial other, despite the fact that most Hmong in college are U.S. born citizens. This is historically the way all Asian immigrants and Asian-Americans have experienced racialized life in the U.S., including me (just consider my experiences in the trailer park). The U.S. government's treatment of its territories of Guam and American Samoa epitomizes this racialize alien othering. These territories are not considered sovereign states, yet are governed by the U.S., and those born there do not receive automatic U.S. citizenship, but they are allowed to join the U.S. military. American Samoa has the highest rate of U.S. military enlistment anywhere (Total Military Recruits, 2004). Guam was acquired in 1898 as part of the Treaty of Paris after the Spanish-America war, while American Samoa was occupied by the U.S. Navy in 1900 and officially named a territory in 1911. A U.S. territory was originally meant to be a short-term political designation that referred to areas that the U.S. was acquiring, particularly during the eighteenth and nineteenth centuries. The long reluctance to make these territories (among others, like Puerto Rico) states suggests the associations of Asians and Pacific Islanders as perpetual foreigners, as racialized alien others.

Angelo Ancheta (1998) shows historically how Asians have been legally deemed the other, denied rights, property, and citizenship. Robert Lee (1999) demonstrates the ways Asians have been represented in U.S. culture over the last century as the racial other, as the "Heathen Chinee" "Coolie," "gook," and "model minority." Vijay Prashad (2000) demonstrates the complex relationship that the U.S. has had with the East as mysterious, filled with menageries, harems, and gurus, but these associations always reinforce the idea of Asians as perpetual foreigners. Christina Klein (2003) shows the way a cold war mentality in the U.S. affected the Orientalism that constructed the ways Americans tend to relate to Asians, most notably through narratives of "sentimental education" that offered cultural and racial integration on a global scale after WWII. And this sentimental education, one of parental guidance for the childlike Asians (similar to the sentimentality voiced in Kipling's "The White Man's Burden") has bearing on Hmong students in Fresno. The parental language that says, "we know what's best for them," is pervasive in schools and college and is the rationale for the EPT and Early Start program, even though the test does not target Hmong students. It does give teachers and schools reason to engage in such narratives.

Klein explains that sentimental education was part of a "global imaginary" that connected and unified U.S. citizens to other parts of the world, most notably the more volatile areas of Asia after WWII, where the threat of communism seemed to be most potent. Klein explains:

> A global imaginary is an ideological creation that maps the world conceptually and defines the primary relations among peoples, nations, and regions ... It produces peoples, nations, and cultures not as isolated entities but as interconnected with

one another. This is not to say that it works through deception or that it mystifies the real, material conditions of global
relations. Rather, a global imaginary articulates the ways in
which people imagine and live those relations. It recreates an
imaginary coherence out of the contradictions and disjunc-
tures of real relations, and thereby provides a stable sense
of individual and national identity. In reducing the infinite
complexity of the world to comprehensible terms, it creates
a common sense about how the world functions as a system
and offers implicit instruction in how to maneuver within
that system; it makes certain attitudes and behaviors easier to
adopt than others. (2003, pp. 22-23)

Klein uses the film *The King and I* (1956), among others, as one example of the
way a sentimental education imagines social relations between whites and Asians
in a global imaginary. Not so ironically, these relations are gendered, with a
white female teacher (played by Deborah Kerr) teaching Asian children (the film
is situated in Siam, or contemporary Thailand) geography, English, etiquette,
and the like (Klein, 2003, pp. 2-3). It would appear she is teaching Asians their
place and relations in the world, to whites, and to English literacies, through
a kind of parental pedagogy.[17] The film not only imagines relations between
whites and Asian school children, but maintains Asians as racially foreign by
associating them with all the tropes that U.S. audiences understand as the Asian
that Lee (1999) and Prashad (2000) discuss. In a pivotal musical performance
of the song, "Getting to Know You," as the teacher sings the song of interracial
relations and etiquette, she is surround by the King's children and his harem,
all decked out in colorful, exotic Siamese dress. At one point, a fan dancer performs. In the background, a map of the world with Siam identified, even central
in the map, is prominent. The only thing missing is a menagerie of animals.

The global imaginary that Klein discusses hasn't changed much. It articulates
the ways teachers and schools in Fresno imagine and live the global relations between them and their Hmong students. This global imaginary offers a common
sense: we can all be full citizens of California and America if, like the Teacher
and her pupils in *The King and I*, we all speak and write the same particular
brand of English. But this set of relations demands a racial hierarchy, one that
imagines a white (female) teacher in charge of helping her Asian students learn
English, while she "gets to know them." Thus we have the EPT and Early Start
programs, which spawn from sentimental, maternal logic. It's only logical and
right, even fair, that the state provide an Early Start experience for underpre-
pared students in Fresno, which happens to include almost the entire Hmong

student population in Fresno. These students need more help with English so that they can succeed in college. This global imaginary functioning in the EPT writing assessment assumes that one key to success in college (and perhaps elsewhere) is a particular kind of English fluency, which is a dominant white middle class English, similar to the kind that Deborah Kerr teaches her Siamese charges in the film (she invokes a British accent in the film). Without this white hegemonic English, students will fail at their work in and out of school. This is the script, the common sense, a part of a global imaginary that reinforces a sense of maternal duty and obligation to straighten out those twisted tongues and words of all Hmong students. I argue this same sensibility, this global imaginary of sentimental education, grounded in past race relations, is alive and thriving in many college writing classrooms, affecting (or infecting) their writing assessments because it determines the ways teachers read and judge writing and create the larger mechanisms for assessment. In one sense, our writing classrooms could be labeled, "The Hmong and I," with the "I" being the teacher, who often is a white female.[18]

It should be remembered that Klein's theory of a global imaginary comes from Edward Said's (1979) powerful and explanatory concept of Orientalism. And the theory is instructive for understanding the Hmong racial formation's position in classroom writing assessments at Fresno State. Through an exhaustive account of various Western scholars, the academy, and government institutions, Said demonstrates how the West generally has constructed and dominated the orient (our Middle East), what it means, what it is, etc. He explains that Orientalism offers the orient as a "system of representations," which can be understood as a "discourse, whose material presence or weight, not the originality of a given author, is really responsible for the texts produced out of it." Academics and their related institutions primarily create this discourse and grant it authority and "prestige" by their act of articulation and *ethos* as Western specialists. Orientalism, as a discourse, perpetuates itself by collecting, organizing, and recycling a "catalogue of *idées reçues*," or "received ideas" (Said, 1979, p. 94).

It isn't that far-fetched to see writing teachers (from high school to college) in Fresno participating in such Orientalist discourse when they read their Hmong students and their writing. Who knows best how to understand and describe the literacy practices of Hmong students? Apparently, the EPT, and those who translate and use its scores: schools and writing teachers in California. This isn't to deny the expertise that many writing teachers develop by teaching multilingual students in classrooms, instead I'm suggesting we question the nature of our expertise in and methods for assessing multilingual and locally diverse students and their writing. We question what informs the judgments we make and what those judgments tell us we should do as teachers, what decisions they seem to demand. Not only might we find a global imaginary of sentimental education functioning in our writing assessments' discourses, processes, and methods, but we may also be constructing our locally diverse students and their writings by a set of racist received ideas that determine the quality of their writing. If Orientalism is anything, it is a discursive field of assessment. It provides its specialists with automatic judgments of the Orient and the Oriental. It is the discourse of Asian and Middle Eastern racial stigmata. Is it possible, then, that there might be an Orientalism occurring in our classroom writing assessments around Hmong students' and their writing, around other Asian racial formations?

In his discussion on early Twentieth century Orientalism, Said shows how Orientalism accomplishes its tasks of consumption, manipulation, and domination by Western academics' "visions" of the oriental and the orient, which has a clear analogue to Hmong taking the EPT and writing teachers' discourses on their writing in college classrooms. Said provides an example in John Buchan, a Scottish born classicist at Oxford in 1922. Buchan illustrates how vision works, and displays several key features of American visions of Chinese during the same period:

> The earth is seething with incoherent power and unorganized intelligence. Have you ever reflected on the case of China? There you have millions of quick brains stifled in trumpery crafts. They have no direction, no driving power, so the sum of their efforts is futile, and the world laughs at China. (Said, 1979, p. 251)

Buchan's "clarity of vision and analysis," common during this part of the twentieth century, "selectively organize[s]" the orient and its objects (including its inhabitants). The Chinese of Buchan's vision is a massive horde of unorganized, incoherent, half-crazed, quick-brained, brown-skinned devils, who might, as Said says, "destroy 'our' [the Occidental] world" (Said, 1979, p. 251). The details that build this analysis are not really details at all but the commonplaces that hold currency in the Western mind, prefabricated judgments, predetermined assessments, serving to uplift the West and suppress the Far East, recreating hierarchical relations of power between whites and Asians. Buchan's passage and its commonplaces are driven by his vision. In fact, Orientalism, in all its manifestations (for Said acknowledges that it's not uniform), is always guided by the Western scholar's vision, coloring all that he sees, helping him make judgments, assess, augmenting his analyses and conclusions.

One might make a similar critique of the way Hmong student writing, or any multilingual student writing, gets typically judged in classrooms, or on the EPT? They are remedial because visions similar to the ones operating in Orientalism determine what is most valuable, visions that are a part of a global imaginary that privileges a particular dominant English and its dispositions, then assumes a parental role toward students. Take the sample 2-essay from the EPT guide previously discussed. The ideal reader described in the guide sees the discussion of the "Great American Boycott" in paragraph three as merely "stream of consciousness," an unorganized, off-topic, and perhaps illogical discussion. The vision required to see such details as stream of consciousness is similar to Said's Orientalist vision since it is reasonable to understand why a Latino/a or Hmong student with a particular relation to advertisements and consumer consumption in California might include this information. This vision fulfills the needs that the narratives of sentimental education create and that circulate in California and the U.S. generally.

The fact that Fresno Hmong students who take the EPT have parents who recently immigrated to California in the last few decades from Laos as political refugees, and who only spoke their native Hmong language upon arrival, and are mostly low-income or living in poverty (Asian-American Center for Advancing Justice, 2013, pp. 20-21) seem not to matter to those who might judge their writing, seem not to matter to those designing or reading the EPT. By the logic of this global imaginary, which uses an Orientalist set of received ideas, these historical exigencies are irrelevant to the assessment of English competency. These historical structures that continue to structure Hmong lives, while not racial in the old-fashion sense of being essential to Hmong (similar factors affect Chinese, Vietnamese, and other students), not biological, pool consistently in Hmong populations in Fresno because they are structuring in nature, perpetuating themselves. But the structures are both subjective, as in the case of Hmong literacies, and projective, as in the case of how those literacies are read and judged by teachers who read them through a global imaginary of sentimental education. Seeing these structures as a part of Hmong racial *habitus* that then work in concert with Orientalist visions of multilingual Asian students and a global imaginary that cast teachers into parental roles in scripts of sentimental education can help teachers rethink and reconstruct classroom writing assessments that do not play power games with students based on factors in their lives they simply cannot control. So to be poor and multilingual are not ethnic or cultural structures, but they are racialized as Hmong in Fresno, which is not to say they are essential but deployed in ways that end up harming Hmong students in college.

It could be said that I'm being overly harsh to local writing teachers, of whom I have been one, and the designers and readers of the EPT. I do not deny that these are well-intentioned, good people, trying hard to offer a quality education to all students in California. I do not deny that writing teachers in the area explicitly attempt to provide educational experiences to Hmong students, most of whom are multilingual, in ways that will help them in their futures in school and careers. But I wonder how many of us have considered the way a Hmong racial *habitus* is or is not accounted for in our writing assessments, in the ways we judge, in the expectations we have for writing, in the processes we design. I wonder if many have considered the white racial *habitus* clearly operating in most writing assessments? I wonder if many have considered the function of a global imaginary of sentimental education in their relations with Hmong students, or Latinos/as, or Blacks? I wonder if many have thought explicitly about the ways race in any way is already in their writing assessments?

A final example I hope will capture the way race functions in classroom writing assessments that cannot help but draw on a global imaginary of sentimental education. For a time, I was the Special Assistant to the Provost for Writing Across the Curriculum at Fresno State. In the first semester I took the job, the dean of the College of Arts and Humanities sent me a package. In it was a memo with an attached marked and graded student draft of a paper from a general education course. The memo was from the professor, whom I'll call Dr. X. The dean said, "here, now you can deal with him. Apparently every semester, Dr. X would send the dean another paper with a similar memo. The memo proclaimed the illiteracy of "our students," with the accompanying draft as proof, complete with his copious markings of grammar issues and errors. Now, I would get his memos and sample drafts each semester.

A few semesters later, Dr. X attended one of my WAC workshops, and I asked him about his memos. I said that I appreciated his concerns for our students' writing, but I wasn't sure what he wanted me to do, since he never made any call to action or offered any ideas. He simply complained. Dr. X looked at me without hesitation, and said, "I want you to feel bad about our students' writing." I told him that I could not feel bad, since what I saw in each draft were opportunities to talk to the student about his or her writing choices. That's what writing in college is about, making mistakes and finding ways out of them.

The one thing I have not said about these memos and drafts is that almost all of them were from Hmong students. I know this because in Fresno we have about 18 Hmong clans represented and they have distinct last names. So if the last name of the student on the draft is one of these 18 names, he or she is almost certainly Hmong.[19] Dr. X seemed to have an Orientalist vision that saw his Hmong students' writing as flawed and illiterate, so much so that he needed to show someone else in power. He needed to show someone that we were not doing our parental duty toward our Hmong students. We weren't educating them, and so we should feel bad because we were shirking our duties, or white man's burden. Dr. X wasn't alone in his assessment of Hmong students' writing abilities on campus, and there were certainly some who didn't see things this way. The point I'm making is that without a global imaginary of sentimental education that determines teachers' judgments, assessments, behavior, pedagogy, and the like when confronted with multilingual Hmong student writing, Dr. X likely would have had a different reaction to his students' drafts. Perhaps, the texts he saw from his Hmong students would have indicated that his assignments didn't fit them very well, or his curriculum might need to be better adapted to his students' needs.

In many ways, this global imaginary creates a vision that may actually augment reality. For instance, I wonder exactly how many students of Dr. X's fit into the category of "illiterate." I asked this question to another professor who complained about a similar occurrence in his general education courses (note: both of these vocal faculty were white males). So I asked him how big the class was? He said 200 students. I asked how many students seem to have these deep language problems in each class? After a few seconds of consideration, he said, "maybe ten." "So 5% of your class have these problems," I reiterated. "Yes," he said. "So 95% of your students are essentially okay," I asked rhetorically? "I don't see a pervasive problem," and I left the conversation at that.

RACE AS A NEXUS OF POWER RELATIONS

Race, *racial habitus*, and racism are about power. So when we avoid it in our writing assessments, we tend to avoid addressing important power relations that create inequality. Paying attention to race in our classroom writing assessments isn't racist. In fact, not paying attention to race often leads to racism. Racism occurs in the nature of assumptions, the production of racial hierarchies, and the effects or consequences of racial projects. And using exclusively cultural or ethnic terms, such as Japanese or Hmong, without connecting them to race (thus leaving them unconnected to racism) have their own problems. Doing so elides the non-cultural and non-ethnic dimensions of human experience in society, defining a social formation primarily by ethnicity or cultural practices that some students may not have experiences with or practice yet still be associated with. Race isn't solely, or even mostly, about culture, as I hope my discussion above about racial *habitus* and racial subjectivity and projection reveal.

Race as an organizing term is primarily about understanding power and privilege, not cultural differences. I'm a good example of the way race is about more than culture or ethnicity. Ethnically I'm Japanese-American, Scottish, English, and some Mediterranean (likely Greek or Italian). My father was Japanese from Hawai'i, but I was raised by my mother, who has always identified as white. This means that I was not raised in a Buddhist or Shinto home, nor did I have the chance to go to Japanese school, or speak Japanese. I wasn't raised with many culturally Japanese practices, yet I am mostly Japanese by blood heritage. I have usually been mistaken for some kind of Latino, depending on the context. I have been the target of many racist remarks, acts, and the like. This is my own racial subjectivity, and I've had to come to my own Japanese-American cultural and ethnic practices, history, and awareness as an adult. Racially, I identify as Asian-American, given the power differentials I've encountered in my life, yet I do this by repressing or denying to some degree my whiteness and white heritage, which I'm sure has helped me in some ways. I do not think that I'm such a strange occurrence. Ethnicity simply is insufficient for me. Race, however, is an identifier of one's political position or relation to power in society, and better captures such complexities of subjectivity.

And so, using ethnic identifiers can make us think that we are looking at ethnic differences, when it is more important to see differences of power and privilege, differences produced by social structures associated with sets of racialized dispositions (or discursive, material, and performative structures), ones that may be subjective (self-identifications) or projected onto groups. Regardless of the structures, we are always seeing differences in power and privilege. Using Manning Marable (2002), Carmen Kynard (2013) explains clearly the relationship between race and power:

> I also define race as the central, power-defining principle of modern states and, today, as a "global apartheid" that has constructed "new racialized ethnic hierarchies" in the context of the global flow of capital under neoliberalism. This means that white privilege can be more specifically understood as the historical accumulation of material benefits in relation to salaries, working conditions, employment, home ownership, life expectancy rates, access to professional positions, and promotions. (Kynard, 2013, p. 10)

The result of the historical accumulation of material benefits to those who inhabit a white racial *habitus* is structural racism that provides power, privilege, and access to opportunities that most folks who inhabit other racial *habitus* simply are denied, and denied for ostensibly non-racial reasons. And this racism amounts to power differentials based on how an individual or group is situated racially in society, school, and the larger global economy. And so, to have an antiracist agenda for classroom writing assessment means that writing assessment is centrally about the construction and distribution of power in all the ways that power is exercised in the classroom. But for the writing classroom, power is mostly exercised through the ability to judge, assess, and grade writing. It is exercised mostly through the assessment ecology.

LOCAL DIVERSITIES

Writing teachers who wish to engage in antiracist writing assessment practices must address race at the local level, considering the racial and linguistic diversity in their classrooms, something very few writing assessment discussions have been able to do. Race is a tangled construct, a clumsy, slippery one. It is not biological, nor even real in the ways that language use or citizenship status are, but race is a way to understand patterns in lived experience that equate a social formation's relation to dominant discourses and a local white racial *habitus*, one's relations to power. If we assume that writing assessments are ecologies (I'll make this argument in the next chapter), then they are local in nature, as others have discussed (Gallagher, 2010; Huot, 2002; O'Neill et al., 2009), and as NCTE and CWPA have recognized as an important consideration for effective writing assessments (CCCC, 2009; NCTE & WPA, n.d.). If they are local, then the populations that participate in them at the local level are important to theorize into our writing assessment practices. So, how can we understand local diversities in particular schools and classrooms in ways that help teachers to assess the writing of racially diverse students in their classrooms?

On today's college campuses, the local student populations are growing in their racial and cultural diversity, and this diversity means different things at different schools. According to The National Center for Educational Statistics enrollment figures for all U.S. colleges and universities, the numbers of Black and Hispanic[20] students have steadily increased: Between 2000 and 2010, the percentage of college students who were Black rose from 11.3% to 14.5%, and the percentage of Hispanic students rose from 9.5% to 13%. For the same years, they show that international ("nonresident alien") student enrollment remains virtually the same at 3.4% of the total student population (U.S. Department of Education & National Center for Education Statistics, 2011). And this doesn't mention the variety of Asian and Asian-American students on college campuses, or the very small but just as complex numbers of Native American students, nor does it adequately complicate what each of these racial categories means at particular schools.

Regardless of the local complexities, with all these students comes more English literacies spoken and written in the classroom. Paul Kei Matsuda highlights the importance of these trends in composition as a field and the classroom by arguing that composition studies must address more directly the "myth of linguistic homogeneity," that is, that writing classrooms and programs work from a false myth in which the teacher's or program's normative image of typical writing students is of "native speakers of a privileged variety of English" (2006, p. 638). Matsuda extends a critique by Bruce Horner and John Trimbur (2002). Horner and Trimbur argue that U.S. college writing classes hold assumptions about the preferred English—the privileged variety of English—used in classrooms, which they call "unidirectional monolingualism." They argue for "an alternative way of thinking about composition programs, the language of our students, and our own language practices that holds monolingualism itself to be a problem and a limitation of U.S. culture and that argues for the benefits of an actively multi-lingual language policy" (2002, p. 597). Matsuda and Horner and Trimbur are talking about writing assessment without saying it. The myth of linguistic ho-mogeneity really boils down to how we read and judge writing of locally diverse students. A writing pedagogy that doesn't assume a unidirectional monolingual-ism is one that assesses writing and writing students by considering more than a single dominant English. But to incorporate their good ideas, to construct writing pedagogies that do more than demand a dominant discourse, we must begin by thinking about local diversities in classroom writing assessments.

In Jay Jordan's (2012) discussion of multilingual classroom realities, he too ar-gues that the Englishes that come to us in writing classrooms are more and more global Englishes, a part of a "globally changing language," and we "cannot afford to continue ignoring the multiple competencies students have developed 'on the ground' and often before entering our classrooms" (p. 53). These are conclu-sions that others have also made about world Englishes (Canagarajah, 2006) and code meshing (Young, 2007, 2011; Young & Martinez, 2011). Claude Hurlbert (2012) makes a convincing argument for considering "international composi-tion," or an English composition classroom that considers epistemologies across the globe as valid and worth learning from and about (p. 52). The bottom line is that the cultural, material, and linguistic diversity in our writing classrooms demands a writing assessment theory that is robust enough to help teachers and WPAs design and deploy writing assessments that are responsibly informed and fair to all students, regardless of their pre-college experiences or cultural and linguistic heritages. Furthermore, this theory of writing assessment should be dynamic enough to account for the ways various racial formations may change when participating in the classrooms that the assessments produce. I could use the conventional assessment language to describe the kinds of writing assessments that I'm speaking of, that the decisions from them be valid enough and reliable writing assessments, or use other terms, such as ethical and meaningful (Lynne, 2004), but the point is that we understand what we are creating and what those creations do in our classrooms to and for our students and teachers.

In our increasingly racially and linguistically diverse writing classrooms, a theory of writing assessment is robust if it can address the difficult question of ethnic and racial diversity among students and teachers, a question addressed publically in 2008 on the Conference on College Composition and Communication's Diversity blog (http://cccc-blog.blogspot.com/). Diversity seems to mean many things to many people. Much like the critique that Joseph Harris makes of "community" in composition studies, that it has no negative binary term (2012, pp. 134-135), an argument he actually draws out from Raymond Williams definition of the term (1976, p. 76), "diversity" may have only positive associations in academia. This isn't a problem until we find that the concept is deployed in ways that function to erase difference, or merely celebrate it without complication (Schroeder, 2011), or as a commodity for institutions to measure themselves by (Kerschbaum, 2014, p.44). In other words, we like to celebrate diversity without dealing with difference. And these complications are different at historical moments and geographic places, at different schools. So it may be best to speak only in terms of local diversity around our writing assessments. This doesn't solve the question of the meaning of "diversity," but it does give us a place to begin understanding so that the writing assessments we have in local places can be developed in ways that meet locally diverse needs.

In the abstract, the idea of designing a writing assessment in response to a local set of diverse students and teachers is no different from best practices in the field of writing assessment. Huot's (2002) calls for "context-sensitive" assessments, meaning they "honor the instructional goals and objectives as well as the cultural and social environment of the institution or agency" (p. 105), seems to say the same thing. But looking closer at Huot's explanation of this principle reveals an absence of any concepts or theories that could explain or inform in some robust way the racial, cultural, or linguistic diversity that any classroom writing assessment might have. Huot explains:

> Developing writing assessment procedures upon an epistemological basis that honors local standards, includes a specific context for both the composing and reading of student writing and allows the communal interpretation of written communication is an important first step in furnishing a new theoretical umbrella for assessing student writing. However, it is only a first step. We must also develop procedures with which to document and validate their use. These validation procedures must be sensitive to the local and contextual nature of the procedures themselves. While traditional writing assessment methods rely on statistical validation and standardization that are important to the beliefs and assumptions

that fuel them, developing procedures will need to employ more qualitative and ethnographic validation procedures like interviews, observations and thick descriptions to understand the role an assessment plays within a specific program or institution. (2002, p. 106)

While it is clear in Huot's discussion that teachers should be taking into account their particular students when developing writing assessments, which makes for "site-based" and "locally-controlled" assessments (2002, p. 105), he focuses attention on procedures and institutional needs, not the ethnic or racial diversity among students who come into contact with those procedures and needs, both of which have been designed before any student arrives on the scene. I don't want to be unfair to Huot. He is concerned with how locally diverse students are treated in writing assessments, and places most of his solution on validation processes, thus on local teachers abilities and intentions to look for and find unfairness or racism. In a broad sense, local teachers have to weed out racism in their assessments. Who else will? But do they? Will they if they aren't prompted to look?

Knowing or being prompted to look is vital. The validation of a writing assessment's decision[21] is usually not designed, nor conceived of, as engaging productively with difference or diversity in student populations or teachers. This is likely why he calls for "qualitative and ethnographic validation procedures," but it's hard to know what exactly these procedures would focus on or reveal. What is the range of hypotheses that teachers begin with? While it is easy to read into the above description of a site, say a writing classroom, as nearly uniform or homogeneous, I do not think Huot means this. But isn't that often the assumption we make when we look to assess writing or design a classroom writing assessment of an essay or a written document of some kind? Procedures and rubrics are usually designed to label and categorize student performances in uniform ways, which means they identify sameness, not surprises or difference. These kinds of procedures and institutional needs (like a need for a standard, local SEAE to be used) enforces homogeneity, and punishes diversity, as we can conclude from both Matsuda (2006) and Horner and Trimbur (2002).

Huot does offer alternatives to validation that could take into account local diversities, procedures that work toward "qualitative and ethnographic validation," but these procedures are mainly to "understand the role an assessment plays within a specific program or institution." This is a worthwhile goal, and while the searching for student difference may be assumed in such procedures for validating an assessment's decisions, terms like "program" homogenize student populations and erase difference. They keep us from thinking about it or seeing it, especially when we are designing such writing assessments. It is simply harder to see local diversities if we do not explicitly name them, or look for them, or account for them. This is even tougher to do in a writing classroom assessment where it has been my experience running writing programs that teachers are not thinking about ways to validate their own grading practices or even feedback practices. Validation is usually a programmatic concern, not a classroom assessment concern. And since it isn't, racism has fertile ground to grow in classrooms.

I should make clear that I believe that we always already are diverse in our classrooms, schools, and geographic locations, which Huot surely is assuming as well. But I'm also suggesting that writing teachers develop writing assessments that explicitly engage with the local diversities in the classroom, that these local diversities be a part of the designing of the assessment's needs and procedures. Designing with local diversities in mind means that we choose to see the inherent multilingual aspects of our students as something other than signs of incomplete students, students who are not quite of the dominant discourses and expectations for college writing (e.g., a local SEAE). I realize that this claim pushes against Bartholomae's (1985) insightful explanation of students needing to "appropriate" the discourses of the academy in his famous essay "Inventing the University," but I'm less sure now that helping students toward the goal of appropriation is a worthwhile social goal, less sure that it helps our society as well as academia break the racist structures that hold all of us back, that limit the work in the academy as much as it limits our ways with words.

This is not to forget or elide the real issues of representation that most people of color face in the academy and U.S. society, nor the real concerns that many have for learning the dominant English of the marketplace. Nor is it lost on me how much I have benefited from a mastery of academic discourse, that this book is a testament to that discourse and how I've made it my own, but I have also been punished by not conforming to it in the past. And like most writing teachers, I am not like my students, in that I have an affinity for language. I love it. Thus I was resilient to the punishments. Most students are not so resilient. The bottom line is that local diversity is something that once we assume it to be a fact, it becomes essential to a healthy, fully functioning, and productive writing assessment ecology.

At Fresno State, Hispanic (which means mostly Mexican-American, but the institution uses "Hispanic") student enrollment has steadily grown since at least 2003 and surpassed Whites in 2010—Whites are a numerical minority on campus. Asian (mostly Hmong) students have also increased in the same period, but at a slower pace. Meanwhile, white student enrollment has decreased each year since 2006. In Fall 2012, 38.8% of all students enrolled where Hispanic, 28.8% were White, 14.8% were Asian (mostly Hmong), 4.4% were African-American,

3.0% were International, and 0.4% were American Indian (CSU, Fresno, n.d.).

Furthermore, in the city of Fresno in 2011, the U.S. Census Bureau states that 44.3% of people aged 5 and older spoke a language other than English at home (Ryan, 2013, p. 13). Of this population, 76.2% spoke Spanish, while 15.5% identified speaking an Asian and Pacific Island language, likely Hmong. The Centers for Disease Control and Prevention corroborate these numbers, noting that in Fresno County the top three spoken languages in homes are English, Spanish, and Hmong (Centers for Disease Control and Prevention, 2007). The U.S. Census Bureau's American Community Survey estimates that in 2011 in Fresno County 44.7% of those who speak Asian and Pacific Island languages at home, speak English less than "very well" (U.S. Census Bureau, 2011). Not surprisingly, of those admitted to Fresno State in Fall 2011, 72.2% of all Asian-Americans were designated as not proficient (remedial) in English (CSU Division of Analytic Studies, 2013), the highest remediation rate of any racial formation, as previously mentioned.[22] The story these statistics tell is one of local diversity, a diversity of people, cultures, and most importantly Englishes. It's also a story that reveals the problems bound to happen in classroom writing assessments that do not account for such local diversity. These issues begin with the EPT and its production of the remedial student, who is primarily Mexican and Hmong.

Now, one could argue against the validity of Fresno State's remediation numbers—that is, the decisions that the EPT makes for Hmong students—especially since they are produced by a dubious standardized test based on judgments that pit student writing against a dominant white *habitus*, a test designed for all California students, a large and complexly diverse state. And the EPT's placement decisions' questionable validity is exactly why local diversities need to be understood better and accounted for in writing assessments. How could it be that so many more Asian-Americans taking the EPT are deemed remedial by that test than any other racial formation at Fresno State? Are they all just bad writers? If a recent survey of all Hmong students conducted in the Writing Across the Curriculum program at Fresno State is accurate (266 students responded), only 10% of Hmong students say they use only English on and off campus on a daily basis to communicate to others. Most (63.4%) say they use mostly English but sometimes another language, while 23.4% say they use half English and half another language. So if this is true, then it's reasonable to say that the Hmong formation at Fresno State is highly literate, at least functional in two different languages. The EPT as a writing assessment doesn't account at all for the local diversity of Fresno State, for the dual languaging of Hmong students. It only cares about the institutional need to promote the myth of the monolingual, native English-speaking student. Local racial diversity, which in this case is constructed by home and school language practices and conditions of immigration to name a few factors, is ignored by the EPT.

The EPT clearly has problems adequately accounting for the multilingual students in Fresno if over 72% of Asian-American students are designated as remedial by it, meanwhile only about 25% of white students are. And we shouldn't be fooled by arguments that claim the EPT, or any writing assessment, could produce fairly such numbers in student populations, populations who come from the same schools, all born in the U.S. The argument is that perhaps the EPT is actually testing writing competency and not biased against Fresno Hmong since it cannot be determined that the EPT measures something different in Hmong students or measures the same construct differently in Hmong students (Inoue & Poe, 2012, pp. 343-344, 352; White & Thomas, 1981, p. 280).

The trouble with this argument is not that it uses conventional, positivistic, psychometric theories of bias (Jensen, 1976; Reynolds 1982a, 1982b; Thorndike, 1971) to determine if the EPT is not a racist test, which it does, but that it ignores the fact that failure (low scores that mean remediation) pool so cleanly, abundantly, and consistently in Hmong racial and linguistic formations in Fresno. It shows us that larger structural racism is happening in schools and classrooms, as much as it is in the test itself. Good writing assessments should be able to identify such structural racism, not work with it to produce more racist effects. Speaking of the EPT historically, Inoue & Poe (2012) explain why this writing assessment can be considered racist:

> The bias of a test, like the EPT, is not just a matter of finding traditionally defined test bias. If this were the case, we most likely must agree with White and Thomas' original judgment that the EPT is not biased against students of color. Bias can also be measured through the consequences of assessments. If an assessment is to respond fairly to the groups on which it makes decisions, then shouldn't its design address the way groups historically perform on the assessment? Thus, we wish to suggest that *understanding an assessment as producing a particular set of racial formations produces educational environments that could be unequal, either in terms of access, opportunities, or possibilities.* (pp. 352-353)

Thus it is the racial consequences of a test that can make it racist and unfair. And these unfair consequences stem from the EPT not addressing local diversity, and arguably only addressing a presumed white majority. So the classrooms at Fresno State are not isolated from the larger structures and previous assessments that construct the students who come. Classroom writing assessments must account for these conditions, and we can do so by understanding better these factors as factors that construct the local racial diversity of our students.

But how do local diversities affect classroom writing assessments in those classrooms? As a teacher if you noticed that 16 out of the 20 students in your writing course were failing their essays, wouldn't you re-examine your assignment, or expectations, or how you judged essays, etc.? Would you assume that those 16 students are all bad writers, and only four in the class are proficient? Of course not. Now, what if your school had a history of accepting students who were conventionally less prepared for college writing, who tended to have trouble approximating the dominant discourse expected, say urban Latino/a and Black students from poor neighborhoods and schools? Given this context, what would you assume? Would you check your methods, your assignments, perhaps even talk to students about how they interpreted the assignment? Now let's say that of those 16 students 14 were Asian-American and multilingual, the rest in the class were white. Now, would you still think your classroom writing assessment is potentially flawed, or would you engage with the global imaginary of a sentimental education that says you know what is best for these less developed Asians, or Blacks, or Latinos/as? Would you imagine your role as parental? Would you imagine that you had an obligation to help these students become more proficient in the dominant English of the classroom for their own good? Would this global imaginary keep you from critically examining the way your writing assessment is or is not explicitly accounting for the locally diverse students you have in your classroom and their relations to a white racial *habitus* that is likely functioning in your assessment? That is, would you change your assessment so that it folded back onto itself instead of pushing back onto your students? Could your assessment assess itself, assess the dominant discourse and not just the discourses of your students?

If your assessment could do this, then it is necessary, vital, that other discourses, other perspectives, other epistemologies exist so that students can compare them to the dominant one the classroom promotes. Notice I'm not saying that the classroom is not promoting a dominant discourse. I'm saying it promotes one alongside other non-dominant ones. And the non-dominant ones become the ways toward critical examination, toward critical assessment practices.

The concept of local diversity ultimately means classroom writing assessments must engage meaningfully with the diverse students in classrooms. It means teachers really cannot develop assessment procedures or expectations without their students' literacies. And this means, local diversities should change the academic discourse, change what is hegemonic in the academy, but this is a difficult task, one requiring a more holistic sense of classroom writing assessments, a theory of classroom writing assessment as an ecology.

CHAPTER 2: ANTIRACIST WRITING ASSESSMENT ECOLOGIES

It is not hard to think of a classroom as an ecology or to think of writing as ecological. Others have discussed it already, and I'll draw on them in this chapter (Coe, 1975; Cooper, 1986; Dobrin & Weisser, 2002). But what exactly is an ecology, and how might we define an ecology in order to use it as a frame for antiracist classroom writing assessments? This is the question that I'll address in this chapter. I'll do so by considering Freirean critical pedagogy, Buddhist theories of interconnection, and Marxian political theory. My goal in using these theories is to provide a structural and political understanding of ecology that doesn't abandon the inherent interconnectedness of all people and things, and maintains the importance of an antiracist agenda for writing assessments. I could easily be talking about any conventional writing assessment ecology, that is ones that do not have explicit antiracist agendas; however, my discussion will focus on understanding what a classroom writing assessment ecology is when it explicitly addresses antiracist work.

An antiracist classroom writing assessment ecology provides for the complexity and holistic nature of assessment systems, the interconnectedness of all people and things, which includes environments, without denying or eliding linguistic, cultural, or racial diversity, and the politics inherent in all uneven social formations. Consider the *OED's* main definitions for the word, ecology:

> 1a. the branch of biology that deals with the relationships between living organisms and their environment. Also: the relationships themselves, esp. those of a specified organism.

> 1b. Chiefly Social. The study of the relationships between people, social groups, and their environment; (also) the system of such relationships in an area of human settlement. Freq. with modifying word, as cultural ecology, social ecology, urban ecology.

> 1c. In extended use: the interrelationship between any system and its environment; the product of this.

> 2. The study of or concern for the effect of human activity on the environment; advocacy of restrictions on industrial and

agricultural development as a political movement; (also) a
political movement dedicated to this. (ecology, 2015)

Several themes from the above definition are instructive. First, the term "ecology" refers to relationships between biological people and their environments. The classrooms, dorm rooms, homes, workplaces, coffee shops, computer labs, libraries, and other environments where students do the work of a writing course have relationships to those students as they work. When the desks in a classroom are bolted to the floor, immoveable, it makes for a rigid classroom environment that can seep into the attitudes and feelings of students as they work in that room. When a dorm room is loud, busy, and cluttered with voices as a student tries to write on her laptop, that environment not only can be distracting but can affect her stance as a reader and writer, keeping her from being open to new ideas, willing to entertain alternative voices or positions, or it may rush her work. The same relationships affect teachers when they read, assess, and grade student writing. The places we do writing assessment, wherever they may be in a particular course, has direct consequences to assessment and the people involved.

Furthermore, places may have important associations with particular groups of people who typically inhabit those places, identified by class, social standing, language use, religion, race, or other social dimensions. Work done in such places can be affected by these associations. For instance, work done at an Historically Black College or University (HBCU) may be done very differently by a Black male student than if that same student was asked to do similar work at a mostly white college in the same state. Being the only student of color, or one of the only, in a classroom, school, or dormitory, can be unnerving, can affect one's ability to do the work asked, even when everyone around you is friendly. My experience as an undergraduate at a mostly white university in a mostly white state was filled with friendly teachers, eager to help, but I couldn't escape the feeling that when I wrote, I was writing at a deficit, that I always had to make up for where I came from and who I was. It seemed obvious to me in class, a brown spot in a class of white milk. Everyone talked and wrote differently than me, it seemed. We shouldn't forget that environments, places, are often (usually) raced, affecting how discourses are valued and judged.

Second, ecologies (re)create the living organisms and environments that constitute them through their relationships with each other. If living organisms and their environments create and recreate each other, then one cannot easily separate people from their environments and expect those people or environments to stay the same. To put this in simpler terms: we are defined by where we live, work, and commune. Places, environments, help make us who we are, and we help make places what they are. The issue that this observation brings up for an antiracist writing assessment ecology is one about the historical relationships between particular racial formations and institutions. White, middle and upper class people have been associated more closely to those who go to college because they have been the ones who have gone to college and who have controlled those institutions. Colleges and writing classrooms have been places of white settlement and communion. And this helps us understand why the dominant discourse of the classroom is a white discourse, and informed by a white racial *habitus*.

To work against this in our writing assessments, I find it helpful to think in terms of labor, in terms of what people do. In one sense, we might think of a student as only a student because of the work she does and the associations she has to particular places, locations, or sites, like a college campus, or a writing classroom. Those locations have certain labors associated with them as much as they have certain people associated with them. A student's relationships to classrooms and a school helps constitute her as a student, and the school is constituted as a school because she and other students like her inhabit and labor in that place. As my earlier discussion of racial *habitus* explains, among other things, the ways that environments affect people are discursively, performatively, and materially, changing us as we dwell and labor because we dwell and labor in those places.

To acquire things by our labors is also seen historically as good and ethical, especially in matters of learning. After making a rousing argument for his young students' willingness to study rhetoric for civic betterment by "disdain[ing] a life of pleasure; when they might have saved expense and lived softly," as many of their contemporaries do, Isocrates argues that his students labor at their studies to know themselves and learn, to be better citizens (2000, pp. 346-347). He ends with an argument for an ethics of labor:

> Pray, what is noble by nature becomes shameful and base
> when one attains it by effort? We shall find that there is no
> such thing, but that, on the contrary, we praise, at least in
> other fields, those who by their own devoted toil are able to
> acquire some good thing more than we praise those who in-
> herit it from their ancestors. And rightly so; for it is well that
> in all activities, and most of all in the art of speaking, credit is
> won, not by gifts of fortune, but by efforts of study. (p. 347)

If our students' gifts of fortune are the racial *habitus* they bring with them, and some *habitus* provide some students an unfair inheritance in today's academy, then we must use something more ethical to assess them by, especially in writing classrooms. Isocrates suggests that we already value in learning those who work hard to attain such learning and that in the study of rhetoric "credit is won" by "efforts of study." While I know Isocrates has particular things in mind that students might learn, but not too particular, since his rhetorical philosophy was at its center *kairotic*, I read him at face value. What we might learn from the study and practice of rhetoric will depend on the practical things that need doing in the now. Our most important asset is the labor we do now, the effort we expend on rhetoric, not our nature gifts, or our racial *habitus*. Adjusting our assessment systems to favor labor over the gifts of racial *habitus* sets up assessment ecologies that are by their nature more ethical and fairer to all.

Thus in antiracist writing assessment ecologies, it is important to focus on labor, as we all can labor, and labor can be measured by duration, quantity, or intensity, not by so-called quality, or against a single standard. This makes for a more equitable ecology, particularly for those who may come to it with discourses or *habitus* other than the dominant ones. Thus, one important aspect of an antiracist writing assessment ecology is an attention to labor, or more precisely, a valuing of labor over so-called quality, even though often our goals may be to help students become more fluent in the dominant discourses of the academy.[23]

Third, ecology often references systems of relationships in areas of human settlement—that is, places people make and call home, or at least create and inhabit purposefully. Thinking in ecological terms is thinking about how we make some place livable and sustainable. The point here is that because ecologies are always in a state of flux, changing, they are in one sense a scene of settlement, a process of constantly making some place livable. If our writing assessment ecologies in our classrooms don't pay attention to the dialectical way those ecologies affect students and the students affect them, or the way they affect and change us as teachers, they may simply be ecologies of measurement, mechanisms of pure accountability. They won't really be doing their job, at least not in its fullest sense.

Antiracist ecological writing assessment references a fuller purpose defined through a set of relationships that form settlement and create sustainable places that depend on local diversity for critical examination of writing and the *habitus* that produce that writing and readers' expectations. I'll explain this set of practices below through Freire's problem-posing methods, a set of practices and priorities that I call *problematizing one's existential writing assessment situation*. In order for a classroom assessment ecology to be sustainable, fair, and resist racism, it needs to question critically the structures and assumptions that make up the reading and judging of all students and teachers in the classroom. To do this, it requires that the assessment ecology is one of settlement, one in which everyone has a stake in making it livable, fair, and sustainable. It doesn't mean the ecology is one that values consensus, or even agreement, about what is "good writing."

It means the ecology's politics continually struggles through disagreement and dissensus, in the way Trimbur (1989) discusses it. The ecology struggles through the ways language comes to mean and be valued and how our bodies and environments affect that meaning and valuing. I'll say more about this below.

Fourth, ecology refers to the actions, effects, and consequences of human and environmental activity. Ecology implies action, or doing things and things being done. It assumes activity and change. The idea that ecologies are fundamentally systems of change and action agrees with the way many have understood language as a system too. Arguing against Saussure's conception of language as understood as either *langue* (a language system) or *parole* (individual, unique utterances of language), V. N. Volosinov (1986) says that there is no such thing as *langue*, only *parole*, that language is a "ceaseless flow of becoming" (p. 66). Volosinov's conception of language as a constantly changing, unstable set of linguistic norms seems a good metaphor for assessment ecologies. Ecologies also are constantly becoming. And if the ecology is in constant flux, so are the people, places, and relationships that form them. Intuitively, this makes sense. From our assessments and feedback on student writing, through peer-review activities and revisions, we hope that our students (and maybe even us as teachers) change, develop, become fuller. This feature of writing assessment ecologies can be turned to antiracist purposes. First, it provides us with at least one rationale for why using a single, static standard to measure student writing performances is unproductive in writing classrooms. Second, in antiracist assessment ecologies, it may mean that we must consider other, larger purposes for our ecology, purposes beyond or instead of measuring or ranking students. For instance, one might see a purpose that aligns with Freirean critical pedagogy that demands the ecology produce some output, some product(s) that demonstrate or observe the ceaseless flow of each students' language practices as it becomes something else. This kind of descriptive assessment process has been promoted in various ways by many already, although none have an explicit antiracist purpose (Bleich, 1997; Broad, 2003; Broad et al., 2009; Guba & Lincoln, 1989; Huot, 2002; Inoue, 2004).

Fifth and finally, the last definition listed above refers to the way all ecologies are associated with political activities, with the ways that people and environments affect each other and the interests that particular groups may have to change or maintain a given environment or place. And so, ecology is always a reference to the political (or power) relations between people and their environments, between people in environments. This directly connects racial *habitus* and racial formations to writing assessment ecologies, since both are centrally defined by power relations. In fact, this last definition makes racial politics, as relations of power that change the environment of the classroom, central to the activities and purposes of a writing assessment. In simpler terms, all writing assessment ecologies are about consciously noticing and perhaps changing the power relations involved so that a more sustainable and equitable ecology is created. Thus antiracist classroom writing assessment ecologies are explicit about their politics, explicit about their attention to reconstructing hierarchical racial power arrangements that are (re)produced through students' performances, their material conditions in which they labor and that affect who they are, and the languages they use.

Putting these five important features together, we might initially think of *an antiracist classroom writing assessment ecology as a complex political system of people, environments, actions, and relations of power that produce consciously understood relationships between and among people and their environments that help students problematize their existential writing assessment situations, which in turn changes or (re)creates the ecology so that it is fairer, more livable, and sustainable for everyone.* This definition is still incomplete however. It doesn't explain the nature of the ecology's complexity as a system, nor how the relationships among elements work. While this definition explains the political purposes for any antiracist writing assessment ecology, it doesn't explain the nature of those politics as constitutive features of the ecology.

In the following sections of this chapter, I'll fill in these gaps in this definition by discussing the way antiracist writing assessment ecologies are "more than" their features or elements, making them complex systems through their holistic natures, and systems that can produce critical or antiracist products and consequences. I'll explain how the interconnectedness of people and environments help writing classrooms understand the importance and necessity of antiracist agendas in writing assessment, and how interconnectedness is vital to the use of difference in discourses, values, and judging. Finally, I'll show how it is best to see antiracist writing assessment ecologies as Marxian ecologies, which reveals the ways power relations work both historically and from the classical Marxian dialectic. Seeing writing assessment ecologies as explicitly Marxian ecologies provides students with language to understand the way all assessment ecologies determine our desires and expectations for discourse, and the evaluations of our writing, and perhaps offers some ways to counter that determining.

What should be clear in the discussion so far is that all classroom writing assessment ecologies are by necessity political, are by necessity racial in orientation, even when we try hard not to consider race in our designs or implementation. Therefore an antiracist project or agenda is crucial to all classroom writing assessment ecologies. To engage in antiracist classroom writing assessment ecologies is a revolutionary or transformative agenda, one akin to Freire's (1970) problem-posing pedagogy described in *Pedagogy of the Oppressed*, which my definition above references. In fact, Freire's description of the process of data collection in the community and its analysis by that community and his literacy workers (1970, p. 112) is strikingly similar to Guba and Lincoln's famous fourth-generation evaluation process that uses a hermeneutic dialectic circle to acquire various judgments (what they call "constructions") by stakeholders in order for a socially constructed evaluation to emerge (Guba & Lincoln, 1989, p. 152). Their process produces a collaborative description that takes into account as many of the stakeholders involved as possible. While they don't focus on it, this process allows for an evaluation to work with the locally diverse people involved and the inherent differences in language and judgment that those people will produce. Freire's pedagogy is very similar. The lens I am asking us to place on Guba and Lincoln's and Freire's processes is an attention to the way language practices participate in larger racialized discourses and *habitus*.

Freire's pedagogy is assessment at just about every level. He says that the dialogical teacher's role is primarily to "re-present" the "thematic universe" uncovered by the team of researchers (which includes community members) as a problem (1970, p. 109), which the community (or students) must take on or use to pose their own problems. This is the heart of what Guba and Lincoln attempt to offer in their assessment model, and at the heart of antiracist writing assessment ecologies. The central work of problem-posing for students in an antiracist writing assessment ecology is to assess and make judgments on language, to re-present colleagues' texts to them from whatever subject position that student inhabits, and to do so self-consciously, calling attention to their own *habitus*, all of which leads to other questions that require more assessments by readers and writers. This makes the assessments more important than the drafts and documents being assessed. Students don't have to label the differences they notice in language practices as racialized, but they can strive to understand the differences as more than idiosyncrasies, more than individual differences unconnected to larger discursive fields, larger social and cultural practices in their lives.

These judgments about language judgments that students exchange in antiracist writing assessment ecologies are focused not on what is right or wrong, conventional or not, but on comparisons between a white racial *habitus* and other *habitus* that students take on. The white racial *habitus* is not a standard by which students must write up to or be judged against, but is understood as a direction everyone heads toward at their own pace and in their own ways. Most important, it is the heading toward, the movement, the "flow of becoming," that is the basis of measuring and grading in antiracist writing assessment ecologies. Because ecologies are fundamentally about change, movement, and actions, judgments about student labor (the engine of movement and change) might best be used to determine things like grades and define expectations for work. This means that it is important not to use measurements of students' approximations to a dominant discourse to determine grades (measures of so-called "quality"). Labor is a more equitable and fair measure. Everyone has 24 hours in every day.[24]

I'll illustrate what this problematizing can look like in an imperfect way in Chapter 4 and offer some ideas toward assessment activities in Chapter 5 that help students problematize their writing assessment situations. For now, this short description is what I mean when I say that the larger goal of any antiracist writing assessment ecology is to encourage students to problematize their existential writing assessment situations. To problematize means students must pose questions about their colleagues' and their own drafts, then investigate those questions, which essentially are ones about the nature of judgment and language, leading students to understanding their own *habitus* and the white racial *habitus* of the academy. This moves discussions and the work of the ecology away from the drafts and into the nature of judgment itself. While I did not use it in the course I describe in Chapter 4, I include in Appendix B an explicit problematizing assignment (a problem-posing letter), which I have used since the course. The problem-posing letter explicitly asks students to problematize their existential writing assessment situations by using the feedback they and their colleagues have written.

I realize the problems with transplanting a pedagogy designed to help illiterate peasants gain language and power in developing countries to a post-industrialized context like U.S. writing classrooms, where our students, even the poorest of them, are not remotely in need of the kind of liberation that Freire is thinking of. Our students are not oppressed in the ways Freire's Brazilian peasants were; however, most U.S. students can be a part of an antiracist, liberatory agenda in the writing classroom. They might help us liberate ourselves from conventional assessment ecologies that keep (re)producing racism through an uncritical promotion of a white racial *habitus*. I'm not saying we know what our students need to know, and that we just have to get them to see things our way. I'm not even saying we need to liberate our students. I'm saying, our classroom writing assessment ecologies themselves need liberating. And our students must do this work with us.

In other words, healthy writing assessment ecologies have at their core dialogue about what students and teachers know, how students and teachers judge language differently, so that students are also agents in the ecology, not simply objects to be measured. I realize that this statement may set up a troubling role for the teacher, the role of liberator or savior, but like Freire's account, the writing teacher in an antiracist writing assessment ecology simply does not have that power, cannot liberate her students. They must do that themselves (Freire, 1970, pp. 93-94). This is an essential part of Freire's problem-posing pedagogy, and any healthy antiracist classroom writing assessment ecology.

Freire's pedagogy works from an important assumption about language. Words offer humans both action and reflection. Language provides us with a mode by which we can transform our world. He explains, "[t]o exist, humanly, is to *name* the world, to change it. Once named, the world in its turn reappears to the namers as a problem and requires of them a new *naming*. Human beings are not built in silence, but in word, in work, in action-reflection" (1970, p. 88). Naming, for Freire, happens in dialogue with others. The act of naming alludes to action and work and material environments that change through our word-acts, or what he calls "praxis," which is "reflection and action which truly transform reality" (Freire, 1970, p. 100). But it's not any dialogue that transforms reality, but a dialogue that engages in critical thinking:

> true dialogue cannot exist unless the dialoguers engage in critical thinking—thinking which discerns an indivisible solidarity between the world and the people and admits of no dichotomy between them—thinking which perceives reality as process, as transformation, rather than as a static entity—thinking which does not separate itself from action, but constantly immerses itself in temporality without fear of the risks involved. (Freire, 1970, p. 92)

Words as actions. Language as action. Action as reflection and reflection as action. To liberate oneself, a student must engage in such labor. And when focusing attention on one's own *habitus* next to a white racial *habitus* expected of students in classrooms, the labor creates the potential for an antiracist praxis. They problematize their existential writing assessment situations. Thus, labor seems the most antiracist measure for any writing assessment ecology because we really don't know what our students can or should ultimately learn.

This brief account of Freire's problem-posing pedagogy offers a way to see Freire's account of language learning as similar to antiracist classroom writing assessment ecologies. Both are defined as a set of relationships and critical dialogue among people, and between people and their environment; as transformative processes that change people and their environments by posing problems through word-acts that name the world, which changes the world and begets more naming; as a scene of settlement in which the ecological transformative processes that occur are always at some level about making a place sustainable and livable, as problem-posing events that liberate the ecology; as action, motion, and processes of becoming something else, as praxis; and as political in nature, or as containing and dealing with power relations among people and their discourses, or the cultivation of liberation and being fully human among others who are doing the same.

AS "MORE THAN"

Antiracist classroom writing assessment ecologies are in one sense complex systems. Understanding this can help teachers and students engage more self-consciously in all their mutual work. Dobrin (2012) and Cooper (2011) discuss the ideas of "complex ecology" and complex systems (respectively), which explains writing as a complex system through theorists like George Van Dyne, Bernard C. Patten, Humberto Maturana, and Francisco Varela. Complex ecologies, like writing assessments, are "holistic" in nature, accounting for the whole as more than an assemblage of parts, yet maintaining a sense of the parts and their mutual interactions. Thus, for Dobrin (and me), there is a "need to address the complex relationships between parts in order to develop more holistic concepts of writing while understating that we will never be able to fully understand all of the complexities and fluctuations of the system" (2012, p. 144). So while an ecology may have aspects we can label and separate out for discussion and design, these aspects and other elements do not account for writing assessment ecologies in total. There is always a bit of mystery, some unknown variables in the system. Antiracist writing assessment ecologies are always more than their elements, more than what they may appear to be. They are always *more than*.

The idea that the teaching and understanding of the process of writing as more than its parts isn't new. While he doesn't speak about writing assessment, Richard Coe (1975) makes a very similar point when arguing for an "eco-logic" for the teaching of writing. He offers this definition of eco-logic:

> [from the modern English, *ecology*; from the Greek *oikos*,
> house or habitation, as in *oikonomia*, economy; the prefix
> *eco-* connotes wholeness] 1. A logic designed for complex
> wholes. 2. Any logic which considers wholes as wholes, not by
> analyzing them into their component parts. 3. *Esp.*, a logical
> model appropriate for ecological phenomena. (p. 232)

In a footnote, Coe explains that the Greek notions for household was of the "smallest self-sufficient unit in the Greek economy," thus "*oiko-* had a connotation of wholeness" (1975, p. 232). Teaching rhetoric this way, as an eco-logic, means for Coe that we not break up the art into smaller units that aren't whole, such as in the case of teaching modes. I doubt today we need to make an argument against teaching writing as modes for many reasons, but for Coe it is because rhetoric in the contemporary writing classroom deals with more complex contemporary phenomena, phenomena less apt to being understood adequately by breaking it up for analysis or practice. From this, he argues that one central eco-logical principle is that "meaning is relative to context" (1975, p. 233). Language gains its meaning and significance only in the context in which it is uttered or used. Most critical in Coe's eco-logical rendering of teaching writing is that we teach it as a socially contextualized activity, something others argue after him (Berlin, 1987). For him, context and relativity mean social context and social relativity. Coe does not make any connection to the judging of writing, but when we think in terms of classroom writing assessment ecologies, the contextual, relative, and contingent nature of language and meaning, at its core, comes from the fact that meaning is derived from people judging and assessing it. To say that language is meaningful because it is contextual and social by nature, because judgments about language can only be made contextually, is to say that the nature of writing assessment is ecological. And to say this is to say that writing assessment ecologies are more than the elements we might list that constitute them.

Dobrin, however, recognizes how limited a biological and organic concept, which Coe stays close to, has been in the past to writing theory (2011, p. 132-33). In part, Dobrin identifies this problem as one of "anthropocentric ecology, focusing on the human agent's relationship with environment, both the agent's influence on the environment and the environment's affect [sic] on the agent." While Coe places his interest in people interacting in ecologies, Dobrin's critique is still applicable, as Coe is anthropocentric, centering only on people and their interactions, disregarding their material environment, the classroom, or other structural factors such as power differentials (i.e., race, gender, etc.). This anthropocentric influence, says Dobrin, is usually "one tied more directly with concepts of social interaction than with ecological relationships" (2011, p. 126). I agree with Dobrin's criticism of older versions of ecological theories of writing, and attempt to focus my attention both on social interaction among students and teacher, and ecological relationships among other elements in the complex systems of writing assessment ecologies, such as processes, the places (physical and figurative) that students and teachers create and inhabit, and the discourses of judgment, all of which I'll look at more closely in Chapter 3.

Thus in any ecology, the material aspects of environments and people in writing assessments must be preserved and understood explicitly. We do not live in conditions of pure theory or discourse. In any writing classroom, we have never, nor could we, simply read and judge words as words that only matter on the page or on a computer screen. Freire's problem-posing pedagogy in both philosophy and method, exemplify this attachment to the material world. Furthermore, the writing our students engage in and submit to be judged in some fashion contains the shadows of labor done, traces of work, references to a body in motion, as well as to places and scenes of writing that produced drafts. Because of this, when we read student writing, we read all of these things simultaneously. We read more than words, more than our students. In fact, as others have discussed in various ways (Brannon & Knoblach, 1982; Sommers, 1982), teachers usually think of their students as they read their writing anyway.

Thinking more intuitively about the scene of reading and responding to student writing (a place in the ecology), teachers have their material students in mind to help them respond effectively. When we formulate feedback, an evaluation, or a grade, we implicitly or explicitly consider that material student, her possible reactions, what she needs, how she needs to hear advice, even nonacademic aspects of her life (e.g., Is she a student-athlete? Does she work, take care of a family, children, etc.? How many future drafts are expected in the course?). And this doesn't include other constraints that a teacher considers that will affect her feedback, such as the amount of time she has to respond to her students' writing, where she can do that reading and writing, the technologies she has available to read and write her feedback, etc.

David Bartholomae's (1985) influential account of students "inventing the university" every time they sit down to write is also an essay that invents those material students, racializing and norming them to a white racial *habitus* through the promotion of a dominant white discourse, as he reads through the excerpts he offers. In fact, Bartholomae's essay can be read as an early primer for inventing types of students through the reading and evaluating of their work. And before Bartholomae, Wayne Booth's (1963) *The Rhetorical Stance* provides an explicit discussion on how to read and construct three types of students by reading their writing, again against a white racial *habitus*. This phenomenon is nowhere clearer stated than in Chris Anson's (2000) discussion of teachers' responses and their relationship to the social construction of error as teachers read student texts. Anson shows how writing teachers construct the severity of the same errors differently depending on the student's ethos created by the teacher-reader (2000, p. 10). While he doesn't say it, the factors Anson mentions, such as the level of neutrality or objectivity of the writer and the writer's perceived bias and "fair-mindedness," are closely wedded to a white racial *habitus*, fitting cleanly into the rubric of whiteness discussed by Barnett (2000), Myser (2002), Brookhiser (1997), and others I discussed in Chapter 1.

While Bartholomae, Booth, and Anson are mostly textual in the ways they suggest teachers invent such students behind their texts, folks like Sommers (1982), Elizabeth Flynn (1989), Edgington (2005), and Scott (2009) in various ways are more explicit about the act of reading being one that is an interaction between reader, text, and student, and they imply actions and decisions by flesh-and-blood writers in the world who work under material conditions that affect that work. Thus, at least in terms of feedback and response to student writing, there is a tradition in composition studies that sees as important the presence of the material student when the teacher is reading, providing feedback, or evaluating. However, if we see these assessment scenes as ecologies, then they are more than the disembodied reading of texts, more than the material conditions that make up students, teachers, and the environments in which they work. What produces the judgments that Bartholomae, Booth, and Anson identify is more than what seems to literally constitute a text and its reading.

What makes up this *more than* attribute of the assessment ecology? Coe might call it rhetorical context. Faigley might say it was historically evolving cultural and disciplinary tastes that affect readers' judgments. Bartholomae and Booth might argue it is the product of students trying to approximate the conventions of discourse communities. Anson might say it is a part of readers' individual idiosyncratic constructions of writers. All of these scholars have at the center of any writing assessment scene judgment and the text being judged. The discourse itself, the writing in our classrooms, including the teacher's discourse of judgment, is an obvious part of the ecology. In short, all these accounts reveal the ways that the social, cultural, disciplinary, and racial *habitus* of writers and readers, with a white racial *habitus* as the standard, clash to form judgments on student writing. This is nowhere clearer seen than in my previous discussion of the EPT sample essay in which I argue it is being read through narratives of a global imaginary of sentimental education that produces particular judgments of the text as remedial and a student in need of help.

This theorizing of assessment agrees with "discursive ecology," a pedagogical approach to writing that argues that writing in the classroom should be seen as such systems. Dobrin and Weisser (2002) explain this pedagogy: "discursive ecology examines the relationships of various acts and forms of discourse ... see[s] writing as an ecological process, to explore writing and writing processes as systems of interaction, economy, and interconnectedness" (p. 581). In a broader sense, this kind of ecocomposition, Dobrin and Weisser say, allows writing theorists and teachers (and perhaps their students), to ask: "[w]hat effects do local environments have on any kind of writing, any kind of writer?" (2002, p. 577). I would add: What effects do local environments, which include the discourses of judgment circulating in those environments, have on the assessment of writing? Thus the substance of the *more than* in an assessment ecology changes and is elusive depending on who is present and where they are when they read and judge.

Thus, environments, like larger ecologies, are more than what they seem. In their own defining of ecocomposition, which mimics Freire's assumptions about language and the world (although they do not cite Freire), Dobrin and Weisser state that "environment is an idea that is created through discourse ... it is through language that we give these things or places [mountains, rivers, oceans] particular meanings" (2002, p. 573). I agree. Our material environments that we live and interact in are more than material. They are also made up of discourse, of language. As Kenneth Burke (1966, 1969) reminds us about image and idea, about the relationship between the symbolic and the material, people do not live in worlds of words alone. Our world constructs our words as much as our words construct our world. Thus each is more than the other. This is also the essence of Freire's critical pedagogy, only he emphasizes that words and the world constantly change because of each other. However, the link between the world and the word is reflection that is action, which is labor, the engine of becoming and change, the engine of ecologies. In antiracist writing assessment ecologies, the *more than* in the ecology is also the evolving critical consciousness about language and *habitus* that the ecology produces.

What shouldn't be lost in antiracist writing assessment ecologies is the way they help students focus on a fuller range of phenomena for assessing language. Dobrin and Weisser explain that people make meaning out of their environments as a response to that environment. The mountain or river is the occasion for discourse. So our lives and relationships with each other and to the environment are connected materially as much as they are connected through our words. But we are connected to our world in a number of other ways, each of which helps us experience and create meaning, helps us assess. We make judgments through emotion and sensation, through analytic and spiritual logics, through kinesthetic movement (e.g., Kroll, 2013), through felt senses and intuition. But we build and articulate judgments through language. Antiracist writing assessment ecologies are more than word-acts. They are emotional and sensual labor, bodily labor that occurs in time and space. These aspects of the ecology teachers cannot control, and often our students cannot either, but they should be accounted for. We can experience them, take note, and articulate.

Through all this, we shouldn't forget the writer or the reader/assessor and their relationship. In Marilyn Cooper's (1986) discussion of writing in the classroom as an ecology, she explains that it can been seen as a collection of "social activities, dependent social structures and processes" (p. 366). She focuses her eye, like many writing scholars at the time, on people and their interactions, saying that "writing is an activity through which a person is continually engaged with a variety of socially constituted systems" (1986, p. 367). These "dynamic and interlocking" social systems are "made and remade by writers in the act of writing" (Cooper, 1986, p. 368). The larger environment that she accounts for in her ecological theory of writing hints at systemic things, but stays close to the writer, making it vulnerable to Dobrin's anthropocentric critique. However, Cooper explains that "writing encompasses much more than the individual writer and her immediate context" (1986, p. 368). It is an interaction with other writers and readers, an interaction with at least five systems that people circulate in (Cooper, 1986, pp. 369-370). The details of her systems are less important to my discussion, except that in each case, she discusses them in social terms, in terms of people interacting and exchanging.

While she speaks only of writing and revision, Cooper's early articulation of writing as ecology can be translated to a theorizing of writing assessment as ecology. In fact, in her example of how an ecological model of writing changes the way we think of and discuss writing in the classroom, she is really discussing classroom writing assessment as ecology. After summarizing Ede and Lunsford (1984), Ong (1975), Park (1982), and Kroll (1984) on audience, she says:

> As should be obvious, the perspective of the ecological model offers a salutary correction of vision on the question of audience. By focusing our attention on the real social context of writing, it enables us to see that writers not only analyze or invent audiences, they, more significantly, communicate with and know their audiences. They learn to employ the devices of audience-adapted writing by handing their texts to colleagues to read and respond to, by revising articles or memos or reports guided by comments from editors or superiors, by reading others' summaries or critiques of their own writing. Just as the ecological model transforms authors (people who have produced texts) into writers (people engaged in writing), it transforms the abstract "general audience" into real readers. (1986, pp. 371-372)

Her example is one of material writers writing and material readers reading, of exchanging drafts, providing feedback to peers, interpreting feedback writers received from others, then revising. It is a more holistic view of most typical classroom writing assessment activities. And what is learned about writing as ecology is that writers learn to write in "real social context[s]," with real people in mind as their audience, from real people's words about their words and worlds, from material action and exchange in material environments. And while she mostly ignores the material classroom and other spaces where students do the labors of reading and writing, the ecology of the writing classroom, according to Cooper, makes students into writers because the ecology calls them to write to real people, exchange ideas about that writing, and continue the process. People and the places they read and write not only become important to the system, but as Dobrin (2012) explains, they are the system. Writers in a writing ecology become assessors, readers of others' texts and makers of judgments, making writers more than writers, and readers more than readers. In fact, if we accept Cooper's account as one also of writing assessment, and I don't see why we wouldn't, then writing assessment ecologies make writers and assessors of writing through their interactions. Without the ecology, you don't have writers or readers. The difference in an antiracist writing assessment ecology is that all this is made explicit, reflected upon, and used to understand the discourses of judgment as indicators of students' *habitus* and the dominant white racial *habitus*.

Cooper's and Coe's early renditions of writing as ecology, while limited to mostly generic (white?) people's interactions and speaking only about writing (not assessing), are still useful precursors to a theory of writing assessment ecology as an antiracist project. None of the composition theorists I've cited so far, however, discuss the ways in which the social, racial, and institutional contexts and histories that follow students and teachers affect ecologies that those people are a part of. How do we account for various racial formations, discourses, and *habitus* in our reading and judging practices, or the privileging of a white racial *habitus* that informs dominant discourses? Cooper and Coe do not make note of the way all students are not simply the same kinds of writers or readers, that where they come from, what languages and backgrounds they bring, what their economic and other social factors are in their lives, affects their abilities to do the work we ask of them in the writing classroom, which has implications to the ways we might assess that writing or the ways they might judge their colleagues' work. Their material conditions while taking the course also affect students' various and uneven chances of doing the work we ask of them.

And yet, the locally diverse student-readers and teacher help any student-writer by being diverse, by essentially posing different problems about their writing to the writer in their own ways, from their own perspectives, through their own problem-posing about the writer's writing. This should allow assessment to reveal judgment as more than meeting an approximation of a white racial *habitus* found in a dominant discourse. In order for the assessment ecology to construct that feedback as antiracist, problem-posing assessment can be the focus. Problem-posing by peers and teacher can help all involved see the local dominant discourse as a part of a local white racial *habitus,* a part of the hegemonic. Thus power and privilege are seen in the ecology as not evenly distributed and as the subject of assessment processes and problems posed.

Thus, an antiracist ecology works differently to some degree for each student and teacher. As Stephanie Kerschbaum (2014) emphasizes in her discussion of the rhetoric of difference and diversity, noticing and using difference, say in a problem-posing assessment activity, isn't about a priori notions of difference but differences that emerge through interactions. The substance of these interactions, I argue, should be about the nature of judgment itself, about the word-acts of assessment. When this happens, when the ecology turns back onto itself, making it the subject of assessment processes, of feedback activities, of reflections on drafting and revisions, the writing assessment ecology takes advantage of the local diversity in the classroom. The local diversity of ideas, languages, judgments, and material contexts that students bring to bear on a text allows for the writing assessment ecology to be more than helping writers improve drafts. It becomes an ecology in which students liberate themselves from conventional assessment.

AS INTERCONNECTED

Understanding explicitly interconnection is important in antiracist writing assessment ecologies, because seeing the ways all aspects of the ecology are interconnected (including students, teacher, and their discourses) helps everyone pose problems about language and judgment through their differences, through the local diversity revealed in writing, assessing, and the material bodies in the classroom. A white racial *habitus* that informs the dominant discourses expected of Fresno State students, for instance, is interconnected to, depends on, local Hmong, Latino/a, and African-American *habitus*. Seeing interconnection helps students understand how dominant discourses need subaltern ones, how we all need everyone and everything around us, how disagreeing with each other can be a critical act of compassion and love.

In another more obvious way, interconnection is a social phenomenon integral to all classrooms. It takes the entire class to have a successful peer review activity, for instance. It takes at least one reader in order for a writer to write and receive feedback. It takes a school to dedicate material classroom space, or virtual space on computer servers, for a writing class to function at all. It takes time and labor on the part of students to do the writing and reading required for a writing class's activities to work. Any student's success is determined by the labors and actions of her colleagues around her in the classroom, by the commitments of institutions and people she may never know, by available space and materials. Conversely, when any student is left behind or fails in some way, the rest of the class fails to some degree, and an integral part of the ecology withers. We all have experienced those classrooms where almost everyone is rowing in the same direction, getting it, engaging in the course's activities in the same spirit, and everything seems to always work. I would argue that when this happens, what we experience in the course is a tangible interconnectedness. In antiracist writing assessment ecologies, this interconnectedness is made explicit, reflected upon and discussed, then used toward problem-posing ends, helping create a sustainable writing assessment ecology.

Robert Yagelski (2011) offers a powerful articulation of both interconnectedness and the ecological nature of writing and its assessment in *Writing As A Way of Being: Writing Instruction, Nonduality, and the Crisis of Sustainability*. Yagelski argues for writing to be taught as an ontological practice that is opposed to conventional process pedagogies that teach it as a purely transactional act, one based on the Cartesian duality of mind vs. body. He calls this old view of writing the "Cartesian view of writing," in which students act as if they are autonomous beings, separated from their environments (2011, p. 47), and from their peers as well who are a part of their environments. In his chapter, "The Crisis of Sustainability," Yagelski explains:

> The basic lesson of conventional schooling, then, is less a matter of learning *what* is outside us than learning *that* there is something outside us that we can see, describe, and understand, a something that is fundamentally separate from our selves. To put it in simpler terms, in school we teach separateness rather than interconnectedness; we see a world defined by duality rather than unity. As a result we promote an idea of community as a collection of discrete, autonomous individuals rather than a complex network of beings who are inherently interconnected and inextricably part of the ecosystems on which all life depends. (2011, p. 17)

And where is the most obvious example in schools of this separateness from each other and our environments in education? According to Yagelski, writing assessment. He says accurately that "students are almost always assessed as individuals" (2011, p. 17). Grades and scores point to this Cartesian way of writing when they define students as only "an intellectual entity, a collection of certain cognitive abilities and/or sanctioned bodies of knowledge," as a "disembodied intellect" (Yagelski, 2011, p. 18). Ultimately, he concludes, "[a]ssessment becomes a process of disembodiment that both reflects and reinforces the Cartesian self" (2011, p. 18). In Yagelski's view, the Cartesian self in school, exemplified in Descartes' *cogito ergo sum* ("I think, therefore I am"), is opposed to an interconnected self, one that sees himself and his education as a part of all that is around him, his colleagues, the teacher, the classroom, the desks, the campus, the buildings, the decisions made in last week's city council meeting, the nearby reservoir, everything.

Although he does not discuss whiteness in his critique, we might hear in Yagelski's criticism of conventional assessment and classroom process pedagogies as a criticism of a white racial *habitus*. The *cogito* is a typical logic in whiteness. It is the logic of hyperindividualism that tends to be the rationale for assessing students individually. Furthermore, the disembodiment of rhetoric from the person speaking (or writing) is not only a denial of our relationship to the material world and our words, but denies that rationality and logic are intimately a part of thinking, feeling, breathing people. Whiteness as a discourse uses this assumption too, one that says logic and rationality can be "objective," are outside of people. In fact, people taint logic and the rational.

While Yagelski isn't making an argument for ecocomposition in the way Dobrin and Weisser or Cooper do, he is assuming a wider net of relationships and actions that make up writing and how we might define it and teach it. He also reminds us that we write from and with our bodies. I'm extending his argument to include the fact that we read, judge, and assess writing in and outside of classrooms from and with our bodies. Our bodies connect us to the earth and each other. Thus, Yagelski sees writing as an ontological act, as "a way of being in the world" (2011, p. 3), which allows us to teach from the interconnectedness of all people and their environments. He draws on post-process theorists, most notably Thomas Kent (1993), to explain that while language is essential to knowing, "it isn't the sole ground for knowing or meaning-making" (Yagelski, 2011, p. 64). In effect, knowing is a three-way exchange among at least two people communicating to each other and a "phenomenal world" that they both experience and interpret together. Thus, communication is "inherently nondualistic," according to Yagelski. He explains, "writing does not demarcate boundaries between the writer and others, because we cannot make meaning without others; furthermore, it begins to erase the boundary between writer as subject and the world as object, because the world is integral to meaning making" (2011, p. 65). While he isn't saying it directly, Yagelski defines writing, through post-process theory, as an ecology, as a holistically experienced process of meaning making. It takes many people, their interactions, a world and its motions to create a single student paper, and equally as many interconnected relations to assess it.

Additionally, one can hear a problem-posing assessment strategy in Yagelski's theory of language. To assess writing ecologically means we pose problems to the writer about what her words mean to the world and how the writer herself is connected to that world being made through words, or we ask what problems appear in her writing when we see it as a part of a white racial *habitus,* or as opposed to one, or as one different from the *habitus* of the reader. In antiracist writing assessment ecologies, local diversity is necessary for critical assessments that ask such questions of writers and their texts. Difference between readers and writers is used to form critical judgments on the reader's and the writer's dispositions in writing and reading. Difference is used to see the white racial *habitus* as such, as just one discursive node in a larger network of interconnected nodes. This antiracist agenda doesn't just examine differences, but examines the ways we interconnect, the ways an individual writer may have connections to—may depend upon—her world, the reader, opposing arguments and ideas. In this way, problem-posing as an antiracist strategy for response or assessment of writing is a process of reading for interconnectedness from various perspectives as much as it is a process of seeing difference.

To give an example, consider two excerpts from student essays, one from Lester Faigley's (1989) "Judging Writing, Judging Selves," a reprint of Rebecca Faery's submission to Coles and Vopat's (1985) *What Makes Writing Good*, and a similar kind of essay from a writing course of mine a few years ago. Faery's student essay comes from Lindsey Lankford, an advanced writing student, who writes about communicating through letters to her family while she spends a year in Paris. Faigley explains that Lindsey "shows awareness of the essay form, beginning with phone bills and check stubs as images of writing in our culture, juxtaposing scenes of intercontinental letter writing, then deftly returning to the empty post office box at the end" (1989, pp. 407-408). Like myself, Faigley says he is "touched by this essay" because of the ideas and images it invokes, familiar ones of Paris and Lindsey as "teacher/critic" of the letters her family writes to her (1989, p. 408). In the middle of the essay, Lindsey writes:

> I loved their letters to me, too. They were never filled with earthshattering news, but they revealed a lot. Actually, most people's lives are dull; it's the way they perceive their lives that is interesting. My sister Allison lives in the Negev Desert, in a tiny trailer. Her world consists of her husband, their two small children, and very little else. Her letters were always wrinkled, smeared with something sticky, covered in crayons and written over extended periods of time. They were a mess: descriptions of the gingerbread village Allison had made for the Christmas party, their plans for moving back to the States, Lauren's latest word, and details of Elizabeth's third birthday party. Allison's letters were disjointed, but ebullient. Living on an army base in the Israeli desert would seem a barren existence, yet Allison's letters describe a busy and happy, if somewhat chaotic, life. (Faigley, 1989, p. 407)

Lindsey knows how to approximate the academic discourse well. In fact, her essay offers a clear picture of a white racial *habitus* that informs her discursive choices and the subject of her essay. She never mentions her own racial or class subjectivity, but like all whiteness, she assumes it as a natural position that her readers will align with and recognize. It is the voice of objective reasoning that she invokes in her essay. Her analysis and voice are the epitome of hyperindividualism and the Cartesian *cogito* that separates Lindsey from her world and even her sister and family. She thinks in conventionally rational and logical ways on the page that fit with the dominant discourse of the academy, allowing her an objective stance that makes observations on her family. Her discussion of her sister's letters and life in an "Israeli desert" makes a stark contrast, one that pits a romantic European city with cafes and wine-fueled discussions of philosophy against a more "disjointed, but ebullient" and "chaotic" life in a "tiny trailer" in a Middle Eastern desert.

It is hard not to read racial undertones in this comparison, one that creates Lindsey as authoritative critic, one who makes interesting insights that construct her as authoritative and detached from her family she discusses, such as "most people's lives are dull; it's the way they perceive their lives that is interesting." Lindsey is outside her sister's life, looking objectively at it, finding it "interesting." Laced in this white racial *habitus* is a posture that is reminiscent of an Orientalist vision that Said (1979) and Klein (2003) theorize. From her topic choice to the way she treats her examples (the letters from her family) to the vision she has of those examples (what they mean), a white racial *habitus* informs Lindsey's writing. This doesn't make Lindsey a bad writer or her essay a bad one. On the contrary, it approximates an academic discourse well, and comes to some interesting conclusions. But an antiracist writing assessment ecology is not about simply measuring how well a student approximates a dominant discourse. The ecology is about problematizing the existential writing assessment situation of writers and readers like Lindsey.

In an antiracist writing assessment ecology, this essay would be read in order to understand the ways Lindsey takes on a white racial *habitus*, then through assessments compares her *habitus* to her colleagues' *habitus*. The comparison would be one in which first interconnection is interrogated. How is Lindsey's leisure, middle-class life in Paris connected to her sister's chaotic life that has fewer signs of middle-classness? How does Lindsey's romantic, intellectual ethos in Paris, exchanging letters in French to her father, need the chaotic, working-class, darker, non-white example of her sister to be meaningful? How does Lindsey's discussion and its insights depend on her performing whiteness?[25] Faigley's discussion of this essay hints at such an assessment when he asks about whether Lindsey could have written a similarly successful essay if she'd "visited a place unfamiliar to us," say the immigrant families from Mexico who temporarily live in storm sewers near Austin, Texas (1989, p. 408). Faigley's example is loaded with implicit questions about racism, class, and capitalism that Lindsey might explore, but in the antiracist assessment ecology I'm suggesting, racism would be placed in the forefront of assessments, and to get at it, we pose questions about her language, her assumptions and conclusions, and the nature of her discourse.

For example, as an Asian-American reader sensitive to issues of Orientalism, like associations of Asian locations and bodies as chaotic, exotic, and hoarde-ish, I might pose questions that reveal such things to Lindsey, not to suggest that her observations are wrong or inaccurate about her sister or the location or manner in which she lives, but to reveal first the dispositions toward such bodies and locations I hear in Lindsey's words, how they work on me as an Asian-American reader in order that Lindsey can pose versions of the questions to herself. How might she tacitly need such Orientalist assumptions when thinking about civil communication and letter writing. In her text, this Orientalist vision of the Israeli desert home of her sister is in contrast to the serene, calm, intellectual place of Paris, a white geographic location that I'd also want to ask about. We can ask explicitly about Lindsey's racial *habitus* that she performs in this essay. How is it connected historically to larger discursive formations in other texts and discourses that may have influenced her, such as Bret Harte's "The Heathen Chinee" (1870), Rudyard Kipling's "White Man's Burden" (1899), or Disney's films like *Aladdin* (1992) and *Mulan* (1998), or films like *300* (2006). So Lindsey's locally diverse colleagues are necessary to help her see her own *habitus*, and she is needed to help her colleagues see their *habitus*. They are needed together to form a critical position toward the dominant discourse expected of everyone in the academy. And the questions posed in assessments come directly from students' own racialized lives, their own material conditions that help them read and judge language. And perhaps the best initial way toward comparing such things in drafts is by working from the interconnection of students, their material lives, and their discourses, by investigating the ways our discourses and texts need one another to be more fully meaningful and critical. So interconnection as a tenant of an antiracist agenda for assessment becomes another way to say that we always, out of necessity, live in and need diversity.

Now, consider Adam's essay on a similar kind of research question that he submitted in a junior-level writing in the major course for me a few years ago. Adam's paper is a research paper, so it's different in scope from Lindsey's, but similar in the kind of question he asks about language and communication. While I don't claim that this course enacted an explicitly antiracist writing assessment ecology, it came close. And race and racism were topics that came up in most students' drafts and assessments of their peers' drafts because that's how I designed the assessment activities. Adam begins his essay:

> Growing up in California, I didn't take much notice of what other people thought of me or what they thought I would be capable of doing. My neighborhood was comprised of mostly low-income families but I didn't recognize that because we always had food to eat and clothes to wear. I remember

learning to read and write at a young age; I was able to read before starting grade school and was also capable of writing a few words. I didn't love reading but I did so when I was told. When I started school I could already read pretty well but I was very shy. I was a "mixed kid" who was considered black to the white kids and not really black to the black kids. I didn't enjoy reading out loud to the teacher or to the class. There was one other black kid in the class, and he wouldn't even attempt to speak out loud in the classroom. When I was in front of the class everyone looked at me with such confusion, this was the first glimpse of black people for many of my classmates. I was becoming a nervous wreck when it came my turn to read or compose sentences aloud. I was so hesitant to participate that my first grade teacher told my Mom that she thought I needed more help with my reading. This talk with my mother precipitated many afterschool reading programs. I have seen my reading and writing skills develop over time but I still have many questions about what lead me to where I am today. This leads me to ask: Does race play a role in written communication? I will review data spanning the past few years, and review what others have published relating to this topic.

Perhaps the most noticeable difference in Adam's approximation of the white academic discourse is his focus on himself as a political entity that stems from his racialized experiences with reading in school. Unlike Lindsey, Adam doesn't begin his inquiry with abstract ideas or details that represent ideas, instead he begins with himself as a poor, "mixed" race kid, located in California. The tensions in his reading practices come from his embodied *habitus*, one that places him in different racial positions (racial projections) depending on who is perceiving him. Adam's research question ("Does race play a role in written communication?") stems from his own racialized subject position in school as a reader, and he doesn't avoid this implication. In fact, it is interconnected with the white racial *habitus* he knows he's expected to take on in school, and the Black racial *habitus* he is expected to take on around Blacks (in fact, he cites Vershawn A. Young (2007) later in his essay). Adam's discourse calls attention to his own racial position, a contextualized and racialized body in time and space, as one connected to his languaging. This is not the same as Lindsey's discourse, which is a white one, and focuses on where she is (location), and what others say to her (others' logos), not how others see her racially. In fact, Lindsey's discourse

divorces her physical, racialized body from the ideas and things she discusse
Adam's cannot. Adam reveals others' racialized perceptions of him that form th
exigency for Adam's inquiries about race and language use. But for Lindsey it
the rumination on the page itself, one that begins with thinking about an emp
mailbox and the labor and care it takes for one to write letters to others, a rum
nating that is disconnected from material, racialized bodies in time and spac
yet connected by her logos, the vignettes she offers of her mother, father, an
sister writing to her. Lindsey's discourse is abstract, rational in the way a whi
habitus tends to articulate things. Adam's is contextualized, social in nature, an
focused on his own subjective meaning making, which centers on racial pro
jections and communication. While there are aspects of Adam's discourse tha
shares in a white *habitus* (he uses a local SEAE), the nature of his question an
its exigency are not.

Adam's discourse isn't better than Lindsey's, only different. And in an antira
ist assessment ecology, the assessments that occur around these texts can use th
texts to compare *habitus*. For instance, Adam brings different things to bear o
his inquiry than Lindsey, such as others' contradictory perceptions of his raci
subject position, which seems to have an effect on his reading practices. Lind
sey's discourse seems to assume that any student could have such thoughts a
she presents, that others might come to similar conclusions if they found them
selves in the same places, doing the same things. Adam's discourse suggests th
contrary, that only he can ask this question from this position. These two essay
and writers can offer a lot to each other, just by reading and posing question
to each other, just by explicitly comparing their methods, if the assumption a
that they are interconnected. Lindsey needs Adam's discourse as much as Adan
needs Lindsey's. Lindsey's *habitus* is one that favors telling details that migh
help Adam see ways his discourse lacks this disposition. Adam's *habitus* is on
that places importance on revealing the writer's subjectivity and its connectio
to others' racial projections of him to his reading practices, which Lindsey avoid
but might do well to consider. In Chapter 5, I offer a heuristic and an exampl
assessment process that may shed light on how a classroom might take advantag
of such interconnectedness in order to form critical insights. For now, I hop
you can see that I'm not favoring one discourse over the other, but instead look
ing to show their differences as *habitus* and how those *habitus* are interconnect
ed. This interconnection is important to make explicit and tangible for students
if they are to help each other in assessment ecologies that do not simply promot
one racial *habitus* over others.

In a crude way, then, Yagelski's explanation of the post-process theory o
Kent says that any act of meaning-making, any languaging that we do, is con
nected not only to our audience but to the world we experience around us in th

act of writing or talking. This interconnectedness of all people and environments is also taught by the Buddhist monk and peace activist, Thich Nhat Hanh. In *Peace Is Every Step*, Hanh (1991) explains the concept of "interbeing" as one centrally about interconnectedness. He asks his reader to consider the sheet of paper in front of him. If one looks deep enough, one can see the trees, a cloud, rain, and sunshine required to make the paper, but if one looks even deeper, one can see the logger who cut the tree and the wheat needed for his meals. In this material way, through the materials of writing, through a sheet of paper itself, Hanh sees everything connected. But he goes further:

> Looking even more deeply, we can see ourselves in this sheet
> of paper too. This is not difficult to see, because when we look
> at a sheet of paper, it is part of our perception. Your mind is
> in here and mine is also. So we can say that everything is in
> here with this sheet of paper. We cannot point out one thing
> that is not here—time, space, the earth, the rain, the min-
> erals in the soil, the sunshine, the cloud, the river, the heat.
> Everything co-exists with this sheet of paper. That is why I
> think the word inter-be should be in the dictionary. "To be" is
> to inter-be. We cannot just *be* by ourselves alone. We have to
> inter-be with every other thing. This sheet of paper is, because
> everything else is. (1991, pp. 95-96)

Thus, for Hanh, like Kent and Yagelski, writing is an act that shows us just how interconnected we are, not just to each other but to the material environments we live in. Furthermore, in contrast to the Cartesian self in which mind and body are separate, Hanh sees one's mind and body as connected in the material of the paper. Your mind and body are in this paper together. In order for any-thing or anyone to exist, everything and everyone else must also. So Lindsey's *habitus* is just as much a part of Adam's paper as Adam's *habitus* is to hers.

Hanh's example is particularly salient for my discussion of writing assessment ecologies. For Hanh, it is the materials, the paper, by which we can enact writ-ing, connecting us to our environment and each other, including our minds. For Kent and Yagelski, it is larger, more abstract connections they are thinking of, yet ones with sensual, material, and phenomenological groundings. In fact, Ya-gelski draws heavily on Couture's (1998) phenomenological rhetoric (Yagelski, pp. 114-115, 132-134), as well as Merleau-Ponty's (2002). What Hanh offers us is a way to see how ecologies are more than environments, more than peo-ple, more than what and who is present at hand. And this more than quality of ecologies also inter-is with the quality of interconnectedness. Our writing assessment ecologies stretch out to other classrooms, places, people, activities, labor, all beyond the immediate paper in our hands that needs to be read because everything and everyone inter-is.

Hanh also offers a way to see inter-being as more than an individual experience, and this is important to my conception of antiracist writing assessment ecologies since much of my thinking about writing assessment has little to do with the individual student working or acting alone. Writing assessment ecologies are a way to see writing assessment holistically, as a larger set of people, environments, relations, labor, and exchanges. Those with antiracist agendas need this social dimension since racism is structural—we seek to change the rule, rather than focus on individuals and exceptions. In *Being Peace* (1987), Hanh explains the *Sangha* which provides a good way to see classroom writing assessment ecologies as harmonious communities:

> The Sangha is the community that lives in harmony and awareness. Sanghakaya is a new Sanskrit term. The Sangha needs a body also. When you are with your family and you practice smiling, breathing, recognizing the Buddha body in yourself and your children, then your family becomes a Sangha. If you have a bell in your home, the bell becomes part of your Sanghakaya, because the bell helps you to practice .... Many things help us practice. The air, for breathing. If you have a park or a river bank near your home, you are very fortunate because you can enjoy practicing walking meditation. You have to discover your Sanghakaya, inviting a friend to come and practice with you, have tea meditation, sit with you, join you for walking meditation. All those efforts are to establish your Sanghakaya at home. Practice is easier if you have a Sanghakaya. (1987, pp. 26-27)

There are three things to notice in this description of a Sangha, or an ecology of practice. First, similar to post-process ideas of writing as communicative exchange, the Sangha works best when more than one person is there practicing. It is social. I think it is safe to say that as humans we thrive emotionally, physically, spiritually, and mentally when we are together. Sangha as a community or family acknowledges this, but it does so because people are interconnected. The Sangha is a way to see this interconnectedness among people in a tangible way, in our daily practices. For example, according to Hanh, when we practice mindfulness with our family members, our family becomes an ecology, a Sangha who are interconnected. I believe, the same can be said for students and teacher in a writing course. We all have the experience of feeling differently about our students after we've gone through a semester in a course with them, after we've sat in conferences with them, exchanged ideas in class with them, read their writing, responded to it, etc. And they too feel differently about each other, feel more connected to one another because they've been with each other in the Sangha-class, the Sangha-ecology.

Thus through assessment practices, the class can become a Sangha if explicitly identified as such and discussed. The benefit is not in the new label for a classroom community. The benefit is in the discussions of what it means to be a locally diverse community of interconnected people and practices. What does it mean to think and act upon the idea that one's colleagues inter-are with oneself, that their reading and writing practices, their reflections, their labors in and out of class inter-are with one's own practices and labors? Identifying and discussing the class and its practices as a Sangha allows for such discussions and reflections. It is not easy, and takes repeated efforts at reflection and discussion, but it helps students feel interconnected because they are.

The second thing to note in Hahn's description is the assumption of inter-being of people and their environments. The home, river bank, and park are all environments that harmonize with the practitioner, and through her practice, the inter-being of these environments with herself and family members becomes apparent. For instance, the bell one might use to signal the start of a mindful practice each day *is* because we *are*. The bell inter-is with the Sangha, and is a symbol of inter-being itself when used to initiate meditation together. The bell symbolically and literally harmonizes one's material environment with the group. Practitioners inter-are the ecology they create with the bell. Classrooms and other learning spaces form similar interconnected relationships with students and teachers through practices like freewriting and weekly group work. But again, students must pause and explicitly reflect and discuss this inter-being of their working environments.

Perhaps the best recent example of how a class might be a sangha is in Barry Kroll's (2013) discussion of his writing classroom, in which they take field trips to a nearby Japanese Zen garden and practice modified Aikido techniques that illustrate ways to argue respectfully with others. Kroll's classroom space not only is extended to other spaces, other environments, offering a wider net of interconnection with the natural world, but inside the classroom the typical activities of learning to write are expanded to include kinesthetic movements and examining the proximity of bodies. Students learn principles of argumentation by physically grappling (and avoiding conflict) with each other in non-violent ways. Kroll's interesting and wonderful class shows how writing and its assessment are labors that are interconnected with our bodies, those around us, and our environments. And when we pay attention to this interconnectedness, we can enhance the assessment of writing, the making of meaning, by understanding how we make value and meaning in and through contexts, how our bodies and environments inter-are by feeling, moving, interacting through our differences in a number of ways.

Third, for Hanh the practice of Buddhism and the Sangha are both practices, rituals and things done each day. They are labor done together with others. We invite friends to join us in walking meditation. We have a family of others whom we engage with and see the Buddha body through. We mediate, practice breathing and smiling. We labor and notice our laboring. Throughout Hanh's description of the Sangha, the Sangha itself is synonymous with practices, acts, doing things, and noticing that one is doing them. Much like the OED's definition of ecology, through the doing of these practices, the Sangha is created and recreated. In antiracist writing assessment ecologies, "labor" can reference this doing of things (Inoue, 2014a), and I use it as a measure of expectations of the classroom, so that we avoid using a dominant discourse as the measure of "good writing," when it's really just one kind of good writing. Labor makes clear that we are speaking of verbs, of processes filled with action that all can agree upon and do. And in these ways, labor is an antiracist measure in classroom writing assessment ecologies. It is through labor and practices that ecologies change, that people interact and affect each other and their environments, so labor is useful to measure, even useful to determine grades because it (re)creates the sangha-ecology. And because one's labor inter-is with others' labors, all classroom labor is the material enactment of interconnectedness whether we see it as such or not.

Interconnection as a way to explicitly understand the relationship between and among people, their labors, drafts, practices, and environments is vital to a fully functioning antiracist writing assessment ecology. It offers students ways out of simply disagreeing, simply seeing difference, or "agreeing to disagree." Seeing difference is a good start, but ultimately, we must work together, help each other in writing classrooms and beyond. We must see how we all inter-are, how we can be a Sangha. Once we act in ways that acknowledge the fluid boundaries between ourselves and others, between our writing and others' judgments of it, we become fuller.

AS MARXIAN ECOLOGY

Given interconnection, it might seem that antiracist writing assessment ecologies can be apolitical, even ahistorical. I don't mean that the people in them or even the environments in which those people interact can be read as apolitical (they too cannot). I mean the ecology as a set of structures itself, as a system itself, could appear to be apolitical, appear to have no politics of its own. This is not true. Antiracist writing assessment ecologies (all assessment ecologies, really) are political and historical by their natures. And these politics are important to make clear to students and be clear for teachers because of the goals or purposes of antiracist writing assessment ecologies (i.e., to help students problematize their existential writing assessment situations). The politics of any writing assessment ecology will determine what is valued, how it gets valued, who benefits most, and the consequences or products of those benefits.

We know from experience that when people get together to judge and make decisions, particularly in classrooms, they do so through relations of power, relations that are a part of larger social structures that come from the mix of languages, genders, racial formations, class, age, ability, etc. in society. We just don't agree about everything, and when we disagree, those with more power in the system have a louder voice. The systems in and through which we make important judgments, such as grading and feedback systems—assessment systems—themselves are political and historical, which is to say they have a politics of their own. To understand the way the politics of antiracist classroom writing assessment ecologies work, I find that Gramscian "historic bloc" and "hegemony" offer sufficient explanations that can be used by writing teachers. In part, this is due to the familiarity of Marxian critiques, even if cursorily understood by some.

Dobrin and Weisser explain ecocomposition as a set of systems in the world. They explain that "humans occupy two spaces: a biosphere, consisting of the earth and its atmosphere, which supports our physical existence, and a semiosphere, consisting of discourse, which shapes our existence and allows us to make sense of it" (2002, p. 574). This binary of connected spheres in which humans inhabit explains a number of important things about environments: discourse's influence on material places, places' influence on discourse, and an accounting of both the material and the discursive. But it doesn't account very well for time, change, or how particular power arrangements maintain themselves, such as unequal racial formations inhabiting the ecology, or whose words get to describe the landscape or environment? Whose discourse shapes whose lived environments? It doesn't really explain, for instance, how a white racial *habitus* remains so universal, even in places where the teachers ascribe to critical and antiracist agendas, or where students are almost all of color, multilingual, or working class.

Gramsci and Marxian theories help explain the grounds by which we can understand the nature of ecological systems as political, material, and discursive ecologies that are inclined toward the hegemonic, or "determined" (in the Marxian sense, discussed below) to produce particular outcomes or products. Seeing antiracist writing assessment ecologies as Marxian systems can provide powerful ways to critique and change unfair and unequal power relations among racial formations in a writing course, and more consciously engage in antiracist agendas in the assessment of writing. It offers language for teachers and students to problem-pose, or problematize the existential writing assessment situations of students. Thus an explicit Marxian analysis of the classroom's writing assessment ecology is important to discuss with students.

Perhaps the most overarching and important term to offer students is one that some may already know, hegemony. Antonio Gramsci, the early twentieth century Italian political philosopher and theorist, articulated a theory of political economy that used the terms "hegemony" and "historic bloc." The term "hegemony" likely comes from the Greek word *egemonia* or *egemon*, which means "leader, ruler, often in the sense of a state other than his own" (Williams, 1985, p. 144; as quoted in Mastroianni, 2012). As a concept, then, hegemony started with having the flavor of rule and leadership. Written while imprisoned during 1927 to 1935, Gramsci articulates hegemony in his prison notebooks, which were written in code to avoid being taken or destroyed by the prison censor. Gramsci describes the term as the multitude of economic, political, moral, and cultural relations of force that produce consent in society between dominated groups (for Gramsci the proletariat and their allies, the peasant classes) for the benefit of political leadership, or the dominant group (the bourgeoisie) (Williams, 1985, pp. 194-195, 200-201). Hegemony, then, is an historically based set of conflicts or clashes of interests among social groups and forces, a gaining and losing ground, all of which produce benefits primarily for a dominant group. Raymond Williams explains hegemony as

> a whole body of practices and expectations, over the whole
> of living: our senses and assignments of energy, our shaping
> perceptions of ourselves and our world. It is a lived system of
> meanings and values —constitutive and constituting —which
> as they are experienced as practices appear as reciprocally
> confirming. (1977, p. 110)

Thus hegemony in our lived experiences is both in our reconfirming practices and in how we understand, justify, and talk about those practices. Hegemony is a way to describe the constitutive set of practices, meanings, perceptions, and values that make up one's whole life, and a way simultaneously to describe the constituting aspects of one's whole life. In a much simplified way, hegemony explains the product and process of culture and ideology. It explains one half of the Freirean problem-posing strategy, the problematizing that is made concrete through examining structures such as discourses and *habitus*, which as Althusser (1971) tells us, is ideology that interpellates us as subjects.[26] The concept of hegemony theorizes the structural part of the problem posed about language explaining the nature of dispositions and discourses and how they are constituted in larger social and economic spheres, and how those discourses and *habitus*, when deployed, create consent.

Williams adds that hegemony is also "a process ... a realized complex of experiences, relationships, and activities, with specific changing pressures and limits" (1977, p. 112). This means there is never one hegemony to understand, even in one concrete historic moment, which is the only real way to explore or investigate it. Instead, hegemony is always plural, always like Volosinov's language, always in the historic act of becoming. Thus it is usually more accurate to speak of the hegemonic, rather than the hegemony. Furthermore, as Williams and others have pointed out, within any hegemonic moment, there is always the counter-hegemonic. Hegemony is always in the process of being reproduced, rearticulated, and revised.

In locally diverse classrooms, however, tensions in the assessment ecology (a product of its politics) often come from an uncritical use of a dominant discourse in judging and assessing student writing. Gramsci's hegemony explains in slightly different terms why these tensions occur. Standardized assessments usually are racist and hegemonic because they are *standardized*, that is, because they use a tacit hegemonic white racial *habitus* as the standard for the test. By enforcing a standard, they measure and fit various shapes of pegs into a one-sized, square hole. Once we see writing assessment ecologies as participating in the (counter)hegemonic, we can see the ways writing assessments create desires and expectations in students and teachers, or change them, shape our perceptions of ourselves and others, or help us critique those perceptions, give us meanings that we live by, or help us see how those meanings are constructed, and constitute ourselves and our environments (interpellating us), or provide ways to reconstitute ourselves and environments. And we see that all these things are a product of a clash of political interests.

As I've mentioned already, there is nothing wrong with a white racial *habitus* in and of itself. What is wrong is that it has been used as a standard by which to place people in hierarchies since the beginning of education itself, at times suggesting people's intelligence and ability, as well as determining their access to future opportunities. Antiracist classroom writing assessment ecologies works against this hegemonic function of writing assessments by not using a standard to rank students, and instead uses labor to focus on the interconnection of various diverse *habitus* that help make critical meaning. Problem-posing as an enactment of interconnection helps students problematize their existential writing assessment situations in the hegemonic by interrogating the ways their texts reveal particular *habitus* and interpellating ideology. Furthermore, when hegemonic writing assessment interpellates students as individuals (as Yagelski claims), and not as interconnected, it reinforces politics and personal interests, constructing difference in hierarchical terms, not on lateral landscapes that inter-are. This is counterproductive to antiracist projects and critical ones that look to understand difference on its own terms.

Keep in mind that antiracist writing assessment ecologies should have a strong ethics to them, but it comes from the entire ecology, not one node or person in it, not the teacher only. Thus, we cannot place our trust in the benevolence of teachers as the key element for an appropriate, effective, and fair writing assessment ecology? We cannot rely on our altruism to solve racism in our classroom writing assessment ecologies. Because if we trust in this paradigm, trust in focusing on teachers' ethics as a good way to design and enact antiracist writing assessment ecologies, then we have to believe that all writing teachers, regardless of their training, backgrounds, ethics, pedagogies, idiosyncrasies, politics, constraints, and contexts in which they teach, will do the right thing most of the time, or will know what to do. I don't think this has happened, nor can it. More important, no amount of good intentions can make up for a structurally racist society, institution, or writing assessment ecology.

Don't get me wrong. I strongly believe in writing teachers' need for strong and explicit ethics, and I believe most (if not all) writing teachers mean well. I believe that a good teacher is like Quintilian's ideal orator, the "good person speaking well." A strong ethical center is important for writing pedagogy and central to what we teach in writing classrooms. Freire, in fact, discusses ethics by saying that the foundation of any liberation or revolution is love, "a profound love for the world and for people," referencing Che Guevara's sentiment that revolution must be seen as "an act of love" by revolutionaries (1970, p. 89). But judging and grading writing have other requirements beyond love in order to be fair and equitable, for example, participation by those who are being judged, by those who have the most stake in the assessment ecology. And participation by those being liberated, by the way, is central to Freire's problem-posing method that leads to critical consciousness through enacting the counter-hegemonic. Even when we love others and wish them the best, we often do not know what that best thing is, nor how to achieve it. Most important, we (teachers) cannot achieve it for students. It is their revolution, not ours.

The above discussion doesn't explain well why such cooperative hegemonic and counter-hegemonic projects and processes in an historic place and time, like Fresno State today, either changes things in one direction, keeps them the same, or simply rearticulates the status quo of social relations, practices, values, etc. This is important because I'm arguing that antiracist writing assessment ecologies are at some level counter-hegemonic. Dominic Mastroianni's explanation of Gramsci's hegemony as historically specific begins to help make sense of this question and of counter-hegemony's ability to change the ecology:

> Gramsci's "hegemony" refers to a process of moral and intel-

lectual leadership through which dominated or subordinate classes of post-1870 industrial Western European nations consent to their own domination by ruling classes, as opposed to being simply forced or coerced into accepting inferior positions. It is important to note that, although Gramsci's prison writings typically avoid using Marxist terms such as "class," "bourgeoisie," and "proletariat" (because his work was read by a Fascist censor), Gramsci defines hegemony as a form of control exercised by a dominant class, in the Marxist sense of a group controlling the means of production. (2012)

So the hegemonic is the mechanisms of control of the means of production of something in a society's historic moment, and it is a process that moves students, teachers, parents, and administrators to consent to things in schools that benefit primarily a dominant group, somehow masking the contradictory outcomes of what they are consenting to. This is a bigger problem for multilingual, working class, and students of color. In a locally diverse writing classroom where the goal is the production of academic literacy practices in students, and where the teacher consciously engages in an antiracist project by asking students to read about racism, racial formations, and whiteness, and even encourages her students to use their own home languages, but still must grade based on a local SEAE and set of academic discursive conventions, say ones found in the popular first-year writing textbook, *They Say / I Say* (Graff & Berkenstein, 2014), it is difficult for the classroom writing assessment ecology to escape reproducing the hegemonic, since both the local SEAE and the textbook by Graff and Berkenstein are hegemonic, both are derived from a white racial *habitus*. The point is, you don't have to be thinking in racial terms for your writing assessment ecology to be racist or only promote a hegemonic, white racial *habitus*. This is the default in most (if not all) classrooms, schools, and disciplines. In fact, not thinking about racism and the hegemonic allows for such things to flourish, allows for consent to be unobstructed. Even in a classroom where the teacher has explicit antiracist readings and agendas, where students are encouraged to critique racism in society, the racism in the classroom's writing assessment ecology can still flourish if it is not addressed explicitly as an ecology with its own unique racial politics that are hegemonic, that move students and teachers to consent to a white racial *habitus* as the standard, and even to desire it.

How does one escape a racist classroom writing assessment ecology? First and foremost, students participation in grading and assessment in the entire ecology is vital. They must liberate themselves. They cannot be liberated.[27] So antiracist writing assessment ecologies are counter-hegemonic in this way, in giving the means of grade production, assessment production, and the production of expectations, over to students, or mostly over to them. There are lots of ways to do this. I'll discuss a few in Chapter 4 (grading contracts) and 5 (a heuristic, and an example assessment activity).

Another key to seeing how the counter-hegemonic can work in antiracist writing assessment ecologies may be in Gramsci's notion of civil society. Mastroianni emphasizes that in order to understand the nature of Gramsci's historically situated hegemony, one needs to understand his concepts of state and civil society. But to understand these concepts, one must understand the Marxian concepts of base and superstructure, which define the structural relationships that create the (counter)hegemonic and the conditions for civil society. We can also see this classic Marxist dialectic (base and superstructure) as one overlay that helps us understand one set of relationships that guide the material and the discursive in an antiracist classroom writing assessment ecology.

Through analyses of the Russian and French revolutions,[28] Gramsci works from the traditional Marxist binary of an economic base (the material practices and economic relations) and theoretical/cultural superstructure (the theories, social relations, and articulations) that describes that base and springs from it, but he doesn't spend a lot of time on the economic. He's more interested in superstructure, in the ways consent is reproduced through structures of language, story, folklore, education, media, etc. He claims that domination in society (Western Europe) doesn't start with the economic base of practices of the proletariat, as traditional Marxism proposes; instead, our practices and theorizing are a dialectical, "interrelated and reciprocal" unity, which he terms an "historic bloc" (2000, p. 192-93).[29] This means that the superstructure is equally important to civil society's manufacturing of consent just as much as the state's military and economic structures are important to coercively regulating broad societal divisions and labor markets when structures of consent break down. Gramsci calls the ways that superstructure works itself out in society as "relations of force," and there are at least three, which correspond roughly to Marx's uses of superstructure in society (Gramsci, 2000, pp. 204-207).

Williams defines these three uses as a way to define Marxian superstructure, and I think also Gramscian superstructure. Williams explains that superstructure can be seen in three senses, as "institutions," "forms of consciousness," and "political and cultural practices" (1977, p. 77). Thus hegemony is stubborn and reproduced through a dialectic between base and superstructure, through the superstructures of educational and disciplinary institutions, classrooms and the like; through forms of consciousness that express a local SEAE and a set of white racial *habitus* as the dominant way by which intelligent and civil people communicate; and through political and cultural practices in schools and academia, in our textual discourses, our journals, department meetings, and ways we read and respond to our students' writing in classrooms and in programs that designate civil exchange. Thus the fight over and in the hegemonic is a complex network of ecologies in which people "fight it out" for control and power, for intellectual, material, and figurative territory over a number of terrains (through institutions, forms of consciousness, and practices). An antiracist classroom assessment ecology, then, is a kind of Marxian dialectic of a base that consists of the material environment(s) and forces that students and teacher enact and work in—all the things we do in a classroom and outside of it—and a superstructure, or a set of relations of force that explain and justify the classroom and its writing assessment practices, (e.g., the use of the local SEAE, the use of a textbook, and conventions privileged, the use of a portfolio, the discourses used to judge writing, a rubric used to explain expectations and evaluate writing, etc.). Antiracist writing assessment ecologies gives students control over the superstructure and by dialectical default also the base of activities and production, both of which help construct that ecology. When students control most of what is called assessment, then the grounds for the counter-hegemonic is fertile.

If base and superstructure are the engine of civil society and its political workings, then they can explain the way civil assessment is produced in a writing classroom. Gramsci explains that

> "civil society" has become a very complex structure and one
> which is resistant to the catastrophic "incursions" of the
> immediate economic element (crises, depressions, etc.). The
> superstructures of civil society are like the trench-systems of
> modern warfare. In war it would sometimes happen that a
> fierce artillery attack seemed to have destroyed the enemy's
> entire defensive system, whereas in fact it had only destroyed
> the outer perimeter; and at the moment of their advance and
> attack the assailants would find themselves confronted by a
> line of defence [sic] which was still effective. (2000, p. 227)

Why is society's defense still effective, why is hegemony so stubborn? Why does the EPT still control the educational futures of students when we have DSP, or a somewhat critically aware WPA, or teachers who consciously do antiracist work in classrooms? Perhaps part of the answer is in the fact that the dialectic of base and superstructure in every classroom writing assessment ecology is hegemonic and most ecologies are not designed to be counter-hegemonic, not designed to see or criticize their own racial politics. This counter-hegemonic characteristic begins with who controls the assessment ecology.

Furthermore, in classroom assessment ecologies, there are many superstructural trenches behind the immediate ones we focus on. A white racial *habitus* is reinforced by other discourses of empiricism: objectivity; neutrality; hyperindividualism; unsentimental, detached discussion; and the pervasive assumption of a Cartesian *Cogito* in grading and assessing of writing. Behind those discourses are ones we see on TV and in popular media that depict intelligent and educated people who speak like Lindsey or as I do in this book. Behind our explanations of our judgments in our classroom writing assessment ecologies (one trench) are the explanations and justifications of the DSP (another trench), and behind that are those that explain Early Start, and behind that are those that explain the EPT, and it goes on. And all these trenches maintain to some degree, in various overlapping ways, the civil society of academia, the civil literacies we teach, the civil assessments we maintain.

Seeing a local SEAE or white racial *habitus* as *the standard* which classroom writing assessments must use doesn't simply come from the discipline of writing studies, from our journals, books, and conferences, or English departments' agreements in meetings and program review discussions, nor is it simply a matter of what our colleagues ask of us from other corners of the university and academy, nor is it just pressure from our local communities. It is all of these forces. The superstructural relations of force, the hegemony of racist writing assessment ecologies that promotes only one version of English, what Horner and Trimbur (2002) called a "unidirectional monolingualism" and Matsuda (2006) explained is associated with the "myth of linguistic homogeneity," *determine* the standard and its dominant discourse, and is reinforced by another trench, the local white racial *habitus*. The trenches of the hegemonic are numerous and overlapping civil writing assessment ecologies.

"Determination" is an important part of Marxian thought and helps explain base and superstructure's relation to consent in the hegemonic, and explains why most civil writing assessments are racist in writing classrooms. I've used the term above, but it demands a bit of explanation. Williams explains that the concept of determination comes from Marx's original use of the word *bestimmen*, which is translated in English as "determine." Williams points out that determine means "setting bounds" or "setting limits" (1977, p. 84); however, "in practice determination is never only the setting of limits; it is also the exertion of pressures," a complex process in real, historic circumstances, something Marxism's base and superstructure often lose when used as abstract categories (p. 87) divorced from real, concrete, historical moments in particular places. The point is that part of the way the hegemonic functions is through processes and practices, values and articulations that are determined in both senses of the word. They are determined in the sense of setting boundaries or limits on, say, choice in a DSP ecology (e.g., a student may choose the one- or two-semester option to meet the same writing requirement at Fresno State), and determined in the sense of exerting pressure toward some end or outcome, such as the fact that there is no option to not take a writing course. There is pressure and obligation to fulfill the university's writing requirement. So while students do have a higher degree of agency through personal choice in a DSP ecology than they would in other placement ecologies, their choice is constrained and pressured. Students are free to choose their courses, but not free to *not* choose a course or to choose just *any* course.

The determination built into classroom writing assessments, particularly ones that produce grades on individual assignments, or that use a dominant discourse only as a standard, have these same two aspects to them. As teachers, we never simply ask students to write or read for us, or their peers, even when we give them choices on what they may write about or read. Their choices are constrained, and they are pressured to labor or face the negative consequences. The question an antiracist writing assessment ecology asks explicitly of teachers is: How clear and explicit are the constraints and pressures that determine student labor and the valuing of the products of those labors in the ecology? The clearer and more explicit determination is in an ecology, the fairer it can be.

As a concept, determination also explains the relationship that our labors and activities (base) and the discourses we use to explain, judge, and justify those labors and activities (superstructure) have to the (counter)hegemonic. It explains how everyone is complicit in the politics of the ecology. In fact, seeing, reflecting on, and discussing with students the ways the classroom's assessment ecology determines their desires and actions, their labor and expectations of writing, their judging of writing, can offer ways to think counter-hegemonically, and perhaps change the ecology toward antiracist ends. In this sense, seeing the way the assessment ecology determines student labor and desires provides a way to see the problematizing that is at the center of the assessment activities in the ecology.

But we have not yet talked about the base, the other half of the Marxian dialectic. If superstructure can be located in "institutions," "forms of consciousness," and "political and cultural practices," base, according to Williams, is "the real social existence of man," or the "real relations of production corresponding to a state of development of material productive forces," or the "mode of production at a particular stage of its development," or as Marx himself put it, "productive activities." Each of these ways of seeing the base in the Marxian dialectic is a bit different, but as Mastroianni, and Marx himself (as well as Engels), makes clear, base isn't a reference to an abstract category, rather it is a reference to a particular instance of material production in "a determined historical form" (Williams, 1977, p. 81). And so, base could be thought of as a particular instance of material production in a determined historic moment that is inextricable from the superstructure that dialectically creates and describes

113

it. Base, then, is the material activities that make up writing assessment in our classrooms. Superstructure is the language we use in our classrooms to explain, rationalize, and explore those activities, or the discourse of assessment. The base cannot be known for sure until a writing course begins, and its superstructure is unique to that course's material base of activities and labor. In short, base and superstructure in an antiracist writing assessment ecology are interconnected. The base of activities inter-is the superstructural ways we talk about those activities.

Base and superstructure offer students and teacher an analysis, a critical description, of the way the hegemonic reproduces itself in an antiracist writing assessment ecology, while also maintaining individual students', teachers', and administrators' agencies by incorporating the more nuanced notion of determine, which provides for choice, boundaries, and pressure. There is always choice in the system. It is just constrained choice. So all must participate in creating both the boundaries and the pressures. As Engels explains, "[w]e make our history ourselves, but, in the first place, under very definite assumptions and conditions" (Williams, 1977, p. 85). This insight, an insight that is the intersection between personal agency and structural constraints that determine one's agency, is what Freire's problem-posing pedagogy attempts to reveal in particular concrete, historical moments for his students. It is also the kind of problems I believe antiracist writing assessment ecologies should encourage students to pose to each other. How does our course, its activities, a student's labors that produce a text, the discourses around these activities and texts determine what ends up on the page, and determine what various readers judge on that page? Are there patterns in the classroom or in any given writing group that might be racial, or that may automatically benefit some and harm others?

Let us not forget that we cannot really know for sure the *habitus* of any given student or group of students, no matter how we group them. Racial *habitus*, like all other dimensions of people, are dynamic and changing. Much like Omi and Winant's (1994) racial formation theory, Gramsci's theorizing is historical and local or specific in nature, accounting for particular dynamic, historical processes of social and economic maintenance and change in society. We can see this in his insistence that base and superstructure form an "historic bloc" (Gramsci, 2000, pp. 192, 197).

"Historic bloc" describes the ways in which societal and economic practices (base) both are created by and create the values, social relations, and theories (superstructure) we use to rationalize and explain our material and economic circumstances. Conversely, the term also describes the ways our theorizing and values (superstructure) are created by and create the material and economic (base) they explain and rationalize. Both elements reinforce one another dialectically, move and slowly change in history, and so are simultaneously socially generative and explanatory. This is the Marxian dialectic of base and superstructure that hegemony describes as processes of determination. The dialectic explains why writing assessment ecologies are holistic in nature and more than their parts, since each part is consubstantial to all others—that is, they inter-are. It should be clear that the dialectic moves in both directions, so base is not simply the foundation, the constitutive, and the superstructure the practices and discourse below it that describe it. Both base and superstructure dialectically constitute and are constituting historical elements. Sometimes it is our explanations of things that instigate change or maintain the status quo, while at others, it is our practices and economic relations that move us to rethink, revise, rearticulate, or maintain how and why we do what we do. Thus because they are a dialectic, base and superstructure inter-are. And because they depend on each other to be in a writing assessment ecology, they inter-are. Gramsci's articulations reveal how even with good people and intentions classroom writing assessment ecologies often reproduce relations of force that arrange people in unequal and unfair ways, cultivate dominant interests, practices, and values, and engender consent by all through particular practices and discourses that justify and explain those practices, coercing some to act and speak in certain ways, and others to accept "failure" or exclusion from the academy.

FEATURES AND PRIORITIES OF ANTIRACIST WRITING ASSESSMENT ECOLOGIES

What I hope I've shown in this chapter is that any antiracist writing assessment ecology is one that contains three important explicit features. The first feature is an attention to its holistic nature (it's sense of being more than the sum of its parts), an attention to critical production beyond itself, which gives the ecology a purpose of helping students problematize their existential writing assessment situations (see Appendix B for an assignment that asks student to problem pose explicitly). This makes labor students do, the reading, writing, and judging, most important. Labor is the engine for liberation or critical output. Second, the ecology explicitly reveals the interconnectedness of all aspects and elements in the ecology. The locally diverse people and their *habitus*, the environments involved, their feedback, and students' labors are all interconnected. They inter-are, making difference not a point of contention as much as a method of comparing and revealing critical insights, revealing how we language and judge language differently, yet paradoxically need one another to be.

Third, Gramsci's theorizing of hegemony and historic bloc offers a theory students and teachers can use to help explain the political nature of the ecology itself, of the way it determines particular practices, ideas, judgments, and *hab-*

itus, so that the counter-hegemonic might flourish. The Marxian dialectic also explains the holistic and interconnected nature of the relationships in ecologies. The language and theory around ecologies tend to avoid the politics inherent in our human and social world. When we avoid the political (power relations) we often avoid race and other social dimensions that embody power differentials because race is an identifier primarily of power differentials, especially in schools. The concept of ecology assumes that people and their environments always form relationships between and among each other, that an aspect of these relationships is one of inter-being, interconnectedness, but just because we are interconnected doesn't mean the nature of our connections to each other are equal, that we each share the same power in a given context of judgment, that how we speak or write is the same or exercises the same degree of power in social settings. Yet despite these uneven power relations, antiracist writing assessment ecologies strive to even power relations by focusing on labor and not quality (determined by comparisons to a single standard) to produce things like grades and expectations, and helping students problematize their writing assessment situations.

However, assuming inter-being in all people and environments is not the same thing as assuming that we are all alike. There is difference, local diversity, but how we understand it and judge it in writing can come from a sense of inter-being, a sense of one student's success or failure as participating in all students' success or failure, and for that matter, the teacher's success or failure in the ecology. We don't need one standard to make judgments on writing in learning contexts—in fact, it's antithetical to learning to write—nor do we need categories and hierarchies, such as grades, which many have already argued against. But let me be clear about it. Antiracist writing assessment ecologies understand the conventional graded classroom as deeply flawed because it needs a single standard by which to rank students and their performances, performances that by their nature are unrankable because they inter-are. Thus grading is racist.

And so, the best learning happens in diverse contexts, in diverse environments, filled with multiple ways of understanding, seeing, and being that are not judged or assessed against one standard of literacy, instead each writer explores the nature of judgment in his own discourse and the dominant one (i.e., a local white racial *habitus*) in order to problematize one's existential writing assessment situation. This makes the discourse of assessment and judgment, one akin to reflection, more important than the drafts we might be judging. Through this problematizing, students can come to an awareness of how they inter-are with others and their *habitus*.

Antiracist classroom writing assessment ecologies imply that people (re)create places of settlement, places we wish to inhabit or make habitable, Sanghas that involve mindful, habitual practices and other actions among groups of people. Enacting classroom writing assessment ecologies as a way to create a humane and inhabitable place for everyone is an antiracist project in intention, process, and outcome. Ecologies are activity systems as much as they are people, environments, and relationships. Thus all writing assessment ecologies imply that our first job when designing and enacting them is to make a place livable in ethical and humane ways for everyone.

Finally, I end with a summary of priorities that construct antiracist writing assessment ecologies for writing classrooms that I've developed through my discussion in this chapter. These are priorities that teachers and students can keep in mind as they design and enact their own ecologies. They provide the grounds by which activities, labors, and discussions can be created or interrogated for antiracist assessment agendas, and are in no particular order of importance.

- Ecologies by their natures are always political, so they should be explicit about the racial politics they promote.
- Places, especially in education, are associated with racial formations and other social groups, which may affect some students' abilities to do the work asked.
- The assessment ecology of the classroom can be discussed as a Sangha ecology in order to help students reflect upon the interconnectedness of themselves, the classroom, and their practices, making difference important to who they are and what they can do.
- Focusing on the amount or intensity of labor can offer fairer ways to respect all students' rights to their own languages, and avoid measuring students' writing against a single standard.
- Focusing on change and movement in student discourses, not comparisons to a single standard in grading or evaluating of student writing, even though students may wish to approximate a dominant discourse, can reduce racism in assessments.
- Ecologies constantly change and with them, students, teachers, and language practices change, thus ecologies can engage in a critical documenting of each student's "ceaseless flow of becoming" in their language practices.

There are also priorities that provide ecologies ways to help students problematize their writing assessment situations, the central activity in antiracist writing assessment ecologies. In Chapter 5, I offer a heuristic that helps teachers and students construct antiracist writing assessment ecologies, and in Appendix B, one assessment activity that does the problematizing I call for here. The following list is meant as a summary of the problematizing theme I've discussed in this chapter.

- Students can discuss how problematizing one's existential writing assessment situation is about making the ecology sustainable, fair, and livable for all.
- Students can continually consider and work from the idea that words are action, language is action, and reflection is action, which makes language and the assessment of it both the means of cultural production (base) and the explaining of that production (superstructure) in assessment activities.
- Assessments and their discourses are more important than the drafts they assess, which means the assessment ecology focuses mostly on the production of the discourses of judgment and assessment.
- Assessment activities use the local diversity in the classroom as a way to create comparisons to a white racial *habitus*, asking students to consider the markers and dispositions in and underneath the texts they read and judge.
- Judgments and questions posed to writers compare *habitus* of students to the dominant white racial *habitus* of the school, discipline, or classroom, or to the *habitus* of readers, not as static entities or dispositions, but as evolving dispositions that change through interaction.
- Interconnection among locally diverse people and *habitus* in ecologies are made explicit and used toward problem-posing ends in the assessment activities—students must reflect upon their need for others who are different from themselves.
- Students need explicit Marxian language to help them understand the politics of the antiracist assessment ecology they participate in and to problematize their existential writing assessment situations; in particular, students can reflect upon the ways rubrics, assignments, or descriptive judgments of their drafts determine their expectations that may have uneven benefits among students in the classroom, or that determine their own desires for their writing or the writing of others.

CHAPTER 3: THE ELEMENTS OF AN ANTIRACIST WRITING ASSESSMENT ECOLOGY

Now, I turn to discussing the seven ecological elements that constitute antiracist classroom writing assessment ecologies, elements that can be used to critique or transform ecologies as revolutionary antiracist projects in order to do more productively the Freirean problem-posing I've already discussed. In my discussion of each ecological element, I will attempt to offer ways that it can be a focal point to design and engage in antiracist writing assessment ecologies, particularly engaging students in problematizing their existential writing assessment situations. My larger argument in this chapter is to show how thinking in terms of these seven elements can help writing teachers develop antiracist classroom writing assessment ecologies that are more critical, sustainable, and fair for everyone. There may be other elements at work in local writing assessment ecologies, but these appear to be the seven basic elements that writing teachers can consider when understanding their own assessment ecologies and turning their efforts toward antiracist purposes.

The seven elements of antiracist writing assessment ecologies may seem commonsensical to many, but not many consider them holistically and interconnected when designing, engaging in, or investigating classroom writing assessments. Furthermore, I discuss them in terms of their potential to explain or aid in antiracist assessment agendas. Because they are inherently interlocking elements, because they inter-are, because they are more than what they are, often sharing in each other's essences and transforming into each other, it easier to discuss them separately, particularly when explaining or designing antiracist classroom writing assessment ecologies. The seven interconnected and holistic elements are: power, parts, purposes, people, processes, products, and places.

Before I discuss each element separately, it is important to consider their complexity as a whole and interconnection to one another. In a recent article in which she argues that agency emerges from actions and reactions among people in the world, Marilyn Cooper (2011) uses complexity theory to explain the system of rhetoric and people, one more nuanced than the writing ecology she explained in 1986. She says that "agency is an emergent property of embodied individuals," and is "based in individuals' lived knowledge that their actions are their own" (2011, p. 421). Emergent rhetorical agency is "a response to a perturbation that is shaped by the rhetor's current goals and past experiences," but it's also an "enactive" system—that is, individuals act without knowing exactly what they are doing or that they may be changing the system (Cooper, 2011, p. 426). Using complexity theorists, Cooper explains the way agency emerges, a process of *"structural determination"* very similar to Marxian determination in which changes in the system, such as persuasion, may be instigated by a person who employs rhetoric but whose specific effects on the system and the individuals who make it up are *"determined by the structure of the disturbed system"* (2011, p. 426). Thus large-scale or systemic changes may not directly affect individuals' behaviors, say changes in writing practices of a student in a classroom. The system is not a linear system, a one-to-one causal system. For instance, it is not always the case that when we give good feedback to a student, the student's draft gets better. Rather, Cooper argues, complexity theory says that it is a circular causal system, termed "structural coupling," in which one person's actions affects others' and those others react, adapting, which continues the chain of mutual adapting. All the elements in any writing assessment ecology work the same way. Change one, and the others change through mutual adapting.

Furthermore, reading these ecological elements as a part of a complex system is important—that is, they are more than the whole of the ecology, but this does not capture all of the complexity Cooper is suggesting. Cooper offers this definition of the way complex systems can be understood:

> Complex systems (an organism, a matter of concern) are self-organizing: order (and change) results from an ongoing process in which a multitude of agents interact frequently and in which the results of interactions feed back into the process. Emergent properties (such as agency) are not epiphenomena, nor "possessions" in any sense, but function as part of the systems in which they originate. And causation in complex systems is nonlinear: change arises not as the effect of a discrete cause, but from the dance of perturbation and response as agents interact. (2011, p.421)

Thus the complex system of an antiracist writing assessment ecology is an assemblage of dancing elements, only one of which is people in the system, that interact and mutually adapt because of the perturbations in the ecology. Consequences (or products, as I'll discuss later in this chapter) occur because of the ecology or complex system, not because of individual actions by students or a teacher or a rubric alone. They may be instigators, causing perturbations in the system, but it is the system, the ecology as a whole, that determines what possible outcomes, effects, changes, or products there will be. Thus any learning or educational benefits to students one might hope from an antiracist writing assessment ecology will be a product of the dance of perturbations and response of elements in the entire complex system.

So while I discuss each element below separately, I hope you will see the complexity in which they inter-are. In one simple sense, all elements create any one given element. People and purposes, for example, help construct the places of the ecology, just as places, power, and processes create people. Likewise, the elements below always work in concert to create a complex system that continually evolves the limits and pressures that form what it determines as outcomes or products.

ECOLOGICAL POWER

The first and perhaps most important element of any antiracist writing assessment ecology that might be considered and developed consciously is power. Power, Foucault (1977) says, is a productive force that moves through society. Thus, "discipline" is itself a technology and a "type of power," which Foucault shows in prisons, the military, and schools (1977, p. 215), each creating "docile bodies" (p. 138) in similar ways. Discipline is made up of "a whole set of instruments, techniques, procedures, levels of application, [and] targets" (Foucault, 1977, p. 215). Foucault defines four strategies constitutive of discipline and characteristic of a docile "individuality" (1977, p. 167), an individuality that moves in power's direction: one, discipline "draws up tables" by enclosing, confining, and defining bodies and "functional sites" (p. 143); two, "it prescribes movements" and activity (p. 149); three, "it imposes exercises" and movement (pp. 151-152); and four, "it arranges tactics" (p. 162), that is, "coded activities and trained aptitudes" (p. 167). It is easy to see how Foucault could be describing any writing assessment ecology. When we design a portfolio system for a writing course often what is most present in our minds as we design it is how we will control students' bodies, their actions, their movements, what they write, how portfolios are put together, how many pages or documents to include, what students should reflect upon, etc. In these material and textual ways, power is exercised through the ways we ask students to labor and submit the products of their labor to us for evaluation. However Foucault says that power is also productive and generative, exists by acting on the individual, and is a "total structure of actions brought to bear upon possible actions," thus it "incites," "induces," and "seduces" (1982, p. 220).

Foucault's description of Bentham's panopticon demonstrates how power operates through the disciplining of bodies and creating spaces that reproduce docile behavior as consent (1977, p. 200), which has clear applications to the typical writing classroom. He explains that power works in the panopticon by

> Automatiz[ing] and disindividualiz[ing] power. Power has its principle not so much in a person as in a certain concerted distribution of bodies, surfaces, lights, gazes; in an arrangement whose internal mechanisms produce the relation in which individuals are caught up. The ceremonies, the rituals, the marks by which the sovereign's surplus power was manifested are useless. There is a machinery that assures dissymmetry, disequilibrium, difference. Consequently, it does not matter who exercises power. Any individual, taken almost at random, can operate the machine (1977, p. 202)

What's striking about Foucault's discussion is how power *is* the environment, which disciplines bodies in and through time and space(s). This disciplining creates visibility and invisibility, docility, and the subjectivity of prisoners themselves. In fact, in the panopticon, the power exercised through the design of the tower and facing cells, defines the inmates as "inmates," as much as it helps them self-regulate, consent to their own imprisonment. Power is consciously constructed and manipulated, used by constructing spaces and experiences that by their natures are or feel like surveillance, or a constant assessment of bodies.

Classrooms are also places in which power is constructed to discipline students and teachers. Desks in rows and facing the teacher are a physical arrangement that many have discussed as one that promotes particular power relationships that work against the kind of pedagogical environment we usually hope to encourage in writing classrooms, one that places too much focus on the teacher as speaker and students as passive listeners. It constructs an environment in which power is exercised as Freire's banking model. This power arrangement is seductive. Students are seduced into easier, passive roles as listeners, while teachers are seduced into attractive roles as knowledge givers, as "professors." This is even more true when it comes to writing assessment ecologies that figuratively face the teacher, ones that demand students "submit" themselves and their writing only to a teacher for judgment, which has its most power(ful) employment in feedback and grading practices.

Antiracist writing assessment ecologies make explicit this power arrangement in grading practices between teacher and students as one that is also racialized through the valuing of hegemonic discourses, dominant ones that use a white racial *habitus* to form expectations and markers of success and failure. The *use* of such standards is discussed explicitly as racialized and hegemonic, then perhaps negotiated with students in order for them to understand their own relations to power embodied in the valuing of the dominant discourse of the classroom.

Interrogating power in an assessment ecology is important because it sets up the rest of students' problematizing practices. Questions that might be posed to students early on about power could be: How are the expectations and standards for grading writing, determining students' progress, or evaluating students as writers used or employed? Why use those standards in the ways that the class or teacher has prescribed, have they been used before in other classrooms, why? What alternative standards and ways might be used? Who exercises the power to grade in the class, and who constructs or negotiates the expectations and standards that regulate evaluations and grading? Why do it that way? Where does the power to grade and make judgments on writing circulate in the course and by whom? How can the classroom productively and safely encourage students to understand, complicate, and challenge the white racial *habitus* in the dominant discourse (the course's writing expectations)? How is the white racial *habitus* of the dominant discourse compared to other *habitus* and discourses existing in the classroom? What reasons are there for valuing some *habitus* over others, and how can the class cultivate assessment practices that do not value one *habitus* over others?

As discussed already, the felt sense of race by students is in part a racial formation's relation to hegemonic power in society or school. Languages are a part of these relations to power. And white discourses (and their *habitus*) have been markers of power, who exercises it, who benefits from its movements, etc. But it is not the use of such discourses that exercises power in writing classrooms. It is the ways in which any discourse is evaluated or judged, making the *habitus* that informs those judgments important to investigate, more so than the drafts that are evaluated in any given moment. Antiracist writing assessment ecologies constantly probe these power relations around the judgment of writing. Who has historically been in this classroom, and who is in it now, being judged and by whom? What kinds of racial *habitus* inhabit a college classroom space in the past and now, how have they submitted to power differently, and which *habitus* are markers of power or of the ideal discourse?

Thus it is important to take note of the local racial diversity in the classroom, the elephant in the room. I know this can be tricky, as race is not a clear feature to notice about anyone, and one's self-identified racial designation does not tell us much about one's linguistic background or heritage, so taking stock in the local diversity of one's classroom might begin with students self-assessing their own language backgrounds and where those backgrounds came from. Then they might trace socially and historically how they and their families, how their churches and local neighborhoods, came to practice the language(s) they do. Finally, students can compare their own language practices and their sources to what they've experienced in writing classrooms as the expected discourse, the ideal discourse. When I do this with my students, I offer them a description of my own language background that uses a history that labels race and racism in my own language practices, and I tell it as an evolving language, one different now than it was when I was 19 years old. I focus on one or two language practices that I engaged in then, and now. For example, the practice of cursing or swearing in public as a way to be emphatic that I picked up while living in North Las Vegas (a poor and almost all-Black community), or the practice of using the double-negative for similar rhetorical reasons that was prevalent in the white working class neighborhood and schools I went to in middle school and high school. I end my narrative with questions about the way these practices' are judged by various people and in various situations, particularly when used by certain racialized bodies. This allows me to open questions about the way my discourse would be judged next to a dominant white academic discourse, revealing its relation to power.

In my language background document, which I sometimes call a literacy narrative or language narrative, I acknowledge that race isn't a biological reality, nor does it tell us essential truths about me, but it does help us talk about larger social linguistic patterns in my life, and U.S. society. It helps us talk about such patterns as Black English Vernacular (BEV), southern U.S. vernaculars, Latino/a Englishes (e.g., Spanglish), and Asian Pacific Islander Englishes (e.g., Chinglish and Hawai'ian creole). Once we do this, we can begin to understand better where we come from when we judge writing, both our own and our colleagues' drafts, which help us begin to identify and reflect upon the *habitus* we enact in judging texts and its relation to the dominant white racial *habitus* that often is used to judge our writing. Collecting such diverse language stories and looking for racial references in them helps us see commonality in our relations to power, in our struggles with a dominant discourse, even as those commonalities are rooted in linguistic and cultural difference. I want to be very clear at the outset of this chapter about the focus of the problematizing I'm speaking of. What antiracist writing assessment ecologies ask students to interrogate and problematize is not language as a discourse or set of practices, although this may happen to some degree. Instead as my description of the language background document above shows, antiracist writing assessment ecologies ask students to interrogate and problematize the judgment of discourses and language as they are occurring in their lives.

Often then, if not consciously identified, reflected upon, and rethought, power can reproduce conventional looking hierarchies when grading student writing, hierarchies that are racist. In antiracist writing assessment ecologies, hegemonic power, power that overdetermines (in the Freudian sense)[30] expectations for writing, can end up being rearticulations of a white racial *habitus* that do not see the negotiation of classroom expectations and norms as an historical landscape of conflict, as a negotiation that doesn't have equal parties, but should. Gramsci's hegemony leaves plenty of room for power to be reconfigured through the counter-hegemonic. But in order for the counter-hegemonic to occur productively in antiracist writing assessment ecologies, power must be reconceived. While choice and actions are explicitly determined, they are not overdetermined. Fairness and more equitable outcomes and products can occur through students' explicit participation in and articulations of the ecology. Students get to be fully involved in the setting of expectations, processes, and the making of judgments and grades, which is what I hope comes out of the questions and investigations of power I've described in this section. The reconstruction of power relations in an assessment ecology is, however, first set up by their nature as explicit, negotiated relations, relations that are racialized but not racist. In short, power is explicit and negotiated with students, then exercised by them and the ecology they help create. These conditions will be made clearer through my discussions of the other elements below, which help create power.

ECOLOGICAL PARTS

The second element of antiracist writing assessment ecologies that can be examined and developed consciously is the parts. Parts refer to the artifacts, documents, and codes that regulate and embody writing, which include the judgments made by people in the ecology. In his discussion of a "critical theory of technology," Andrew Feenberg defines the literal materials of technology, which is a good way to explain the ecological parts of any antiracist writing assessment ecology. He offers two useful elements: (1) "artifacts," or the sum of all objects and processes involved; and (2) a "technical code," or networks of cultural, institutional, and personal values, rules, and decisions (Feenberg, 1991, p. 80). When we talk about writing assessment, it is the instruments, scores, grades, portfolios, essay prompts, students' and teachers' responses, or scoring rubrics that we often refer to. The parts of an antiracist writing assessment ecology are what is most visible about it, and often become a synecdoche for the entire ecology, potentially eliding the relationships those parts have to other ecological elements.

For instance, a portfolio as an ecological part of an assessment ecology can exist for a number of reasons or purposes. It can also be read in a number of ways and by a number of different people. It can be understood to represent a number of different constructs and student dispositions, behaviors, or competencies. It could be a demonstration of knowledge, of development of writing competencies in the course, or of the best work accomplished. It could function

125

to produce the final grade, or simply inform discussions on students' writing development. Thus, the portfolio itself is just a part, a part in the ecology that has significance and meaning only when it interacts with other ecological elements, such as people, their purposes, or the products (outcomes and consequences) their decisions intend to encourage. Another way to put this is to say that like all the other ecological elements, any part of an assessment ecology, a rubric, some feedback, a paper, inter-is with the other ecological elements. Thus the part in question can only be meaningful, can only be what it is, when all the other ecological elements are as well. The easiest demonstration of this is to consider the changes in students' attitudes (people) in a course in which a portfolio (part) is graded (another part) next to the same course when the same portfolio is not graded. The presence of the grade-part changes students' attitudes, the portfolio, processes, and the entire ecology.

One important aspect of the parts that can be the focus of students problematizing in an antiracist writing assessment ecology is the biases that are inherent in those parts. While there can be many kinds of biases, I'm particularly interested in racialized biases, or biases that have historically in the U.S. and academia been associated closely to particular racial formations and their language practices. Again, Feenberg's discussion of technology can help us. Through a careful consideration of Foucault and Marcuse, Feenberg rejects the instrumentalist view of technology and claims that all technology has inherent biases toward the hegemonic, which have been articulated in Madaus' (1990, 1993, 1994) and Madaus & Horn's (2000) descriptions of testing as technology. Feenberg's "bias" draws on Marcuse, who explains that

> [t]echnology, as a mode of production, as the totality of
> instruments, devices and contrivances which characterize the
> machine age is thus at the same time a mode of organizing
> and perpetuating (or changing) social relationships, a manifes-
> tation of prevalent thought and behavior patterns, an instru-
> ment for control and domination. (Marcuse, 1998, p. 41)

This is strikingly similar to Gramsci's theorizing of historical bloc and hegemony, only Feenberg focuses on the instrumentality of technology, on the instruments, devices, and contrivances that make up technology. While he is making the point that technology is not simply machinery, he is revealing how the instruments, how the parts of technology are themselves loci of networks of other devices and contrivances, of biases. This means that a part in an antiracist writing assessment ecology is not bias-free and is interconnected to many other devices, contrivances, social relationships, and instruments of control. These biases are what gets explored and form the problems that students pose to themselves and their colleagues. One important set of biases I've already discussed in detail is a dominant white racial *habitus* that informs writing rubrics and expectations for writing in classrooms, even ones that ask students to help develop expectations for their writing.

Feenberg further argues that "all action within its [technology's] framework tends to reproduce that hegemony" (1991, p. 65). To explain why technology has hegemonic bias built in, Feenberg draws on Marcuse's notion of "techno-logical rationality," which "constitutes the basis for elite control of society," by being "internal" to the "structure" of technology itself. When translated to writing assessment ecologies, bias is built into an assessment's ecological parts, its artifacts and technical codes (Feenberg, 1991, p. 69). Thus parts have ecological biases that often amount to racial biases, such as the biases of a local white racial *habitus* or a local SEAE. Marcuse himself uses the illustration of a highway, perhaps a technology better understood as an ecology, that directs drivers to various destinations, prescribing routes and norms of behavior through signs, cement, and laws (1998, p. 46). Marcuse explains that if one must get anywhere, one must take the highway in a car, which automatically "dissolves all actions into a sequence of semi-spontaneous reactions to prescribed mechanical norms." Everything appears "perfectly rational" and "reasonable" (Marcuse, 1998, p. 46). The technology of the highway defines what is rational, such that "individual protest and liberation appear not only as hopeless but as utterly irrational" (Marcuse, 1998, p. 48). Through parts, with their ecological biases, writing assessment ecologies construct power, as in Foucault's panopticon, but do so hegemonically because the parts come with biases that tend to be determined by the hegemonic. Yet like Marcuse's highway, people's actions and behaviors may be determined, but they aren't prescribed completely. One could take a number of routes to get to one's destination, but there are only so many routes to that destination. This is Marcuse's way of theorizing Marxian determination, and it is explained through the biases inherent in the system's parts.

Resistance, then, to an assessment ecology's rationality, to a teacher's demanding of a portfolio in a classroom or the use of a rubric to grade writing—just like a California high school student resisting the demand to take the EPT or the ACT—appears utterly irrational. You want to get a grade in the class, don't you? You want a college degree, don't you? Then you take this test, or submit a portfolio in this prescribed way. The bias in the assessment ecology that the classroom creates, makes such resistance or questioning of whatever part is used (i.e., a portfolio, an essay, a series of documents, a rubric, etc.) unreasonable since the reasonable responses are dictated by the biases in the parts of the assessment ecology.

Consider, for instance, the ecological parts of a rubric, say, the construct of reflection, a typical expectation in writing classrooms for portfolios or other reflective writing that one might find on a rubric or an assignment sheet, or even in course goals or outcomes statements. Often reflection is thought of as a discourse that women perform more fluently than men (at least in popular cultural contexts), which suggests possible gender biases, and a particular kind of rationality itself built into the parts of portfolio assessment ecologies.[31] Once enacted, the judgment on "reflection" provided to students becomes "rational." Additionally, like the cells and tower of the panopticon, one important bias in reflective parts is the way in which power is generated by and moves through them in very distinct directions, which is the nature of bias. As an artifact of power, the portfolio letter itself is a "functional site" in which the body of the student is controlled and made to obey. Write the letter in a particular way and pass the portfolio, then the student may take the next course. Fail, and she must take the present one again, or perhaps leave the university.

As the teacher, I have not forced her to do anything by failing her portfolio, yet the portfolio, as an ecological part has drawn up a site that disciplines the student, and controls her material, bodily movement in the university and possibly elsewhere. The reflection letter also disciplines her, arguably in a more explicit way, pushing her to claim a progress narrative, something many (Conway, 1994; Inoue & Richmond, in press; Scott, 2005; Weiser, 1997) mention is common in their research on portfolios. It subtly urges the student to consent through its naturalized rationality, norming students, making individual resistance or difference irrational (unnatural). Power is often exercised through the bias of parts in an ecology.

In an antiracist writing assessment ecology, however, the class would consider the construct of reflection as an explicitly racialized set of dispositions, ones that likely have biases formed from a white racial *habitus*. When judging instances of reflection in portfolios, readers would not use comparisons to a white racial *habitus* in order to determine student success, grades, or progress in the course and portfolios. Instead, the class might use labor as a marker of success, completion, or development. This doesn't mean teachers do not discuss ways to reflect that push students toward demonstrating reflective *habitus* that match a local (white racial) dominant *habitus*. It just means students aren't graded against that dominant *habitus* when they reflect in ways that do not match the dispositions in it, instead assessment is an occasion to discuss choices, audience expectations, and diverse ways of judging reflection, connecting those judgments to possible racialized *habitus* with no consequences to their grade. Assessment is an occasion to problematize existential writing assessment situations within reflective practices. This kind of problematizing centers on the biases of parts in an assessment ecology that create the valuing of reflective discourse in particular ways.

The literature on reflection offers us plenty of evidence for the assumption that most reflection in writing classrooms asked of students is of a white racial *habitus*. The scripts and codes of reflection as a classroom discourse and *habitus* that many scholars have described (Beach, 1976; Dewey, 1910; Pianko, 1979; Schon, 1987) match most if not all of the dispositions of a white racial *habitus*. This is evident in the research I've done on the Hmong racial formation at Fresno State (Inoue & Richmond, in press). For instance, as I mentioned earlier, the Hmong racial formation has the highest percentage of students who are designated as remedial by the EPT. Between 2007-2012, based on average EPT scores, 77% of all Hmong students taking the EPT were designated as remedial (the white population was roughly 23%). In the Early Start English program in the summer of 2013, the average rating on reflection in Hmong final portfolios was just below proficient (2.97 out of 6, with 3 the lower threshold for proficient), which seems to coincide with their EPT scores.[32] However, in the final ratings of similar portfolios in Engl 5B (the second course in a two-course sequence of FYW), Hmong students averaged the highest ratings among all racial formations on the same scale in final portfolios (Inoue, 2012, p. 88).

So what happened? The construct of reflection as a discourse didn't change. The same teachers taught both the Early Start and the FYW courses. The curricula of both programs matched, using the same outcomes and language. By all accounts, both portfolios in the Early Start English and in Engl 5B measured the same thing, the same construct (reflection). What might best account for the change? Time? Instruction? Practice? Perhaps. But there are many teachers and sections, some TAs, some adjuncts, all with a variety of teaching experiences and different assignments and readings in their courses. There is one thing that is constant in both programs and curricula, one thing that dictates the nature of time, instruction, and practice: the classroom writing assessment ecology, which I'm arguing leaned toward antiracist ends.

Here's how. All teachers in the program used a grading contract and a portfolio in both the Early Start English course and the Engl 5A course, the course before Engl 5B. In my own program reviews, about 80% of all teachers continued to use grading contracts for their Engl 5B courses. Most students stay with the same teacher for 5A and 5B. Portfolios are required in all three courses. So the apparent linear progression from just below proficient (2.97) in Early Start to well within the proficient category (between 3.47-3.81) by the end of their FYW experience is associated with consistent classroom writing assessment ecologies used. Those ecologies are created by the use of two ecological parts: a grading contract, which is provided to all teachers in template form and negotiated with students; and a portfolio system, which requires only that there be a certain amount of polished writing in it and a letter of reflection.

The most obvious feature of the contract is its focus on labor, not quality, to determine course grades.[33] The contract and portfolio kept grades off of day-to-day and major assignments in all courses, and focused students' attention toward the labor they did each day or week, which is a feature of assessment ecologies that can be antiracist. The rubrics and assignments, the parts (the codes and documents), did not produce grades, rather they were used differently in the classroom. Writing, rubrics, feedback and other ecological parts circulated in different writing assessment ecologies, making reflection in portfolios different in nature, and learning different (arguably better).

The contract constructed labor as the main criterion for determining course grades, while their writing itself was used to help form writing practices and discussions about how to value that writing, which comes close to my description of problematizing the existential writing assessment situation of students. Thus the assessment ecologies at Fresno State tended not to be overdetermined by rubrics and other ecological parts that have a bias toward a white racial *habitus* through their grading and ranking of students. This, I argue, allowed multilingual students, such as Hmong students, to find confidence, perseverance, and other non-cognitive writing dispositions that helped them succeed and excel in reflection, a key program outcome, even though that outcome was still informed by a white racial *habitus*. I've made a more complete argument for contracts concerning the Hmong racial formation in another place (Inoue, 2012a), and the way they can change the nature of failure in writing classrooms (Inoue, 2014b), which confirm this conclusion.

What should be noted of antiracist (or any) writing assessment ecology is that the hegemonic nature of its parts' biases is self-reinforcing. This self-reinforcement offers a response to criticisms about lowering or ignoring standards in antiracist assessment ecologies, such as the one I've just described. Feenberg addresses this phenomenon by explaining that "the 'universe of discourse,' public and eventually even private speech and thought, is limited to posing and resolving technical problems" (Feenberg, 1991, p. 70) —that is, problems the system creates in order to solve them itself, problems it can solve with the same old results. Thus, hegemonic writing assessment parts present to us problems we solve with hegemonic solutions because we are given only the hegemonic. This helps us defend antiracist assessment ecologies like the one I've described above from criticisms that question its ability to keep standards. Standards are specific code (hegemonic parts) in an assessment ecology, which I argue are always racialized to some degree because they are informed by a white racial *habitus*. When on invokes them, they assume particular racial *habitus* that are the standard, which are hegemonic. Questions about writing classrooms not keeping standards tend to be the same old hegemonic questions that assume (require) hegemonic answers, or a particular set of biases.

Thus a question like, "how can the above assessment ecology that doesn't grade students' reflective writing on quality guarantee that students will be able to meet particular writing standards?" is really a question that asks, "how can we maintain the hegemonic if we are not judging and grading it, if we aren't holding students accountable for it?" Another way to say this is: "how can we get students to reflect like white, middle class language users if we don't grade them on that standard?" I could reply to this criticism by saying that just because a teacher doesn't grade writing doesn't mean students aren't held accountable for particular standards, or better yet, are not responsible for such standards. But a better response is that this question of standards is the wrong question to ask in our increasingly diverse classrooms. In fact, its premise (that we need a standard to judge students against) is racist. When our classrooms were homogenous and white, when most students came from a particular socioeconomic strata, it might have been fair to enforce standards through writing assessments, but it's not today. In fact, it is overly limiting, binding students and the academy, holding us back. Perhaps better questions are: what *are* our students doing when asked to reflect? How do our students reflect in writing differently from what we initially expected? What are the biases in the reflective discourse produced in classrooms? How do those reflective ways meet (or not) the challenges we understand reflection addressing for students? In what ways do our students' reflective ways innovate our old ways of reflecting? How do our initial biases in the reflective discourse we ask for create unfairness and limit the cultural and linguistic production of the classroom?

These questions not only help reveal the hegemonic biases in the parts of our assessment ecologies, but are good ways to focus student assessment activities that lead to problematizing their writing assessment situations in the class around reflection as a practice. I realize that some will not accept conceiving of classroom writing assessment practices as explorative and descriptive of the hegemonic and other *habitus* that students bring. They will say that such ecologies do not necessarily help students become successful writers in our current world. Instead these critics may say that the writing classroom is meant to prepare students for future success in writing in either school or civic life, which isn't a completely false assumption, but it is an assumption about a dominant white racial *habitus*, as well as what direct instruction on a dominant discourse will offer students. We can and should have other biases, other discourses and *habitus*, which all can be equally productive. Furthermore, there is no guarantee that using language in particular ways in society or the academy will guarantee success to any given student, however one wishes to define it. But the definition of successful writing, or a successful writer, is a product of all antiracist writing assessment ecologies. In fact, the definition of success in writing is central to the larger ecological purpose of antiracist writing assessment ecologies. Success is explicitly investigated and defined as certain ways of judging writing or writing practices that are relate to dominant and non-dominant *habitus*.

My example of the construct of reflection shows that one way to radically change the parts of an assessment ecology is to rethink the terms by which course grades and credit are given so that reflection, both as a practice and as a racialized bias in rubrics and assignments, functions differently than to hierarchize students. In the above case, the classroom writing assessment ecologies in question used labor, not quality of writing, to determine course grades. This sufficiently changed the biases in the parts and what was done with them, like the portfolio, feedback from the teacher, or daily assignments. So there are no unbiased parts, but parts that have explicit biases that students and teacher explore and discuss together, then use to pose problems about the judgment of language (in this case, reflection as a construct). The contract and portfolio have their biases too, and they are different, depending on how they get constructed, situated, and used in classrooms. Thus in antiracist writing assessment ecologies, students become aware of the biases in the ecological parts they use, work with them more than against them, and discuss them and negotiate them with other students. Furthermore, this problematizing allows them to realize the nature of the judgment of writing as overdetermined, as hegemonic.

In one sense, what I'm arguing for in antiracist writing assessment ecologies are parts that are counter-hegemonic. The biases of a rubric that articulate local SEAE expectations for a writing assignment in a course, or a grading contract that uses labor to determine grades, can potentially be counter-hegemonic structures. For instance, a rubric could be translated or used to identify and question deviations of a local SEAE but not as error or writing done wrong. Instead, the rubric could be a way to notice and validate local non-SEAE practices, first by not penalizing students for using such subaltern discourses, and second by allowing the rubric to be a heuristic for asking questions about ways of knowing and articulating that are open-ended, not closed and narrowing. Thus differences from the dominant discourse are read as meaningful and productive.

Teachers and students may co-construct evaluation rubrics, which may articulate expectations that are not "standardized" to the larger writing assessment ecologies of the program or school, then use those rubrics to examine and critique not just their own writing but more conventional rubrics and texts that adhere to a local SEAE, or to a local white racial *habitus*. Students may respond in original or alternative ways to conventional calls for a portfolio, and engender a teacher's response that moves her to compare the portfolio next to (not against) the local SEAE or white racial *habitus*. A classroom might incorporate critical and other pedagogies that focus students and teacher interaction on negotiating the meaning of error (Horner, 1992; Horner & Lu, 1999) or articulating and using alternative and code-meshed discourses (Young, 2004, 2007; Young & Martinez, 2011). The bottom line is that ecological bias and counter-bias should work side by side in the parts of an antiracist writing assessment ecology so that power doesn't simply overdetermine what students do, or how well they do it, but allows the determination in the system to function both hegemonically and counter-hegemonically. In short, the parts of any antiracist classroom writing assessment ecology are the places where students and teacher can generate problems to writers and readers about the biases that those parts inherently have.

In order for these kinds of biases to work counter-hegemonically in the rubric, they must be reinforced superstructurally, reinforced in the ways the class explains them and justifies them to each other, in the ways they use the rubric in feedback and reflection activities, in other words, in the base of the class, in the processes and labors of students and teacher that produce writing and its assessment. Students have to understand how to read the rubric, why they are doing this kind of questioning, what it means to question in this way, and have reading and judgment practices that keep them away from making judgments that penalize or assume deviations to a local dominant discourse are error or wrong. Antiracist writing assessment ecologies do this kind of work through the parts they set up, which determine much in the classroom.

ECOLOGICAL PURPOSE

The third aspect of antiracist writing assessment ecologies to reconsider and design is purpose. Most who discuss writing assessment tend to place this first, or as a key element in any writing assessment that determines its effectiveness, products, outcomes, and even existence (CCCC, 2009; Huot, 2002; White, 1994, 2007). George Madaus explains that agents' purposes and uses for a test are defining elements of it as a technology, calling a test technology "something put together for a purpose to satisfy a pressing or immediate need, or to solve a problem" (Madaus, 1993, pp. 12-13; see also Madaus, 1990, p. 6). Teachers and WPAs always have purposes for their writing assessments, just as students have purposes or reasons for taking (or not taking) such assessments, and institutions have reasons for imposing writing assessments. In writing assessment ecologies, these various purposes may be different for different people (stakeholders) in the ecology, and usually fall into a few categories for teachers and WPAs: to check for students comprehension of material or proficiency in writing, to place students in courses, to predict future performance in college writing generally, to motivate students to do work in a class, or to provide feedback for revisions and future practices. For students, the purposes may be similar and may also include: to get a good grade in the class, to follow orders (like a good student would) or because that's what you do in school, to get feedback for revisions for future writing practices. For institutions, purposes often deal with their needs for accountability, consistency, and maintaining the institution itself: to find out how many students are remedial writers, to gain funding from various outside sources, or to produce evidence of the institution's effectiveness, value, and worth. These may not be the only possible purposes for teachers, WPAs, students, or institutions, but the point is that purposes are determined by the people and institutions involved in a writing assessment, and in fact, even within these groups of people, purposes will vary (I'll say more about people in the next section).

Everyone has some evolving sense of why they are involved in a classroom writing assessment ecology, even if they may feel coerced into it. And that's important to keep in mind. Not everyone, including teachers, are always crazy about being involved in an assessment ecology, so their purposes for the ecology are shaded by these feelings. Furthermore, many of these feelings and purposes come from society, the school, personal histories, and from cultural, racial, or other social formations' practices stemming from the local diversity in a school. The hegemonic, then, is a strong force in producing the needs and purposes for classroom writing assessment ecologies. While I'll say more below about the shaping effects of people (stakeholders) on classroom writing assessment ecologies, here I would like to focus on the larger purposes that shape antiracist writing assessment ecologies, which influence students' evolving purposes.

As you might expect, antiracist writing assessment ecologies have explicit purposes that students and teachers negotiate. This negotiation helps share power, albeit still unevenly, with students by providing them with the opportunity to discuss and articulate the larger purposes of the assessment ecology, affecting all assessment activities in the course. Thus, I am not talking about the purposes for writing particular drafts or assignments, nor the purposes for an individual assessment activity of a draft. The purposes for an antiracist writing assessment ecology address the larger problem that the ecology means to confront, in the present case, racism in the assessment of writing in the class. More generally, we might call this larger purpose fairness. A student's purpose for participating in an assessment ecology may be to get a grade, but the expressed purpose of the ecology itself is to problematize the student's existential writing assessment situation.

To address the gaps between purposes of students and the ecology, it should be noted that all ecological purposes change or evolve. For instance, consider the purposes for Lake Mead, the human-made reservoir outside of Las Vegas. There is Hoover Dam that provides hydroelectric power and water to mostly California, but it also is the "Lake Mead National Recreation Area," where millions of tourists and visitors come every year to see the dam and use the lake. The purposes are multiple and the area, the terrain, was designed over time to accommodate multiple purposes that serve local communities, tourists, and the cost of its own maintenance. However, much of the terrain was already there before humans came along and built the dam, made roads, etc. In fact, the dam was built by Roosevelt's Works Progress Administration (renamed Work Projects Administration in 1939). The dam's initial purpose was to employ people during the Great Depression. We responded to the environment and our own economic needs, as much as made the Hoover Dam environment, which later served energy and recreational needs. One lesson we learn from this is that all ecologies have purposes that shape them, then those purposes evolve, which continue to shape the ecology. The act of making or shaping usually dictates an environment's purposes, such as a classroom or a course website, but once it is made, other purposes can be placed onto or evolve out of the ecology that forms there. Writing assessment ecologies are no different.

Antiracist writing assessment ecologies take advantage of the evolution of purposes by taking time out to consider, reflect, and articulate the evolving individual purposes within the ecology. This helps classrooms determine effects on the larger purpose of the ecology, which may also evolve. Thus not only do students negotiate and articulate the larger purpose of the ecology, but they pay attention to the way their own personal purposes for their assessment work evolve. They learn to look at their own judging practices and see important problems that help them understand the way language is or can be valued, which evolves their purposes if they are given the chance to reflect upon those problems as ones that pose alternative purposes for their labor.

Let's say a teacher has assigned writing to her students. If you assign writing, you have to collect it and evaluate it, grade it. That's what teachers do with writing. It's almost a knee-jerk reaction on the part of teachers, and even students come to expect that anything assigned will be graded or have "credit" attached to it, meaning it is "submitted" to the teacher. Peter Elbow (1993) discusses this phenomenon at length and offers several ways out of the conundrum, all of which take grading, ranking, and evaluating out of the assessment activities, leaving only description, response, and dialogue, modes of judgment that resist hierarchizing students' written performances. Most students feel that if an assignment is not graded, it's just busywork, not worth doing, which is counter to the impulse that produced the writing assignment (writing for writing's sake, or writing for some other purpose). The catch is, students are correct. When grades are present and calculated by points and percentages, an assignment that isn't graded is busywork. It is work that keeps them busy until they do something that is graded. Grades become the purpose, not the labor involved in producing the things that get grades.

But what if there were an explicit, larger purpose, one discussed and negotiated with students, one that may evolve as students' figure things out over time. If the larger purpose of the assessment ecology is to help students problematize their existential writing assessment situations, then assessment processes and practices in the ecology should have related purposes, ones that provide ways to develop that problematizing. The *content* of these purposes, as I've said, is to help students see the hegemonic in our language practices and standards—to become critically conscious of the ways their writing practices are valued—then make writerly decisions from this knowledge, while the *method* of this antiracist purpose might be to engage in assessing as an act that is itself edifying by the mere doing of it over and over.

How does this assessment-for-assessment's-sake method lead to problematizing? Because if we are to problematize our existential writing assessment situations, we must read and judge writing (our own and others') in self-conscious ways. This takes practice and repetition to do it self-consciously, and to see the patterns that begin to emerge. Assessment is then articulated as method, as labor, as processes with content and goals. This method is essentially assessment for assessment's sake, since it is through the labor of assessment that students learn the lessons of the hegemonic, lessons about white racial *habitus*, lessons about their own critical awareness of how their language practices and *habitus* are valued and judged. You cannot become critically aware of how you value and how others value your languaging without problematizing those language practices, making judgments about them over and over, then discussing such judgments over and over—without repeatedly engaging in assessing as method for its own sake. The purpose of all assessment has to begin as labor worth doing because it is good to do it, because it is the labor of problematizing, because it is the process that gives students more power in the ecology and over their own languaging.

However if ecological purposes evolve, then we must be prepared for the changes in our classrooms. For example, the EPT was originally designed then instituted in 1977 by CSU English faculty (most notably Ed White) and ETS to determine English writing competency in order for CSU campuses to determine writing course placements. And because each campus has always had different courses and requirements, the EPT couldn't simply provide a placement. It had to provide a score that would then be translated to a placement. Because the EPT uses a timed writing component—real student writing—it was argued that it was more valid for making placement decisions than the old tests that were only multiple choice tests. The new EPT assessment ecology's purposes were more in line with what students did in the classes in which those scores helped place them (White, 2001, p. 309). Over the next twenty years, the cut-scores for remedial status determined by the EPT became reified, although the actual numbers changed. The EPT assessment ecology no longer was thought of as just a way to place students in writing courses, but as a way to find out who was remedial and who not.

This came from institutions making sense of and using the data that the EPT produced in response to periodic literacy crises that cropped up cyclically, as many have discussed (Fox, 1999; Hull & Rose, 1989; Soliday, 2002). Defining remediation was not the EPT's primary purpose when originally designed. It was a placement test. The cut-scores used have changed, so they too are artificial. A few years ago, the CSU Chancellor's Office required all incoming students who scored below the cut-score that designated them as remedial to take an Early Start English course in the summer before their first fall semester. If they didn't take the summer course or didn't pass it, they could not be admitted into the university. By default, this makes the EPT an entrance exam, a new and very different purpose than determining competency so that individual campuses can then decide course placements. Not only did a new purpose evolve for the EPT ecology, but that purpose changed the ecology, and changed the ecologies of writing classrooms, since it designated new places to which students must go (e.g., Early Start courses in the summers), and other uneven consequences (e.g., added costs to some students, mostly students of color and multilingual students). Because of these evolving purposes for the EPT ecology, racist effects occur, most notably the higher cost of education for students of color and multilingual students.

In antiracist writing assessment ecologies, the larger, explicit purpose is to engage students in problematizing their existential writing assessment situations, which means the focus of most activities is on the labor of writing assessment, the labor of judging writing and understanding that judgment as connected to larger discursive fields, dispositions, biases, and values, or *habitus*, some of which are hegemonic and some not. This purpose should be negotiated with students, and discussed with them periodically, so that the purpose of all assessment in the ecology is clearly understood and articulated by students, and so that the ecological purpose has a chance to evolve as students learn more and understand more about the nature of judgment. Because many students may find it difficult to understand this larger antiracist ecological purpose, or use it to guide their assessment labors, a focus on method seems most prudent. With gentle guidance, asking students to assess for assessment's sake can lead to posing the kinds of problems that work best in an antiracist writing assessment ecology.

ECOLOGICAL PEOPLE

While Madaus doesn't say it, assumed in his "purpose" and "problem" that constitute a testing technology (1990, p. 6; 1993, pp. 12-13) is *whose* purpose and *whose* problem. People, social pressures, and institutions define the purposes of writing assessment ecologies. And so, people is the fourth ecological element in an antiracist writing assessment ecology that might be designed or considered. When I say designed, I don't mean that a teacher or program should try to engineer who enters writing classrooms, particularly by markers of local diversity, such as by racial formation. What I mean is that students in any classroom will constitute an element of the assessment ecology that is quite diverse racially, culturally, and otherwise, therefore this element of the ecology will require some discussion and articulation to understand its relation to the ecology by the teacher and students.

People always inhabit spaces and places on any terrain. They often change that very terrain. It may be obvious to say that people live and work in ecologies. Sometimes those people move or migrate to particular places, and some have long histories in a particular place. The local diversities that make up the students and teachers of a writing assessment ecology have their own purposes for the environment and may even design the assessment ecology itself. These same people, such as students, could also be the ones being assessed, while others in the ecology may have some other stake in the ecology or its consequences. When discussing the similar ways writing and ecological systems function, Cooper (1986) cites Lewontin, Rose, & Kamin's (1984) critique of sociobiology, which explains how ecological systems and the people in them work together:

> all organisms—but especially human beings—are not simply the results but are also the causes of their own environments .... While it may be true that at some instant the environment poses a problem or challenge to the organism, in the process of response to that challenge the organism alters the terms of its relation to the outer world and recreates the relevant aspects of that world. The relation between organism and environment is not simply one of interaction of internal and external factors, but of a dialectical development of organism and milieu in response to each other. (p. 275; as quoted in Cooper, 1986, p. 68)

So according to the way sociobiological ecological systems work, people (organisms) are simultaneously the result and causes of their environments. These two ecological elements, people and places, form a kind of Marxian dialectic, and are closely interconnected.

We should be careful with such a proposition. When we consider the local diversities in any community and writing assessment ecology, saying that people and their environments dialectically cause and are the result of each other could be misleading. In fact, it could be a version of blaming the victim, or blaming African-Americans or Hmong students in Fresno for inhabiting the remedial location in the EPT ecology or remedial classrooms. Is it true that African-Americans and Hmong are remedial because they are not prepared to write in college, or is it true that the designation of remedial, among other elements in the system, such as the bias toward a white racial *habitus* in the EPT, constructed such racial formations as remedial? There's too much research that reveals remediation as an historically complex construction (Fox, 1999; Horner & Lu, 1999; Hull & Rose, 1989; Soliday, 2002; Stanley, 2009), produced by larger institutional and other forces that explain it as more than simply referring to the illiterate or semiliterate in our midst. Regardless, my point is that a variety of people move, interact, and change the landscape of a writing assessment ecology, each person may have a different relation to the environment (place) than his peers. Not everyone controls the same degree of power in the ecology. Antiracist writing assessment ecologies attempt to take these multiple relations into account.

It should be clear, then, that I am not saying that people are their environments, nor am I saying that people who reside or congregate in particular places and spaces in an environment are "naturally" supposed to be there, want to be there, or belong there. But I am saying that people who inhabit places in a writing assessment ecology tend to be influenced by those locations, and those locations, because particular people inhabit them, are influenced by those people. The phenomenon of particular racial formations inhabiting particular places in most conventional writing assessment ecologies—white, middle class students in areas of success, African-Americans and Latinos/as in areas of failure—should be expected (but critiqued and resisted) since, as Charles Mills (1997) convincingly argues at the societal level, the racial contract of Western society norms and races spaces (discussed below), and thus norms and races bodies as well (pp. 53, 61). Understanding this phenomenon can be the beginning of discussions with students about them as an element in an antiracist writing assessment ecology. To do this, one can use simple grade distributions from classes in the writing program (not the course), disaggregated by racial formation (among other locally important dimensions of diversity), to begin discussing the relations each racial formation seems to have to the assessment ecologies in the program. What might cause such differences (if there are any)? How might the present class' antiracist assessment ecology take these data into consideration?

But students also need some theory, even if translated by the teacher to help them make sense of the numbers and material conditions in classrooms that they might bring up. I find Charles Mills (1997) account of the racial contract to be easy and helpful. Mills explains that in Western society the aesthetic and somatic norm is the white male body, which gets continually rearticulated over time (1997, p. 72), something the hegemonic and Omi and Winant's racial formation theory (1994; 2015) have helped us see. He demonstrates this historically, particularly through the social contract theory of Hobbes, Locke, Rousseau, and Kant that dictate civil and savage societies, reasonable people and "wild beasts." Mills argues that people are raced through white norming processes of history, which are underwritten by social contract theory that regulated the minds and social conflicts of Western societies. Mills' argument agrees with others who have written accounts of how race was historically constructed, justified, and maintained for particular social hierarchical purposes (Baker, 1998; Goldberg, 1993, Takaki, 2000). This idea of norming and racing bodies also agrees with accounts of the construction of white populations and whiteness in the U.S. through particular groups' conflicts and self-articulations of whiteness, most notably the Irish (Ignatiev, 1995; Lipsitz, 1998; Painter, 2010; Roediger, 1991).

Thus the ecological parts of antiracist writing assessment ecologies often compose one node in the system that function as a self-conscious site of norming and racing (usually to a white racial *habitus*) the people of that ecology, while in conventional assessment ecologies this norming occurs with little attention paid to it, as Matsuda's (2006) myth of linguistic homogeneity, and Horner and Trimbur's (2002) unidirectional monolingualism each suggest. In antiracist writing assessment ecologies, this norming of people is made a topic of ongoing discussion, since it influences students' judging practices and abilities to problematize.

The point that all bodies are normed to the white male body and raced in particular ways complicates the way one can understand people as an ecological element in an antiracist writing assessment ecology. The obvious observation that all people inserted into an ecology will be raced differently and normed against the white male body hardly needs arguing. Thus all people will not have the same relations to the other ecological elements in the ecology, nor have the same relations to power, but they should. Therefore, the consequences of the ecology will be uneven.

This means the ecological element of people should be discussed by students as an element that creates that assessment ecology in the classroom. They might discuss the ways labor (processes) and judgments (parts) are generated in diverse ways because of who is in the classroom. These discussions do not attempt to form consensus over how to judge or translate things, but understand the diversity of ways of judging that may happen and why. Giving students the ability to articulate and figure out how to handle uneven power relations that stem from gender, race, language practices, or other dimensions of diversity is key to avoiding stereotyping and other assumptions that can harm or misrepresent students. It's not important that students identify themselves racially when discussing their own relations to, say, a rubric used, or a process put forward as the method for producing assessment labor, instead such reflection on people could begin with students' individual responses to such ecological elements that move them to do a tiny bit of research that informs and deepens their response.

One reflection activity that asks students to consider their various positions as ecological people with different relations to power and parts in the assessment ecology might ask for an individual response in class, say in a five minute writing prompt. The prompt might ask them to look at their rubric, the expectations for the writing assignment ahead, perhaps one they've helped create, and consider: (1) what their individual labor will look like if they are to meet those expectations; and (2) what problems they foresee in that labor and in producing the ideal draft they believe the rubric asks for. The class might then share these responses and discuss the sources of their expectations, translations of the rubric, and assumptions about labor and its written products or outcomes.

As homework, the teacher might offer a short list of resources, each about three to five pages in length, excerpts from academic discussions on whiteness and language diversity, ones that can encourage discussions about judgment of diverse language and diverse racial *habitus*. Students would choose one that most interests them and helps them either rethink their initial response to the rubric or consider more deeply their expectations, translations, or assumptions about judging drafts with it. They would go home and do more prompted reflecting after reading their chosen text. Here are a few sources I've mentioned already that could be excerpted:

White Discourses
- Barnett, T. (2000). Reading "Whiteness" in English studies
- Delgado, R., & Stefancic, J. (Eds.). (1997). *Critical white studies: Looking behind the mirror*
- Faigley, L. (1992). *Fragments of Rationality: Postmodernity and the Subject of Composition*
- Frankenberg, R. (1993). *White Women, Race Matters: The Social Construction of Whiteness*
- Morrison, T. (1992). *Playing in the Dark: Whiteness and the Literary*

Imagination
- Myser, C. (2003). *Differences from Somewhere: The Normativity of Whiteness in Bioethics in the United States*

African-American and Latino/a Discourses
- Ball, A. F., & Lardner, T. (2005). *African American Literacy Unleashed: Vernacular English and the Composition Classroom*
- Fowler, J., & Ochsner, R. (2012). *Evaluating Essays across Institutional Boundaries: Teacher Attitudes toward Dialect, Race, and Writing*
- Young, V. A. (2007). *Your Average Nigga: Performing Race, Literacy, and Masculinity*

Asian-American Discourses
- Inoue, A. B. & Richmond, T. (in press). *Theorizing the Reflection Practices of Female Hmong College Students: Is "Reflection" A Racialized Discourse?*
- Lee, R. (1999). *Orientals: Asian Americans in Popular Culture*

Linguistic Diversity and Racism
- Greenfield, L. (2011). *The "Standard English" Fairy Tale: A Rhetorical Analysis of Racist Pedagogies and Commonplace Assumptions about Language Diversity*
- Lippi-Green, R. (1997). *English with an Accent: Language, Ideology, and Discrimination in the United States*
- Villanueva, V. (2006). *Blind: Talking about the New Racism*

The lists above are not meant to be exhaustive, only illustrative. They illustrate the kinds of discussions that might help students consider their responses to the rubric and the accompanying labor that the rubric assumes for them as practices and as *habitus* that are connected to larger social and racialized structures in their lives. Subsequent discussions about these reflections might focus on the relations that each student has to the rubric, and what it may mean in terms of that student's judgments of writing in the future. The focus would be on understanding how the student comes to make particular kinds of judgments and do particular kinds of labor (i.e., the sources of their labor practices). These discussions would only be the start of ongoing discussions about students' *habitus*, continuing once they begin engaging in assessing each other's drafts. Furthermore, it should be clear that as Kerschbaum (2014) argues, difference is complex and evolves through interactions (pp. 6, 69). So the reflective labor I'm suggesting above focuses less on static notions of racial *habitus* and more on dynamic, evolving racial *habitus* in the classroom.

It could be productive, for instance, in a classroom with white, Hmong and

Latino/a students to read Myser's (2003) discussion of whiteness as a discourse in bioethics. Myser associates whiteness to a "hyperindividualism," to a persona who is detached, objective, and demonstrates abstract reasoning (2003, p. 6). She includes a table (2003, pp. 6-7) identifying non-cognitive and cognitive dispositions of whiteness that characterize this discourse. The table could be used by students to help them think about the sources of their own assumptions about their labor and what that labor is assumed to produce in writing. Furthermore, this new information may offer students ways to deepen their understandings of the problems they originally reflected upon in class. The teacher might lead discussions in critiquing her own assignment instructions and expectations, given these white dispositions (one articulation of a white racial *habitus*). How might seeing whiteness in the assignment expectations help students and the teacher problematize the judgments of writing implied by—determined in—the writing assignment at hand? In what ways might students write with or against the white racial *habitus* inherent in the assignment? How will students' dispositions, their *habitus*, harmonize and conflict with the white racial *habitus* of the assignment?

At this point, I think it important to heed Mills' own words concerning the effects of the racial contract on people, which includes those in writing assessment ecologies, no matter how those ecologies are designed, who deploys them, or for what purposes:

> the norming of the individual also involves a specific norming of the *body*, an aesthetic norming. Judgments of moral worth are obviously conceptually distinct from judgments of aesthetic worth, but there is a psychological tendency to conflate the two, as illustrated by conventions of children's (and some adults') fairy tales, with their cast of handsome heroes, beautiful heroines, and ugly villains .... George Mosse points out that the Enlightenment involved "the establishment of a stereotype of human beauty fashioned after classical models as the measure of all human worth .... Beauty and ugliness became as much principles of human classification as material factors of measurement, climate, and the environment." The Racial Contract makes the white body the somatic norm, so that in early racist theories one finds not only moral but aesthetic judgments, with beautiful and fair races pitted against ugly and dark races. (1997, p. 62)

Thus the norming of bodies is often ambiguously confused with the aesthetic and moral. What this means for writing assessment ecologies is hinted at in Mills' own words. The norming and racing of bodies influences people's judgments of aesthetic and moral worth. Aesthetic and moral worth, often linked to nationalist values, certainly have a tradition in our writing pedagogies and histories of judgments on student writing, which some have discussed as taste and expectations (Faigley, 1992; Miller, 1991; Watkins, 2009). Thus when we discuss people as an ecological element, it is important to remember that all people are not socially or linguistically constructed equal, nor do they have equal relations to other elements in the ecology. It's not a fair situation, but it is one the ecology is explicitly trying to make fair. Just as important, what Mills reveals through the focus on the norming and racing of bodies as a function of and influence on the various human judgments made in the world is that writing assessment ecologies are themselves ecologies of norming and racing. This is why all writing assessment ecologies are racial projects of some kind.

Antiracist writing assessment ecologies will be resisted by some students. This should be expected. For instance, at Fresno State, often white, middle class students in my writing classes had more problems than students of color with our use of a grading contract, while Latinos/as and Hmong students had fewer resistances to the contract. They generally found it fair and reasonable.

Spidell and Thelin's (2006) study on student resistance to grading contracts confirms the white, middle class resistance I've experienced, which they do not link to race, but I explain elsewhere can be seen as a white resistance (2012b). Spidell and Thelin assume an unspoken, silent, white student norm in their conclusions (Inoue, 2012b, p. 131). They say students find the contract too much work and possibly unfair. They find that (white) students are still too attached to conventional grading systems. In another place (Inoue, 2012a), I've discussed the difference in responses to contracts by various local diversities at Fresno State. The point I'm making here is that many white students would reasonably have difficulty with a writing assessment ecology that seems at its face to not reward them for the normed discourse (a white racial *habitus*) that many of them have been rewarded for in past writing assessment ecologies. Since they are not the aesthetic or somatic norm in this new ecology, and they've always been the norm, everything seems unfair, which is what their Hmong and Latino/a colleagues have felt all along. White, middle class students would, of course, yearn for conventional grading systems that produce grades on papers, since higher grades have always had a direct, positive relationship to their uses of a local SEAE and their own instantiation of a white racial *habitus* in their writing. They no longer exist in the ecology in a privileged position. These resistances, as we'll see in a few cases in Chapter 4 in my own classroom, are soothed through continual reflection on people as an element in the assessment ecology.

Reflection on people, or more precisely on *habitus*, offer ways to understand student judging practices, values, and biases, as well as dominant ones experienced by students through past teacher evaluations. In her socio-historical discussion of technology, Ruth Cowan (1997) can help us consider the role people play in forming or enacting *habitus* that affect the valuing of writing in an ecology. Cowan explains that in order for a technology, like a cup, to be meaningful, it requires people to make, use, manipulate, and change it (e.g., I drink out of a cup, or I may put pencils in it and use it as a pencil holder, etc.). This has an interesting by-product for Cowan: people's ideas about a technology, how we conceive of, value, and use it, are always in "relation to something else," often an abstract value or concept. For instance, the social and historical outcomes of a cup, car, or cell phone are shaped by the ways in which people conceive of each technology's relation to, say, social status, skill, progress, function, gender roles, God, or politics (Cowan, 1997, p. 204). Thus the abstractions people use to make meaningful a device binds them to that device.

If there's one lesson we learn from many of the U.S. histories of composition studies and the teaching and testing of English (Crowley, 1998; Miller, 1991; Ohmann, 1996), it is that various writing assessment ecologies have been developed as responses to people's relations to abstractions like "taste" and "bourgeois reason" (Crowley, 1998, pp. 41-44, 57; 76; Faigley, 1989, 1992; Miller, 1991, p. 54), and merit and progress (Ohmann, 1996, p. 130). People's responses that are linked to abstractions like these produce ecological purposes, which are often simultaneously hegemonic in nature because the values tend to be hegemonic. These abstract values are articulated and used by people, as well as bound to them. This is not to say that all African-American students will engage in some kind of Black English Vernacular (BEV) and associated *habitus*, nor would we say the same about white students and the dominant white discourse, or Latinos/as and stereotypical Latino/a *habitus*, but an antiracist assessment ecology would encourage such discussions and the noticing of such patterns historically. It would consider how such discourses and *habitus* have been valued in writing classrooms, in drafts, without linking such patterns to individuals in the class a priori (or as essential to students who may seem to fit into racial formations that match those *habitus*). The important thing is to reveal just how important the racialized body has been to the valuing of discourse and its success in assessment ecologies.

Additionally, one might discover local values that can affect how various people behave and interact in the assessment ecology of the classroom, what purposes they may wish to evolve, etc. For example, Hmong have particular historical associations, narratives, and stories about language and "The Book" that symbolize freedom, escape from prosecution, and a king who will bring back their book and free the Hmong people from oppression and return them to their homelands (Duffy, 2007, p. 40). Language holds a sacred place in the minds and hearts of many Hmong. A Hmong faculty colleague, Kao-Ly Yang, who teaches Hmong and French at Fresno State, explained to me at a WAC workshop that many Hmong think of language, particularly written language, as sacred, so being concise is best—no wasting of words—and revising text can be seen as disrespectful or irreverent. People in writing assessment ecologies bring their own abstractions and values that can shape their purposes in the environment, their responses to it, and create various, uneven consequences.

Still some teachers may feel uncomfortable paying such obvious and explicit attention to students in their classrooms as racialized subjects that may judge writing differently because of such racialization. Others have articulated ways to talk with students about dominant discourses, what I'm calling a white racial *habitus*, without linking it to whiteness or the white body. To address such concerns, I now turn to Ed White's popular rendering of stakeholders in classroom writing assessment, the closest term to people who are racialized in antiracist writing assessment ecologies.

Ed White (1996) offers a conventional and useful way to see the various kinds of people involved in a writing assessment ecology, using the familiar assessment term, stakeholders, which I'll critique in a friendly way in order to show why we must focus more attention on the relations made with local diversities that inhabit writing assessment ecologies (why the term should be people, not stakeholders). White organizes his discussion around the wants or purposes that help construct each group of people, connecting the various (and sometimes competing) purposes for a writing assessment ecology with the people, or stakeholders, involved. He identifies four groups of stakeholders: (1) teachers, (2) researchers and theorists, (3) testing firms and governing bodies, and (4) students, identifying particularly students of color and other marginalized groups. White explains that teachers tend to experience two kinds of purposes for writing assessment: "evaluation as an administrative sorting device, to make institutions more efficient, more accountable, and more objective; and evaluation as a personalized teaching device, to help students learn more effectively" (1996, p. 12). This causes, he explains, a tension or conflict in teachers. Teachers realize both the problems with testing and grading students, yet also find it necessary in their classrooms to evaluate, even grade, their students' writing (1996, p. 13). The bottom line is teachers want writing assessment to do at least four things: "suppor[t] their work" in the classroom, "recognize[e] the complexity of writing" and how it is taught, respect teachers as professionals and students as individuals, and not be misused in ways that cause damaging or misleading information about the classroom, students, or program (White, 1996, p. 14).

This is an accurate account of teachers, I think, if we assume that all teachers teach in similar environments, work with homogenous students, and are themselves homogenous in their racial, ethnic, and even disciplinary backgrounds. While I doubt that the local diversities of teachers at Fresno State and those at Pennsylvania State University, for example, would disagree with a statement like, "recognize the complexity of writing" in their classrooms and students, I do think that a purpose like that (or any of the one's White lists) change dramatically when particular racialized teachers step into particular classrooms of racialized students.

"Recognition" and "complexity" will mean very different things, and where such values come from matter since some people, by luck or birth, have had more access to the *habitus* that produce them in the ways expected in school. A teacher's purposes could be in part to establish her as an authority in the classroom, or as a coach and guide, or as mentor who questions, pushes, and instigates deeper thinking and more research, or as a past professional working in a particular field. Thus at a general level, White's teacher purposes surely work, but at the level of actual, living teachers, each of these things mean something quite different. As a new teacher, I recall feeling enormous pressure to be "hard on my students," to demand a lot of effort and high quality from them. So much so, that my first term's course evaluations were the lowest in the writing program. This ecological purpose of mine, a version of White's second one, came from my tacit and lived experience as the only person of color in any English classroom at that university. I knew how students would see me and what kinds of assumptions they'd make just from my name printed on their schedules. My response was to reshape the purposes of the writing assessment ecology to ones that demonstrated me as authoritative and knowledgeable, which I thought meant I had to be rigorous and have overly demanding standards. My purpose, in part, was to demonstrate that I belonged in front of them as their teacher. These were values cultivated from my racialized experiences with writing assessment in school.

The next group of people, researchers and theorists, says White, tend to ask questions that cause teachers to feel uneasy by interrogating current practices, not necessarily upholding them or supporting them (1996, p. 15). While I'd argue against White's contention that researchers and theorists are concerned more about critiquing current practices, more about measures and theories, and less about students (1996, p. 15), it is important to see that researchers and theorists do have other primary interests and purposes for writing assessments, which White reveals. For theorists and researchers, the immediate purposes for the work at hand is not to teach students, but usually to support such efforts. However, theorists do not critique current practices because they are there or because they can. They do it because they assume that the act of critiquing will help develop better or more careful writing assessment practices, thus better pedagogies and fairer practices for students' benefit. This focus on students' benefit can be heard in what White identifies as the four things that researchers and theorists generally want writing assessment to do, even if he denies this underlying purpose: "suppor[t] the gathering of reliable data," "recognize[e] the complexity of writing and of teaching writing," "not privilege existing practice but ... explor[e] a variety of potential practices," and "produc[e] new knowledge and theories" (1996, p. 17).

I won't belabor this point, since I've made it in another place in a slightly different way (Inoue, 2012b), but White misses an important problem within the discipline of writing assessment (although to be fair, this isn't his goal in the chapter). The problem is that there are no people of color doing research or scholarship on writing assessment, except for myself. It is mostly white men, with a few white women. There are one or two scholars of color like Arnetha Ball who have done some important work in the field, but they tend to be scholars who do other work first. For instance, I would characterize Ball as one who primarily does work in literacy studies, learning environments, and research on impact on students and secondary educational settings. The lack of any scholars of color doing sustained work in college writing assessment is a big problem, particularly since composition studies and the academy tend to acknowledge the need and importance of having diverse voices and people on problems and in disciplines. Would White's purposes change if we had some African-American, or Latino/a scholars working on writing assessment theory? Would the "potential practices" "explored" by White's researchers look different than they do now, if scholars of color were involved in that work? This isn't White's fault, of course, and I do not blame any current scholars in the field for the lack of writing assessment scholars of color, but I think we do have an ethical responsibility to encourage and bring new scholars and researchers into the field, and part of this responsibility is paying attention to who those people are, what cultural and educational experiences they have, and how they may help make the field more racially diverse.

Testing firms and governmental bodies make up White's third group, and are mostly involved in writing assessment ecologies to make money or to find out "how many students failed a particular test and who should be blamed" (1996, p. 19). According to White, these stakeholders want writing assessment that: "produces scores quickly and cheaply," "reduces the complexity of writing" and teaching that "impl[ies] complex measurement," "weighs heavily surface features" and a local SEAE, "sort[s] ... students according to existing social patterns," and leans on "statistical explanations, of sufficient complexity to invite misuse of scores" (1996, p. 20). While framed mostly in the negative and implying possible nefarious motivations, White's expressed purposes likely would be framed differently by actual testing firms and governmental bodies. And while I agree with White that surface features of a local SEAE likely do not tell us enough about the writing competencies of locally diverse students, yet when used tend to sort students according to racial and class-based patterns, or rather against linguistic dispositions characteristic of a white racial *habitus*; and those complex statistical analyses invite misuse of scores in writing assessments; testing firms want to use such purposes because they are more reliable ones to measure given the available large-scale writing assessment options, or so they think. Testing firms likely would argue from different disciplinary assumptions about how to measure writing competencies (say, from psychometric ones), or predict future success in college, assumptions that most composition theorists and writing assessment theorists do not agree with (Huot, 2002; Lynne, 2004).

Arguably his weakest discussion, students, White's fourth and final stakeholder group, is characterized by White as diverse (although this diversity is not explained). Students are seen as anxious. He explains a student response to a writing prompt in a "remedial English class" that was titled, "Why Write?" One student responded, "They make you write ... so they can *getcha*!" (1996, p. 21). Thus, students in White's description are said to be diverse but are described as homogenous in their anxieties, purposes, and needs for assessment. And the purposes that shape White's version of the student stakeholder group is equally homogenous. White says that students want at least five things in writing assessment: a stressing of "the social and situational context of the writer," "maximum and speedy feedback," a breakdown of "the complexity of writing into focused units," the production of "data principally for the use of learners and teachers," a focus on "critical thinking and creativity" that also "places surface features of dialect and usage in a large social context" (1996, p. 22).

While I think that White's rendition of student purposes seems reasonable enough, and certainly if we polled random students across the nation on whether they agreed with this list of wants or purposes for writing assessment done on them, many would agree. But I wonder about the disagreement and who might disagree and why. For instance, I'm not convinced that all or even most students uniformly want a focus on critical thinking and creativity that places surface features of dialect and usage in a large social context, which I think means that they want the substantive thinking parts of their writing to be most important in any judgment of their writing and not superficial errors or deviations to the local SEAE. This sounds more like what teachers want students to want. However, I know many students every semester in my upper-division writing intensive course for all majors who ask for and demand surface-level correction or feedback on how their writing can better match the local SEAE that most of their other professors demand and expect of them, and that they know will be expected of them in their jobs in industry and society. Furthermore, this need by students is patterned. That is, it's mostly asked by white students and multilingual Hmong students, but for very different reasons. For white students, it is a part of their reaction to the grading contract's use of labor and not quality. For Hmong and other multilingual students, it's often a response to what they hope to get or expect from a writing course, and their desires to write better in the eyes of other teachers. Meanwhile the rest of the class, the majority, who are mostly Latino/a, have no strong opinion about the matter.

Furthermore, when I consider the local diversity in the classrooms at Fresno State generally, there are patterns. When surveyed at the end of their first-year writing courses, Hmong students still express anxiety and concern about their "grammar" and other superficial linguistic markers in their writing, and for good reason. They know how they are read by others in the university. They know that their next professor will see those markers as signs of illiteracy or failure. So I'm sure most Hmong students likely want feedback on such superficial features of their writing, as problematic as this is for writing teachers. They want direct instruction and feedback on the local SEAE because whether they can identify it or not, they know that to succeed in a society that values and rewards a white racial *habitus*, one must take on the markers and dispositions of *whiteness*. That's why they are in college in some sense.

To many faculty at Fresno State and to those in the community at large, the Hmong racial formation tends to be seen as one linked to illiteracy and remediation. In this case, Hmong students tend to want feedback in writing assessment ecologies that help them directly learn the local SEAE, a white, middle-class discourse, a discourse that most Fresno Hmong and many (maybe most) Latino/a in Fresno do not practice outside of school. But even those who do feel the problems of walking around with other dispositions, non-linguistic ones that mark them with a different racial *habitus* than the white one, find a tension in what they expect from any writing assessment ecology that is intended to be educative. From personal experience, I know that one must appear more than white, or as my Japanese-American ancestors used to say after World War II and internment (American concentration camps), we had to be "more American" than others, particularly whites. This mentality surely played a part in the "model minority" stereotype.

We could make similar arguments about each group that White (1996) defines, and it would require that we know the local diversity of a particular writing assessment ecology. What can be pointed out in White's description of these kinds of people in an ecology is that they are defined by their purposes for the ecology. Their purposes are formed usually from very different disciplinary, economic, and social origins, but people should be defined as more than their purposes, since their judging practices are influenced by more than purposes. If students investigate their own *habitus*, then compare it to the dominant one of the classroom, they can see their assessment practices as more than subjective, more than personal opinion, more than "just what I think," but interconnected to larger, social, cultural, and racial *habitus*.

The people in ecologies are always a complex, classed, gendered, and racialized set of formations with particular historically and locally constructed concerns and conflicts, who also have different relations to power and to the hegemonic. One hint of how seeing the people of a writing assessment ecology as more than homogenous stakeholders can be seen in Arnetha ball's (1997) important study of African-American and European readers (teachers) who rated student writing along several dimensions. European-American teachers rated European-American student writing higher (both holistically and on each dimension) than African-American student writing; however, African-American teachers rated African-American student writing higher (both holistically and on each dimension) than European student writing (Ball, 1997, pp. 177-179). This suggests that the racial formations that make up the teachers in a local program affect how they read and respond to student writing. By the same logic, teachers' racial *habitus* (and their students') affect what happens in the assessment ecology. Similar patterns of judgment were found in feedback on midterm portfolios in the first-year writing program at Fresno State. The results of that study were presented at CCCCs in San Francisco in 2009.[34]

Antiracist writing assessment ecologies pay close attention to the people who change it, asking students to reflect upon their own *habitus* and judging practices, and examining the interconnection of those *habitus* to larger social, cultural, and racial *habitus*. The ecology doesn't assume *a priori* or essential notions of the racial *habitus* of students, but it does ask them to look for patterns of judgment in their own histories in order to find the sources of their dispositions toward valuing language, and look for difference through interactions with colleagues.

ECOLOGICAL PROCESSES

In Maxine Hairston's (1982), "The Winds of Change: Thomas Kuhn and the Revolution in the Teaching of Writing," she argues that at that time the field was entering a paradigm shift, one that focused on writing as a process. The herald to this change that she mentions is Donald Murray's (1972/2011) short piece, "Teach Writing as Process, Not Product." Since then, this is a given in the field, so much so that no one questions how important teaching process(es) is, or that writing itself is a process. Just like writing, assessing writing can be understood as a process, which is the fifth designable element in antiracist writing assessment ecologies.

In their important book, *Designing Writing Tasks for the Assessment of Writ-*

ing, Ruth and Murphy offer an important conception of the "writing assessment episode" (1988, p. 128) as their way of making sense of the moments of reading and interpretation that occur in any writing assessment. Their writing assessment episode makes explicit the way writing assessment is also a process. The three key moments in any writing assessment episode starts with (1) the test-maker, who designs a writing topic or prompt; (2) moves to the test-taker, who reads and interprets the topic, then writes a response; and (3) the test-rater who reads and interprets, both the initial topic and the response in order to produce a rating or score (Ruth & Murphy, 1988, p. 129). While the process may change with different kinds of decisions, purposes, parts, and people, the important aspect of the writing assessment episode that shouldn't be lost is the simple fact that class-room writing assessment ecologies, from their conception and the identifying of a dominant need or purpose, to development and use, involves processes that move chronologically, as all life does. Thus processes make up the fifth ecological element, and makes writing assessment ecologies historical in nature in the ways historical bloc helps us understand them as political.

In one sense, processes of a writing assessment ecology are the labor and actions that happen in the ecology that have some import. Chronology, or the order in which these actions happen, is important, at least in terms of understanding their influence on the other ecological elements, particularly the products (explained in the next section). For instance, the simple truism that feedback and revision helps students' drafts get better proves my point. Implied in this truism is a process that starts with one draft, moves to some kind of feedback activity (a process itself), then moves to a revision activity or practice (another process), which produces a second draft that may be judged or graded. If the entire process is designed well and focused in the right places, places that match what students need most help improving in their drafts at that time, then the process may produce better drafts, so goes the logic. Thus, even if we do not explicitly ask students to engage in them, teachers always assume by necessity that students will engage in processes of assessment.

As post-process theorists have argued, however, teaching a particular process is not the key to learning to write better, since there is no one process to master, rather ideas about the nature of writing as public, interpretive, and situated are more important when constructing writing processes (Kastman Breuch, 2002/2011, p. 104). For antiracist writing assessment ecologies, assessment processes, which are typically exchanges among teachers and students about drafts and the judgments made on those drafts, are at least public and situated through their negotiated manner. The grading contract is a good example of how negotiating processes can work toward antiracist ends. Students gain power and control over how they do their work, as much as over the nature of that work.

Negotiating labor, or the processes of assessment, provides access to power and opportunity to reflect. This makes the articulated processes students negotiate a description of their ideal labor, at least as it is initially conceived.

As one might guess from my discussion so far, the key to improvement in antiracist writing assessment ecologies is students' engagement in the assessment processes of their work. The best way to maintain that engagement is reflection activities on judgment and assessment processes. The literature on reflection in writing (Belanoff & Dickson, 1991; Black, Daiker, Sommers, & Stygall, 1994; Hamp-Lyons & Condon, 2000; Yancey, 1998; Yancey & Weiser, 1997) and on reflective practices (Brookfield, 1995; Dewey, 1993; Schon, 1987) suggests some processes that could be inserted into such writing assessment ecologies in order to help writers at least become more self-aware of their practices. I've written on ways to insert reflection and self-assessment into larger writing assessment processes in other places (Inoue, 2004, 2010). However, one should be mindful of the ways that reflection as a discourse may be a racialized discourse informed by a white racial *habitus* (Inoue & Richmond, in press). This isn't a reason not to use reflection, only to make it a part of the problem-posing processes of the ecology—that is, as discussed earlier, reflection as a construct should be examined as a set of dispositions that may be different from the way some students already reflect in writing.

Using labor to determine progress and grades can provide for ways to more effectively ask students to reflect upon their *habitus*. The processes that students negotiate will be what the class uses to determine grades. Do the labor that the process dictates and you get full credit for the assignment. What students produce from the assessment processes and their reflection activities is less important than them self-consciously engaging in the process and reflecting upon that doing. This can produce problematizing of their existential writing assessment situations.

Some teachers may worry that they can't be sure that students are doing the labor that they say they are unless they grade drafts. Students have to be accountable if teachers are to know in some reasonable fashion that they have done the labor, goes the argument. If our main criterion for grading is how many hours of labor a student engages in, then we've set up a system in which we cannot know how well a student is doing (we cannot really grade them), since we have little access to students' out-of-class labors. The problem with this argument is that it is based on an assumption about students that is negative and caustic to the ecology. It assumes that the norm will be for students to lie or be dishonest when they say they've done the labor asked of them. This assumption creates writing assessment ecologies that have no faith in students, no trust, and so little room for them to build their own ways of intrinsic engagement and interest in the course's labors. These kinds of ecologies interpellate students as suspect and untrustworthy, and students feel this interpellation, then either live down to this subject position or against it. Not trusting students in the most fundamental aspect of any course is counter to healthy, sustainable ecologies. Often, what's in a draft doesn't come close to explaining the labor and thinking involved—this is why we have reflection components in portfolios, to explain the gaps, to reveal some of what is not there.

But there are ways to make more visible student labor. It still requires that we trust our students though. Students can keep labor journals that keep track of labor sessions for the class in terms of their time of day, duration, location, and even their level of engagement. Recently, I've used spreadsheets on Google Drive (Google Sheets) that are accessible and can be easily filled in during the week when students labor for the class. Twitter is another way to see labor as it happens. A teacher can ask students to tweet their labor. I do this by incorporating in my labor instructions for every assignment moments when students pause in their reading or writing and tweet something to the class with our hashtag. The tweets usually help us see something they are engaged in, a question, an interesting quote, an idea. This archives a bit of their labor as they do it, and provides a moment to pause and reflect on what they are doing, a method that helps them be more mindful of the labor process they are engaged in. My point is not that one needs to use Google or Twitter, but that if one uses labor as a way to grade, there should be mechanisms that students use to keep track of labor, reflect upon it, and make it visible to the class.

It is important to keep in mind that as Ruth and Murphy (1988) show us, processes of writing assessment are fundamentally reading and interpretive activities. Even writing drafts is a set of reading and interpretive processes. One must read the prompt, figure out the assignment, its goals, and how to proceed. As writers draft, they often reread sections or paragraphs they've just written in order to see continuity, logic, structure. Proofing and polishing are also reading processes. These are things that Nancy Sommers (1980) and Sandra Perl (1979) found in experienced and successful writers, that they draft and revise using recursive processes, going back over their texts, reading them over and over. At their core, all these reading processes are assessment processes, judgment processes, which means even when we are teaching writing processes, we are really teaching assessment processes. Antiracist assessment ecologies simply make this relationship explicit for students through a focus on processes of assessment.

Many assessment processes can have uneven consequences on different local diversities. In Fresno, for instance, the mostly affluent white (and some Latino/a) students of the nearby Clovis school district come from classrooms that heavily emphasize testing and scoring high on standardized tests, so they practice timed-writing exams a lot. But at most of the Fresno unified schools, where most of the Latino/a, Hmong, and African-American students attend, and where most are poor and on free-lunch, there is less of a focus on standardized testing (but they do still engage in a lot of testing). The consequences of a timed-writing exam process for students, then, from the Clovis-Fresno area are clear.

Clovis students score higher than those from Fresno unified.[35] Of those students from Clovis High who took the EPT for entrance into a CSU for the Fall 2012 semester, 73% of them scored above a 147, which is the cut-score for a remedial designation, thus they were deemed "proficient in English." At Clovis North High School and at Clovis West High School, 83% of students at each school were designated by the EPT as proficient. Meanwhile at Fresno High School, only 35% of their students for the same year scored proficient on the EPT. At Sunnyside (another Fresno unified school), 36% of their students scored as proficient. At McLane High, 41% of their students are proficient according to the EPT—and McLane is just blocks from Fresno State. Even a school that is situated in a more affluent neighborhood in Fresno, in some ways similar to the affluence in Clovis, but still in the Fresno unified school district, Bullard High School, has lower EPT scores than those in Clovis schools, achieving a more respectable 67% proficiency rate.

What are the differences beyond curriculum that create such uniform performances on the EPT? The answer is surely complex, but part of it I'm arguing has to do with how student populations from these schools, which are defined in large part by the local racial and economic diversities in Fresno and Clovis, are trained and practiced at timed-writing exam processes. Thus, the processes students experience in any classroom writing assessment ecology have consequences, but do students from these schools understand that their performances on the EPT are affected by the writing and assessment processes they practice in high school? Antiracist writing assessment ecologies attempt to make this connection explicit: assessment processes are the labor students do to understand the nature of judgment about their language. Thus understanding and controlling one's assessment labor offers students the opportunity to form critical writing and reading practices, which is another way of saying assessment practices.

ECOLOGICAL PRODUCTS

Products make up the sixth designable element of an antiracist writing assessment ecology. Like the term suggests, products refer to all of the direct and indirect consequences that occur in and from writing assessment ecologies. Direct consequences typically are things like scores, grades, decisions, the language that constitutes the actual feedback given on a draft by a teacher (which can also act as a part), etc. In other instances, direct consequences could be the written articulations of students that explain to peers, the teacher, or themselves how well theirs or others' drafts meet the expectations of a writing assignment. The indirect consequences are those that typically occur because of the direct consequences. Because a draft is graded (direct consequence), students focus on superficial editing in the draft (indirect consequence), or the grades tell them something about their abilities (good or bad) and that in turn affects their confidence or future performances in the class. The low score on the EPT that designates a student as remedial places that student in a mandatory, summer Early Start English course, which costs her more money, time, and perhaps erodes her confidence, suggesting to her that she is not ready for college. Clearly the indirect consequences of writing assessment environments appear more severe and have more long-term effects as the direct ones. But the two are connected. You cannot have indirect consequences without direct ones. Both kinds of consequences, however, are ecological products because they are produced by the ecological processes, parts, people, power arrangements, and purposes of the writing assessment ecology.

In a classroom, the grade on a portfolio isn't the final product of the portfolio assessment ecology, the course grade or decision is, since typically that is the real decision the portfolio makes. However, my version of an antiracist writing assessment ecology doesn't produce grades from portfolios, but it does use portfolios. In my writing classes, the portfolio assessment ecology produces a set of articulations (usually five assessment documents: three from peers, a self-assessment, and my own) that are pitched not toward justifying a grade, or even a simple assessment of meeting expectations from a rubric, instead peers and I articulated three things to the writer and myself for discussion in a final conference: (1) what picture of the writer as a learner do you see in the portfolio; (2) what did you, the assessor, learn from this writer in this portfolio; and (3) what potential do you think the writer has as a writer and should most work on in the future? The articulations of these questions are used only for discussion of the writer in a final, one-on-one conference that discusses what she has done in the portfolio and where she might go as a writer in the future.

Because grades are determined already by a grading contract that bases course grades on labor only, these articulations are not about justifying grades, or figuring out the course grade. The main product I hope to encourage from the portfolio assessment is to allow writers and assessors to learn something about themselves as writers and assessors from various diverse perspectives, what I call a landscape of judgment. Like all classroom writing assessment ecologies, I do not control much of the indirect consequences, but I can control the direct consequences, in this case, the production of grades and articulations of learning by writers and readers. Antiracist assessment ecologies mostly produce complex, descriptive products that focus on the local diversity in judgments, such as my portfolio assessment, and resist hierarchizing judgments (like grades).

While I'll discuss this final assessment process in more detail in the next chapter, it is important here to point out the fluidity of ecological products and parts. In the larger writing assessment ecology of the course, the final assessment documents by group members that are discussed in our final meetings are both parts and products. They are an ecological part because they are the artifacts the writer and I use to understand the landscape of judgment about her as a learner in the class. The individual assessment documents about the writer are parts to larger assessment processes that only chronologically finishes at the end of our conference, which produces a more complex set of judgments about the writer—that is, once all the documents are read, then we discuss the differences and similarities. We discuss the landscape of judgment, which only then becomes the direct product of several processes. While this scenario may seem atypical, if one looks more closely at the way articulations of judgments and other artifacts function in any writing assessment ecology, even very conventional ones with grades and with only the teacher reading drafts, we'll likely find parts morphing into products, and products, like the feedback on a draft, morphing into parts of subsequence processes, in the same fashion.

Note, however, that the key to figuring out whether a document or portfolio is a product or a part (an artifact) in the process that leads to another product is in figuring out the relations between the document, the process of judging the writing, and the purpose for the assessing process. This is the nature of all ecological systems, transformation, or the inter-being of all elements, which is why products also are more than decisions, grades, or culminating judgments.

Furthermore, all ecological elements are productive in some fashion—that is, they have some influence on the ecological products that come from an ecology. They are productive. They produce things in the ecology. For instance, bringing in different, perhaps atypical people into the writing assessment ecology of the classroom as judges can change the products of that environment in unexpected ways. A technical writing class could bring in technical writers and managers working in the field to offer formative feedback on student writing. This in turn could alter the way teacher feedback is enacted, perhaps making it more collaborative, focusing on how to meet the demands that the outside professionals have placed on the writing. In antiracist writing assessment ecologies, this might be an occasion to examine *habitus* outside the classroom that arguably exist in professional settings. Students might interpret teacher feedback as coaching, or collaborating, and less evaluative. The product of teacher feedback could be an investigation or inquiry into why this technical writer or industry manager values these particular things in this kind of document for this audience. What *habitus* can be described in the judgments and how do those dispositions compare next to the ones the class has negotiated in its rubrics or assignment? What indirect products or consequences to students do these *habitus* reasonably encourage when used to judge writing/writers?

As mentioned already, Arnetha Ball's (1997) research suggests that who the teacher is, what racial formation she participates in or what racial *habitus* she enacts in the assessment ecology matters and can produce different products, different grades, scores, and perhaps feedback. I see no reason why this same claim cannot be made about students as well. The same can be said about using different ecological parts, say a new rubric or prompt, a different process, such as a different kind of feedback method, etc., or different power arrangements (e.g., who gets to grade, or how students interact with each other).

The ecological products of an antiracist writing assessment ecology are products and not parts because they are the learning that occurs because of the ecology. Sometimes, however, the products of an ecology may get circulated back into the ecology as parts, in which case, the ecology may change. Using reflection activities to "close the loop" is one way classrooms can do this. The best recent examples of closing the loop processes that I've seen are from dynamic criteria mapping (Broad, 2003; Broad et al., 2009), in which the point of the assessment process is to produce a document that exemplifies what the participants have learned about the writing program and its values (an articulation of products), which then helps the program understand and perhaps change their practices by its use of the document as a part.

ECOLOGICAL PLACES

Using Plato's *Gorgias*, as an opening example, Nedra Reynolds (2004) offers this introduction to thinking about the importance of place in the teaching of writing: "[p]laces evoke powerful human emotions because they become layered, like sediment or a palimpsest, with histories and stories and memories ... they become embodied with the kinds of stories, myths, and legends that the spot beside the Ilissus holds" (p. 2). Place, however, is more than geography that acquires meaning. In considering a "macro-view" of writing as process, James Reither (1985) re-explains writing in terms of systems and contexts, and sees writing as an ecology, which helps us understand place as a part of that ecology:

> writing is not merely a process that occurs within contexts.
> That is, writing and what writers do during writing cannot
> be artificially separated from the social-rhetorical situations

in which writing gets done, from the conditions that enable writers to do what they do, and from the motives writers have for doing what they do. Writing is not to context what a fried egg is to its pan. Writing is, in fact, one of those processes which, in its use, creates and constitutes its own contexts. (p. 621)

Reither's identification of writing as a generative force that constructs contexts is very similar to Ede and Lunsford's (1984) claim a year earlier about audiences constructing writers and writers constructing audiences (p. 158). In short, the people and their labor and processes of writing create contexts that dialectically create that very writing. Writing creates contexts as much as contexts create writing.

These earlier versions of writing as contextual tend to see context in the above rhetorical ways, bound in or around the text itself, or in the superstructural, but it is also in the base of the classroom, in the material production of culture and ideas, namely the processes and environments in which assessment occurs. While context is rhetorical in the ways Reither and Ede and Lunsford describe, it is also material in nature. So I use the term place to identify both the rhetorical context and material conditions of the production of assessment (judgment) of writing in the classroom, which includes places like writing groups, the remedial location, an evaluation rubric, success, failure, a course's Internet discussion board, the classroom, the dorm room, etc. The ecological places, the seventh and final element that makes up an antiracist writing assessment ecology, can also be explicitly examined and designed. In fact, the places of an ecology may be the most important element in the system because they inter-are the entire system. Just like Reither's writing situations, we (teachers and students) create conditions and places of assessment through our interactions with the other ecological elements. Additionally, material bodies make up locations and define them by occupying places.

Drawing on Lefebvre and geographer Yi-Fu Tuan, Dobrin (2012) explains the way space and place have been defined relationally. Space, the larger more abstract term, is "freedom" and "movement," while place "offers security" and is "pause," according to Tuan (Dobrin, 2012, p. 36). Dobrin uses Tuan: "The ideas of 'space' and 'place' require each other for definition. From security and stability of place we are aware of the openness, freedom, and threat of space, and vice versa." (Tuan, 1977, p. 6; as quoted in Dobrin, 2012, p. 36). For de Certeau, "place is the 'order (of whatever kind) in accord with which elements are distributed in relationships of coexistence'" (Dobrin, 2012, p. 39). Dobrin highlights an important aspect of place that de Certeau explains. Place is created by whatever occupies it, but "occupation is limited." Ultimately, Dobrin says that the order that is imposed through occupation is "imposed through power" (2012, p. 40). His conclusion, then is that "[s]pace is the site of ideological struggle; place is the result of that struggle. Place is the hegemonic made visible, readable. Space is where bodies combat to make meaning and, in doing so, make place, produce the location of hegemony" (2012, p. 42).

I'll come back to this idea of combat and conflict in places (not spaces) shortly, but I want to call attention to past theorizing of place as a site that is a result of ideological and physical conflict. I do not wish to engage in the interesting distinctions between space and place, except to reveal that before places are created in an antiracist writing assessment ecology, they are broader, often more abstract, ideological and material spaces of conflict, which continue to get worked out through conflict and difference once they become identifiable places. It is, I think, enough to know that places in an antiracist ecology are not produced out of thin air. They come from larger, more abstract spaces of conflict.

Dobrin (2012) makes much of the way place is defined by the notion of occupation. Occupation, in fact, constructs places through an association with the bodies that rest in those places, that occupy and have occupations in those places. Ultimately, he says, this means that occupation is "a struggle of power" to "inscribe meaning"; it is a result of the action of occupying a place; it is a "taking up or filling up of space," that is, occupation is spatial and temporal in nature; and it is "the manner in which individuals occupy their time through engagement or the pursuit of an activity" (2012, pp. 43-44). And so according to Dobrin (who cites Lefebvre), by this logic, bodies cannot define the space they occupy because it is through bodies' deployment and occupation of space that they then create places, which are more ordered, hierarchical, and hegemonic. As I'll discuss below, this seems to contradict Charles Mills' important theory of racing places and bodies. While bodies may not define spaces, they do define places, and places tautologically define bodies.

But even at face value, the material places in which the processes of writing assessment ecologies occur, the schools, dorm rooms, and offices where students are judged or judge themselves, are important to negotiate and make clear in antiracist writing assessment ecologies. If assessment only happens outside the classroom in the privacy of teachers' offices, what Belanoff described as "the dirty thing we have to do in the dark of our own offices" (1991, p. 61), then those private processes and perhaps private products define the classroom as a public space in the assessment ecology in which grades and the evaluation of writing are not done. If teachers use student work to discuss and evaluate patterns in all students' writing in a class, then the classroom or the Internet discussion forum become material places where such interactions, or public assessment, are acceptable. In antiracist writing assessment ecologies, assessment processes and the parts and products they produce are usually public. There is no private learning or private assessment, because any given product associated with a student or her writing inter-is with the places that learning comes from. Students and their learning inter-are in ecologies. Everyone must come to benefit from everyone else's assessments in the Sangha ecology.

In some ecologies, assessment happens in lots of places. In others, it happens in only one place. Is it okay to make judgments of worth on student writing in public places, such as a classroom or in a writing group with other students? To ask this question more broadly: where are the appropriate or condoned places in which a student, or all students, may be graded, evaluated, or given feedback? Where are the places in which that feedback or those evaluations are generated initially, or shared individually or publically? Who in those places have authority, by the nature of those places, to give evaluations or assess writing? The classroom is an institutionally authorized place for teachers to say pretty much whatever they want about student writing, but are students also authorized in that material place to do so, should they be? How might they become authorized? What about their dorm room or their home, an Internet discussion forum? What about in someone else's class? Places matter to how antiracist writing assessment ecologies function and what they produce, which includes producing different notions of authority in the assessment ecology for students and teacher. The questions above should be asked and negotiated with students, explicitly inquired into, so that students can see that there are other options for how the places of assessment are created, which can make a difference in how fair and equitable the ecology is for everyone.

We should also keep in mind the nature of places as discussed by others in composition studies, which work from concepts like community, consensus, conflict, difference, negotiation, and borderland. For instance, likely working from Pratt's (1991) contact zone metaphor, Ed White (2001) argues that assessment is "a site of conflict" (pp. 315-316) and illustrates this in his narrative of the establishment of the EPT in California in the 1970s. He urges writing teachers and administrators to acknowledge that they come to places of writing assessment with particular values, perspectives, and needs, while administrators and others come with different ones. There will be a difference of opinion on many things, but to get the work done, negotiation is needed. In some sense, this is common sense in composition studies, where we hardly contest the idea that within students' drafts and in the classroom itself there are "contact zones" (Pratt, 1991), ones filled with conflict and difference, ones that demand we understand different perspectives that simply do not agree with one another. The field has pedagogies and theories about contact zones and borderlands

(Anzaldúa, 1999/1987; Horner & Lu, 1999), about how teachers create differing personae and assumptions of students (Anson, 2000; Williams, 1981), and about how to use difference and negotiation productively (Horner, 1992; Trimbur, 1989). However, within Pratt's own example, one of the Spanish imperial conquest of Peru, we see the problem presented by such a view of the classroom community, or rather the problem that "contact zones" can reveal to students in antiracist writing assessment ecologies that construct various diverse places in the ecology from the bodies of students.

For Pratt, contact zones are "social spaces where cultures meet, clash, and grapple with each other, often in contexts of highly asymmetrical relations of power, such as colonialism, slavery, or their aftermaths as they are lived out in many parts of the world today" (1991, p. 34). She explains that "[t]he idea of the contact zone is intended in part to contrast with ideas of community that underlie much of the thinking about language, communication, and culture that gets done in the academy" (1991, p. 37). Likely, Pratt is referring to—and criticizing—discussions like Bruffee's (1984) on collaboration and community building in the classroom that work from unqualified versions of Oakeshott's "unending conversation" (1991, pp. 638-639) and Rorty's concepts of "normal" and "abnormal" discourse in communities (1991, pp. 640-641). A similar critique of "community" was put forth around the same time by Joseph Harris (1989). Harris promoted a way of seeing the classroom space, for instance, as a conflict-filled, diverse, public space, like a city (1989, p. 20), not a cozy place where people can simply come to agree or find consensus. But Harris finds problems with Pratt's contact zone too. He sees Pratt giving conflicting messages in her text, and concludes that the idea of a contact zone promoted by Pratt's argument tends to be a mostly harmless, exoticizing of the multicultural other, in which students and perspectives harmlessly bump into each other, "banging or sliding or bouncing off each other" (Harris, 2012, p. 163). In line with his public city metaphor, Harris urges us to find pedagogical ways "to make such a meeting of differences less like a battle and more like a negotiation ... to learn not only how to articulate our differences but how to bring them into useful relation with each other," which moves him to focus on negotiation that doesn't entail full agreement (p. 165).

Others have made similar arguments about the problems of consensus in collaborative activities and unqualified notions of community in classrooms. From a Marxian perspective, Myers (1986) argues against Bruffee's (1984) notions of collaboration and community by discussing the way any society reproduces ideology through acceptance and consent of mundane ideas and actions, then argues that conflict is thus necessary for change. When we see a community as mainly one in which folks agree or only search for agreement, Myers argues, we blindly reproduce ideology (or the hegemonic), and miss how the system changes or can change (1986, p. 156). Trimbur (1989) also disagrees with the clean and unqualified notion of community that Bruffee claims can support a collaborative classroom, and thus writing processes. He argues, similar to Harris, that conflict is necessary and can be used for students' benefit, and puts forth the idea of "dissensus," "a process of identifying differences and locating these differences in relation to each other" (1989, p. 610). The product of such writing classroom processes is not about "an agreement that reconciles differences through an ideal conversation," instead it is about "the desire of humans to live and work together with differences" (Trimbur, 1989, p. 615). Thus one key to designing ecological places that resist norming everyone to a white racial *habitus* is to see them as sites of negotiation in which students focus on their relations to others through an attention to their evolving differences.

The places that are constructed by and make up an antiracist writing assessment ecology are not benign mini-communities, or less benign but ultimately harmless contact zones. These places in the ecology are places of true conflict and irreconcilable differences, places of colonization. While Pratt's concept has problems, it can be a powerful way to help students see their differing stances and the places they create in the ecology as colonizing places, such as their writing groups, the classroom generally, discussion board exchanges, and anywhere multiple assessments and reflections on judgments occur. If places in antiracist writing assessment ecologies colonize, then they norm students to particular *habitus*, which should be made explicit so that students have as much power and choice as possible. It is unavoidable that the writing classroom's assessment ecology colonizes students, especially those who come with non-dominant racialized *habitus*, but we can make this fact known and discussed, even negotiated, so that students understand what they are consenting to, and make conscious choices to do so, or not.

I am, however, persuaded by Harris' and Trimbur's separate arguments about the intrinsic difference in all places where people and ideas inhabit, but they should be tempered with the spirit of Myer's Marxian critique that focuses on the reproductive nature of the hegemonic in all systems. And I'm convinced that as teachers, we must keep foremost in our minds the conflicting nature of all places—especially ones we create—and how conflict and difference can be a way to learn, develop, and make changes in our world. Yet I'm also wary of how stubborn the hegemonic is, even in a classroom that focuses on situating difference (of opinion, of ideas, of making meaning, of languages, of histories and cultures, of *habitus* etc.) without trying to harmonize, as I think Harris' good example in the Interchapter that follows his "Process" chapter shows (2012). No matter what our political or pedagogical stances are on how to read multilingual writers, how (or whether) to teach a local dominant discourse, or what the subject of any writing classroom is, it is difficult to escape the privileging of a white racial *habitus* that is so closely associated with the academy. Thus, the hegemonic will be a powerful part of the dissensus in any ecological place. It may even create the boundaries of that place.

Gloria Anzaldúa's (1987/1999) concept of borderlands offers a corrective or refocusing of Pratt's contact zone, Trimbur's idea of dissensus, and Harris' public-natured city metaphor. Anzaldúa focuses on the border between the U.S. and Mexico, a border between white and brown, English and Spanish, the dominant and subaltern. It is also a place of struggle and conflict, of *"un choque,* [shock] a cultural collision" (Anzaldúa, 1897/1999; p. 100). The idea of the borderlands attends to the geographic, linguistic, physiological, and figurative border places, places on landscapes that define insiders and outsiders. Anzaldúa provides a powerful geographic metaphor that reveals the places where changes occur, where transgressions appear, and where action and drama happen. These are places perfect for people to confront their existential situations. She states the borderland this way:

> The U.S.-Mexican border *es una herida abierta* where the
> Third World grates against the first and bleeds. And before a
> scab forms it hemorrhages again, the lifeblood of two worlds
> merging to form a third country—a border culture. Borders
> are set up to define the places that are safe and unsafe, to
> distinguish *us* from *them.* A border is a dividing line, a narrow
> strip along a steep edge. A borderland is a vague and undeter-
> mined place created by the emotional residue of an unnatural
> boundary. It is in a constant state of transition. The prohibit-
> ed and forbidden are its inhabitants. *Los atravesados* live here:
> the squinted-eyed, the perverse, the queer, the troublesome,
> the mongrel, the mulato, the half-breed, the half-dead; in
> short, those who cross over, pass over, or go through the con-
> fines of the "normal." Gringos in the U.S. Southwest consider
> the inhabitants of the borderlands transgressors, aliens—
> whether they possess documents or not, whether they're
> Chicanos, Indians or Blacks. Do not enter, trespassers will be
> raped, maimed, strangled, gassed, shot. The only "legitimate"
> inhabitants are those in power, the whites and those who align
> themselves with whites. Tension grips the inhabitants of the
> borderlands like a virus. Ambivalence and unrest reside there
> and death is no stranger. (1987/1999, pp. 25-26)

While not as encouraging of a picture of place as perhaps Harris' ideas of a city or Trimbur's dissensus, Anzaldúa's borderland reveals how places where local diversities meet the hegemonic can generate serious conflict and wounding. Race and racial formations, "Chicanos, Indians or Blacks," and whites who are in power, is central to Anzaldúa's metaphor of place, which is not the case for either Trimbur or Harris (although it is more so for Pratt). Somebody, and it's almost always the subaltern,[36] gets hurt or worse. But borderlands also reveal something important about the nature of places and landscape that often goes unnoticed. All places are loci for drama and action, thus they are also in constant states of change, just as the concept of ecology makes present for us. However, most of the time that change is incremental, almost imperceptible, like the slow eroding of the Grand Canyon by the Colorado river. And because the changes are so slow, by the time they are perceivable, they are already coopted by the hegemonic, even if at one time those changes, those shocks to the system were counter-hegemonic. Thus, in some sense, change is hegemonic, is essentially systemic.

Therefore, I prefer to mix the metaphors of place so that the places constructed in an antiracist writing assessment ecology refer at once to public cities of negotiation and getting along, spaces where dissensus is inherent and important to see and confront, not ignore, yet are borderlands that inherently have the potential for violent racial and cultural collisions, wounding, and change. This last element of place is at the heart of my reading of Freire's revolutionary pedagogy (1970), in which much of his discussion is about folks going into the community, the place where the subaltern inhabit, the borderland, and understanding how words work there. But there is wounding and hurt. It's not always safe.

Recall that ecology has an association with settlement and making some place inhabitable, livable, sustainable; however, places themselves, like people and parts, are usually already connected to larger colonizing structures in history. The material places of schools and classrooms, and the figurative places of the English paper and evaluation rubric, as well as the places of the remedial and mainstream writer, are all locations in which the colonizing project occurs and is reproduced through writing assessment ecologies. This is nowhere better illustrated than in Soliday's (2002) discussion of the politics of remediation, and others' discussions of remediation and access to higher education (Fox, 1999; Kynard, 2013; Miller, 1991; Stanley, 2009; Trachsel, 1992). This means we should be most conscious of the ways antiracist writing assessment ecologies' construct places that affect differently the local diversities in our classrooms and schools. We may create places that produce discomfort and unease in some, anger in others. But we should not confuse discomfort with the safety required in a successful learning environment. Learning requires us to be uncomfortable and safe. Safety in writing assessment ecologies demands that students' judgments and opinions not be graded, but counted and heard.

Victor Villanueva (1997) offers an illustration of the uneven hurt that can occur in any assessment ecology through a complicating of the notion of multiculturalism. He says that there is "a colonial sensibility [that] remains for us in the United States—in America—and that America's people of color are most affected by that sensibility" (1997, p. 184). Students of color are "forced" in many ways to assimilate to local SEAEs and dominant, white ways of knowledge making and discourse, most notably to a white racial *habitus*, yet this forcing often is voiced by students of color as consent. Consent is achieved through writing assessment ecologies, by doing what it takes to get the grade or receive credit, by achieving. Assessment decisions reward or punish the subaltern, which is not just the student of color but often all students, since students are subordinate by their nature in assessment ecologies (there are degrees to the subaltern). Not only are students of color coerced through the assessment of writing, but are also made to consent, as we all are, only students of color tend to move through a process of internal colonialism (Villanueva, 1997, p. 186), which Villanueva identifies as having two impulses: "economic ascension and cultural resignation" (p. 189; as cited in Altbach & Kelly, 1978). We go to school and learn a local dominant academic discourse because it means economic and other opportunities, or so the myth goes. The point I'm making is that when places are created in antiracist writing assessment ecologies, they are also locations of potential internal colonializing, which limit the ideas and discourses available to judge in the ecology, and these dynamics of ecological places should be made explicit and negotiated.

Thus, the ecological places in an antiracist writing assessment ecology are inherently borderlands because they are sites of action, change, and drama, locations where colonizing occurs forcefully and willingly, through hegemonic means of coercion and consent. No matter how we design classroom writing assessment ecologies, no matter how much we desire to change the hegemonic in the academy, ecological places—like most places on the planet—tend to be places of colonization at some historical point, thus they are places of norming and racing. This is to say, conventional writing assessment ecologies colonize primarily by norming bodies to a white racial *habitus*, and as Charles Mills (1997) has pointed out, this is simultaneously a racing of bodies. Mills says,

> The norming of space is partially done in terms of the *racing* of space, the depiction of space as dominated by individuals (whether persons or subpersons) of a certain race. At the same time, the norming of the individual is partially achieved by *spacing* it, that is, representing it as imprinted with the

characteristics of a certain kind of space. So this is a mutually supporting characterization that, for subpersons [people of color or the subaltern], becomes a circular indictment: "You are what you are in part because you originate from a certain kind of space, and that space has those properties in part because it is inhabited by creatures like yourself." (1997, pp. 41-42, emphasis in original)

Mills does not make a distinction between places and spaces. At face, Mills would seem to contradict Lefebvre and Dobrin since they say bodies do not define the spaces they come to occupy, but if we replace Mill's looser term "space" for "place," then Mills' racing of spaces theory agrees with them. Racialized places are constructed by the occupation of the racialized bodies in that place, while simultaneously those racialized bodies are also constructed by the racialized places they occupy. However, Dobrin reveals that even the broader, more abstract spaces (pre- or proto-places) is not devoid of the influence of occupying bodies: "space can be seen as a factor in constructing the occupier's identity, not the opposite—though, of course, this is an illusion. The relationship becomes eventually reciprocal in that those who come to occupy a space—say, the space of the university—must mold their identities to fit the space as defined by previous occupiers/occupations" (Mills, 1997, p. 48). But even with this explanation, the question remains, at some earlier, historic point a raced place, like remediation, the remedial classroom, failure, or success, was a space, and thus not raced initially, according to Lefebvre. Race, however, is an attribution of people, and so a construction attached to bodies and their *habitus*. How do we get to a moment in history when Mills' racing of place can be accounted for or explained? Surely, students in a writing classroom won't always accept this claim. We have to look back at the history of race itself to understand its influence on places, which has great bearing on antiracist writing assessment ecologies as counter-hegemonic historic blocs. Understanding the development of race as a concept can provide students and teachers in antiracist writing assessment ecologies ways to be critical of the colonizing that occurs in places that race students to a white racial *habitus* through assessment processes, and perhaps additional ways to problematize existential writing assessment situations.

The racing of places, as Mills suggests, can be traced back to the beginnings of the use of the term "race" in Western societies and literature. In his extensive study of "race" as a concept in Western philosophy and history, Ivan Hannaford (1996) explains that the word "race" did not enter Western languages until the middle of the sixteenth century. There was no Hebrew, Greek, or Roman equivalent, and its original meaning tended to be "lineage, family, and breed" (Hannaford, 1996, p. 5). The *Oxford Dictionary of Word Origins* explains the word as an Old English derivative that meant "rapid forward movement," which came from the Old Norse word, *rás*, or "current." These origins allowed the word to be developed in use to mean a "contest of speed," a "channel" or "path," ("race"). I find it interesting in a number ways that the concept of "race," so important to Anzaldúa's notion of borderlands, a place of change, also has etymological roots in Western languages that draw on a metaphor of dynamism and change, a current of water, a path, a contest of speed, and forward movement.

Drawing on at least ten different etymological sources, Hannaford explains that the term "race" "entered the Spanish, Italian, French, English, and Scottish languages during the period of 1200-1500 CE and did not have the meaning that we attach to it now. In most Western languages its earliest meaning related to the swift course or current of a river or a trial of speed" (Hannaford, 1996, pp. 4-5). In English, the word's first appearance has been attributed to a 1508 poem by Scottish poet William Dunbar called, "The Dance of the Seven Deadly Sins" (Banton, 1998, p. 17; Goldberg, 1993, p. 62; Satzewich, 1998, p. 26). The one reference comes in the fifth stanza, where the narrator is describing the dance of Envy and his family or troupe of followers "of sindry racis," all with "fenyeit wirdis quhyte," or "false white words," which was akin to "little white lies" (Conlee, 2004). In his discussion of race as a concept, Vic Satzewich explains that during the sixteenth century, the word race referred "only to a class or category of people or things. These classes or categories were not seen as biologically distinct, nor were they seen as situated in a hierarchy of superiority and inferiority" (Satzewich, 1998, p. 27). This is the way we might read Dunbar's use of the term, as a way to identify the family or category of dancers in his poem, a way to relate them together as the family of Envy, but not necessarily associate any biological traits or physiognomy to them. However, the evil, ugly, dark, or negative associations readers are supposed to make about envy are there, and they are organized by the term race.

A similar use of the term can be found in Shakespeare's *The Merchant of Venice* (1600), in which Lorenzo speaks to Jessica about listening to music in the night. Shakespeare uses race to refer to a group of horses in Lorenzo's rebuff to Jessica, saying, "The reason is your spirits are attentive/ For do but note a wild and wanton herd/ Or race of youthful and unhandled colts/ Fetching mad bounds, bellowing and neighing loud,/ Which is the hot condition of their blood" (V.i.70-74). While race groups the horses into a common category, that category has associated with it negative or less than mature attributes. Thus race, even at this early historical point, appears to begin being used with negative references to people, but not places.

So what does this have to do with the norming or racing of places in writing assessment ecologies? People and places have always been intimately connected for obvious reasons. Without people in them, places become less socially significant. Beyond this, while race as a term had no origins or associations to geography, except to refer to the running of water or streams, it appeared to be used to group people and animals together as common. Places in this rudimentary way, raced people, only in different terms, in more conceptual ways, as immature or as a family with similar attributes.

But by 1684—just eighty some years after Shakespeare's *Merchant of Venice*—François Bernier published what is considered the first reference to the modern concept of race in "Nouvelle Division de la Terre par les Differents Espèces ou Races qui l'Habitent" ("A New Division of Earth and the Different Species or Races Living There") in *Journal des Sçavans*. In the article, Bernier proposed four races based mostly on geography, color, and physical traits. He identified them as: (1) Europe, South Asia, North Africa, and America; (2) Africa; (3) Asia; and (4) Lapps (Hannaford, 1996, p. 203; Painter, 2010, pp. 43-44). While published in a prestigious academic journal of his day, Bernier's "new division" seemed to have been "idiosyncratic" and not referenced by later writers; however, Pierre Boulle concludes his study of Bernier's influence on racial discourse by saying that Bernier's text was indicative of the "shift in thought that occurred in the second half of the seventeenth century," a shift to racial discourse as we know it today (Boulle, 2003, p. 20). This shift in the use of the term race was one linked closely to geographic places, making places a primary way people are raced, or gain racial qualities and characteristics. This shift in discourse and racial thinking is more clearly seen in the more influential early writers and texts on race that came just decades later, such as Carolus Linnaeus's *Systema Naturae* (1735), Georges-Louis Leclerc, Comte de Buffon's *Histoire Naturelle, Gènèrelle et Particulière* (*A Natural History, General and Particular*) (1749-1788, 36 volumes), and perhaps most notably, Johann Friedrich Blumenbach's *De Generis Humani Varietate Nativa* (*On the Natural Variety of Mankind*) (1775). In each case, beginning with Bernier, geographic location, places on the globe, became racialized. Places began to racialize people. Through this most basic associative logic used by all the early writers of race theories, the territories on Earth are raced and have remained so.

The most influential early writer of race was Johann Friedrich Blumenbach (1752-1840). His methods were consciously empirical, considering physical features (including examining fetuses, pictures, and drawings), leaning heavily on craniology (the measuring of skulls), considering geographic location, and inserting his own notions of beauty (Bhopal, 2007, p. 1309). From these methods, Blumenbach induced a degenerate theory of races in which all races are degenerate versions of the Caucasian race (named after a group of people who lived around the Caucasus Mountains, located between the Black Sea and Caspian Sea). Each of Blumenbach's five races, the Malay, Ethiopian, American, Mongolian, and Caucasian, are distinguished by physical characteristics: cranial size and shape, the color and texture of skin and hair, body proportions, outward demeanor, shape of eyes and nose, etc. But Blumenbach's thinking begins with geographic location, with places in which these bodies dwell.[37] As Raj Bhopal explains, the purpose for Blumenbach's research was to figure out if humans comprised a single species (monogeny), which he concluded was the case, or whether the popular view of the time was correct, that there were many species of humans (polygeny) (2007, p. 1308). Thus, for Blumenbach, the varieties of humans he catalogued were degenerations of the perfect one, the Caucasian, which had a geographic origin. And so, places and races are not only associated closely to each other but become hierarchized somatically, geographically, and aesthetically.

From a consideration of Blumenbach's collected treatises, edited by Thomas Bendyshe, published in 1865, Bhopal (2007) argues that Blumenbach has been misunderstood. He was not promoting a racist theory at all. He was promoting "the unity of humanity (monogeny)." In fact, "Blumenbach wrote favourably [sic] about 'negroes,' extolling their beauty, mental abilities, and achievements in literature and other fields. He pointed to variations in opportunity as the cause of differences" (Bhopal, 2007, p. 1309). However, even if we accept this antiracist position on Blumenbach's work (his motivation and perhaps purpose), which I see no reason to doubt, it is clear that the categorizing of bodies from empirical evidence (e.g., cranial size, geography, or physiognomy), in order to justify a theory of monogeny (a worthwhile goal at the time), and linking it to locations on the globe, easily gets deployed for a number of other racial projects at the time and later on, all of which associate race with place. It doesn't matter what Blumenbach's motives were. Even though Blumenbach was not making the argument that any one race is inferior to another (beyond beauty), that was the message that others took.

What makes the deployment of Blumenbach's theory so enticing is how it is a rhetoric with substantial power, the way it uses empiricism and categorization to form a tacit hierarchy. Degeneration is a hierarchical logic, much like the religious hierarchy of the chain of being from God to humanity. This logic is arranged in a calm, reasonable, rational, and seemingly objective voice, a voice that carefully explains the data, which places at the top of the racial hierarchy a white racial category. The use of empirical skull measurements, observations of physical features, and geographic location of groups of people, all of which create the categories, make it hard to argue that Blumenbach is biased, or that what he presents is anything but the truth. He is a scientist who is simply categorizing naturally occurring phenomena in different geographic places (something Aristotle is famous for). In the process, however, he also begins the project of norming and racing places to the white norm, the white *habitus*, which for him was the Caucasian. If all races are degenerated from the Caucasian, then it's not hard to see colonization as a process of norming bodies, ideas, values, languages, and *habitus* to the dominant white ones of the time. In short, the racing of place is, as Mills points out from other sources, simultaneously done by racing people, and through other historical, racial projects, Blumenbach's theory and categories become a way to assert the white, European norm as the spatial and racial ideal.

From this brief history of the concept of race, the questions we might ask our students in antiracist writing assessment ecologies lead to reflections on the function of places in the ecology. What is the function of the our rubric as a place, for example? In what ways does it colonize some through assessment processes that norm everyone to a white racial *habitus*? How might we understand our rubric, as one articulation of the writing expectations of the class, as interconnected to larger histories of racing bodies in classrooms and other societal spaces? What alternative purposes might we employ so that the places we create in the ecology work to critique and change racist outcomes or products, such as the blind norming (colonizing) of people in the ecological places of writing groups, feedback documents, and the like?

Beyond the hierarchy inherent in Blumenbach's degeneration theory, using geographic location suggests a kind of hierarchy connected to colonial conquest that would be familiar to Europeans of the time, one of center and periphery, which brings us back to Pratt's original thinking about contact zones. But there are hierarchies of places and people in Anzaldúa's borderlands that are historical in their making. Lothrop Stoddard's *The Rising Tide of Color Against White World-Supremacy* (1920) sees the world divided by "inner" and "outer" dikes, regions of white racial control or settlement (p. 226). Regardless of the metaphor, the white European is the center, the norm. In both Stoddard's and Blumenbach's cases, Europe is constructed as the center or origin from which all races degenerate, using geographic location as an empirical logic in concert (in several cases) with appearance.[38] The more distant one is located from the European center, the more degenerated, and the less value the race and place have. This primacy of the white racial center as norm is no more obvious than in typical maps of the globe, where Europe sits at the center. These maps could be situated in any number of ways, but they typically are not. So is the assumption of the racing and norming of places. This could be a metaphor for the way conventional writing classroom assessment ecologies situate racialized places of evaluation as well.

The theory that Dobrin cites that accounts for the ways in which bodies occupy spaces, thus creating places, such as writing assessment ecologies' places, does not account well for actual history and actual places, actual people who inhabit and settle places, and the way place has been raced and race has been placed through historically changing, politically motivated colonizing, which includes the scientific colonizing that race scientists engaged in. As Marxian theory (particularly base and superstructure) teaches us, his notion of place is too abstract. We need historical details to help us think carefully about place. Places have always been sites of conquest and colonization, of hierarchy, and after the seventeenth century a site of racing bodies, languages, customs, etc.

In more specific terms, Dobrin's notion of place does not account for the fact that during the Enlightenment period, groups of non-white or non-European people were associated to geography and places on the globe, many places Europeans had very little knowledge of, and those places and people were racialized and formed into hierarchies of bodies, creating racialized places from racialized spaces and racialized bodies. The spaces were racialized because that is how the science presented it. A particular tautology was born, racialized bodies defined racialized spaces that defined racialized places that defined racialized bodies. Thus today, all places are racialized places by default, and most important, contrary to Dobrin and Lefebvre, there is no such thing as a non-racial space. Every space and place is racialized in practice, even if we might say that in the abstract and theoretical, (racialized) bodies do not define (racialized) spaces. What is a non-racialized space? It is a white racialized space since conceptions of space are defined by white logics, rhetorics, and epistemologies, as my discussion of whiteness has already argued. The writing assessment ecologies we construct thus are always racialized because the spaces we use to cultivate such ecologies and the places we create in those ecologies are not only inhabited by racialized bodies, local diversities, but always already normed and raced by those bodies as well.

Historically then, the logic of spaces and who dwells in each are associated with hierarchies, inherent goodness and beauty, as well as virtue and perfection. The racing of spaces and places also affirms the discussions of remediation as inherently a racial and racist set of projects (e.g., Fox, 1999; Horner & Lu, 1999; Hull & Rose, 1989; Soliday, 2002; Stanley, 2009). But my discussion of place also suggests another reason for why all writing assessment ecologies that construct remedial places are racist, and why it's important to account fully for the places created by any assessment ecology.

Foucault (Foucault & Miskowiec, 1986) identifies two kinds of places in society, utopias and heterotopias. Utopias are unreal places, and it is the heterotopias that Foucault is most interested in because they are places defined by their relation to other sites, and are "outside of all places, even though it may be possible to indicate their location in reality" (Foucault & Miskowiec, 1986, p. 24). Every culture has these sites, and Foucault explains that earlier in Western culture, they were "crisis heterotopias," "privileged or sacred or forbidden places, reserved for individuals who are, in relation to society and to the human environment in which they live, in a state of crisis: adolescents, menstruating women, pregnant women, the elderly, etc." (1986, p. 24). These were sites of change, but were temporary. They were permeable borderlands, and the expectation was that everyone moved through them at some point in his or her life. Today, however, we are more likely to find "heterotopias of deviation, those in which individuals whose behavior is deviant in relation to the required mean or norm are placed" (Foucault & Miskowiec, 1986, p. 25). Foucault gives the example of rest homes, psychiatric hospitals, and prisons. These are less permeable places, and the typical assumption is that people avoid them. These borderlands are harder to leave or exit. They are on the fringe of society both geographically and figuratively. They are not the center of life or activity. It is not hard to read failure, all subaltern or code-meshed discourses, remediation, remedial classes, and the remedial student, as places of deviation, as heterotopias of deviation that are raced by their natures since all places are raced. Thus, like common notions of race as static (one doesn't change one's race in the middle of one's life) heterotopias of deviation can easily become, by racial association, static and fix in bodies that occupy that place.

In antiracist writing assessment ecologies, crisis heterotopias are promoted, rather than heterotopias of deviation. Our assessments of each other's words and ideas should lead to crises, big and small. This is the nature of problematizing existential writing assessment situations, a revealing of paradoxes in the judgments of writing. The purposes of places in such ecologies should be to move all students through crisis and change, not avoid such dynamism.

Finally, explicit discussions of the historical ways that places in an antiracist assessment ecology are sites of racing and norming is critical to the larger purpose of the ecology. The use of the concept of place has both an intellectual history involving conflict among locally diverse social formations, material histories of colonialism (as in the Orientalism and the global imaginary), and racialized histories that set value to geographic locations and have normed people to a white racial *habitus*. Places are raced, classed, and gendered, as much as they are hierarchized and defined by borderlands. I realize it is very difficult to know exactly how the creation of particular places in our writing assessment ecologies will play out in the short or long term, but one thing is certain. We can look to the way Western society and the academy have typically constructed places as centers of norming and racing, usually through assessment ecologies, and attempt to self-consciously create places that work as critical sites of problematizing the judgments made about our students' writing, and not simply as sites of colonizing.

CONCLUSION

The ecological power, parts, purposes, people, processes, products, and places that dialectically make up and are created in antiracist classroom writing assessment ecologies reveal the complexities of simply judging writing in a class without doing more harm to students who do not already come to the class demonstrating a white racial *habitus*. These elements offer ways to explicitly reflect upon a number of questions that help students understand the fuller conditions under which their writing is judged and produces other products (learning), which then provides them power to change those conditions and products. While not all of these ecological elements can be interrogated in any given class. My hope is that teachers and students figure out which elements offer them the most productive investigations into antiracist writing assessment practices. Since all elements inter-are with the others in the ecology, focusing on one or two can often lead to discussions of other elements.

Power is the overarching element within ecologies that is constructed by techniques, spaces, processes, and other disciplining tactics. Reflecting upon it and negotiating its terms, such as negotiating what control students have to design assignments, assessment processes, and expectations, students can determine better their own relations in the ecology. This provides agency and better chances to problematize their writing assessment situations, which will mean critiquing the dominant discourse and the white racial *habitus* that informs it.

Parts are the codes and artifacts, with their own internal biases, that are used to discipline bodies and writing, and to identify and judge. Parts, such as evaluation rubrics and dominant discourses valued in ideal texts, have historical associations with a white racial *habitus*, which usually end up privileging students who come to the classroom performing those dispositions already and disenfranchising local diversities. Parts are often the most immediate and easiest element to reflect upon and negotiate in an assessment ecology with students.

Purposes for any antiracist writing assessment ecology is vital to its functioning and should be discussed and negotiated carefully with students. A clear antiracist dominant purpose provides ways for students to understand and act in the ecology, to understand the fuller implications of their labor as an antiracist project. The dominant purpose I've offered for antiracist assessment ecologies is one that interrogates racism in writing assessment and judgment practices. It asks students to problematize their existential writing assessment situations over and over, posing problems about the way they and their colleagues judge their language, considering as part of the problems a comparison to their understandings of a white racial *habitus* that informs the dominant discourse promoted in the classroom.

People in antiracist writing assessment ecologies are not considered homogenous, nor are they simply stakeholder groups with uniform needs and wants. Like any geographic or urban environment, people in antiracist writing assessment ecologies who move about on the landscape are diverse in many ways, which affect their ways of reading and judging, and the entire system. Students can reflect upon their own subject positions as informed by historically shifting racial, cultural, and social formations that compel particular *habitus*, which they may be using to assess texts. Paying attention to who they are, without falling into the trap of *a priori* and essentializing assumptions about people, can help students problematize.

The processes that make up an antiracist assessment ecology are the actions and drama that occur, and are the means by which products come about. Like power, purposes, and parts, processes should be negotiated with students so that they have stake in them, understand them, and find them fair. Processes are the articulations and expectations of labor in the ecology, and can be focused on as the primary element of the ecology for any given assignment or task. Focusing on labor and processes can be criteria for success, grades, development, and work completed, which is often a good beginning for cultivating an antiracist writing assessment ecology.

Products are the decisions and consequences of the ecology, which may be direct or indirect, and may be different for each student. Products explain the learning that has or is occurring in the ecology, and can be a way to focus later reflections in the course. Products may also be turned back into the ecology as parts in order to change or improve the ecology.

Finally, the material and figurative places that make up antiracist writing assessment ecologies characterize and determine interactions, power relations, and the people who get to be there or not. Places also are the occasion and context for processes. Mostly, however, places are by their historical natures locations of norming to a white racial *habitus* and of racing people into hierarchies. Places, therefore, are themselves always informed by the historical racial projects that raced all places, which means that teachers and students must be aware of this fact and make decisions about it together so that their classroom ecology is not simply a place of colonizing, coercion, or uncritical, hegemonic control. Paying explicit attention—calling attention to—the places that the ecology creates, how it creates them, who seems to reside in those places, and why they do, can help antiracist writing assessment ecologies become more critical of their effects on students, and perhaps find alternative locations that are defined in alternative ways that are more responsive to students and their needs.

I offer Figure 1 as an initial way to visualize the interconnection of all seven elements. Place is primary with people situated firmly in place, and place constituted by people. Their most distinguishing feature is their consubstantiality. Processes, parts, and products are most connected to people, since they enact, create, and manipulate them, yet this means that they have a clear relationship with places of writing assessment. Finally power and purposes are connected to places and people of writing assessment ecologies, which produce processes, parts, and products. While this diagram is incomplete and does not show all of the relationships, no diagram can. Writing assessment ecologies are complex systems, resisting simple explanations and visual representations. Ecologies are more than visual. More than textual. They are more than this figure. The figure represents a small portion of the relationships of the seven interconnected elements of a writing assessment ecology.

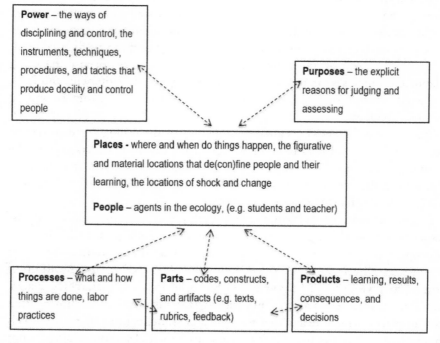

Figure 1. Seven interrelated elements constitute a writing assessment ecology.

CHAPTER 4: APPROACHING ANTIRACIST WORK IN AN ASSESSMENT ECOLOGY

In this chapter, I look closely at my own classroom's writing assessment ecology, which used a grading contract. My purpose is to make sense of what happened, to understand the class as a burgeoning antiracist writing assessment ecology. I did not design the course's writing assessment ecology to be antiracist, but believe in places it comes close. This chapter considers how my assessment ecology helped locally diverse students develop as readers and writers, and my discussion suggests ways for future pedagogical change that is inevitably personal and local. It offers useful ways to think through any writing assessment ecology in order to transform it into an antiracist one.

Up to this point, I've discussed racism in classrooms as larger, social patterns that we must understand and address in structural ways. But when a teacher steps into her classroom and people are present in all their diverse complexities, when students write and do all that they do, when our lives as teachers become tangled in the day-to-day workings of a course and academic life, racist patterns become less visible because life and people are messy and unpredictable. This is a part of Kerschbaum's (2014) point about understanding diversity's evolving character, best seen in relation to others. So this chapter is less about showing patterns, although some exist, and more about seeing the ecology. Doing so leads us to antiracist work. Let me be clear: An antiracist writing assessment ecology is a classroom that makes more visible the ecology since racist patterns are always less visible in real life.

In another place (Inoue, 2014a), I discuss how to use grading contracts in writing classrooms, highlighting three important themes or questions that guide students in my classrooms. These questions come up in this chapter, but I do not focus on them. In another study (Inoue, 2012a), I discuss the effectiveness of grading contracts on various racial formations in Fresno State's first-year writing program, finding that they do in fact have differential consequences on Fresno State's local Hmong, Latino/a, African-American, and white student formations. My past research shows that contracts that focus on labor as a way to calculate course grades helps most students of color and multilingual students perform well in writing classrooms. I theorize these findings in fuller detail for writing classrooms (Inoue, 2014b) by discussing the nature and distribution of failure based on quality and labor in writing courses. By focusing on labor as a way to assess for development and produce grades, the nature and distribution of failure, particularly course failure, changes. With these changes, the assessment ecology becomes more antiracist. I've also discussed the ways that past grading contract research, which is very limited, has neglected to account for racial formations by not seeing students as racialized bodies in the classroom, thus not parsing the data by racial formation or making conclusions that consider race as a factor (Inoue, 2012b). All of this past work informs my observations and conclusions in this chapter. I'm not trying to argue for grading contract ecologies; instead, I wish to illustrate how any teacher might understand his or her classroom writing assessment ecology as potentially antiracist. Because grades are so destructive to student learning in writing classrooms and grades produced by quality (comparisons to a dominant standard) are themselves racist, grading contracts are the best antiracist solution I've found.

What follows is a description of the course and its work. I discuss the central part (artifact) and conceptual place of the course, the grading contract, which used labor and assessing as a way to organize and conceptualize the course and responsibilities. I discuss the way students engaged in labor, since labor was the primarily way in which course grades were determined, and the main way students constructed their own places in the assessment ecology. I then look closely at the assessment practices of students in order to show the main pathways of learning in the class that our writing assessment ecology produced. Finally, I end by considering students' exit from the assessment ecology. Throughout, I draw on students' writing and reflecting in the course, as well as my notes from that semester. All students gave me written permission to use their work, and were shown the chapter before publication. I use students' real first names, unless they asked me to use a pseudonym, which I note.

ENGLISH 160W

In Fall 2012, I taught Engl 160W, an upper division writing intensive course at Fresno State, intended for third and fourth year undergraduates to fulfill their upper division writing intensive requirement. Most students who enroll in this particular course are not English majors. For instance, in Fall of 2012, there were seven fourth year (four females, three males) and 16 third year students (nine females, seven males) in the class. The 11 majors represented in the course were as follows:

- Psychology (4)
- Business (9)
- Business- accountancy (2)

- Viticulture (1)
- Communication (1)
- Political Science (1)
- Computer Science (1)
- Criminology (1)
- Health Science- Occupational Health (1)
- Communication Disorders- Deaf Education (1)
- Chemistry (1)

Because I asked students to introduce themselves as readers and writers in a number of ways in the first few weeks of class (in writing, in group work, on Blackboard, etc.), and because I introduced myself as a product of racial projects in my own school history, as a former remedial reading student in schools who attended public schools in North Las Vegas (a mostly African-American "ghetto" at the time) and who was always the only brown kid in class in college, they felt more authorized to bring up their own racialized experiences and *habitus*. I did not explicitly ask them to do this though. I learned the racial and cultural makeup of the class, as well as other aspects of their material lives that had import on their work in our course. As you'll see below, the course in some ways encouraged students to talk about, draw on, and consider their own histories and material conditions that affected their work in the course. While I realize this can be a delicate set of discussions, some being more uncomfortable with talking about things like race than others, I tried hard to give students options. They did not have to reveal anything about their past or their own sense of racial, class, or gendered identities, but everyone did.

I contextualized the sharing of this personal information early and throughout the course by explaining how racial, gender, cultural, and other personal factors can influence the ways we read each other's work and judge it, so while they do not dictate how anyone will read or value another's writing, our racial, cultural, economic, and linguistic heritages inform our reading and writing and may offer reflective insights into how we value language. While I didn't use the term, the point I tried to convey was that our racial *habitus* does matter to us and to those whom we offer judgments. Just because we identify ourselves as African-American, White, or Hmong, or from a poor family, doesn't mean we are prejudice, it simply means we have important histories and experiences that bias us in necessary ways, which writers should know and readers might use to help explain why they value certain things in texts. I asked them to consider reading as an inherently biased activity, one requiring bias in order to make sense of things, thus it is good to know explicitly the biases that make up how we read, even if only personally.

The students in this course were close to the larger Fresno State student population's racial makeup. Our course's ethnic breakdown looked like this, which amounts to four racial formations:

- Latino/a, Mexican America (7)
- White (7)
- African-American (3)
- Asian-American: Hmong (2); Chinese (2); Southeast Asian Indian (1); Laotian (1)

As you may recall, Fresno State is classified as an Hispanic Serving Institution (HSI), because it has a total enrollment of at least 25% Hispanic students. In Fall 2012, 38.8% of all students enrolled where Hispanic, 28.8% were White, 14.8% were Asian (mostly Hmong), 4.4% were African-American, 3.0% were International, and 0.4% were American Indian (CSU, Fresno, n.d.).[39] Thus the racial formations that made up the class was mostly consistent with students at Fresno State that semester; however, the class's African-American formation was out of balance with the larger percentage at the university. This was simply luck or happenchance, since in the last six or so years prior to the class, I had never had three African-Americans in the same course.

I designed the course according to the department's description of it in the catalogue, as a project-based course in which each student writes two research projects, each based on some question in her major or discipline. When I put students in their writing groups around week 4, which they choose to keep for the entire semester, I tried to shuffle the groups as best I could so that they contained different majors, were racially and linguistically diverse, and had a roughly equal number of males and females, which didn't always work, given that a few students moved in and out of the course in the first few weeks. The groups were between four and five students each. Most of their work on their projects occurred in the groups, so the writing groups made up much of the class's day to day work. For some students, the groups also ended up characterizing the class, and to some extent the grading contract, which I'll discuss below. Most important, in several ways that will become clear later, the writing groups were one primary ecological place initiated by me, but created, cultivated, and settled (colonized) by students over the course of the semester, and the place of their writing groups tended to determine a number of processes, use of parts, purposes for assessing, and even products.

The course was organized around formal labors, or processes of assessment that overlapped and connected to each other, scaffolding student work toward two culminating documents, their projects' final documents. Our course consisted of several reoccurring activities. I am not calling them assignments since the philosophy and language of the course was that of labor, not products. "Assignments" seems too close to product-oriented writing assessment ecologies. However, I will admit that in the class, we did refer to "assignments" as much as we did activities, processes, or labor. It made things clearer for many students. It can be confusing to never talk explicitly about "assignments," when in one sense we did have them. I would characterize this aspect of the course as being focused on writing assessment processes that have ideal parts (artifacts) in mind as their goals, but a student's successful completion of those processes was not contingent on submitting an ideal artifact. Instead, the nature of "ideal" for our class in any given activity's artifact tended to be defined in terms of time spent on the activity, length of the document, and whether the writing addressed the prompt or instructions in the spirit that the work was given (did the document accomplish its purposes?). So in some senses, we did care about the nature of the writing that students produced. We cared about quality all the time in discussions and feedback, but we did not use quality to determine credit for or a grade on an assignment, nor did we use it to determine if someone met some standard of our local SEAE or a dominant discourse of the classroom. The labor we did was the following:

- *Reading.* These activities occurred between class sessions. Every act of reading produced an artifact (part): some postings on Blackboard (Bb), a list of items, a freewrite/quickwrite done during or after the reading, a focused paragraph response or summary as one read a text, or an annotated passage or page from the reading. Each activity and its artifact had explicit purposes that connected that labor to students' projects. I asked students often to consider where they did their reading and why they did it there, particularly in labor journals (see below), which helped them be conscious of the places that their reading labors were most productive or intense. I also asked students to consider all reading as a kind of assessment, a set of judgments they make about a text in order to make some sense or meaning out of it. Reading was assessment because it was a set of judgments for some purpose (i.e., to understand, to summarize, to find particular information, to make other judgments, etc.). We defined these activities, like all of the activities, in terms of the time spent on the activity and the kind of labor we expected to engage in. Instructions looked and sounded like process directions, or procedures with a description of the artifacts expected to be used in class.

- *Writing.* These activities happen at home and in class. I wanted the places of writing to be varied, since the places of assessment would be. Students produced artifacts that were used in class, in groups, or to begin discussions. Depending on what we agreed upon, or where we were in the semester, our writing activities invented, researched, thought about, drafted, and revised their two projects. In most cases, I couched these shorter writing assignments as ones fundamentally asking students to assess and make judgments for some purpose. We decided together on parameters of these labors, and most of those directions were cues for timing (how much time to spend) and what to do in each stage of laboring (how to do the labor or how the labor should be focused). For the projects, we also conducted more formal rubric building activities (discussed below). Again, the prompts and instructions looked a lot like procedures. On average, we did one activity a week, taking a few hours to do, stretched over a few days.

- *Reflecting*. These were reading and writing activities done each week-end and discussed in the Monday session of the following week. Students read excerpts from their reflections that I chose, and the class sometimes discussed them, but usually we just listened. I wanted students to hear the good thinking and questioning happening in the class, and I wanted the classroom to be a place where their ideas and theorizing about writing and reading were center stage, were import-ant, public, and explicit. I wanted to value all the writing in the class, so I made a point to keep track of who had read their reflections each week, with the goal of getting every student to read at some point. At times, students responded to a prompt that asked them to do some metacognitive thinking (e.g., "What did you learn about 'entering academic conversations' from your group this week? How did it come to you? What rhetorical patterns did you find occurring in the most effective written feedback you received?"). At other times, they were free to reflect on anything that was on their minds (and that pertained to our class). This reflective labor was defined most explicitly as self-assessment and assessing the activities of the class for lessons learned or questions revealed. The prompts for each weekly reflection activity was similar in nature as all the other activities. I defined each reflection activity by the amount of time students should spend reading and reflecting in writing, usually 20-30 minutes, then asked them to spend another 10-20 minutes reading other students' postings. Finally, they replied to at least three others with something substantive and mean-ingful.
- *Labor Journaling*. In class each day, we spent five minutes freewriting

a journal entry about the labor for our course that we did just before that class session. The labor journals attempted to help students see and quantify exactly the labor they were doing for the course. Their entries were designed to help them determine whether the labor they were doing was enough and what its nature was (What were they doing when they were most engaged? What did that labor produce for them? How engaging or intense was it?). In my prompts, I tried to push them each week a bit more, little by little, to develop their labor habits into more intense, effective, and productive behaviors. Again, like their weekly reflections, labor journals were self-assessment activities, only focused on the nature and intensity of their labor. More recently, I've incorporated Twitter as a way to capture some of my students' labor practices during the week as it occurs, which I discussed in Chapter 3. In class we spend a few minutes looking over those tweets in order to write their journal entry for that day. Students can also tweet back to others in the class, as I sometimes do, if they so choose.[40]

- *Assessing.* If it's not clear already, assessing in a number of ways is the center of the course, the central activity. It was the way I articulated most activities and all reading and writing activities. At its center, assessing is about reading and making judgments on artifacts from frameworks of value and expectations for particular purposes. At around week six, the writing groups moved into full swing. Each week students did the reading and writing labors (above) that worked toward their projects (below). The assessing activities directed students through processes that asked them to read artifacts and articulate judgments in a variety of ways on those artifacts. To guide assessing labors, there were two sets of collaboratively created expectations or rubrics: a set of project expectations (what they should demonstrate in a final draft of the project) and labor expectations (what they should demonstrate in their labors in and out of class to produce the project), which I discuss below.[41] On average, I asked students to spend at least 20-45 minutes on each assessment activity (including the reading time) for each artifact being assessed (some drafts varied greatly in length). Near the end of the semester, students also wrote assessment letters to their group members, which their colleagues and I used in final one-on-one conferences, which I discuss later in this chapter. Instructions for assessments were similar to all other activities. I gave directions on how much time to spend on the reading of peers' drafts, and the writing of the associated assessment documents. Additionally, I provided general guidelines for what we expected students to produce in those assessment documents, but at a midpoint, students helped decide this aspect of their assessing as well.

- *Projecting*. These labors were the culmination of all their work in the course (everything above). All the scaffolded activities led to two research-based, written inquiries on subjects in the students' major or discipline that dealt with some aspect of rhetoric. Usually the projects were traditional looking research papers, but one student did a report, while another student did a brochure. Another student attempted a video, but realized midway through how much more labor that required, so she changed to a traditional research essay. All projecting required the same amount of research and writing, which amounted to all the activities above—all labors fed into the projects' final documents, which tended to be multimodal constructions, using videos and images. Some produced six to eight page research papers, while a few produced 12-15 page research papers. In this grading ecology, all labor in the class was a student's project*ing* of her chosen research topic/question; her learning about writing and the question; her understanding and articulating of ideas, texts, and writing processes; her enacting of her own learning journey to exactly the place that she can achieve. My only limitations on the writing and research was that writers had to have an academic audience in mind, deal with rhetoric in some way, and use academic sources to help them engage with their projects.

LABOR AND THE GRADING CONTRACT ECOLOGY

Engaging explicitly and self-consciously in discussions about the course's writing assessment ecology makes the ecology itself visible to students and is vital to antiracist work. We began this work by engaging in discussions of our grading contract as a part that articulates how course grades will be produced. These discussions were on-going and led to negotiations about the conditions and expectations of their labor, the codes we used to determine acceptable labor and behaviors. Reflecting and discussing our contract was the most obvious ecological place to start since I knew that most students would care about their course grades and would have some investment in determining them.

The scholarship on grading is almost unanimous about the unreliability or inconsistency and subjectivity (in the bad sense of being too idiosyncratic) of grades (Bowman, 1973; Charnley, 1978; Dulek & Shelby, 1981; Elbow, 1997; Tchudi, 1997; Starch & Elliott, 1912), and just as much research shows how grades and other kinds of rewards and punishments de-motivate and harm students and their abilities to learn anything (Elbow, 1999; Kohn, 1993; Pulfrey,

Buchs, & Butera, 2011). Thus grades as the primary ecological products of writing assessment ecologies often work against issues of language diversity and difference (e.g., class, gender, race, religious view, sexual orientation, ability, etc.), reinforce a norming to a white racial *habitus*, and the racing of academic places. For instance, conventional grading systems often construct a student's text as a place of norming to a white racial *habitus*. Grading uses a dominant standard, seen in rubrics and assignment expectations, to produce a grade for a writing performance. This creates the student text as a place, not of problematizing the judgment of language practices (both the dominant and the student's), but one of colonizing the student to a dominant set of dispositions, which are indirectly seen through textual markers. This is more the case with multilingual students and students of color, although white working class students surely feel colonized as well. In short, grading students' writing on its quality is a racist practice, despite the fact that it is arguably important for students to learn (about) dominant discourses.

But knowing how well one is doing in a class is important. One central grading problem that is revealed when one sees one's class as an antiracist writing assessment ecology is this: *when we value quality, particularly by assigning grades by using judgments of quality, we have no control over the valuing labor or processes; yet when we value labor and processes, we have an equally hard time valuing quality (as compared to a dominant discourse) as an outcome or artifact.*

However, if we can value labor and processes that have collaboratively defined ideal artifacts (parts) in mind, dictated by agreements that students and teacher make together that maintain and interrogate the difference inherent in the local diversity of the classroom (i.e., keep difference present), and keep grades out of the ecology, then it is possible to create productive antiracist borderlands in the course's writing assessment ecology because the parts can reflect the local diversity of language use while not penalizing students through ecological products like grades. These borderlands offer students landscapes to problematize their existential writing assessment situations, revealing how their language is judged and perhaps why.

I used a grading contract in this course similar to Danielewicz and Elbow's (2009) in order to consciously value labor, processes, particular purposes for assessing the documents produced by those processes, and products. The grading contract was ideal since it almost always requires lots of discussion for students to understand it, and reveals the assumptions students and teachers make about grades. But I also incorporated the good use of democratic negotiation that Shor (2007) emphasizes in his contracts. Unlike both Danielewicz and Elbow, and Shor, I started the conversation of grading and course grades with the idea of labor. The idea of writing as labor, while intuitive at some level, is not intuitive for many students when it is used to determine their course grades, or when helping them understand how well they are doing on a task or generally in the course. As Elbow (1997, 1999) has discussed in a similar way, most students are thoroughly conditioned to thinking in terms of documents, page counts, and grades rather than in terms of labor, quantity, time, and how to do an activity.

The grading contract (see Appendix A) was emailed to students a few weeks before the semester began, and was discussed on the first day of class. After the first day's introduction to the contract, I asked students to go home, read carefully the contract again, and mark it with questions they had and things they would like to negotiate or change. We discussed and negotiated the contract again on the second day of class, a Wednesday (the course met Monday and Wednesday at 4:00 P.M. for 80 minutes each day). After Wednesday's discussion, I asked them to reflect upon the contract and our negotiations, since I knew many at this early stage would have a hard time questioning the contract—and they did—but might open up when writing to their colleagues and themselves (this was an in-class freewrite).

While there was, as usual, very little that changed in the contract, the discussions helped reveal three important questions that organized the course's writing assessment ecology as a semester-long historic bloc. These questions came from my students' writing, which I rearticulated to them in class since I had anticipated the questions, and in fact encouraged them through my prompting of their reflective writing. The questions were:

- What does labor mean in our writing class?
- How do we know how well we are doing if there are no grades?
- What does assessing mean in our class?[42]

It may seem odd that students inquired about the nature of their labor unless you take into account my prompting them in a number of ways. The grading contract is defined by the concept of labor, and I made a point to read and discuss this aspect of the course's grading contract on the first day. Additionally, one of the course's weekly assignments is a labor journal, in which I prompted them one to two times a week to write about what they experienced when they did the physical labor of the course that week, we discussed this as well on the first day. If labor is important to students' course grades, I argued, then we needed some way to see it, understand it, and reflect upon it—in effect, we each needed to evaluate it, only not for a grade or accountability, but in order to find ways to improve our own labor, making it more intense, productive, or effective. The contract also explains the grading of the course in terms of student labor and trust, stating on its first page:

> This contract is based on a simple principle and a few import-

ant assumptions, which are not typical in most classrooms. First, the principle: how much *labor* you do is more important to your learning and growth as a reader and writer than the quality of your writing. Our grading contract calculates grades by how much *labor* you do and the manner in which you do it. The more you work, the better your grade—no matter what folks think of the product of your labor—but we assume that you'll be striving in your labors to improve, learn, and take risks. The other important assumption that this principle depends upon for success is that we must assume that all students will try their hardest, work their hardest, and not deceive anyone, when it comes to their labor. If we ask for an hour of writing at home, and someone says they did that and produced X, then we must believe them. This is a culture of trust. We must trust one another, and know that deception and lying hurts mostly the liar and his/her learning and growth.

Thus not only did I prompt them about labor in their writing and discussions, but I also planted the seeds of thinking about the course's assessment ecology in terms of their labor in the contract. Because the contract is the main articulation of how course grades are determined, it is central to the writing assessment ecology. It is the most important ecological part, which in other ways is an ecological place, a site of negotiation and orientation. In a sense, the contract was a place of norming, only not to a local dominant discourse or a local SEAE, or a white racial *habitus*, but to a negotiated set of practices and discourses about assessment and labor.

This norming in the place of the contract was not a one-way, hierarchical norming, but was a norming that students negotiated and had more control over than in typical academic places of norming and racing. In class discussions, I began by asking them: what responsibility do you have to your colleagues in our class and in your writing groups? What responsibilities do you expect of your colleagues around you? How does that responsibility translate into your own behaviors and labor in this class? What happens when someone doesn't meet his or her responsibilities to others in the class? These discussions, because they implicitly built a rationale for our writing assessment ecology, especially the places of writing groups, which originates in the ecological part and place of the contract, were crucial to my students' acceptance of the grading contract and to their abilities to do the labor required.

So, the grading contract and our discussions in the first week of the course dictated that the writing, reading, and other work of the course was conceived of as labor, as activities, as processes, as doing things. We'd care most about the quantity of our labor, but increasingly about the nature of one's labor (more on this below). If a student met the contract's labor guidelines, she would earn a "B" course grade, no matter what. On the last page, the contract provides a table that sets out clearly the labor needed for each course grade and how we would tabulate that labor:

Table 3. The grading contract calculated course grades by the amount of labor students produced

	Absences	Late Assigns.	Missed Assigns.	Ignored Assigns.
A	4 or less	5	0	0
B	4 or less	5	0	0
C	5	6	1	0
D	6	7	2	1
F	7	8 or more	2	2 or more

Note that the assumption in my bookkeeping is that all students are doing the work appropriately and adequately. My assumption was, and I said this to the class, everyone will do the work, or is doing the work, to earn a "B." It is only when someone doesn't turn something in, or turns in something incomplete, that a mark in my grade book is recorded. Items #4, #5, and #6 in the contract explain the differences between a late, missed, and ignored assignment.[43] In essence, the main differences lie in how much time goes by before the assignment is turned in. In addition to the above table, the contract stipulates a "plea" or a "gimme," which amounts to a get-out-of-jail-free card. A student can use one plea at any time in the course to erase an absence, a late assignment, a missed (which becomes a late) assignment, etc.

Note that there is no difference between an "A" and a "B" course grade on this grid. This is because in this course, the number or quantity of assignments for students striving for "As" was technically the same as those who were okay with a "B," but if a student wanted an "A," then her two projects would have to be twice the length and depth as her peers shooting for a "B." This roughly amounted to 10 academic sources researched and incorporated into each project's final document and that document needed to be around 10-12 pages in length.

Negotiating the grading contract moved students away from focusing on grades, and refocused their attention on their labors, in particular on the processes of reading, writing, and assessing their own and others' drafts. My hope was that focusing on the processes of writing assessment in the course, processes

I was largely absent from (except in their design), would also reorient students to other kinds of purposes for their writing and emphasize other ecological products. Thus the assessment of writing framed the course at large through the contract, the writing group's primary activities, and the projects' activities. This re-orienting to new processes of assessment, assessment products, and purposes for writing and its assessment did seem to occur, and I consider it important to any antiracist writing assessment ecology.

Reorientation in the environment can be productive, unproductive, helpful, ambiguous, or harmful to students, but I argue that some kind of reorientation always occurs. And it affects the culture of the classroom and students' learning. In the next section, I discuss the way students oriented themselves in our writing assessment ecology, particularly through the renegotiation of the contract at the midpoint of the semester. The absence of grades and refocus on labor was central to this reorientation.

Most students reoriented themselves in the ecology by rethinking the nature of their labor, not the perceived quality of their texts. The labors of the ecology, of writing and reading (judging), are fundamentally ontological acts that connect us to places in the ecology, as well as to other people. It is through our labors that we experience inter-being, which help us negotiate the problematizing in the borderlands of the ecology—in fact, one critical labor is problem posing. Robert Yagelski (2011) offers a good way to understand the labors of writing as a way of (inter)being by describing his own act of writing:

> As I write, I *am*—but not *because* of the writing; rather, the
> writing intensifies my awareness of myself, my sense of being,
> which is prior to but, right now, coterminous with this act
> of writing. And if I attend to my awareness—if I become
> aware of that awareness, as it were; if I focus my attention
> on my attention during this act of writing, as I am doing
> right now—it is not my sense of self as a separate, thinking
> being that is intensified but my sense of self as existing in this
> moment and at the same time "inhabiting" the physical place
> where I am sitting as well as the scene in the coffee shop that
> I am imagining and trying to describe, a scene removed from
> me in time and space at *this* moment; thus, I am connected
> to this moment and those other moments I have been trying
> to describe and indeed to all those other selves I've mentioned
> and many I have not mentioned and the things around me
> now and those that were around me then and even you, the
> reader I am imagining who will, I think, at some point, really

> *be* a reader of this text and thus be connected to me as well
> in a very real way through your act of reading at some future
> date, which means that this moment of writing right now
> somehow encompasses that future moment, too.

> It is in this sense that I *am* as I am writing. The *writing* does
> not create me, but in the *act* of writing I *am*; by writing I
> reaffirm and proclaim my being in the here and now. The act
> of writing, in this sense, is a way of being; it is an ontological
> act. (p. 104)

I wish I could say that I showed my class this passage when dscussing what labor means in our class, but I didn't. What I hope you can hear or see in Yagelski's rendering of the act of writing as a way of (inter)being in the world is that place is vital to a writer's or reader's inter-being. Place is vital to the ontological meaning of the labors we do in the class. I wanted students to see that the labor of writing, for instance, is the only access we have to writing. And if our goals are in some way to write more self-consciously, more critically, more problematically—to do *more than* write right now—then we must have access to ourselves as writers in the act of writing, and we must see the places in which those labors are done as part of that access, part of the labors of writing and judging. Thus is the nature of the inter-being of labor and place, of writing and one's acts of being that inter-are with where we write and who we write for.

And why is the notion of labor as processes of inter-being important to an antiracist writing assessment ecology? Because it allows locally diverse students and teacher to share in the ontological essence of others' writing, no matter how different that writing is from our own writing or from our expectations of it. It allows us to access place as part of the labor of writing and its judgment. It allows us to realize that no matter who you are, another reader, a very different person, can inter-be with you, and in fact, must inter-be with you, which provides grounds for compassionate problematizing, posing tough questions that come from a place of shared essence. It helps us feel as we judge. This inter-being of place, people, and their labors connects us in tangible ways through our labor, our work, our doing of things, through our bodies, not just our minds. Other's writing and its success and failure, then are our own successes and failures. When students share in the ontological essence of locally diverse writing, they have a good chance at confronting difference from a white racial *habitus* and posing problems about the nature of judgment to each other.

Still, you may be wondering why "labor" as the central metaphor for our grading contract and the classroom writing assessment ecology? Why not "work" or "process"? The idea of labor as valuable isn't that strange for most students.

U.S. culture rewards labor by paying for it by the hour, and the paradigm of mandatory labor hours and overtime hours are familiar to Fresno State students, most of whom work in labor economies. At some point, I wanted them to question these paradigms, question the idea that the rewards we get out of our labors correlate positively to the time and effort we put into them, that learning is a linear equation, that more time spent on writing can always be apparent in the development and quality of drafts, or even writers. I do not think this is entirely true, but it is not entirely false, and it is more true than false. So for the assessment ecology's purposes, it was safe to say that writing well and producing effective documents takes effort and time. Thus the dominant purpose of the ecology was not to produce grades as ecological products. It was to produce labor, which is another way of saying to produce sustainable places, which by their nature in this ecology would become borderlands of problematizing, antiracist places to inhabit.

I should note that in retrospect I see a problem with defining and discussing the contract's calculus for course grades purely in terms of the labor in capitalist market economies. While students get this metaphor easily, and usually agree with it philosophically, as a scholar of Marxian stripes, I can see how my contract may look like some version of exploitation, in which a ruling class (the teacher) expects a certain amount of labor for a lower price (course grade) than what might reasonably be expected from a subordinate class (students). The power dynamics work in the teacher's favor, labor's price is set by the teacher. There is no equal exchange or true negotiation, despite the fact that most (if not all) writing teachers do not wish to exploit their students.

Exploitation, though, is subjective. What I see as fair, my students may see as unfair and exploitative. Two white female students, Susan, a middle-aged women returning to school, majoring in business-accountancy, and Jane, a former Minnesotan in her early twenties, majoring in business, voiced this concern, discussing it as fairness and too much work. Both were traditionally, high performers in classes, and both came into the course writing the local SEAE quite well. They each embodied well a white racial *habitus* in their writing and reading dispositions.

As I've discussed in another place (Inoue, 2012a), students from white racial formations at Fresno State often have difficulty with the contract because they no longer automatically sit at the top of the grading pyramid in the class. The labors that required an "A" grade before are now insufficient, or seem so initially. Additionally, these students often feel it unfair that now "As" are more available to more students in the class (Inoue, 2012a, p. 92). Their "A's" mean less.[44] These findings from Fresno State's first-year writing courses also align with other research on white student reactions to grading contracts (Spidell & Thelin, 2006).[45] Susan's and Jane's concerns, along with a few other students, were important to our mid-point re-negotiations of the contract, and important to enacting more equitable power arrangements in the writing assessment ecology of the course by encouraging difference and conflict, and providing a method for the exercising of their own agency and power in determining their course grades. So when such resistances came up, even if they were the minority opinions, I made sure they were heard and discussed.

I'm not sure this alleviated the sense that the contract was not an exploitative one. I am sure that conventional teacher-student power relations are unavoidable, and so regardless of how I presented things or offered ways to negotiate the contract, it may still have ended up feeling to some as an exploitative contract, because some students may have felt coerced into agreeing with the contract and not voicing their real concerns. But even in conventionally graded classrooms, students are automatically placed in less powerful positions and more likely to be exploited. They get no say in grading. Students frequently mentioned in reflections how helpful and rewarding it was to construct or negotiate the course's terms. And as I show in the next section, monolingual Latina and white students in the class had uniformly positive orientations toward the grading contract ecology. The theme of labor was important to the sense of fairness in these orientations.

Allowing my students to negotiate the terms of the contract in weeks 1 and 10 (we have a 16 week semester) was my attempt to negotiate a "fair price" for their labor in the course. I reasoned that after a significant portion of the class had gone by, after students had experienced the contract in good faith, they would be more comfortable and inclined to negotiate the contract or make a judgment on its fairness at that point. And so, my students were given multiple opportunities to be involved in the setting of the terms of their labor through the contract as an ecological part, an artifact that represented what labor meant and what its consequences were in our ecology. In week 10, we did make an important change to the contract. The original contract allowed for three or fewer late assignments in order to meet the contract's guidelines for a "B" course grade, but after discussions, the class agreed to five or fewer late assignments, with the caveat listed below the breakdown table (see the contract in Appendix A). The caveat attempted to reward in some fashion the significant number of students (the vast majority of the class) who were still meeting the original contract guidelines and expected to meet them by semester's end. In fact, when all was said and done, 16 out of 23 met the original contract's guidelines for a "B" grade.

But philosophically, there is still tension with the economic metaphor of labor. There is something about using grades as the unit of exchange in an assessment ecology that doesn't do justice to what we usually attempt to accomplish in a writing classroom. If students accepted this as the main way our contract worked (and I cannot say with certainty they did not), then one might say the contract created an ecology in which students were somewhat alienated from the ecological products of their labor, that is, alienated from learning, alienated from the reading and writing practices they were expected to improve. Students would be focused on grades as products, not attaining better writing or reading practices, not laboring with increased awareness of that labor's intensity or productivity (i.e., its ability to generate future learning products). But one can also make this same criticism of any conventional grading ecology because in both cases, it's not the focus on labor that is the problem, it is the focus on grades that alienates students from the real products of their labor. The surrogate product of grades substitutes a student's purposes, swapping out the goal of laboring to learn (about their writing and reading practices) for laboring to earn (a grade). I asked my students to labor to learn, not labor to earn, but it was up to them to accept.

Labor is also traditionally the productive activity that results in a child. To be in labor is to be giving birth, to be generating, to be creating. Creating and generating is at the heart of all writing classrooms. And when we create things, difference and originality are most valued, even expected or assumed. No two babies are alike, and no one would ever say they were. Even with identical twins (I am an identical twin), people look for differences as often as they look for similarities. Difference is valued and assumed. Thus, labor in childbirth suggests to me the unknown or unexpected consequences of our energies because that labor is associated with creativity, originality, difference, and the unexpected, all of which are embraced as the norm.

Similarly in the writing classroom, we ask our students to generate readings of texts, to form arguments, to create feedback for colleagues, to create texts of all sorts. Usually, these creations, like babies, take on a life of their own when they are distributed and read by others. There is no better way to see this than in a writing group in which readers interpret or judge a text (a peer's or a published one). Each reader sees or argues for something different, sees different things in the text. These readings are the life that comes from the original text, whose author may not have intended at all those discussions, yet there they are. A focus on labor in the ecology, as a painful, generative, exciting, and unknown activity, keeps students from thinking in terms of grades and simple, less-useful rewards, and moves them to embracing and problematizing difference in language use. This alone makes grading by labor an antiracist assessment practice.

While he doesn't use the metaphor of childbirth or labor, Alfie Kohn (1993) makes a supportive argument against grades and other hierarchical rewards in education, work, and parenting. In fact, citing educational research and research in behavioral psychology, Kohn finds that students learn more when they are asked to reflect and self-assess on their work but aren't graded (Brophy & Kher,

1986, p. 264; as quoted in Kohn, 1999, p. 156). Furthermore, Kohn explains that students who are "led to think mostly about how well they are doing—or even worse, how well they are doing compared to everyone else—are less likely to do well" (1999, p. 156). Using the metaphor of labor, particularly the labor of assessment (reading and judging), makes more visible several elements of the ecology: the processes of reading and assessing; the places created in the ecology that connect, norm, shock, and change people; and the people around us who labor together and whom we are always trying to connect to because we already feel our latent inter-being, or to use Burke, we try through our rhetoric to identify with others (1969, p. 55).

I'm not saying that we can escape giving course grades (I didn't in this class), but I am saying we can pay attention to the power and influence that grades have over our students, and ask our students also to pay attention in order to explicitly form critical stances against grades. This work begins with revealing the ecology as structured by grading and assessment. I tried to cultivate places in our conversations in which I inserted this problem, which is central to the second question students developed in their initial thinking on the grading contract ("how do we know how well we are doing if there are no grades?"). The assessment ecology we created did focus most students' attentions on their labor, thus implicating it in their purposes and in the dominant purpose I articulated in the contract's language (to write and assess for its own sake). I would also argue that this refocusing of purposes changes the nature of any products students can get out of a classroom writing assessment ecology. The best way to see how students were able to explicitly form critical stances against grades, and perhaps problematize the judgment of their own language practices, is to look closer at our contract renegotiation processes during week 10.

STUDENT ORIENTATIONS IN THE WRITING ASSESSMENT ECOLOGY

To say that most students changed their orientations toward their labor in the classroom writing assessment ecology from laboring to earn grades (a conventional purpose) to laboring to learn about the ways their language is judged is a significant claim. I argue that it happened uniformly, and we can see perhaps how it occurred by seeing the way various ecological elements intersected for students. It is in the intersections of various elements where the products of our assessment ecologies become clearest. These intersections are the places in the ecology that show the inter-being of elements.

The renegotiation of our contract in week 10 perhaps best illustrates the dramas in the ecology that revealed students' evolving ecological purposes and products. This significant moment in the semester when we consciously looked at and altered the most important ecological part of our assessment ecology, appears to suggest that most students did have productive purposes that came from the dominant one I offered (i.e., laboring to learn). However, these orientations to the writing assessment ecology also had patterns. They tended to congeal by racial-linguistic formations, mostly defined by their monolingual or multilingual statuses. But as I'll show later in their assessing of each other's drafts and the reflections on those labors and activities, these patterns didn't always hold up.

The monolingual students in the course usually experienced the contract positively and in unambiguous terms, however, several, particularly the white students, did mention grades as an ecological product they were striving for. Jane (a white student, mentioned above), for instance, says, "[t]he grading contract is something I was unsure of at first as well, but I actually love it. I love knowing exactly what I need to do in order to get the grade I want, no questions asked. It is a little stressful at times, but I would take our grading contract over the typical grading any day."[46] While she doesn't go into detail, she is unambiguous about the fact that the contract works for her, and this was clear in her enthusiasm and hard work in the course, particularly in her writing and class discussions. It would seem that Jane cared most about the grade, since that is where her reflection appears to be focused, but in the fuller reflection, this statement is surrounded by a discussion of her appreciation for her group discussions and the ways those processes worked well for her learning. Still, Jane suggests a somewhat dual orientation in the writing assessment ecology, one that has one eye on the learning she gets in the ecological place of her group and one eye on what she has to do in order to get the product (grade) she wants.

Zach, a white student majoring in viticulture, a first-generation student from a farming family near the central coast, on the other hand, reflects in more detail:

> First I want to say that I greatly respect and enjoy the contract because it provides me the ability to always do my best and makes me want to better my writing. Also it gives me the opportunity to write what I want to write and not feel as if it's going to be compared to everyone else's work, instead I get to discover my own capabilities and be completely unique in the way I put my ideas on paper. Lastly the greatest part of the contract is the idea of our labor being taken [in]to consideration, I have taken many English classes in my life and in most I know for a fact I have worked harder than some of my colleagues and yet be graded lower than them which has always discouraged me as a writer, but in this class It's finally

being recognized that if I work hard I still can be successful regardless if my writing is not considered the best in class. To be completely honest I really don't have any negative thoughts about the contract because none of the work in this class has made me feel as if it's unfair or I'm not capable of meeting the expectations. I do work very hard in this class, but my hard work is being recognized so there are no complaints from me.

Zach describes his past writing experiences as ones that did not reward or value his labor, his hard work. And Zach is not exaggerating about his hard work, something he likely learned working on his family's farm, which we discussed several times during the semester. This aspect of his labor, seen through each activity and assignment from the very first day, was characteristic of him as a student. He worked long and hard, producing copious amounts of text, and followed the directions for each assignment to the letter. So it makes sense that he'd find value in the way the contract focuses on labor and work, not on a teacher's judgment of the results of that work, or on "compar[ing his work] to everyone else's work." And for Zach, this allows him to turn his writing labors into learning products—that is, the contract "provides [him] the ability to always do [his] best and makes [him] want to better [his] writing." The emphasis in Zach's orientation in our assessment ecology is on the contract as a part, as an articulation ("the part of the contract I like most") of labor that defines the codes for success in the class. In effect, Zach focuses on labor and our processes of reading, writing, and assessing, which the contract asks the class to value first. Additionally, the absence of grades as one product and the presence of his labor as valued processes created for Zach a fair system. This is different from Jane's sense of fairness. Hers is more oriented toward a grade-product she wants and can clearly see how to attain.

Amanda, a Latina majoring in business-accountancy, discusses in a typical way for the class the grading contract in week 10's reflection posting:

My first initial response to the syllabus was, "shit, that's a lot of writing" and we've actually done a lot more writing than what the syllabus stated but the writing has come, surprisingly, fairly easy to me. I really do like the grading contract. It's fair enough and I like the degree of freedom given to us because of it. We don't have to be worried about being judged on quality so we can get away with stepping outside our boundaries.

Many other students commented similarly on the workload that the syllabus and contract identified for the "B" grade. Most found it to be quite steep, more writing than they'd ever done before or been expected to do for a "B" or an "A" grade. Yet all that writing without being "judged on quality" allows Amanda to take risks, step "outside our boundaries." Zach affirms Amanda's comment in his reply to her: "It's funny that you mention the 'O Shit' moment while reading the syllabus at the beginning of the semester because I said the same thing, I really thought at first I wasn't going to be able to keep up. But as for most of us we found out this class isn't really that hard it's just a lot of work." The other two students who replied to Amanda also affirmed her sense that the work was steep, but producing the amount of writing wasn't actually that hard. Amanda and Zach's exchange about the class not being hard but "a lot of work" is significant. What this identifies to me is the felt sense by these students around the tension in quality-based writing assessment ecologies that are less predictable for students. In those ecologies, the amount of labor involved in any writing assignment does not necessarily equate to success, credit, or a good grade. You can work hard but still do poorly. This unpredictability causes students to find writing in those courses "hard." Thus, when Amanda and Zach say our ecology isn't hard, what I hear them saying is that their labor is valued in predicable ways. They explicitly connect this predictability to fairness. Fairness seems constructed by a number of ecological elements working in concert: the contract's guidelines and our use of them (an ecological part that regulates processes/labor), students' participation in the negotiation of the contract (shared ecological power), and valuing in real ways the worth of student labor (ecological processes that lead to parts and products).

Kyler, a hard-working, white student majoring in criminology, in his reply to Amanda sums up the three most prevalent themes in that week's reflections:

> The way you first described the syllabus was the same way I
> felt, I mean 5-6 for a B and 9-10 for an A, like that's a lot of
> writing. I agree with how easy it has become, at first I started
> off a little shaky but now with knowing how the process works
> I'm much better prepared. Not being judged on quality and
> rather on effort is nice, writing just is too subjective to grade.

Klyer identifies that there is a lot of labor for "A" and "B" grades, however that labor, which seemed daunting in the beginning has turned out to be easier than expected. The question underneath this statement, I think, is one about exploitation, but he moves quickly to a positive outcome of his labor. It feels good not to be judged on quality, not to be judged against a white racial *habitus*.[47] Judgments based on quality (as compared to a white racial *habitus*) produce grade-products in assessment ecologies that are often unfair or unwanted (writing is "too subjective to grade"). Kyler senses these contradictions. In one sense, Kyler is voicing the same argument that Zach, Amanda, and Jane seem to be making, that the lack of grades, despite the heavy workload, makes for less exploitation because it's fairer than grading on quality. Why? Predictability. Their labor is directly rewarded.

Kyler ends on a good point that hints at larger institutional conditions in which all my students must work. These grading conditions are not new or hidden to those in the fields of writing assessment or linguistics. Many studies have been done on the unreliability of the grading of student writing over the last 100 years (Diederich, 1974; Finkelstein, 1913; Starch & Elliott, 1912), but locally diverse students complicate further this unreliability in grading because of the complex *habitus* they embody when writing.

Paul Diederich sums up these conclusions best when describing the famous factor analysis study done by John French, Sydell Carlton, and himself in 1961 at ETS, and it illustrates an insight about the "subjectivity" of grading that students, like Kyle, can figure out. Diederich and his colleagues presented 300 college papers to 53 readers, and asked them to grade the papers. They found that 101 papers "received every grade from 1 to 9; 94 percent received either seven, eight, or nine different grades; and no essay received less than five different grades" (1974, p. 6). The median correlation, or agreement among all the readers, was a very low .31—that means, their model could account for or predict only 9.6% of the variance in grades. Most of the variance was unknown, or as Kyler says, "too subjective." Moving from class to class, teacher to teacher, students, even white students like Kyler who arguably share more in a white racial *habitus* (the norm), feel this unevenness in grading and perceive it as unfair, unpredictable. More important, this unevenness affects students' abilities to engage deeply in writing, and orient themselves appropriately in each writing assessment ecology. This affects their abilities to learn, their ecological products. Clearly students, if given the chance, can see this unfairness, and make productive (as in producing ecological products) sense of it if the writing assessment ecology offers the conditions to do so. In our classroom, we used reflection on the contract to help us build these conditions.

Diederich, however, also explains this problem from the teacher's side of things. In his next chapter when concluding about a different ETS study done by Benjamin Rosner on the effects of bias in grading practices, Diederich says, "grading is such a suggestible process that we find what we expect to find. If we think a paper came from an honors class, we expect it to be pretty good, and that is what we find. If we think it came from a regular class, we expect it to be only so-so, and that is what we find" (1974, p. 12). This is a phenomenon that I have found to be true at every institution at which I've taught, where the bias does not just come from a stamp on the student's writing ("honors" or "regular"), as in Rosner's study, but comes from an association with the body of color and that body's assumed linguistic capabilities, particularly those of Latino/a and Hmong students (at Fresno State).

In fact, Shaughnessy (1977) makes this association to the basic writer explicit, suggesting some historical precedent of such associations. She describes remedial students as "true outsiders," "strangers in academia," all from "New York's ethnic or racial enclaves," who speak "other languages or dialects at home" (1977, pp. 2-3). Otte and Mlynarchzyk (2010) describe Shaughnessy's rendering of the basic writer as "above all as urban and 'other'" (p. 49). The association of race to language use and its differential valuing by others is a finding that linguists have confirmed in several studies (Richardson, 2003; Greenfield, 2011), and those in rhetoric and composition have reported on and discussed already (Gilyard, 1991; Kubota & Ward, 2000). And it is also a phenomenon closely tied to the norming and racing of places, classroom places, textual places, and remedial places, as others have suggested about the assumption of the remedial student as a student of color in institutions (Soliday, 2002; Stanley, 2009). The biases in judging that create racist patterns in classrooms, however, may be hard to see by individual teachers in their own assessment practices. We need our students to tell us about the degree of fairness in our assessment ecologies, and we need to ask them to help us investigate the construction of fairness in the ecology.

To get a sense of the grading conditions at Fresno State that influence my students, like Kyle, Zach, Amanda, and Jane, consider the grade distributions of different colleges. In these grade distributions, there appears to be an association between grades and the particular racial formations in those colleges. In Fall 2012 for example, 92.8% of all grades given in the Honors College, an ecological place where mostly white students inhabit, were A's. Meanwhile, in the School of Business, where a large number of Hmong students take majors, only 22.1% of all grades given were A's and 35.9% were B's. In Criminology, where there are more majors than in any other department, and the vast majority of them are Latino/a, just 35.2% of all grades were A's and 35.5% were B's.[48] Of course, there are many factors that go into a course grade, and given the wide range of courses involved in these numbers, it's hard to know what exactly could be common influences. I'm not arguing for a causal relationship here.

My point is not to suggest that grades are determined by racial bias in teachers' grading practices. Certainly there are more factors that go into those grade distributions. I merely wish to show that throughout the institution's assessment ecologies, where grades are conventionally given to student writing based on quality (or comparisons to local SEAEs and a white racial *habitus*), students experience uneven terrains that are not easily predicable by them without explicit attention to the way each assessment ecology constructs grades—and in part, constructs them by processes of norming to various versions of the domain discourse. Their own racial *habitus* affect this unevenness and their immediate success or failure, despite the good intentions of teachers. The results of the pervasiveness of these grading ecologies is for students to be hyper-conscious of grades and how their writing is graded. They see and feel the unpredictability in it all. I take this deviation from Kyle's orientation in our writing assessment ecology to point out how complex his response, which seems straightforward, really is, and how interconnected our writing assessment ecology is to others at Fresno State. Perhaps one lesson from this a teacher might take is that no teacher ever grades on an island. Students experience the inter-being of the various assessment ecologies they move through, and their membership in one ecology likely will affect their movement in another.

Interestingly, Kyle's reference to grades is one of the two or three explicit references to any actual grades in all of the reflections during that week. Most students in my class discussed the contract in terms of work, effort, or labor in the above ways, and what it produced for them as readers and writers. This suggests that in fact our writing assessment ecology had shifted their ecological purposes and re-oriented monolingual students to other products by first focusing their attention on the assessment processes, which asked them to labor over drafts and texts in the course, staying away from using quality as a way to measure success in any given writing or reading activity.

It should be noted also that Jane, Zach, and Kyler were white students that I would consider conventionally higher performing students at Fresno State, while Amanda was a Latina who also was high performing in the same ways. I'm not saying that all of them came into the class as superior writers of academic discourses in their fields or of our local version of SEAE, but I am saying that they each were highly motivated students, following the contract very carefully, doing all the work according to the directions, always highly engaged in class discussions and group work, and were each from monolingual, dominant English-speaking households. So the amount of labor to be done to earn the same kind of grade they typically received in other courses might reasonably be the most noticeable difference from other courses. Thus orienting themselves by their labor and the absence of quality-based grades on drafts is not surprising to me.

Yet most if not all of the monolingual students, who were almost all white and Latina in my class, found the contract's emphasis on labor as a fairer system than quality-based, conventional ones that produce course grades. Monolingual students also tended to orient themselves in the assessment ecology toward the labor processes of the class and against quality judgments of writing produced by those processes, like Amanda, Jane, Zach, and Kyler. They voiced enjoyment and engagement. They were usually unambiguous about their feelings toward the contract system. And they all mention in some fashion alternative products for the labor processes of reading, writing, and assessing. For example, Jane explains in the same reflection cited above that "[r]eading my peers papers also lets me evaluate my own writing and gives me ideas on how to improve"; Zach mentions the products of "always doing his best," and "discover[ing] my own capabilities"; Amanda finds she attains "a degree of freedom" in her writing so that she can "ste[p] outside our boundaries"; Kyler later in his reflection on the contract says that it helped him to be more adventurous in his revising, "[i]ncorporating new concepts" into his writing. Beyond the implied purpose of achieving course grades as direct products of our assessment ecology, monolingual students tended to articulate their purposes as simply being involved in a fairer, predicable, more democratic system, one that values their hard work, and provides freedom to explore and take risks, and this ecology was in stark contrast to other writing assessment ecologies they inhabited in the past.

In contrast, consider a few of the multilingual students, who likely had difficulties meeting the SEAE and white racial *habitus* expectations in school and who may have had trouble engaging as deeply as Amanda, Zach, Jane, and Kyler in past reading and writing activities. Multilingual students had more uneven responses to the grading contract, and tended to orient themselves toward different ecological elements in the assessment ecology, which allowed them to articulate a variety of purposes beyond the dominant one. They were still mostly positive in orientation to the contract, but those orientations had more tension in them, often because of the multilingual aspects of their own *habitus*. In the same week's reflection on the contract at midpoint, Ashe,[49] a quiet, soft-spoken, multilingual, Hmong, female student, majoring in business administration-management, seemed more ambivalent than most students in the class:

> After meeting with Professor Inoue, I seem to be on track
> with my previous assignments. I plan to continue to turning
> in assignments on time. This second assignment doesn't seem
> easy as other classmates may say, things still are the same.
> Researching, outlining, drafting, and deciding whether what
> you've done is enough ... is still a complicated matter to take
> on, in my opinion. I guess I need to continue to read and
> write to get use to writing in college. The only thing that I
> think bothers me at the moment in regards to the Grading
> Contract is the amount of work that we do (pages of writing
> that we produce) determines our grade. The subject that I
> chose to do my first project, I would say limited me to pro-

> duce a large amount of writing. I wrote as much as I could to
> prove my point, but then again, I guess it may challenge me
> to find other ways to go around proving my topic.

It would appear that unlike many of her colleagues in class, Ashe still needed me (the teacher) to validate her progress and labor in class—that is, she had yet to judge the effectiveness of her own labor and thus the fairness of the contract. She leaned on me to make those judgments. Unlike all of the monolingual students, Ashe wouldn't make that judgment without citing my approval. It would seem then, for her, that power arrangements in class flow from the teacher, perhaps her way of giving me respect. The writing assessment ecology had not shifted as much power and agency to Ashe as it had to the monolingual students. And Ashe contrasts her difficulties with Project 2 to what "other classmates may say" about the ease of the labor asked of everyone. She's aware that her position in our assessment ecology is different in nature than other students, perhaps a lingering effect of all those other institutional assessment ecologies in which she was normed in the past. She was quiet and shy, not often willing to talk in class or even in her group, but was highly engaged, doing each assignment fully and carefully. My sense is that Ashe was very aware of her linguistic difference from the local SEAEs expected in college, hence the comment, "I guess I need to continue to read and write to get use to writing in college," and her contrasting of her difficulties to her classmates. This is perhaps one example of the psychological effects of Matsuda's "myth of linguistic homogeneity" on multilingual students in writing classrooms, a need to compare one's own performances to others, particularly monolingual peers.

However, Ashe concludes that this demand of more labor in our assessment ecology, a demand of many "pages of writing that we produce," can challenge her to "find other ways" to prove her topic, to urge her to invent other writing strategies. Despite her needing my validation, her orientation in the ecology, like her colleagues, is *not* concerned with grades, instead it is about what labor she needs to do and what she can learn once she's validated that labor with me. This, I think, is a step in the right direction. The products of the ecology for her are true learning products, not grades. They spring from her sense of her subject position in the place of her writing group, and her knowledge of her capabilities as a multilingual writer in a writing class that still assumes a local SEAE and dominant versions of disciplinary discourses (for her, business), all of which come in part from her contrasting herself to her colleagues.

However, I may be assuming wrongly that Ashe requires full, unfettered power and agency in order to develop as a writer and reader, that my validation is somehow either unnecessary or harmful to her. I've made these arguments to students before, but Ashe complicates these assumptions. Her reflection suggests, I think, that maybe this isn't the best assumption to make about what's best for Ashe's growth as a writer. I might be leaving her without any oar or anchor in a choppy sea of discourse if I didn't offer some ideas and validation, validation that none of the monolingual students seemed to require from me.

While it seems that our assessment ecology allowed Ashe not to have unfettered agency, she still claims her learning in useful ways. Similar to the monolingual students, Ashe focuses on ecological products and the power to determine things in the assessment ecology, even if tentatively ("it may challenge me to find other ways to go around proving my topic"). She ends her reflection this way:

> I am not sure that I have developed as a writer, I still feel like
> I am still the same as I was before. What has been challeng-
> ing for me is the layout of this new approach in a English
> course, such as the power that we have to create our own
> rubric. As a writer, I would like to have readers understand
> my writing, but that I know will still take years and years to
> get across; with more reading and daily writing incorporated
> in my life, hopefully it can happen. I think I may have to set
> a schedule of the labor needed for specific homework assign-
> ments to keep myself from procrastinating and losing track
> of time.

Despite her own admission to not seeing any growth in her writing, Ashe offers an elegant theory of learning to write, which comes from the labor-based assessment ecology of the course. Her theory is based on "years and years" of work and "a schedule of the labor needed" to accomplish writing that her "readers [can] understand." Thus even though she doesn't seem aware of any learning, Ashe demonstrates a reorientation in the ecology to labor that has a particular purpose for her and a learning product, revolving around her future writing practices. The contract set the grounds for such self-assessment and reorientation. The rubric and the contract may be "challenging" for Ashe, and she may still feel that she has "years and years" to go, but she is making these claims about her learning on her own and in spite of the "challenging" "layout" of the course. This to me is healthy agency and an exercise of her power to control the products of her labor in the class.

On the other hand, Gloria, a multilingual, Latina, who was a third-year student majoring in psychology, offered a more optimistic reflection on the fairness of the grading contract, but like Ashe, moves to discussing the assessment ecology's products, only this time through a discussion of what she learned as a reader/assessor of her colleagues' drafts:

> As far as the contract goes, I think it has expectations that we
> can meet as students. It has been very helpful that the con-
> tract puts emphasis on the labor the we do, and not in the
> quality of our work. Although, I do believe that because we
> have been given flexibility, we are developing as better writ-
> ers. Thus far, as a reader I have learned how to provide better
> commentary to someone's writing; not judging the quality of
> their work, but by providing commentaries that will induce
> the writer the reader's understanding of the writing, while
> at the same time invoking critical thinking on the writer to
> better develop their work.

Like the majority of the students in this class, Gloria didn't talk about grades
as products explicitly when asked to reflect upon our grading contract and any
problems with it. Instead, she thinks about the assessment ecology and its learning products (i.e., "flexibility" and "developing as better writers"), and affirms
that it is a fair environment ("it has expectations that we can meet as students").
Most important to Gloria are the products of her labor, the labor of reading
and providing descriptive feedback to colleagues, feedback that stays away from
evaluating quality in drafts and focuses on "invoking critical thinking." These
are the day to day processes, expectations, and artifacts that help form each
writing group as a place in the assessment ecology. Most interesting, Gloria does
not argue that the writing assessment ecology produces better documents. The
environment's "emphasis on the labor [that] we do, and not in the quality of
our work" gives "flexibility" in the ecology to "develop[p] as better writers." So
the products of the writing assessment ecology, at least for Gloria, centers on
developing *students* through assessment processes, not documents. This important insight, a learning product itself, is a result of the focus on labor, something
she mentions above. Because Gloria wasn't thinking of assignments as points or
grades to be acquired, she could instead focus on what she was doing each week,
moving her to focus on herself as a writer, which then revealed this insight.

The presence and importance of the people in the writing assessment ecology
was a major theme for most multilingual and many monolingual students reflecting on the contract in week 10. But arguably, it was a stronger way that multilingual students oriented themselves in the writing assessment ecology. Lyna,
a multilingual, Cambodian student, majoring in business, who often produced
a lot of text in her assignments, had lots of language issues that often tangled
up her sentences, more so than Gloria or Ashe. However, both Gloria and Lyna
center on the consequences for the people in the assessment ecology. In Lyna's

reflection, she focuses on the writing groups, how helpful and encouraging they were for her as a writer, then moves to her own difficulties in writing:

> It is appropriate that we all help one another be on the same track. The power of determining the contract help ease the tension of whether or not we are able to reach our goals. Personally I actually enjoy working as a group more than I can ever re-call at college level. In some ways that I have grown is that I am more accustom to having my peers reading my issues with out having an overly extorted anxiety of having my papers read other than an instructor. I just realized now we work in a group in a way of a support group to help one another with our issues and share our concerns. I more used to writing in my own style. This is typing away as what my brain works. What makes sense to me does not always make since to others. One main reason is that I happen to work in how my ideas flow. Upon reading it to myself, I would fine it a paper that I can say put forth my ideas until some one comes along (usually my English teacher in High school) would tell me the sequence is not in a "logical" order. There are many orders you can go buy because there are many styles you can use. But sometimes I forget that we don't write just to write. But we must write in order for our readers to understand our work. If our readers do not then the paper would be useless. You not only lose your readers but your reasoning is also lost too. I find it the hardest when I actually plan for my paper to flow a certain way but only to realize it would not meet my readers like I expected to do. Like having your work nearly down but to only have to rebuild it. I find this task the most challenging and the most disheartening thing in writing. Does not matter if this is just a leisure piece that I am writing or an assignment that is given in class. Correcting things when they are small can save you a lot of time than catching it way later in your paper. But there are so many things that can affect our writing that I just find it horribly overwhelming …. I'm going to have to do much more research than I originally did. I only wish my researching skills were up to par in my writing like I would find in finding new recipes and searching what would work for me and I should remind myself I should not cripple myself in writing.

It is revealing that one of the two or three writers in the class who had the most challenges with meeting conventional notions of our local SEAE, when asked to reflect on the grading contract and how well it was working at week 10, discussed most substantively the people (her group), the processes of her labor, and their direct products (good and bad) for her in the ecology. She begins her discussion by couching everything in terms of students having the power to determine the grounds by which their writing will be assessed, and that this ability helped students, or at least her, meet their goals (i.e., "The power of determining the contract help ease the tension of whether or not we are able to reach our goals."). Power is something, I'm guessing, Lyna has rarely felt or exercised in writing assessment ecologies, as suggested in her parenthetical aside about past English teachers identifying her writing as "not in a 'logical' order." Not so surprisingly, being able to exercise some degree of power is key to Lyna's success. I imagine the norming and racing enacted through the place of her writing, the documents judged by past teachers and those at Fresno State in other classes, was reduced tremendously in our class. And I think, to some degree, Lyna is aware of the ecology having people, processes, products, and power relations that affect her ability to write successfully. Hers is the most developed reflection in this way, offering the fullest sense of the way negotiating the contract's details about the labor requirements allowed groups to do more effective and supportive work, which in turn, reduced anxiety on her part because a grader, a teacher, was not the primary assessor of her work.

Her comment about past teachers judging her writing as illogically arranged is particularly interesting to me in the way it reveals the dynamics of past writing assessment ecologies, suggesting the paper as a place of norming and racing in writing assessment ecologies, particularly for multilingual students of color. Like Kyler, other assessment ecologies affect Lyna's movement in ours, only her lessons are different. They are more comparative. It is a strong power move by a teacher to make such claims about a student's text, regardless of the evidence offered in support of such claims. And because such claims about her text likely were in the context of grades as motivators, Lyna was forced to worry about grades first, then about her writing (her logic and arrangement only mattered because it was graded). Perhaps she saw the indirect products of her labors, labors which likely were never rewarded or acknowledged, as anxiety.

Since this reflection was typical of Lyna's writing in the course, I'm guessing it was typical of her past writing. I would not characterize her writing, however, as lacking a logical structure. It has transitions from one idea to the next, and all the things discussed are related. Logic is not Lyna's problem here. Her ability to use a locally accepted SEAE does create dissonance and tangles in her sentences (particularly around sentence boundaries). Her natural inclination to write associatively may lead some teachers to see a lack of organization, since this isn't a top-down, topic-oriented discourse. Her associative logical arrangement may cue some readers to hear/see a non-white racial *habitus* in her discourse. When a teacher (either knowingly or not) associates this kind of text to her material raced body and slightly accented speech, the teacher likely will categorized Lyna as remedial, as the literature tells us. Logic will not be found in the remedial, error will.

But Lyna acknowledges that she has her own "style," one that mimics the way her "brain works," and she realizes that not all readers understand this style. Her group as an ecological place helps her to write to them. Through the power arrangements and the local place of her group, constructed by our labor processes and the people engaged in those labors, Lyna has some room to begin writing from her own associative discourse without an immediate comparison to a white racial *habitus* as norm that previously devalued her writing and labor. Her own discussion of these issues, stemming from past teachers judging her texts, is evidence of this self-awareness as an ecological product. Her orientation to the ecology is positive, connected to the positive experiences in her group, but comparative to other less positive experiences with teachers correcting her writing, so her ecological products (her orientation to labor) is not without its tensions.

Norming to a white discourse is, I think, important to reading Lyna's reflection and her relations to other people in the ecology. Lyna continues by focusing her positive comments on the place of the writing group, a place in the ecology that is relatively anxiety-free for her. She explains that the writing group was a "support group" and perhaps offered a less stressful set of readers than a teacher. This leads her to discuss her own writing anxieties and problems in the past, realizing that "we don't write just to write ... we must write in order for our readers to understand our work" —how beautifully Burkean her theory is. I would argue that perhaps one might read Lyna's progress, which I think this reflection shows, as progress predicated on her needing to physically know and interact with her readers, which is most directly and materially her group members, something akin to Ede and Lunsford's "audience addressed" (1984). Furthermore, Lyna's focus on the place that her writing group created in the process of writing, reading, and providing feedback, which always included face-to-face talking over each other's drafts, suggests an interesting translation of Ede and Lunsford's good criticism of the audience as addressed position. And place as a site of norming and racing is important to this translation.

Ede and Lunsford criticize those who only consider audience as addressed in writing processes by saying they miss "a recognition of the crucial importance of this internal dialogue, through which writers analyze inventional problems and conceptualize patterns of discourse" (1984, p. 158). Furthermore, they say that the audience-addressed position misses the fact that "no matter how much feedback writers may receive after they have written something (or in breaks while they write), as they compose writers must rely in large part upon their own vision of the reader, which they create, as readers do their vision of writers, according to their own experiences and expectations" (1984, p. 158). Thus, writers need or do already address real, material audiences and invoke imagined ones simultaneously. Lyna exemplifies this dual nature of audience. Lyna's construction of her readers is a product of her experiences and expectations that are formed by her multilingual, Cambodian heritage, and the deep, semester-long discussions with her writing group members.

Lyna's group was locally diverse, and so not a unified audience, which I find many teachers, perhaps even Ede and Lunsford, assume to be the audience for any writing assignment in classes.[50] Her group consisted of Amanda (from above); Kevin, a monolingual, fourth-year basketball player from Florida but originally born in Jamaica, majoring in communications, who had a girlfriend and a small child, whom he took care of, which took up much of his limited time after class; Claudia, a multilingual Latina, majoring in communication disorders—deaf education; and Rachel, a monolingual, Latina, majoring in chemistry who was quiet but an astute reader of her colleagues' work. Lyna's group consisted of all students of color, with four Latinas and one African-American male. There was a spectrum of multilingual and monolingual English language users in the group, and everyone had a different major from the others. It was a diverse group in many ways. These locally diverse *habitus* make her audience plural, which complicates the way Ede and Lunsford explain writers conceiving of invoked audience. This complication comes from Lyna's interaction with her addressed audience. So not only is there a gap between Lyna's addressed audience and her invoked audience, but there are gaps among her addressed audience members and potentially how she translates those variations into a set of invoked audiences. Lyna, however, seems unworried about this. Then again, to be fair to Lyna, I did not prompt students to discuss such issues.

Arguably just as important to her group dynamic was the absence of a white student in the group. I'm not arguing to exclude white students from groups or writing courses, or that they taint in some way writing groups for students of color. I am saying that because Lyna's group had a textured set of non-white racial *habitus*, a range of multilingual and monolingual writers in the group, and a range of majors represented, the group could resist simply being a place of norming to a white racial *habitus*. There was no representative of a white racial *habitus* in the group, which made their group a place that had an easier time problematizing writers' existential writing assessment situations since any criticism of the dominant discourse in the rubric or a text might more easily be criticisms of discourse outside the place of the writing group. It was a safer place to be critical of the dominant white discourse. It was a borderland.

Additionally in the group, there could be some assurance that most group members, maybe all, shared a felt sense of the influence of norming to a white racial *habitus* in past judgments of their writing in school. Their discussions could be more open to exploring whiteness, even if covertly stated. This made it a less stressful and more productive ecology for a multilingual, female writer like Lyna, who was a little shy in class, but not in her group, who had difficulty with producing local SEAE texts but no difficulty doing the labor of the course and producing lots of text and thinking, even if that text may not be conventionally arranged (topic-oriented) or follow local SEAE conventions. The place of her writing group, then, was a racialized location, a place in our assessment ecology unlike any of the other four writing groups in the class, each with their own dynamics. And because the ecology placed as top priority the processes of assessment each week and the labor individuals did in preparation for each day, there was no need to compare and rank writing performances against a white racial *habitus*. Lyna's writing could be valued and she could be a valuable member of her writing group, not a hindrance. And all of this hinged on Lyna's getting to know intimately her group members as a pluralized primary audience.

Our rubrics also resisted norming to a local dominant discourse, although not completely. So I don't want to give the false impression that somehow Lyna's group didn't attempt to discuss local dominant academic conventions or expectations that matched a white racial *habitus*. Like all groups, they did. So I'm not claiming that conventional norming didn't occur in Lyna's group, or that there wasn't pressure in peer assessment activities to compare and thus norm Lyna to our local white racial *habitus*. Yes, this surely happened. But the fact that it happened in a locally diverse group of non-white students, slowly over time, in which grades were not the products of assessments of drafts, but working and laboring was, something Lyna could do very effectively, made the difference for her. She could show her value to the group, and offer publically valuable texts.

Lyna doesn't let herself off the hook though. Her orientation to the ecology is still filled with tension. Much like Ashe's contrasting to her colleagues, Lyna assumes a tacit monolingual, white racial *habitus* as norm, which she must stack up against. She knows she has difficultly producing writing that meets such expectations. She focuses on her struggles mostly in her reflection on the contract. The process of the class, of drafting, redrafting, reading others' drafts and writing up feedback, then revising, and redrafting is "challenging" and "disheartening," since it feels like "rebuilding" each draft. Much like Ashe, Lyna's tension in her orientation to the assessment ecology stems from her accepting a comparison of her writing to a local dominant discourse, which is informed by a white racial *habitus* that other teachers in her past used to devalue her writing. In a reply to

Lyna, Rachel, one of her group members, attempts to reassure her:

> I feel like I have very challenging courses and this class is
> one of the toughest. The material is not that difficult but the
> amount of work and time in each assignment is very challeng-
> ing. I also wrote in my reflection that I liked being in groups
> the most because it clears up confusion and questions I have
> for my peers. My group is very supportive when I mess up
> and I am grateful for that.

Interestingly, the only person to reply to Lyna's long reflection, of which the
above is only part, is Rachel, a monolingual, Latina group member. Perhaps Rachel felt obligated to reply to Lyna, or maybe she was looking to read her group
members' posts first and found Lyna's worth a reply. It's hard to know, but it is
interesting that most other students' posts received replies from students outside
their writing groups, but not Lyna. Rachel shores up this problem, proving Lyna's point about the supportive nature of the place of her group. While Rachel
does not reply directly to any comment or item in Lyna's original post, she does
implicitly comfort Lyna by agreeing about the challenging workload. But she
ends on the supportive nature of their group, which mimics Lyna's "support
group" discussion. And the nature of that group, Rachel reminds Lyna, is one
of clearing up confusions and questions. In essence, the job of their group is to
help rebuild drafts.

At the end of her reflection, Lyna makes an interesting, and I think productive, comparison to her own more organic research practices around recipes
and cooking.[51] Would she have come to these insights without the grading contract? Perhaps, but what about in a different writing assessment ecology, one
not characterized by the labor of drafting and redrafting that create places like
support groups, or assessment in a locally diverse place that was less influenced
by a mandatory norming to a white racial *habitus*? It is less likely, especially for
a multilingual writer who might find her private receipt research and writing
quite effective and productive, but not worth a comparison to academic research. However, in our ecology, she sees a connection.

Interestingly, groups also offered an ecological place that produced learning
products for an introverted, mature (in his mid-to late- 20s), white male student, Dwight, a business major, who explains: "the good thing about this class
so far is the interaction in our group circles. I feel more comfortable talking in
front of people the more and more I have been doing it lately. I really really really struggle with talking in groups, I get really nervous and awkward and I do
not know how to fix it, but I can say lately it has been better." Dwight focuses
on his own locally diverse group (consisting of Ashe, a monolingual Latina,

and another monolingual white male student) as a place that offered him ways to more comfortably talk to people, but he doesn't link his writing group with writing or reading products as Lyna does. I think it is significant, however, that Dwight's group is mostly monolingual students, and perhaps suggests the ambiguity of Ashe's reflections on the grading contract. Ashe and Dwight's group wasn't as racially or linguistically diverse as Lyna's. In fact, Dwight's reflection on the contract describes his future work on project two as mostly changes in his individual effort and labor practices, not in what his group offers him. Dwight orients himself differently than his multilingual colleague, Lyna, even when they find value in the same ecological place in the assessment ecology.

It wasn't just multilingual or introverted students who found the groups most helpful in creating ecological places where they could thrive. Jane, who was extraverted, lively and outspoken in large class discussions, also found the groups the most valuable aspect of the writing assessment ecology: "I enjoy our group discussion the most, I always leave class in a great mood and have lot of laughs. Reading my peers papers also lets me evaluate my own writing and gives me ideas on how to improve. I think by going through the evaluation process in such an in-depth way, my writing has really improved." As Lyna's, Dwight's, and Jane's reflections suggest, group work offered ecological places that produced unexpected consequences for them, products that were more than grades, which came from processes, recognized labor, and power arrangements that gave students more flexibility and control over what they did. However, as Ashe and Lyna's reflections show, there was tension in multilingual students' orientations to the ecology, which tended to stem from their own self-norming to the white racial *habitus* often expected of them in their writing.

The way the monolingual Latina and white students (e.g., Amanda, Zach, Jane, and Kyler) oriented themselves in our writing assessment environment is striking next to the way all the multilingual female students did (e.g., Ashe, Gloria, and Lyna).[52] As my analysis above shows, the monolingual white and Latina/o students tended to orient themselves in the ecology by the power and freedom (usually from stress or writing constraints) generated through the class's labor processes and the absence of grades. Often they focused on the negotiation and creation of ecological parts to articulate this power, such as the contract negotiation and rubric creation processes. They also tended to articulate the dominant purposes I had offered for our assessment environment (i.e., laboring to learn). The multilingual Latina and Asian students tended to orient themselves by their own purposes for the assessment processes and their relationships with people in the places cultivated by their writing groups. As ecological places, the groups also arguably provided multilingual students valuable tensions in several areas: between addressed and invoked audiences, among locally diverse addressed audiences, and between past norming by teachers and our classroom's more complex norming and counter-norming. In some ways, one could say the ecological place of the groups, when they were locally diverse, provided tacit ways for students to problematize their existential assessment situations, even white students like Kyler and Zach.

I'm convinced that most students understood at some significant level these elements of the writing assessment ecology we were creating, even though we did not talk explicitly about them in these ways. Gideon, a tall, monolingual, white student,[53] majoring in computer science, who always sat in the middle of the room, nicely sums up what most of the students were saying, but does so in terms of the contract as an ecological part of a larger system of related elements, namely purposes, processes, and products, which help people (students):

> The grading contract is one of the most interesting things. At first I saw it as just the grading guidelines and it bored me. But really it's about the process and constantly considering and re considering how to construct a more professional and effective message on paper. It is a lot less about the grade than I initially took it to be. It's more a reminder to work work and re work your writing, because there really isn't any reason to let a piece of writing rest as if it were perfect and there was no room for improvement. At least for us at this level. In other courses you write, get your grade, and then move on and never look back. This course has reminded me to carry over the attitude of constant analysis and criticism of my life efforts into my written communications.

Gideon was one of those students who didn't initially seem that motivated or interested in the class, but as the semester moved on, his level of engagement in groups and on our Bb forums, such as in this reflection, quickly became more intense, producing insights like this one. He captures exactly the way I saw our ecology, one that did produce course grades, but was mostly about doing reading and writing labors and processes, about "work work and re work" for other learning purposes that help students in their "life efforts."

But Gideon makes an astute observation, one we had not discussed in class, that any piece of writing can be improved, and that if we are here to learn how to write, then we have no reason to let any piece of writing sit idle. There is always work to be done, places where we can continue to learn, labor to do. The contract isn't about grades, but about changing orientations toward many other elements in the writing assessment ecology of the classroom. And perhaps most interestingly, Gideon contextualizes these insights about our contract by contrasting them with "other courses" ecologies. He illustrates how more meaningful our ecology became, how more productive when students had opportunities to compare it to the way other ecologies treat them and their writing, which is a first important step in problematizing his existential writing assessment situations.

The labor of the course, as articulated in the ecological parts of the contract and our discussions of it, was arguably accepted by most students by week 10 and articulated as well or better by them. This can be seen in their orientations toward labor in the ecology. Their power in the negotiations and renegotiations of the contract, determining the ecology itself, was critical to their orientations. The writing groups also were important because they were ecological places that were personalized, semi-private, and characterized by the local diversity of students. This created productive (counter)hegemonic places of norming and counter-norming, which upon reflection offered some students ways to begin to problematize their assessment situations, but not everyone. The places of writing groups provided the borderlands needed for posing problems about judgment, their language practices, and the dominant white racial *habitus* they had come to expect to be compared against.

The ecological products of such places were sometimes unanticipated, but were connected to the dominant purpose of the ecology (i.e., laboring to learn). These places helped students orient themselves in the ecology in productive ways, ways that could produce antiracist products, and certainly opportunities to problematize their existential writing assessment situations. As Gideon's reflection above illustrates, students appeared to reorient themselves in the ecology because of the grading contract and how it changed fundamentally their orientations toward most of the ecological elements of the course. For the most part, students labored to learn, instead of laboring to earn. The ecology was more visible. Because of this visibility, students could more consciously create the places they felt they could learn in and from, which made the ecology more antiracist in its nature.

MORE INTENSE, ENGAGED, AND PRODUCTIVE LABOR

My focus on the ecological processes (labor), parts, and purposes in all assignment instructions, particularly those that constituted the writing and feedback cycles in the class, was intentional. These were the ecological elements I thought students would quickly understand and take advantage of. They were also the elements I wanted students to reflect upon periodically in order to pose questions about the nature of judging language. Focusing students' attention on these elements, asking them to help create them, negotiate them, and reflect upon those processes and their use of them, did begin to work toward antiracist ends. Most important, focus on these elements in this way gave students opportunities to problematize their own existential writing assessment situations, which some were able to do. My assumption was that if students focused mostly on what they had to do in any given week, how long they had to do it, and why they were doing it, then the parts (the artifacts) would improve, as would their reading and writing behaviors, the real ecological products we were aiming for. Additionally, by focusing mostly on processes (labor), students could slowly build over the semester more effective, intense, and productive labor by reflecting upon that labor in labor journals and weekly reflections. This would, I thought, translate to better writers, but not necessarily, as Gloria suggests above, better documents.

However, while the course's discussions used the concept of labor to describe and acknowledge the degree of effort expected in the class, which was articulated as time, discomfort (occasionally), and hard work, I made it clear that students should be increasing each week the intensity, duration, or productivity of all their labors. At times, it should be painful if they were doing the labor right, maybe not all the time, but sometimes. For instance, when one labors hard at anything one is often in physical pain or discomfort. Lyna's and Dwight's recounting of the painful processes of writing and speaking exemplify some pain in the processes of the class. Amanda's and Zach's "oh shit" moments suggest the discomfort from the expectation of more time in their labors. Additionally, many of my students said things like, "it's always been hard to read textbooks," or "I've often found writing for school painful," or "I haven't really enjoyed writing in school," so I wanted to acknowledge the sensual and emotional aspects of the labors of reading, writing, and receiving assessments of their writing, not to change students' minds about how they feel about the labor, but to acknowledge and potentially explore those feelings that accompany any labor, and perhaps allow those feelings to be some initial indication of productive labor. I reasoned that most students have such experiences with writing, reading and assessment in school because of unreflective, hegemonic, and often racist, writing assessment ecologies that those labors usually exist in. What multilingual Latino student would find reading or writing for school engaging when the ecological places that construct him and his educational products are formed in a racist assessment ecology, when every part and place norms him against a white racial *habitus* that often is ill-fitting?

In another very real sense, focusing on the labor as labor was my way of asking students to pay attention to the way writing and reading (or assessing) are ontological activities that give students something worthwhile in the doing of them, as in the way Yagelski (2011) discusses writing as a way of being. Tacitly, I was asking them to just be in the labor, to stop trying to be somewhere else when they write or read, stop trying to think about the final product or what they were to produce, or how hard it is, or how uninteresting the text is, and try to be in the physical, sensual, and emotional experiences of the reading and writing processes of the course. Just be in the writing or reading labors, just labor, and the ecological products will already be there. If it is boring and uninteresting, notice that that is your feeling of the text at that moment, then in a non-judgmental way ask yourself why. What's boring me here? Why is that boring to me? These answers can be valuable to understanding and managing one's labor.

If they were doing our processes right, their labor would often be uncomfortable and painful, but at some point that discomfort should give way to pleasure in a job well done, in feelings of accomplishment, in satisfaction, success, pride, growth. Pain and discomfort can signal the quality of work and effort put into something, and my students, many of whom came from families who were seasonal workers, laborers, folks whose family members did honorable, hard, sweaty work, understand and usually respect this kind of labor. The class generally saw the value and honor in such labor, and our discussions were meant to connect writing with that kind of hard, sometimes painful, sweaty doing of things, because it should be that kind of labor. We write and read with our bodies. And it is hard, tough, exhausting, fun, exciting, and energizing labor.

If labor was at the center of what students experienced, and if we expected to look closely at those labors in order to make them more intense, engaged, and productive, then we needed some public articulation of labor as much as we needed a public articulation of what the goals of that labor should be in their projects' culminating documents. So over several weeks near the beginning of the semester, we inductively created two rubrics, a project rubric, explaining the dimensions of writing we expected to practice, judge, and explore in project drafts, and a writer's rubric, which articulated the labor we expected from writers as they worked on drafts and engaged in the assessment activities that accompanied each draft. The writer's rubric would be the way we figured out how intense, engaged, and productive our labor was, while the project rubric would give us our textual goals for our labors.

We started with the project rubric since it was a more familiar kind of rubric to most students. Using similar inductive processes that I have described in another place (Inoue, 2004), we began by reading some of the students' own researched articles from their projects in order to identify how those published articles in various fields accomplished their purposes (e.g., made and supported claims, appealed to audiences, displayed past discussions on the topic, introduced their arguments, used sources, etc.). In the broadest terms, each student reread a published article from her research, asking essentially: What aspects or elements in this piece of academic writing do I want to practice in my own project drafts? I was not asking students to explicitly think about what made these articles good writing, although those discussions did come up quite a bit. I asked students to read looking for rhetorical and academic moves that they wanted to explore in their own writing. Students annotated their articles in focused ways, then they discussed those dimensions in groups, both the ones that seemed common to all and those that seemed particular to a writer or a discipline.

We inductively created the project rubric by gathering each writing group's observations, then through a similar but simplified process as Guba and Lincoln's (1989) fourth-generation evaluation process and Broad's (2003) dynamic criteria mapping, formed the categories we cared most about and what those broad categories meant more specifically. This gave us an articulation of the dimensions of writing we could see in drafts, judge in some fashion, and discuss with writers. It was not a scoring guide or even a rubric that delineated "developing," "proficient," or "advanced" categories of performance. It was a rubric that identified the broader dimensions in their writing that they wanted to explore, understand, and problematize for their writing purposes (see Figure 2 below). Thus the project rubric was a place of norming to a locally generated SEAE and a white racial *habitus* represented in the articles students used to induce writing dimensions. I do not deny that there is this feature to all rubrics, including this one. But the project rubric came from students' concerns, and did not tell students how exactly to value each writing dimension. It was an articulation of what we wanted to explore and problematize.

In some ways, our rubric activities and the artifact they produced, fit Bruffee's (1984) definition of normal discourse. Citing Rorty, Bruffee explains normal discourse as that discourse that

> everyone agrees on the "set of conventions about what counts as a relevant contribution, what counts as a question, what counts as having a good argument for that answer or a good criticism of it." The product of normal discourse is "the sort of statement that can be agreed to be true by all participants whom the other participants count as 'rational.'" (p. 643)

However, our project rubric was a rubric negotiated by students that explicitly attempted to include disagreements and areas of tension. Students' exercise of power to create the rubric gave some room for the rubric not to be simply another exercise of disciplinary hegemony, or just another teacher telling students what he wants in their writing. It was not simply a document based on some false sense of consensus in the ways that Myers (1986) and Trimbur (1989) criticize Bruffee's (1984) consensus-based collaborative pedagogy being. It was a set of writing dimensions that we later had to figured out through our reading labors how to ascribe value to and what our expectations for those dimensions would be. It was a rubric that offered dimensions of writing to be understood and explored in locally diverse ways by locally diverse groups in projects. It was not a conventional description of "good writing," instead it was an articulation of dimensions of academic writing that we wanted to practice in our drafts, explore ways to enact, and discuss in assessment activities. It was a point of origin, not an endpoint or outcome.

The project rubric evolved into four broad categories or dimensions, with lists of more descriptive but contentious features underneath each category. The categories were imperatives, actions, which oriented writers (and readers) toward laboring and our labor rubric (the writer's rubric). Some of the features describing each category were specific and told the writer directly how to accomplish the dimension in their writing, such as, "offer a conclusion that summarizes the argument/discussion." Some features were less specific, only providing a general idea of what we wanted, such as, "address multiple perspectives," which were often areas of less agreement in the class. We chose to articulate the features this way because these were the statements we could most agree upon, providing flexibility to writers and readers, but were not definitive of the dimension in question. This, as well as competing features attempted to preserve difference of opinion and conflicting ideas about categories.

The bottom line is that we tried hard not to simply agree on everything, although students still wanted to agree more than find differences. I asked the class to try to preserve options and the diversity of opinions and perspectives on writing we found existing in the classroom, no matter how small. I encouraged students to disagree, even asked them at times to list disagreements in their groups, explaining that the point of our conversations and rubric-building wasn't about finding a consensus, but creating *hard agreements* that we could all live with, preserving those ideas that may seem out of place, wrong, or too radical for us. Hard agreements offer a way to move on with the business of the class, to move forward with the labor, but preserve the sense that some of us do not agree about the details that create value and expectations in our writing. And those disagreements are somehow acknowledged and captured, so that they can be used later because they may help us rethink and revolutionize our practices.

This was my attempt to use Trimbur's idea of dissensus as a method to create our rubrics, particularly since I understood writing assessment ecologies and their parts, such as rubrics, as functioning often as places that norm students to a white racial *habitus* and race non-white students and discourses as remedial. I wanted our rubrics, even if only in method, to attempt to work against these hegemonic structures. I wanted our rubric processes to be ones of problematizing our collective existential writing assessment situation, to model what I hoped they would end up doing on their own. Through Trimbur's explanation of dissensus' function in abnormal discourse, he explains the method I was shooting for:

> Abnormal discourse is not so much a homeostatic mechanism that keeps the conversation and thereby the community renewed and refreshed. Instead, it refers to dissensus, to marginalized voices, the resistance and contestation both within and outside the conversation, what Roland Barthes calls acratic discourse—the discourses out of power. Abnormal discourse, that is, refers not only to surprises and accidents that emerge when normal discourse reaches a dead end, when, as Wittgenstein puts it, "language goes on holiday." In the account I'm suggesting, it also refers to the relations of power that determine what falls within the current consensus and what is assigned the status of dissent. (1989, p. 608)

So our method for honing down the possible meanings (features) of each writing dimension (broader category) on our rubric was not to form a consensus about what each category meant, but to find statements that everyone could reasonably see could define some aspect of that dimension in question, see the acratic discourses, the languages and ideas that were "out of power" as much as those in power. We called each set of features "the range of possibilities" that we might be looking for as readers when judging drafts, but we would be on the lookout for new ways as well. The purpose for this activity, then, was to engage in the process of finding, explaining, and agreeing upon the writing dimensions we wanted to practice, explore, and problematize as a local racially diverse class of various majors, who are each working on different disciplinary projects. How we valued each dimension in actual drafts would need to develop in the group assessment discussions. In locally diverse places, as Anzaldúa reminds us of borderlands, values often come from the clash of different people and the contradictory outcomes of their labors. When ecological parts rub and wound one another, producing tension, questions, and problems, they become borderland-places where problematizing clashes can occur.

In retrospect, I could have done more to help students develop the abnormal discourse incorporated in the rubrics, and problematize their existential assessment situations through the processes of creating and using the rubrics. Students often talked about and used the project rubric as if it was a more conventional rubric, one that told them what to do in their drafts, perhaps one like other rubrics they had used in other classes. This makes sense, and is helpful for students at one level, but doesn't offer them much critical perspective, and thus ways to see the hegemonic or counter-hegemonic in the language practices they are asked to demonstrate. The fact that our rubric looked like all those other rubrics to some degree didn't help matters. So while it wasn't a scoring guide by any means, it did appear to be a list of expectations, not a statement of hard agreements about the normal and abnormal discourses we were attempting to explore and problematize. I did not have good ways to help them better see these aspects.

A good start might have been to change the codes and artifact of the rubric. We might have included in the rubric a dual listing of normal and abnormal expectations for each dimension, maybe list the dimensions as questions, not topics or statements. I could have prompted them with different purposes for their assessment processes of various drafts, such as asking readers to look for and discuss the abnormal discourse (e.g., what is the abnormal discourse in your colleague's draft? How does your colleague's draft problematize or complicate a dimension on our rubric?). I could have asked writers to take that feedback and rewrite a section of their drafts, creating an abnormal draft. The difficulty with doing such activities is that many students didn't have a firm handle on the normal discourse of their fields, so it might be difficult for some to see what is normal and abnormal in any disciplinary discourse. Regardless, we attempted to include both normal and abnormal expectations in our rubric by including room for an articulation of differences in what dimensions meant.

To illustrate the presence of difference and disagreement in the project rubric, one must look closely at the features. For instance, when creating the dimension, "Clearly Structure and Focus the Document," there was lots of disagreement about what "focus" could mean, and what kind of "structure" should the class most value and expect from writers? Some felt that a classical pattern that began with a thesis statement was best, since that was what most others outside our course expected. Others felt we needed more room for other organic organizational structures, perhaps allow the thesis to be the conclusion, or be implicit. Some wanted very explicit and unambiguous wording, while others thought that was too confining—there were too many things excluded when we got too specific. So we carefully crafted two features: "focus on one research question (topic) and present the question early in the document (within the first three paragraphs)"; and "offer a conclusion that summarizes the argument/discussion." Some did not agree with these features, hence the parenthetical additions. I also reminded them that these features were merely reminders to students about the discussions we'd had concerning the broader category, not hard and fast rules that all had to go by in order to meet expectations. The features listed were to give us a sense of the range of possibilities, so they were not prescriptive, as in scoring guides or conventional rubrics.

This could mean a writer might find an effective way to include her research question in the first three paragraphs of her paper, but there was an understanding that maybe someone might find another ingenious way to focus her paper. These features described the dominant ways the class understood the category, a mixture of normal and abnormal discourse. However, I must admit that it was mostly normal discourse, an acceptable statement that most agreed upon (Bruffee, 1984, pp. 642-643) and that came from examples in their researched articles. I'm not going to pretend as if most students tried to consciously work against this feature, to find abnormal ways of accomplishing focus or clear structure in their project drafts. They mostly attempted what Bruffee sees as normal discourse, but we did have the conversation, and that conversation carried over into their writing groups and discussions on drafts (discussed below). What I wanted first was for students to be aware of how they created focus and how they structured their drafts, where those ideas and practices came from, and their choices as writers—to see that they had other choices, even if those choices might create drafts that were confusing. I also wanted them to see that their ability to have choice, to disagree, to exhibit difference from the norm, in our ecology was acceptable and accounted for in our rubric-building processes.

Another instance of disagreement was in the third feature in the same category, "personalize the subject or inquiry." In the first few iterations of the rubric, this feature wasn't there at all until Jane and Gideon's group asked this question: "What's the right balance of research and personalization? Is there a limit as to how much personalization can be included in your paper?" When the class asked them to explain a bit more, they said they wanted to know whether we expected writers to leave themselves out of their papers or include some personal references. Could they refer to themselves (e.g., use "I")? Was it okay to use personal experience to illustrate or provide examples? Or should we make a rule that writers not do this in the class's academic writing?

In the same activity, Kyler's group also brought up a related issue. They asked two connected questions: "What happens if we want to compare and contrast an article (non-scholarly) to a scholarly source?" and "[m]ultiple perspectives, how do we address those?" The second question was referring to the second feature in the second category of the rubric (see Figure 2), but it and their first question related to the first group's question about the personal. I suggested that both groups were asking important questions about how to treat evidence and information that writers felt were important to inquiring about their topics. I asked them: if you are interested in your research question, is it reasonable to think that you will have some personal connection or experience with your topic? Is the source of your interest a part of your perspective on the question? What value do we place on the

Project Rubric (what should we demonstrate in writing?)	Writer's Rubric (what should we do to write?)
Clearly Structure and Focus the Document	**Drafting and Revising**
• Focus on one research question (topic) and present the question early in the document (within the first three paragraphs) • Offer a conclusion that summarizes the argument/discussion • Personalize the subject or inquiry	• Outline your document • Illustrate the ideas of the project and incorporate rhetoric • Reread your essay with a purpose in mind (purposefully) • Spend time formatting and editing your documents appropriately
Use Rhetorical Methods, Purposes, and Strategies	**Doing Research Continuously**
• Use rhetorical methods by discussing or incorporating in some fashion the concepts from class (e.g., Kairos, ethos, pathos, logos, stasis, etc.) • Address multiple perspectives • Attempt to provoke a purposeful response in readers • Use and discuss appropriate examples that help illustrate and/or complicate the ideas of the project	• Start your research early and follow up on it (update your research) • Read and acknowledge what is out there before coming up with your own position/argument • Explore different areas and multiple perspectives on the question (look for different ways to answer the question) • Find and use peer-reviewed articles (academic articles), especially opposing viewpoints • Research your research (don't settle on the first idea or perspective)
Provide Multiple Perspectives Fairly	
• Listen closely and respect the ideas of others, especially those who disagree with you (the writer) • Address or acknowledge multiple sides to the issue or question and substantiate those experiences with research	**Receiving and Giving Feedback** • Share your draft and ask for different perspectives (readings) of it from colleagues • Listen to and respect diverse opinions on your draft and writing (learn from and do something with their feedback)
Use Appropriate Format, Grammar, and Mechanics	• Challenge the writer in your feedback on drafts
• Cite appropriate sources (no non-scholarly sources) • Format the culminating document in a way that is appropriate for the question and research conducted • Use appropriate grammar and mechanics, so that readers can clearly understand the project's ideas	

Figure 2. The project and writer's rubrics offered evolving dimensions from hard agreements among students.

personal as one of the multiple perspectives we already say we must engage with?

Some students felt that including the personal was too much, possibly too revealing, too intimate. They were not comfortable doing that. For example, Barry, an African-American, third-year student around 20 from an affluent, Southern California family, and majoring in political science, who was in Jane and Gideon's group, was not sure he wanted to include the personal in his writing, while Jane was okay with it. Some students loved the idea and felt that it was a way to engage more deeply with their questions, while others felt that it was a good rhetorical strategy to draw in readers, and still others didn't know or were not sure. It was an irreconcilable set of opinions, a clear borderland we had created in the place of our rubric, so we included it. In follow-up group work, a different group, Lyna's, offered the articulation of this feature that the class felt most comfortable with, and we put that version on the rubric.

If the project rubric identified what students wanted to practice in drafts, the writer's rubric was a public articulation of the expectations they had for their labor. It was a set of behaviors and orientations to labor that they expected of each other to practice over the course of the semester, things they'd reflect upon (and had been reflecting upon already) in their labor journals. Most of these behaviors were difficult to directly see in any draft. They were things they had to talk to each other about. The process for this rubric was similar to the first, except that they also had the first rubric to consider. Our conversations that led to the writer's rubric essentially asked students to articulate what they felt was reasonable labor. What will they need to do in order to accomplish the goals of the first rubric and the course? I asked them also to look at our grading contract since that established the ecology of the course, and set out some assumptions and expectations of labor that we'd already agreed upon. The writer's rubric they settled on had three categories or dimensions of labor that they cared most about, that they said they wanted to practice and get better at doing. And like the project rubric, each writer's rubric category had a list of evolving and contentious features.

Thus by week 10 after several revisions, our two rubrics were combined for easy use in class and in writing assessment activities. Figure 2 shows the way in which the rubrics were joined and displayed for our use. The statements in both rubrics were conceptual placeholders for the on-going classroom discussions, feedback activities, labor journal entries, and reflections. The rubrics were not posed to the class as a final statement on what we wanted out of the projects' culminating documents, nor what we expected writers to do in their labors. They were a way to focus our discussions and assessment processes toward particular dimensions that we had inductively come up with and negotiated as a class. They were an ecological part constructed through our differences, an articulation of hard agreements.

The statements of labor gained meaning contextually, slightly changing over the semester. For instance, "doing research continuously" initially meant the third, fourth, and fifth items listed; however, at the start of Project 2, when we revisited formally the rubrics, students decide to add the first two items, "start your research early and follow up on it (update your research)," and "read and acknowledge what is out there before coming up with your own position/argument." These came from reflections on their assessments and labor practices, in which many students tended to start writing with a thesis in mind, which stalled them out, and limited what they could explore. Ashe's earlier reflection on the contract and its labor hints at this problem when she reflected, "The subject that I chose to do my first project, I would say limited me to produce a large amount of writing. I wrote as much as I could to prove my point."

Some students felt that promoting labor that started early by reading the research before writers attempted to write would help them write more informed questions and drafts. These two added features also seemed to give a slightly new purpose to our annotated bibliography and a research question assignments. For some in class, "updating" research literally meant rethinking and revising those research questions to be more about inquiring than about proving a pre-existing idea in their heads. To others, it meant finding related research that helped them consider claims they originally made in drafts and assumed to be true. To students, these actions were more connected to their behaviors, their research, reading, and writing labors, rather than to the products they were shooting for.

In retrospect, I missed opportunities to take full advantage of the writer's rubric as an ecological part that developed more intense, engaged, and productive student labors. I missed this because I saw it more as a part, rather than a place of problematizing, a borderland. I could have used the writer's rubric's language and dimensions as cues for later week's tasks and processes. This would have shifted the power arrangements in the assessment ecology even more, allowing students to directly dictate processes and purposes of the ecology. If I had used the writer's rubric's dimensions as goals for each week's activities, then students would have literally created the labor expectations and the activities. For example, I could have asked writers to locate key claims or positions they were making in their papers, then research and find an alternative argument to those claims. I could have couched this activity in terms of the labor they articulated on the rubric (i.e., "[f]ind and use peer-reviewed articles (academic articles), especially opposing viewpoints").

When discussing in groups the assessment documents that provided writers with feedback, I could have asked each writer to end each discussion by asking her readers for opposing ways to read or judge her draft from those just given, which would draw on the rubric feature, "[s]hare your draft and ask for different perspectives (readings) of it from colleagues." So readers would be obligated to provide the writer with opposing or contradictory judgments about the draft, discussing both as reasonable ways to see the draft. In a very tangible way, this would have been an exercise in *dissoi logoi*, which we'd discussed already (the first six weeks of the semester focused on readings and discussions on rhetorical concepts). These activities not only would have helped writers and readers see the merits and flaws in their drafts but in the various judgments on their drafts, problematizing those judgments, all of which coming from students' expectations about the labor of the course.

Ultimately, the rubrics, like the contract, functioned as an ecological part with biases toward our local SEAE and a mostly white racial *habitus*, yet they produced processes and places we created together that were meant to problematize students' existential writing assessment situations by continually creating borderlands of conflicting values, judgments, and reflections on those judgments. The rubrics, like all rubrics, were places of norming to discursive behaviors and dispositions, but by employing dissensus as a method for creating the rubrics and having the purpose for such processes be to articulate hard agreements (a mixture of normal and abnormal statements about writing and labor expectations), the rubrics were not simply places of norming to a white racial *habitus*. They were also places of conflict, hard agreements, borderlands in which locally diverse students attempted to articulate a fuller range of values and expectations. Were we completely successful? I doubt it. But these purposes and processes were explicit, which gave us grounds to reflect upon them, and I argue, offered students the possibility of stronger future labor practices by being more aware of the contingent nature of how texts are judged and valued by various, locally diverse readers.

I had a least another missed opportunity around the rubrics, one equally important to an antiracist classroom writing assessment ecology. As I discuss through Gramscian hegemony and historic bloc and the Marxian dialectic of base and superstructure, part of being critical surely is being able to see the structural influences in our language practices next to the way language also is experienced as personal choice and subjectivity. There are points, of course, where the structural or social are different from personal or individual choice, yet at other points, these two things inter-are, as in how the rubrics' seemed to agree with the ways students personally value certain kinds of texts or labor. In other words, the degree to which the rubrics felt right or accurate to individuals was simultaneously the degree to which those students' values and feelings about writing were consubstantial to larger, dominant discourses, such as our local SEAE and white racial *habitus*. Questioning this aspect of the rubrics, problematizing our writing assessment situations from the rubric, might have given us ways to see the structural and the determined in our individual and diverse practices, or see the ways we colonize ourselves through consent to a white racial *habitus*. Additionally, much like the way the rubrics themselves are both ecological parts and places, students are both people and parts that norm and race each other. They embody shock, conflict, and negotiation.

Problematizing ones existential writing assessment situation, as a practice, offers a way to investigate the rubrics and the labors they embodied as "limit-situations," which would have offered my students more ecologically productive labor practices. To see this better, Freire explains the coming to critical consciousness by explaining the way humans become "conscious beings":

> As they separate themselves from the world, which they
> objectify, as they separate themselves from their own activity,
> as they locate the seat of their decisions in themselves and in
> their relations with the world and others, people overcome
> the situations which limit them: the "limit-situations." Once
> perceived by individuals as fetters, as obstacles to their libera-
> tion, these situations stand out in relief from the background,
> revealing their true nature as concrete historical dimensions of
> a given reality. Men and women respond to the challenge with
> actions which Vieira Pinto calls "limit-acts": those directed at
> negating and overcoming, rather than passively accepting, the
> "given." (1970, p. 99)

Thus, the key to critical consciousness, for Freire, is a person's separation from the material life of his limit-situations, and one good way to separate one's ideas and feelings, one's experiences of the world, is to abstract them into language. The rubrics were in some sense an embodiment of students' separations from their discursive worlds, a set of rhetorical abstractions about writing academic texts, about laboring to create those texts. The processes and labors we focused on were processes of objectifying their values and feelings about writing. I did not make a point to discuss or prompt them about this separation and abstraction of labors and outcomes. I should have. It would have given us a chance, as Freire says, to locate the seat of our decisions in ourselves and in our relations to the world, in other places that determine (limit and pressure) what we end up valuing in our classroom and the ecological parts we focus our attentions on. This would have helped us see the project rubric, for instance, as an articulation of limit-situations that revealed the concrete historic dimensions of their own writing realities in and outside our classroom. This would have offered us a chance not simply to passively accept the rubrics, which I'm not arguing happened, but could have easily.

The kind of liberation Freire discusses comes from a very different context than mine. My students are not Brazilian peasants struggling to read and write in order to gain political rights and voice. They were U.S. college students, who are mostly of color and multilingual, at a large state university in California. So the kind of liberation through critical consciousness I see possible through our antiracist writing assessment ecology is in one sense trickier to accomplish, since one could argue that becoming completely normed to our local SEAE and white racial *habitus* is the key to liberation, at least at the individual level, if we define individual liberation as power and access to the dominant discourse, yet it is this very dominant discourse, a white racial *habitus,* that oppresses many (most) of my students because they don't quite have mastery over it. The hegemonic forces us to consent, while that consent reinforces the hegemonic and people's own oppression in the system.

What I'm arguing, and what Freire, Villanueva, and many others would agree with, is that individual economic success, while wonderful (and likely a part of most of my students' goals for their education) is not liberation from the aspects of the hegemonic that produce social inequality, larger patterns of poverty and imprisonment that pool in populations of color in the U.S., or liberation from the way certain kinds of language are perceived and used as a reason to keep jobs and other opportunities away from many non-white, multilingual, poor, or working class citizens. These tensions between the social and the individual, between the structural determination in our lives and our own freewill and agency could have been questioned through the place of the rubric—that is, through seeing the rubric as a place and not a part in the ecology. The writing assessment ecology was set up perfectly for it. I just didn't take advantage of it. The method to do so could have been reflective activities that considered the dual nature of the project rubric as (1) a list of conflicting values and expectations created by us and (2) a borderland-place that normed and raced us to a dominant discourse. What do inhabitants of this rubric-place look and sound like if everyone is doing what we think they should be? Do any of us look and sound like this ideal person? Yet the rubrics incorporated hard agreements, abnormal discourse, acratic discourse, locally diverse ways of languaging that countered this one-way norming. If this is true, how did our rubric allow for heterogeneous inhabitants in the rubric-place?

The action, the labor of the rubric-place would be reflection and dialogue among students. Freire too understood dialogue among people as central to investigations of "limit-situations" that produce critical consciousness. Freire believed that only through dialogue can one understand fully "the word," which has two important, dialectical dimensions: "reflection and action." Once these two dimensions of the word are realized in educational settings, then praxis occurs, and praxis is the product sought after, since it leads to change and liberation (Freire, 2000/1970, p. 87). In a footnote on the same page, he offers this equation for what action and reflection involve: "word = work = praxis." Thus implicated in the word's dialectic, in reflection and action, in words, work, and praxis, is the individual in community, is people dialoguing, using words, and laboring. There are no words without people, and people are not people without words. Freire makes this last point clear later in the chapter in his discussion of animals as distinct from humans because humans can reflect upon their actions, thus without words humans are simply animals that are "unable to separate themselves from their activity" (2000/1970, p. 97). This is strikingly similar to Burke's (1966) famous semiotic definition of humanity. And so, our rubrics were artifacts composed of students' words, which came literally from their dialogue and interactions, places of separation. But the rubrics could have been more if they had been more explicitly ecological places where the limit-situations of students' words and judgments opened discussions that investigated the ways larger disciplinary and other structures determined (i.e., limited and pressured) their own values and expectations in drafts and writing labors.

And as Freire's articulation of the process of critical consciousness references, the rubrics were also a "reflection" of students' values and expectations for their writing. In Marxian traditions, the concept of reflection first referred to the dialectical relationship between the economic base of material practices and the philosophical superstructure that imagined or described those practices (Williams, 1977, p. 93). So one might say the superstructure encapsulated in the project rubric reflected the material classroom's drafts (base), while the superstructural articulation of the writer's rubric reflected the students' labor practices (base). At another level, the two rubrics mimicked their own dialectic: the project rubric (superstructure) reflected students labor practices (base). Thus we might see why Freire defines "true words" and praxis as synonymous to each other and to reflection and action (2000/1970, p. 87). The act of reflecting, of seeing a word as both an abstraction and as an embodiment of one's existential and material situation in the real world, one's relations to the world and others, is the process of engaging with the Marxian dialectic of base and superstructure, the process of critical consciousness. Thus both rubrics were necessary to be fully critical in the way Freire describes, and I'd add to be antiracist in action. They allow us to confront the paradoxes in our ideas about writing and our material practices that produce our real-world drafts.

Williams (1977) explains that Adorno provided a way out of the dilemma that the concept of reflection created when trying to understand the relationship between base and superstructure, providing a replacement term, mediation, which Freire's account does not use, but would benefit from. And this helps us see why rubric-building processes are vital to writing assessment ecologies that aim to create critical places for students to do antiracist work with language. Williams describes mediation as an inseparable process between base and superstructure, between my students and their rubric. It is a "positive process in social reality, rather than a process added to it by way of projection, disguise, or interpretation" (Williams, 1977, pp. 98-99). So like Freire's incorporation of reflection into word and praxis, the concept of mediation also assumes a consubstantial essence of base and superstructure. This means that if the rubrics are a reflection of students' values and labors, then they are not external to those processes. They dialectically re-present and influence—they mediate—writing and assessing processes. They inter-are those ecological elements. The ecological people (students), the parts they generated (rubrics and assessment documents), and the places of their writing groups mediate each other, making them inter-be. This is what complex system theory tell us is inherent in open systems, flux and change, interconnection of parts within the system (Dobrin, 2012, p. 144). My missed opportunity was not finding ways to help students see our rubrics in these ways, as places of mediation among our values-drafts-selves-labors-groups that in turn led them to interrogate limit-situations that the rubrics pointed us to.

Perhaps I could have asked them to engage with the structural in the rubric and in their drafts. What institutional and disciplinary sources or origins might they see in their drafts, in the kind of decisions they make, in the way readers interpret and value certain kinds of textual patterns and practices? What structural or disciplinary origins might we find in our project rubric's dimensions, such as, "clearly structure and focus the document," and why do individuals agree with such ideas? Who does it serve to have such a concern or value in discourse? Is it really that this is a universal "best practice" in writing or could there be other sources for such a value, or other textual values? And if there are, then why do we promote these particular ideas in our writing? And of course, I could have introduced some of the research on whiteness, allowing us to ask: How similar to a white racial *habitus* is our rubric and our ways of translating it? Are there ways in which it does not match up?

Regardless of how I might see the missed opportunities, the opportunities I did not miss were to focus students' attention on the labor in the ecology and to make visible the elements of the ecology. These things began with our negotiations of the contract and moved to our work on the rubrics, which self-consciously defined and reflected upon the labor and texts of the ecology. This created the conditions for students to engage in stronger, more aware—and perhaps more critical—labor practices, which by their nature have the potential to be antiracist.

STRONGER, MORE AWARE LABOR

These stronger future labor practices began with students making sense of the rubric-creation activities, which I asked them to do in reflections on the rubrics. My goal in these reflections was to encourage students to be more self-aware readers and writers. During the later stages of refining our rubrics, I asked them to reflect upon the entire process, comparing it to their past experiences with rubrics and writing expectations. Zach offered a typical reflection:

> [I]n the past the instructor would just hand us a piece of
> paper with a prompt and all the guidelines expected to be
> incorporated within the assignment. Furthermore it meant for
> the class there were no choices or decisions to be had or dis-
> cussions regarding the assignment because we were just simply
> expected to write about what was on the simple piece of
> paper. For our class it was much more engaging do to the fact
> that we had complete freedom on the topic/question in which
> we are going to be writing about in addition we were in full
> control on what standards and expectations as a class we were
> going to have to meet in order to complete the assignment.

Zach makes clear he saw the class more engaged in understanding the guidelines and prompt for the projects because they had more control over the "standards and expectations" of their writing. While perhaps not seeing that the rubric represented the range of possibilities, just a point of origin, and not static standards, it should be remembered that this was still in the later stages of the rubric-building process, midway through the semester. We had not yet officially used the final versions of the rubrics on drafts. So his coming to awareness of future practices that might question the white racial *habitus* of the rubric, something that Zach himself benefitted from, being a monolingual, English-speaking, white male, starts with seeing and feeling shifts in power in our writing assessment ecology. Furthermore, seeing this shift in power provided Zach with more agency, which in turn pushed him to labor more intensively and productively in his assessment documents on colleagues' drafts. In one sense, I read Zach coming to his own problematizing of his past writing assessment situations, but at this early stage this problematizing is seeing problems in the assessment of his writing in the past, not in the present or future.

Several others in the class agreed with Zach's comparison. Barry takes Zach's ideas one step further. He replies,

> After careful thought I do agree with your opinion. Giving
> students the ability to critique and critically think about the
> rubric which they will be judged on does sound reasonable.
> It also makes it more exciting for students. I also agree with
> your idea about voicing our opinions. This not only allows
> for creative thinking and discussion, but this type of activity
> allows us to become better adults.

Interestingly, Barry sees the control and power exercised in our ecology, located
in the part-place of the rubric, as not just producing products related to writing, but "makes it more exciting" and produces ways to become "better adults."
What he means by this is less clear, but it does appear that becoming a better
adult is associated with the exercise of power and control in constructing the
rubric, in making decisions about expectations, and in critiquing and thinking
"critically" about the rubric. In short, being a better adult, for Barry, appears
to be about exercising agency through one's labors in meaningful contexts and
understanding the significance of that agency to expectations in the community.

Lyna also explains how pleased she was with the rubric creation process,
discussing how students could give themselves an advantage by having control
over the rubric:

> Being able to create our own 'rubric' was a first for me. Just
> like negotiating our social contract it was pretty much a new
> thing to me. Besides being new it almost felt foreign—very
> foreign indeed. Even though the course is a writing workshop
> it much different from taking a critical thinking class that
> challenge and stimulate our mind. Then again this is a writing
> workshop class and we, students, are our own instructors and
> we are able to set our own 'standards'. It is nice being able to
> set our own standard without manipulating too much to give
> ourselves the upper hand.

It almost sounds as if Lyna is voicing a bit of dissonance in friendly terms. Creating the rubric and being in control of their own standards "without manipulat-
ing too much to give [themselves] the upper hand" admits that they could have
set the rules of the game in their own favor, and that they had the power to do
so. But like Barry suggests about being a better adult, the power of creating the
rubric allowed them not to do this—that is, it gave them the opportunity to be
adults and make a decision that eventually will help them learn. Lyna reinforces

this idea of power and being an adult by proclaiming that "we, students, are our own instructors," suggesting also a level of responsibility to both teach and learn. Like Zach and Barry, Lyna's critical awareness of future writing and assessing practices comes from the way exercising power to control expectations provided her with ways to act responsibly and conscientiously.

And Lyna's labor journal reinforces these responsible and self-aware labor practices. In the labor journal entry immediately after the rubric revision activities that asked them to discuss their own assessment labors on their group members' Project 2 explorative drafts, Lyna offers a long discussion (786 words) about her labors. She explains her process for reading her colleagues' drafts and creating the assessment documents needed for class discussion:

> I have to admit I took more time than I originally like to
> have. For each of my group's draft I took an hour writing up
> their responses though the content was short. Now I know
> that with the additionally time I took in my peer's draft. I
> know for sure to add this to my new calculation of how longs
> it will take me. I thought long and hard about what to write
> [concerning] their paper. I did not realize that one of my
> mates did not post theirs up until later. I actually had them
> read the previous evening. I had them out on display to read
> once again in the morning. I found this much easier. My flaw
> was that I did not check Blackboard again in the morning
> to see if she had posted her inquiry or not. It turned out she
> did but it was under a different section than I had checked. I
> checked in the Literature Review part and did not check any
> other part thoroughly.

Surely the place in the ecology created by her writing group (her support group) was important to Lyna's sense of responsibility to her colleagues. It seems clear to me that she saw her labors of reading and offering feedback as more than an assignment. She was conscientious about her reading labors, doing them twice, and managing her time so that she could sleep between both readings. Additionally, Lyna produced just as copious discussions in her assessment documents to colleagues. For instance, her discussion of Claudia's 857-word explorative essay was 475 words, over half the length of the original essay. Lyna's labors, similar to Zach's, improved, got longer, more carefully planned, and more productive. These more intense and longer labors in their assessment activities I attribute to Zach's and Lyna's self-conscious awareness of the way they labored and why, and having control over most of the ecology in which these labors were situated.

Ashe, however, had a harder time shedding the yoke of past writing experiences and the feelings of being a substandard writer of multilingual heritage, which likely came from the constant norming and racing that occurred around other rubrics in other ecologies at Fresno State and in her past. She was the only one who had these kinds of struggles. These struggles affected how she could talk about her labors in complex ways. In the same reflection activity after the revision of the rubrics, Ashe explains:

> The process we engaged in class as we produced the rubric was in different, first of all, is we get to make our own rubric, that clearly is not normal in any class! Compared to my last English classes, there were rubrics that the teachers designed themselves, or none were provided at all, just a set of guidelines of what not to do.
>
> My expectations in my past course were to get an A or of not then a B on my essays. This motivated me to write better. I was able to kind of move away from my nonstop fragment sentences and be able to write in complete and meaningful sentences. However, I had no interaction with other students with my writing. The only person who criticized my writing was my sister, I took all of her criticism to heart. I felt that I had gradually improved with the help of her criticism over every little thing that I did that didn't make sense to her or would make me sound like a motor [moron?]. In this class, I think it will allow me to start writing again, I have not written paper all summer long. This has caused me to lose my sense of writing. I recently wrote an essay and it felt like high school again, my writing has worsen over the summer, not writing. I think this class will help me enhance my writing again, with, not only the criticism of my sister, but my classmates.

It is fascinating that Ashe, a Hmong student, discusses her sister's help—the only student who mentioned help from family members—but it is not surprising. In a survey of 265 Hmong students at Fresno State in the Spring 2013 (the semester after this course), about 70% of the respondents said they lived in their parents' home, and 92% said they lived with family members.[54] So Ashe appears to be calling upon common material conditions of the Hmong racial formation at Fresno State. Der, a Hmong female, third year, pre-business major, affirms Ashe's claims about her sister: "When it comes to someone looking over my essays I do think that an older sibling is very useful. They are at times very truthful as to what we write." It is unclear if Der is referring only to Hmong students in the final "we," but Gloria, a third year, Latina, psychology major, offers the only other response to Ashe's reflection, and it suggests differences in the material conditions of Hmong and Latina students. Gloria replies, "Ashe, I don't usually have anybody criticizing my writing at home, especially since I'm the first one in my family to attend college. However, my writing has been criticized at my work. I can really say that the criticism from my coworkers, has really helped me develop my English writing skills as English Learner."

While both Ashe and Gloria are multilingual, first generation college students, Gloria reveals different conditions in her home, but then offers the comment about her writing being criticized at work, the result of those criticisms is the same as Ashe's experiences with her sister. Her writing improves. For Ashe, Der, and Gloria, our rubrics may still call up past writing problems, but they see them in the context of their own material conditions, not as static problems with their writing outside of the material conditions and contexts of their family and work lives. This finding, one that connects Hmong students' writing practices with the material conditions of their lives, has been duplicated in a recent study I completed with a colleague on Hmong reflection practices (Inoue & Richmond, in press). In that study, we found that female Hmong students always contextualized lessons learned in reflection letters of final portfolios in terms of the material conditions of school and home. Additionally, the lessons they learned, like Ashe's and Der's lessons, were ones that were about the tensions they saw and felt between their own racial *habitus* and the white racial *habitus* expected of them in the classroom, which often revolved around gender and cultural expectations and language practice differences.

For Ashe and Der, the success or failure of their writing appears to be connected to the other people around them in the ecology, which for Ashe (and maybe Der) includes family members not in the class, and for Gloria, coworkers. Gloria ends her own reflection on this very note, connecting the processes we used the rubric for to the purposes she must figure out for her writing, and its assessment: "Using this rubric will not only help me understand what and how I'm producing my writing, but I think that most importantly, by collaborating with my group and classmates, it will help me understand why I'm producing my writing." The ecological product of "why I'm producing my writing" seems to be also her purpose for writing. This evolving purpose, for Gloria, is produced through her interactions with the people who form the ecological place of her writing group, which seems also to involve others outside the classroom, coworkers (or family members for Der and Ashe). Gloria's labor becomes more aware through her interactions with her group members. It isn't clear how strong or aware Ashe's own labors are. Yet her labor in the class, similar to Der (the other multilingual, Hmong writer of the class) was always very copious and dutiful.

Despite the difficulty that Ashe has with acknowledging or voicing the power and control of ecological parts and processes, she does articulate writing-based purposes that seem productive for her. But her labor is disguised in her reflection, more so than her colleagues, which makes me wonder if the writer's rubric worked in the same ways for Ashe as it did for most of her classmates, both monolingual and multilingual. Ashe reflects in her labor journal just after our rubric revisions:

> On Tuesday, after I came home from school (around 6pm) I read one of the Inquiry Paper of my colleagues. I was in the kitchen, everyone in my family were doing their own thing. I started on one of the papers and when I opened all of the three documents of my colleagues I knew that it wasn't going to be the same, they were all different lengths. So the first one I responded page by page.
>
> On Wednesday morning, in my quiet-dark room, I finished the second paper, since it was shorter compared to the other ones. I responded by every two paragraphs. In the last paper, I had to respond by every three paragraphs. What I think I did better here was actually being able to connect with what each person was writing about. In addition, I was able to ask more questions that I wanted to know in terms of each of their topics.

In part, her short labor journal entry could be due to her need for more time to generate text (we spend only five minutes or so in class writing these entries), or it could be related to Hmong cultural issues around the sanctity of language and its valuing of concision. What her labor journal entry does offer is a self-conscious, contextual method for reading and producing her assessment documents. Each paper is read differently, taking different lengths of time, and she concludes that this time around her labors have provided better products, "more questions" that pertained to her colleagues' topics. Yet the question of how effective or more intense her labors were in the class is more difficult to ascertain, as is her acceptance of power and her articulation of control over most elements in the assessment ecology. She does, however, seem to grow in awareness of how she labors, which is a good first step.

Do Hmong students, or multilingual students, labor differently from their white, Latina, African-American, or monolingual peers in our writing assessment ecology? Perhaps. Ashe may have been a special case. It's hard to know.

Der, the other multilingual Hmong student in the class, in her reflection on the rubrics, is more optimistic than Ashe, more similar to the rest of the class, focusing on power in the ecology, as well as the methods and the labor that the class expects in order to achieve their goals. She offers a different narrative of the intensity of her labors. In similar ways as her monolingual colleagues, Der describes past experiences with rubrics forced upon her by teachers:

> The expectations for those classes were always "write what the teacher would want you to and do a good job at it". Most times, it is simply to just follow what they want us to write, but it was not very influential of a practice to do. It was very hard to get into the topic, so it was hard to get a good start on the paper ....

> The process of making this rubric makes me feel, as a writer, more in tune with what I would like to write about for the class. I seem to know more as to how I should go about with my writing with this class. Writing in this class, even though it may have prompts, seemed more freeing and flexible. Going through the ways in which we get our end results is very different from any class I have ever gone through. Most classes do not focus at all at how we get to where we are at in the end. This class gives us the time to reflect on things.

Der sees the writer's rubric as crucial to understanding the labor and processes of drafting and revising, which helps them "get to where we are at the end," yet somehow, a focus on labor appears related to the time to "reflect on things." I'm not completely sure what this connection is, but given Der's ability to produce lots of reflective text when prompted, this isn't a surprising product of her labor processes, which was more copious than Ashe's textual output. Was this key to Der accepting more power and being more aware, the fact that she could produce more text at will? It's hard to know for sure. Another possibility is the difference between Der's and Ashe's writing groups. Ashe's group contained mostly quiet students, a Latina, and two white males. Der's group was a diverse, mostly talkative group of students, consisting of Jane (monolingual white female), Gideon (monolingual white male), Barry (monolingual Black male), and Gloria (multilingual Latina). The places each group cultivated by their labors, which includes their discussions in class, surely affected the strength and awareness of their labor practices.

Still Der's reflection is ambiguous about the intensity of her evolving labor practices, which is unlike Lyna's more managed and longer labors, or even

Ashe's evolving labors that are contingent upon who she's reading. In Der's labor journal entry just after the rubric reflection activity, she explains her labors for assessing her colleagues' drafts:

> When I was reading my group members' inquiry papers I felt like was half asleep or more so just half paying attention. I fear this is because I have been feeling a little lost in my own project at the moment. When I was writing up the responses I usually had questions as to how things will go or to what are they specifically going to answer. I fear that I maybe have been more lacking now then I was in Project 1 with the responses. But it might have been from the fact that most of my group members are still a little unclear as to how to approach their question or the question itself is going under some construction at the moment.

Thus, like her Hmong colleague (Ashe), Der seems to offer ambiguous information about the intensity or length of her labors. They changed and were contingent on what her colleagues gave her. She felt "half asleep" when she read, but maybe it was because her colleagues were "a little unclear as to how to approach their question." In much the way Lyna describes her group as a support group, it appears that multilingual Asian students in our writing assessment ecology were more affected by the contingencies and fluctuations of the place of their group than others in the class.

While there was some unevenness in the way students reacted to and used the project and writer's rubrics, all (except perhaps Ashe) found the process of generating the rubrics helpful in a number of ways, most noticeably in how they changed the power relations in the writing assessment ecology. In reflections on the rubric and our rubric building process, these changes were articulated as different ecological products for each student. Some found it liberating, freeing, and helpful in understanding what was expected, such as Zach, Der, and Barry. Some found the processes helpful in discovering labor practices that would make them better people in the environment, and perhaps better people period, like Barry and Lyna. Still others had more complex or ambiguous relations to the rubrics and the labors they represented, as Ashe's sparse discussion of her labor practices that produced more copious assessment documents and Der's connection between the class's rubric building activities and the time to reflect upon things.

There were no discernible patterns in monolingual or multilingual formations, except that the two Hmong female students in the class (Der and Ashe) both connected outside people (family members) to their labor processes, and the other responding student, a multilingual, Latina student (Gloria), connected outside co-workers in her labor processes. This seemed to make ecological place and people important to how strong and aware their labors appeared to be in reflections. But for most students, the parts that we created, the processes that used those parts to write and assess each other's drafts, and the power that students claimed in the ecology helped them develop stronger and more aware labor practices that could be seen as ones that problematized at least past writing assessment situations. But for everyone, the key to more awareness about the complexities of judgment and the valuing of language was the frequent formalized moments of reflection on assessment, the rubrics, and our labors.

I still missed important opportunities to encourage students to explicitly problematize their existential assessment situations in the reflections by not calling attention to the limit-situations that the rubric afforded us. I missed opportunities to use the difference and borderlands existing in the rubric, our writing, our groups, and our labors, in ways that could have revealed the hegemonic, as well as racialized *habitus* that affect judgments on writing. I also missed chances to have students compare directly the ways that our rubric as our version of a hegemonic discourse, a white racial *habitus*, norms and races us and our writing already. This would have given us a chance to question our own reading and writing practices (our labors) as practices that constitute who we are, as ontological, as ways of being in our classroom and as locally diverse people.

ASSESSING AS PROBLEMATIZING IN THE ECOLOGY

Up to this point, I've focused on the parts and processes of the assessment ecology as deeply involved in asking students to inquire about assessment and grading, which I feel offers students some way to be critical of how their writing is and should be assessed, and how grades affect their learning to write. But I have avoided showing any actual assessment documents, which was the meat of the course.

Like any writing course, assessment of student writing—in this case, students' assessments of their colleagues' drafts—is the engine that regulates the learning and development on drafts and in writers. This idea was explicit in my course, since we began with the assumption that if students can practice and improve their reading and assessing of colleagues' drafts, then they were learning to be better writers by their own measures. Part of the discussions on the grading contract in the early weeks of the class attempted to make this clear. In fact, the third question that students came up with directly addressed this assumption: "What does assessment mean in our class?" I've made this argument in at least two other places in different ways. I (Inoue, 2004) argue that when students control the articulation of rubrics and reflect upon them, they do valuable intellectual work that helps them as writers and gives them necessary power to make their educational experiences more potent and critical. I (Inoue, 2010) also argue that teaching students the rhetoric of writing assessment, teaching them to theorize their reading and judging practices on each other's drafts, exercises the same competencies that is valued in the academy through dominant discourses.

Now, I add to these discussions a third argument for such a focus or theme in a writing classroom: by giving explicit access to such rhetorics of assessment, teachers can help students become more critical of dominant discourses in much the same way (through contrast) that the grading contract makes explicit potentially harmful assumptions in other conventional assessment ecologies. In other words, posing the problem of what does assessment mean in our class is a way to confront students with their existential writing assessment situations as racialized situations, as situations mediated by a hegemonic discourse. I'm not saying I did this in my class, but it is a possibility that I see now. So I am not arguing that my students in any uniform way challenged significantly the dominant discourses of their fields or the class, or that they were able to critique the local white racial *habitus* effectively. They mostly did not, and I take the blame for this, since my ecology's purpose wasn't explicitly asking students to problematize their existential writing assessment situations. I didn't develop the explicit problem posing activity in Appendix B until after this course. But a critical stance, like those promoted by Freire or Marxian critiques, is difficult to accomplish in just sixteen weeks for anyone. I didn't expect this. I merely wanted to plant the seeds of critique, to give them glimpses of a critical stance they might grow into.

Most of the time, the processes of assessing were to respond formatively, and the activities were structured so that all responses in a group were similar in format and focus, but different in what they discussed. Students made no overt judgments about how they valued drafts in binary or final ways (e.g., "this is good," "that is bad," "I like X," etc.), instead I guided them to make descriptive judgments. Assessment documents began with observations that could be debated (e.g., "this sentence is clear to me because," "I'm confused in paragraph 4 when you say," "the statement about Wilson feels judgmental by using the words," etc.). In terms of stasis theory, these were still judgments of quality, only starting from questions or statements of fact or definition.[55] Our assessment documents usually asked students to do three things (in this order) in some fashion:

- Provide a judgment or observation that states carefully the view of the reader about the document, page, or section of text in question (sometimes generally, sometimes regarding a rubric dimension),

- Support those observations about the text with quotes or references to the actual text of the writer, and
- Reveal assumptions that allowed the reader to judge or see things in the above ways (why do you read the text in that way? What assumptions about the rubric dimension in question are you making, or how do you understand what it means?).

It is a typical, academic discursive pattern, a set of moves that we also found in the articles we used to build our rubric, which I pointed out. Most importantly, in all assessment processes, I asked students *not* to offer advice on how to revise anything since writers must decide how to revise on their own after considering all the assessments from their peers. Telling someone what to do in a draft tends to prematurely stop the writer from reflecting on the meaning and value of a particular observation about her draft, or creates an unnecessary debate between the writer and reader about what the text should say or do. Instead, I wanted to encourage critical, subjective conversations between readers and writer, situating all observations in the subjective stances and *habitus* of readers. This made the third move above most important.

In one sense, the assessments of colleagues' drafts were equally about learning how the reader reads and values texts herself. To help everyone keep these ideas in mind, we had two mantras that came from our early reading of a chapter from Peter Elbow's *Writing Without Teachers* (1973): (1) explain to the writer how you experienced her text and why you experienced it in that way; and (2) writers make decisions, they don't follow orders, so do not give orders to writers.

I designed several processes or methods for the weekly assessment activities that students conducted on various drafts. During the first project, I developed the processes for them, but later gave them more freedom to determine their own processes, but required everyone in a group to have the same purposes and processes. So they had to discuss and agree upon the best purposes, processes, and parts for their writing groups. Often groups chose to follow one of our established processes for assessing, while others designed ones that better fit their group's evolving purposes for their assessment documents. A favorite process of most students was the first one:

METHOD 1: STOP AND WRITE

Read carefully your colleague's text. While you read, stop at the bottom of each page (or after every 2 paragraphs) and do some writing. Spend 2-3 minutes just writing. Talk to the writer directly. What did you just read? What are the ideas, concepts, or questions that come to your mind at this pausing point. Most important, do NOT tell the writer what to do, or how to revise things, or even how well the writer has or has not accomplished the goals described in our rubric. Try not to judge how good or bad your colleague's writing is in your responses. At this early stage, instead, your job is to help the writer consider what is on the page and what expectations you think the rubric's dimensions demand. In other words, show the writer what you, as a reader, hear and see, as well as how you feel or respond to those ideas, in the text she/he has created. You should pause a total of 3 times to write about what you just read. Here are some questions that may help you start writing at each 2-3 minute pause:

- What did you just read? Describe to the writer what you think the last page says and what ideas are most important.
- What did the last page make you think about?
- How did you feel when you read particular parts, paragraphs, or sentences on the last page? Point to them. What responses did you have as a reader?

Your final product should consist of 3 separate paragraphs, 1 for each stopping or pausing moment in your reading. This should extend your reading of each draft by about 9-10 minutes.

The most important thing to see in these instructions is that it focuses students' energies on the process they go through to first read, then write about their colleagues' drafts. Assessments are not thought of as documents but as ecological processes that happened to produce a document. In middle and later drafts, they did end up making judgments that were organized by the rubric dimensions, which I asked them not to do in this method, which we first used in early drafts, where our dominant purposes revolved around formative assessing, generating ideas, and creating more complex analysis in drafts. In general, the dominant purpose of every assessment process was to generate discussions of some specified kind, first written by readers then discussed face-to-face in groups in class, that reflected back to writers the experiences of readers. In the process, writers were to look for ways these discussions led to rethinking, adding to, and changing their drafts. Later on, we slightly altered this same procedure so that we could focus on one rubric dimension only, but the process remained the same.

In most assessment ecologies when things are working well, drafts tend to function as parts (artifacts) that reveal some of the learning and development of students. But by their nature, they are incomplete records of learning, especially learning to write. Drafts are like ancient artifacts that an archeologist digs up and examines. They tell the scientist something valuable of the society and people who made or used the artifacts, but they only give incomplete or indirect evidence of how those artifacts were made, and more important, of the social and material practices around those objects (e.g., how were they used? What did people think of them? What was their significance to people in their daily lives? etc.). If we are interested in the ways people develop and learn as writers, how students make drafts, what significance and learning they take from that labor, then it is the social and material practices that we should care most about, not the draft itself. Drafts, while important, are in many ways incidental to learning to be a better writer. The *Framework for Success in Postsecondary Writing*'s (CWPA et al., 2011) emphasis on habits of mind instead of textual outcomes speaks to this need in writing instruction and its assessment, as does the importance of reflection and self-assessment over other classroom documents (Dewey, 1910; Yancey, 1999). My research on failure (Inoue, 2014b) that reveals the power-ful role that non-cognitive dimensions of writing play in success and failure in learning to write also suggests how insignificant creating perfect documents (as a pedagogical goal) are to learning to write.

In the present course, the assessment documents, because they document the reading and judgment practices of students, and because they are often re-flective in nature, tell us more directly what and how students learn, although they will still be incomplete. To use the archeological analogy again, assessment documents as ecological parts are akin to diaries, journals, and travelogues, in which the people of an ancient society speak directly about their social and material existence (in this case, about reading and judging writing). This isn't to say that all assessment documents will function in assessment ecologies in this way, but as should be clear from my description of just one assessment process and its part (the stop and write method above), I attempted to make these as-sessment documents function as reflective parts that might become productive places of learning, ecological places where students might experience borderland clashes between individual judgment and hegemonic structures of valuing texts (e.g., structures of a white racial *habitus*, of local SEAEs, of the local dominant discourse of our classroom, of subaltern discourses read and written in drafts, etc.). Since this class, my labor instructions are more explicit about being labor (i.e., steps in a process), so they make visible our labor as processes that we can abstract. When labor is visible, students can see their own drafts mediated by a base of practices.

Assessment documents can also be places where readers and writers focus on problematizing the existential writing assessment situations of readers and writers by exploring the judgments made and their sources. A small tweak to the second of the three questions that students respond to at each pausing point would be needed, asking something like, "why are the ideas you summarized most important on this page? What ideas or values do you have as a reader that make those ideas important? Where in your life and education did you acquire these ideas about language and writing?" This could allow writing groups to discuss how readers came to judgments, revealing assumptions and *habitus* active in their group, which can be compared to each other, not as a process of finding right and wrong, but as a way to reveal different places (or subject positions) within the place of the writing group, or the place of the draft in question. In this revised process, the purpose of writing assessment changes so that the center of discussions is not the writer or her draft, but the readers and their reading process, their *habitus*. I think this works best when students see the draft and the writing group as ecological places, not parts or collections of people. Places can be borderlands, sites of contestation, and require understanding perspectives.

The clearest example of a student who attempted to problematize his own existential writing assessment situation was Zach. He enthusiastically took to the assessment processes of the course from the beginning. He also shows the typical ways most students tended to develop as assessors and struggle in the borderlands that their assessment documents created. As mentioned in the previous sections, Zach initially gained some agency by recognizing how power shifted in the writing assessment ecology of our class from those in his past. I suggested that this translated into stronger more aware labor for him, seen through his reflection on the rubric building process. In his next labor journal entry after the rubric revision activities, and as we began the drafting of the explorative essays for Project 2, Zach explains his process of assessing his colleagues' explorative drafts in which I assigned the above stop and write method:

> I directly highlighted certain parts of their text that I found
> to be interesting, informative, and valuable. By doing so it
> helped me make notes on what was being said during the sec-
> tions that I broke off in each inquiry. Lastly I wrote the para-
> graphs on each of the sections as the assignment asked of me,
> what I discussed was 1. what I read in the text. 2 if I felt there
> was significance to what was understood or presented. 3 how
> it could be argued or what questions I might have regarding
> the text. Lastly I took this assignment much more seriously
> this time because I know that this early state is what's going
> to determine how my group members are going to further
> structure and create the rest of their document.

Zach rearticulates his reading process in slightly different terms from the instructions, and makes the assessment practice his own. According to his labor journal entry, these annotations on each draft took him about 12 minutes each. Figure 3 below shows what Zach produced for the first page of Cristina's paper, which was typical of him for all three pages and all four colleagues in this round of assessing. Zach's labor worked well for him and Cristina, a multilingual Latina, third year student, majoring in Business. It was intense and productive. It is clear he took this process more seriously this time around because of its implications to his colleagues' future project drafts. He felt more responsible for Cristina's success.

Walking through the entrance of Walmart have you ever noticed the Missing signs of those who

have not returned to their homes for whatever reason? When we hear the names Laci Peterson,

Chandra Levy, or Natalee Holloway we can somewhat describe who they are and what

> **Section 1**
>
> In this first section you bring up many great points and examples of different people involved in serious tragedies. Also you mentioned the difference between the ones that made headline news and the ones that did not. Furthermore you made a statement that asked whether or not race was a role or reason some made headline news and others did not. As for this section it seems you are on the right track, maybe you could go into a little more detail regarding the situation/story of each of the names and could compare and see if the same things happened or didn't happen to each of the individual mentioned. A great way to complicate what you brought to attention would to see if there are differences in the case situations and explain maybe the reason for receiving headline news is due to the severity of the crime committed to these individuals. Or you might find that race dose have a role and all the crimes were exactly the same just white, middle class, females get all the attention. Lastly you could also see if the same goes for white, middle class, males.

happened to them because of their tragic stories which made headlines for months. Do you

recognize the stories of these women: Evelyn Hemandez, LaToya Figueroa, or Tamika Huston?

Just like the first names that were mentioned previously, these women's lives also ended

tragically and deserved national headlines, based on the circumstances. You may also notice that

the first names are of white, young, beautiful, middle classed women. The other names

mentioned were the names of a Hispanic woman, African American/Hispanic woman, and an

African American woman. Why is it that the majority of us recognize the first names, but not the

second list of names mentioned? Is it because of their skin color or is it much deeper than that.

With this in mind, I then asked myself, how does race play a role in the media coverage of

victims of crime?

Figure 3. A page from Zach's assessment document for Cristina's Project 2 that began to problematize his own existential writing assessment situation.

In his assessment document (Figure 3 above), Zach focuses first on describing what he reads in the draft, then on the significant details, which he had highlighted first in his reading labors. While he moves to telling Cristina what to do, these details lead him to thinking with Cristina about rival hypotheses for why there is more media coverage of white female victims in news outlets, and why there might be a lack of coverage of victims of color. His attention is not on making Cristina's exploration of her question, "how does race play a role in the media coverage of victims of crime?" simple or easy to answer, instead Zach tries to find ways to "complicate" what she has begun to think about. Finally, it is interesting that he ends on a suggestion for future inquiry that implicates himself, asking her to investigate the coverage of white, middle class males. I'd like to believe that our course's assessment ecology's attention to difference and constructing borderlands in the rubric and in our discussions of drafts (the assessment processes) allowed Zach to make this dangerous proposition that implicated himself in Cristina's project. This would be a kind of problematizing of his own existential situation. No matter the impulse, Zach's labors seem not only to be self-aware but racially problematizing in nature. Assessment becomes a critical process, a process that implicates Zach's own subjectivity in his colleague's writing, a potentially problematizing process for both Zach and Cristina.

These impulses toward questioning assumptions and claims of texts and ideas began to develop in Zach's own writing of his Project 2 drafts. It should be noted that like Lyna, Zach produced a lot of text for assignments, and always followed our process directions carefully. But while he was very good at reflecting on his work and assessing his colleagues' papers, like Lyna, Zach had trouble managing the dominant academic discourse of his field (viticulture), and the conventions of our local SEAE in his own project drafts. It appears that when he felt free of the obligations to make "arguments" or write a research paper, Zach could think clearly and cogently, ask good questions, and ponder tentatively on the page, as his reflections, labor journal, and the above assessment document show. However, in project drafts, his language was often riddled with errors, oddly used words, and tangled syntax. He was less sure about how to cite and quote sources appropriately, as well as integrate them into his own thoughts and ideas. And yet there were moments of more clarity and a coming to "appropriate the discourse" of the academy (although I would not say Zach was equally appropriated by his academic discourse), as Bartholomae (1985) has said. In his later drafts, which I'm arguing are linked to his assessing practices, Zach tries to question and manipulate sources, practices he migrated from his assessment processes.

A few weeks later in the second full draft of Zach's Project 2, he explores his research question, "what are the cultural perceptions of the wine industry and how does the media play in those perceptions," by looking at one example, the movie *Sideways* (2004). Late in the draft, Zach incorporates his assessment process as a rhetorical pattern into his project's draft:

> One example of media directly relating to the wine industry would be shown by the devastating wine market change from the release of the movie "Sideways". " The movie sideways was released on October 22, 2004, nominated for 5 Academy Awards on January 25, 2005, winning one (best adapted screenplay) , and closed in theaters on May 19, 2005. In the 30 weeks the movie was in theaters, gross domestic ticket sales were over $70 million with worldwide sales reaching just over $100 million, making it the 40th highest grossing movie of the year." (Cuellar, Karnowsky, Acosta, 2009) the reason this is being presented is to show the magnitude of the movie, also it represents the size of audience that viewed the film for those who have not seen or heard about the movie. "In the movie *Sideways*, there is a memorable scene in which the lead character adamantly refuses to drink Merlot … the effect of the move has become folklore in the wine industry and has even started what is known as the "Sideways effect". (Cuellar, Karnowsky, Acosta, 2009) … After the large study being done by those in the particular article being represented the "Results suggest that Sideways did have a small negative impact on the consumption of Merlot while increasing the consumption of Pinot Noir. However, far from having a "devastating" affect, the positive impact on Pinot Noir appears greater than the negative impact on Merlot. For example, while the sales of merlot slow following the movie, sales of Pinot Noir Increases significantly." (Cuellar, Karnowsky, Acosta, 2009) Now as we can see that this is a prime example of media and its power to change the perceptions of a whole industry more specifically the wine industry. As we can see just by a couple of lines form a movie has the power to take sales of two products and drastically change them. As for the perception goes the movie was able to negatively portray Merlot, and glorify Pinot, in result the public perception followed.

Zach has trouble with the local SEAE and citing and incorporating sources into his own thoughts, but he does make the right kind of rhetorical moves that most academic discourses expect. And these moves mimic what he did well in assessment processes. This was also something the dominant translation of our project rubric seemed to be prompting students to explore in their drafts. Our project rubric asked students to "provide multiple perspectives fairly," and suggested it might be seen in a project as "[a]ddress[ing] or acknowledge[ing] multiple sides to the issue or question[ing] and substantiat[ing] those experiences with research." From the feedback that Zach received from his group members, it appears they all accepted this dominant way to translate the rubric. And Zach attempts to use sources in his text, but he tends to lean on one. Still, he uses a quotation from a source, inserts a parenthetical citation in APA style, then explains what readers are to make of the quoted material. While there are issues with each of these moves in his draft, the details he brings to bear on his question about the media's influence on people's perceptions of the wine industry are all relevant and appropriate.

More important, Zach uses the same rhetorical pattern provided in the process instructions in the stop and write assessment method, which amounted to three moves truncated to two moves: (1) point to a source text which offered the claim/observation about the "Sideways effect," then (2) explain or analyze that source. What he still lacks is enough contact with academic discussions that would provide him examples of the kinds of appropriate and meaningful things to say after those quotations, or the kinds of counters an academic audience might reasonably have to the "Sideways effect." The fact that he truncates his own observation is also a problem, but a minor one in this early- to mid-draft. The discourse has not appropriated him, nor has he fully approximated it. But this is where Zach is at, which is much farther along than where he began the course, and he is conscious of it, since he made these same rhetorical moves consistently throughout his paper.

While Zach transfers the course's assessment processes to his drafting processes, I wonder about his ability to problematize his existential situation in his own writing. That is, does he question his role as a white male with some affluence (his family does own a farm and he has aspirations to be a grape grower and winery owner)? What is his stake in his essay's question? Perhaps expecting a discussion from Zach along these lines is unfair. It would require a cultural studies orientation to this project that he likely was unprepared to undertake. It may also have required him to change much of his purposes for his project. But he could problematize his writing labors as ones that are informed by a white racial *habitus*. He could see the rhetorical moves he makes as ones that are in some way implicated in the hegemonic that he simultaneously takes advantage of (white skin privilege) and is penalized by (in his own inability to fully mimic the dominant discourse of the academy). Again, these are difficult problems to pose for any student because they are paradoxes.

Note that I'm not making the argument that Zach's paper was mimicking well the academic discourse expected of him, nor am I saying that his paper was one of the best in the class. Instead, I'm saying that these judgments of success, like "better papers" or "improved drafts," whatever that may mean in any given assessment ecology, are less important to Zach's appropriation of the dominant academic discourse, a discourse he wanted to appropriate. And it was less important to his success in our writing assessment ecology, less important to Zach's ecological products, his learning, his coming to critical consciousness. Zach's academic goals were never to be an academic. They were to help his family with their farm and open his own vineyard and winery. He and I had several discussions about these goals. So entering academic conversations and reproducing fluently our local SEAE—being appropriated by an academic discourse—are mostly intellectual exercises that, to his credit, he valiantly attempted, but were not on his career horizon, at least as he saw it at that point in his life. Zach's purposes for writing in the course and for the assessments on his writing, then, were to produce some other learning product. This is the case for the vast majority of college writing students, particularly those in first-year writing courses.[56]

For the above draft, Zach's group decided to use a version of the stop and write method for assessing, only they used the comment feature in Word. Like Lyna's group, Zach's group exhibited a locally diverse character. Susan, an older, white, monolingual, third-year student, whom I mentioned earlier in this chapter as vocal about grades, was a strong and articulate assessor and a strong writer of the local SEAE. Her assessments on Zach's draft focused often at the sentence level, whereas his other group members tended to offer their annotations after each paragraph or page. At the end of the above paragraph, Susan comments: "This whole paragraph is really good, but again, check your grammar and use of certain words. Sometimes the misuse of a word changes the intended meaning." And in her overall comment on his draft, she explains,

> I also felt like some of your points could use a little further
> discussion by way of examples or research. You talk about
> owners being passionate and I would be curious to know what
> causes that passion. Since you are majoring in this field, you
> might consider discussing your own passion and what makes
> you want to own a vineyard. Is it tradition? I know your
> family farms but not wine grapes, so where did your passion
> come from?

Susan is pushing Zach to do at least two things in his draft. One, she wants him to look for those errors in his attempts at the local SEAE so that his meaning comes out clearly; and two, she sees a need to have alternative voices, perhaps ones that challenge the ideas or claims he already has in his draft. One place he might start, she thinks, is his own reasons for his passion for the wine industry.

The use of more voices, more "examples and research," is a common theme in his other colleagues' assessments. Adam, a monolingual, African-American business major, a junior with a wife and two children, offered this comment on the same paragraph: "The discussion about the movie is a strong point for me. What other sources agree or disagree with its said impact?" In his global comments on the draft, Adam makes similar observations about his own expectations: "I don't see an end to the paper right here. A good argument to me would be discussing if there is another influence over the wine market. What else creates perceptions other than the media?" Additionally, Adam wonders if Zach might be able to criticize his sources more, "attack them fairly," and asks, "do you agree with all of your sources or do you feel that they could be wrong? If so I would like to hear about it."

Cristina, a multilingual Latina, in similar fashion as Susan, mentions Zach's troubles with the local SEAE, but focuses her overall feedback on her interest in knowing more about Zach's position in the project, and perhaps on the ideas he quotes from others. Cristina explains: "What I would have like to have read more about was your opinion. You had a lot of great information about your topic, but being able to see where you stand in your arguments would show us the reader why you are so passionate about viticulture and your take on the arguments being discussed." His assessors were uniform in their readings of his draft as not meeting the local SEAE expectations, and wanting more perspectives represented, particularly ones that challenged the ideas he had in the early drafts. He received similar kinds of comments from his colleagues on his Project 1 drafts, but at this point in the semester, Zach held on to his own purposes for his writing. He wasn't, for example, trying to force a purpose like perfecting a local SEAE in drafts, and perhaps he wasn't sure how to insert his own ideas and opinion yet. But the ecology allowed him to ignore or put aside these suggestions. Things seemed okay to him. He could have his own purposes for writing.

However, when Zach tried to force-fit our dominant purpose into his assessment and drafting processes, it seemed to cause him a good deal of frustration and cognitive dissonance. In a reflection around the same time as the above draft was submitted to his group, he reflects on the differences between his colleague's assessments of Project 1's later draft and my assessments of it, focusing on the contradictory ecological products of those assessments:

> So after reading my reviews that my colleagues wrote about
> my project one I truly didn't seem to find anything said to be
> constructive. All of the comments that were left were basical-
> ly checking off to see if I meet our rubric or not. According
> to 2 of the 2 individuals that read my paper I have indeed

completed my project according to the rubric. So this leaves me with a bigger question "where do I go from here?" I do understand that there are probably a lot of grammar errors to be fixed. And I'm sure there is some part of my project that's weak and could use some more attention. So my bigger concern is what areas does my project need some improvement. This leads me to the comments left by Dr. Asao, which were very constructive but yet made it very clear that I was no where near meeting any of our rubric benchmarks which is the contradiction. So I do respect what was said about my article by Dr. Asao, but at the same time I feel that all of the group work in class has just been a huge waste of time. To clarify, I do respect my group members and feel as if they have helped me in many ways, but I just don't understand how I can be so close, but way off at the same time. For the future I plan on going through my document and closely analyzing it to see how I might be able to make the changes needed to get me back on track. And hopefully change a few things to make my project to be more rhetorically acceptable. For my future project 2 I have no idea on how I will be able to change my writing practices but for now I just plan on working hard and continue to improve day by day.

Zach appeared to be unsure of what to do. He was frustrated. He saw a contradiction in the assessments of his writing, between what I said on his Project 1 draft, which was mostly about helping him come closer to the dominant academic discourse, and what his colleagues had said, who appeared generally to be less concerned with those things. Because they used versions of the stop and write method, and because I had coached the class not to make judgments about passing or meeting expectations in assessments, instead I asked them to make observational judgments, ones that described their reading experiences. Zach's colleagues' assessments didn't include the binary judgments mine did (i.e., "meets expectations" or " does not meet expectations"). Keep in mind, this frustration is a true frustration about learning, not earning. Grades aren't a part of assessments, as our grading contract stipulates. Zach knows that no matter what folks think of his writing, he's getting at least a "B" course grade, and probably an "A," something he makes a point to mention in his final self-assessment letter in the course. So the real issue here for him is "how I [Zach] can be so close, but way off at the same time"? His concern is about what to make of the locally diverse set of readers' judgments of his writing.

What was difficult for Zach, and many of his colleagues in class at this point, was how to read and use assessments that didn't try to grade or judge his writing as passing or not. Instead, colleague assessments presented writers with a series of ambiguous decisions that were framed in personal terms, as Susan's, Adam's, and Cristina's assessments of Zach's Project 2 illustrate above. This creates a borderland for Zach, which he experiences as conflicting judgments on his writing when he gets my assessment. In my assessment documents, I explicitly listed the project rubric's codes, the dimensions, and stated a clear judgment of "meets expectations," or "does not meet expectations." But the rest of my assessment document looked similar to Zach's colleagues' documents, in that I attempted to describe my experience of their texts and my expectations as a reader along each dimension.

The simple act of judging whether they met or didn't meet my expectations created a lot of confusion and frustration in the class. I seemed to be saying dramatically different things than their colleagues in groups. Additionally, I seemed to say contradictory things in my judgment and discussion of each dimension. And in a way, I was. When placing a judgment like "does not meet expectations" next to a descriptive assessment that may say similar things as their group members' assessments of their writing did (as in the case of Zach), a writer cannot help but focus on the binary judgment, even a student as dedicated as Zach. That judgment feels and acts much like a grade, a final, summative decision, even though it wasn't a part of the calculation of course grades.

My students, even after 10 or so weeks in our class, reacted to the codes in my assessments (my summative judgments), in ways they had been acculturated to do in school. The other writing assessment ecologies were bleeding into ours, affecting the ways in which they read my feedback. They reacted to them as parts, not as borderland-places of negotiation and conflict. If they could see the contradictory assessments of their drafts as a place, a landscape of judgments, then they might see a dialogue, a conversation about their writing that is equally about readers' different *habitus*.

Instead of using the differences between my assessments and their colleagues' as an opportunity to investigate the differences in assumptions and how those differences may help them as writers to problematize, my students tended to see the differences initially as a result of a flawed system. Why listen to students when they cannot read like our teacher? Isn't it all just a "waste of time" if the teacher says something different from our colleagues? In retrospect, while my summative judgments did offer students like Zach a chance to dwell in a borderland that was uncomfortable and dissonant, shocking, one he would eventually emerge from, I'm not sure that all the angst and frustration in the class was necessary. Perhaps I should have prepared them for my assessments before they received them. Maybe I should not have provided the judgments on each dimension. One thing is for sure, our classroom writing assessment ecology did not prepare them well for my binary judgments, but the confusion and angst that they created in most of the class was productive for many. It posed a problem about the judgments on their writing.

Like many in the class, Zach's cognitive dissonance occurred because he had difficulty rectifying the two seemingly contradicting sets of assessments on his writing. For instance, my assessments of Zach's project focused on the same two issues that his colleagues' assessments did on both of his projects (i.e., his issues with our local SEAE, and his need for more sources or counter arguments). But as the stop and write method illustrates, readers framed their assessments in personal ways, drawing on their own inventories and feelings about the text in order to translate the rubric's dimensions (e.g., "[a]ddress or acknowledge multiple sides to the issue or question and substantiate those experiences with research"). This was intended to produce assessment documents that offered a variety of interpretations of what the draft was doing and what the rubric dimension meant, which could lead to investigating assumptions and values that inform those personal judgments. The assessment ecology, then, worked as I had planned it, at least initially. But because I didn't incorporate critical consciousness raising activities to explicitly investigate the borderlands created by the conflicting assessment documents, students may have dwelled too long in those borderlands without any way to navigate them and see the structural in the personal feedback of their colleagues. What Zach's reflections suggest is that he saw my feedback coming from larger, structural and disciplinary sources, but didn't see his colleagues' feedback in the same way. Their feedback seemed to be more personal in nature, maybe even random or merely idiosyncratic, but certainly less relevant than mine.

Additionally, I think, Zach and the class may have been looking for direction at this point, a point in the semester when teachers typically give direction to students, but our assessment ecology resisted providing this to him in an unambiguous way. He was not able to simply follow my orders. Ideally, I should have offered some additional ways to help students like Zach through the borderlands that at this point stymied and frustrated them. Maybe I should have modeled the process of making a decision from conflicting judgments on a draft, focusing on the way all the assessment documents create a conversation, a place where people are talking about a writer's draft or him as a writer. Then again, Zach and his colleagues needed to sit with difference and conflict for a time, then figure out how to make decisions as writers. I did not always know how students should negotiate these borderlands. Zach was frustrated because in his eyes in a perfect world, his colleagues' and my assessments would be clear and unambiguous about their judgments. They would agree. But in our assessment ecology, these things didn't happened because the people were locally diverse in a number of ways and the processes and parts embraced that diversity.

In our discussions in class after the reflection activity comparing my assessments to their colleagues', I asked students if they felt I was a substantively different reader than their colleagues. They said, yes of course. I was the teacher. I was an expert in composition theory. I had more experience in writing and teaching writing than they did in school.[57] I asked them if they were experts in their own readings of texts—that is, did they feel that what they said in assessment documents was truthful and honest, or was truthful to their experiences of the texts at hand? Of course, they said. So I wondered aloud in front of them if it's possible that all of us could be right about each other's drafts at the same time, and why we as a class generally might want to measure everyone's judgments against mine. In other areas of our lives, did we do this kind of comparing of judgments to validate them, to make sure they were correct? In those other places in our lives, is there always a right or correct answer or response? Is there always a yardstick to measure by?

I didn't ask them these questions directly, since I only wanted them to think about them. I reminded them of our on-going discussions about difference and conflict and about writers making decisions. This didn't solve their problems, but that wasn't my goal. I wanted them to sit with the differences and find a way out as writers in the places of their groups, since we still had more assessments and drafts to engage in. Finally, I reminded them that these were good tensions to have and to try to solve, and fortunately for us, these contradictions of judgment do not affect one important product of our assessment ecology, their course grades. They were free to make decisions without risking a lower course grade. The question was not what decisions do they make, but *how* and *why* do they make them. So in a tacit or covert way, I was asking them to problematize their existential writing assessment situations, which came to a head in the contradictions between my assessments and their colleagues'.

What I didn't connect to this problematizing is the ways that my judgments, and the *habitus* I enacted in my assessments, was deeply informed by a white racial *habitus*. I didn't show them how our stop and write assessment process has roots in a white racial *habitus*, and this is both a good thing and something that could harm us if we used it to grade one another. Thus our assessment ecology, one that didn't grade using a white racial *habitus* to form judgments of writing, was antiracist in this respect, but it didn't use this antiracist method very effectively to help students become critically conscious of such racism in all writing assessment.

The key to understanding and working through the contradictions in judgments is seeing the assessments as a place in the ecology. Their writing groups were also places, ones that resisted norming (to my expectations or those of a white racial *habitus*), even as those places attempted to norm students to a dominant discourse and our local SEAE. This norming and anti-norming could only happen if students exercised enough power in the assessment ecology, which I argue they did, and that the power they exercised allowed for the presence of alternative interpretations of what we expected in writing. So while Zach may have left Project 1 and entered Project 2 confused and frustrated, it did make him more alert, more vigilant, which is a step toward critical consciousness. The assessment of his writing was clearly not going to be about correcting his drafts, but about constructing and negotiating a borderland of diverse judgments.

In his final portfolio's reflection letter, Zach returns to this moment in the course, in part because it was a potent moment for him and because he included both the Project 2 and the above reflection in his portfolio. He reflects:

> The last aspect that I truly struggled with project two would be speeding up my conversation. Ever since receiving this feedback [on project 1] from Dr. Asao I have always been left with this final question. "How does one speed up their conversation? And what does this exactly mean?" as for me I do not have the time nor energy to properly attack this allegation but I defiantly feel that it should be a place where I could use some improvement.

> As for the journal entry that I provided I would like to briefly say that this is the best example of how emotion will change my tone or attitude within my text. At the time I was very upset with the reply I received from Dr. Asao regarding my project one. I just simply felt as if I let myself down because I truly put so much time and effort into that project just to receive what I took at the time to be negative feedback. Later I realized that he actually was providing me with the best feedback I could possibly have gotten. Lastly I just want this journal to be recognized for the sheer emotion that was represented. Now looking back at it I sometimes wish I could write in such a manor or emulate this in other texts.

Is Zach's reflection proof that our assessment processes led him to all the answers he sought, to a critical consciousness about his own language practices, about the judgment of his writing in the class? I think he is more ambivalent than that, but ambivalence is an important characteristic in good, critical reflection.

It reveals the student's willingness to acknowledge ambiguity and complexity, to resist in some way the powerful pull of the progress narrative that so many portfolio reflection letters tend to engage in since the genre itself leads students toward that disposition, as Tony Scott (2005) shows in his research on the Kentucky portfolio project. While I'm positive Zach got much from our class, this reflection engages in, among other things, two interesting questions that are never given a final answer. Both come from the contradictions he saw between my assessment of his writing and his colleagues in his writing group. And because I was not the bearer of grades, he initially struggled with how to answer these questions.

The first question he raises, "how does one speed up their conversation?" comes from a comment I gave him in which I said that as a reader I was looking for him to stop summarizing so much and move to his argument, his ideas, his questions (this is tied to the way he tended to truncate the rhetorical moves he was mimicking from our assessment processes, mentioned above). As a reader, I expressed a need, one that urged him to move more quickly to his ideas and perhaps wrestle with his sources. In the above reflection, he seems to agree with me but uses some strong language to do so, which could be simply some language miscues, but these decisions lead to a sentence with interesting tension in it. The first half of his conclusion, meant to be an answer to the question, seems on the verge of attacking my assessment: "I do not have the time nor energy to properly attack this allegation." The clause sounds defensive and oppositional. Does Zach see that he's used two phrases that could be read as defensive or even attacking me? He doesn't have time or energy to take my assessment seriously, to "attack" it as an "allegation," suggesting that my assessment is false. What student in a conventional writing assessment ecology, where the teacher holds most of the power, would make such a statement?

This statement shows agency, a willingness to suggest that the teacher's own assessment is wrong, or could reasonably be seen as wrong. I wish he had the time to follow up on my assessment. It would have told us more, and more important, told him more. The second clause begins in the same way, but quickly warms to a kinder, gentler, more humble voice, one I had come to associate closely with Zach: "but I defiantly feel that it should be a place where I could use some improvement." So he "defiantly" (or is it "definitely"?) agrees with my assessment. I like to think that the statement ends on a note of defiance, a defiance that opposes my own judgment of his work, yet he sees my judgment as reasonable, worth some consideration that may lead to "improvement." This is the kind of agency that our ecology attempted to encourage and develop in students. The ability to talk back to the hegemonic. I realize I could be reading too much into this final statement of Zach's, but given the way Lu (1994) demonstrates that such language miscues could be read as a writer making conscious choices that are counter-hegemonic, not errors or miscues, suggests that this kind of reading is worthwhile. It reveals an exercise of some degree of power, agency, critical consciousness.

The second question that Zach ends this section of his letter on deals with a question of how to infuse more emotion and passion into "other texts," which I'm assuming are academic texts since he's referring to his informal reflection as the one filled with emotion. He sees the value in "how emotion will change my tone or attitude within my text," which is extraordinary in a class based on helping students appropriate academic discourses, ones that typically do not value emotion and passion, at least not in the ways Zach is describing it here. His emotional reflection, however, gives him access to another contradiction that I had hoped students would confront, that time and labor in writing may not always lead to improvement, that learning isn't a linear process. While he doesn't explain why my feedback was "the best feedback [he] could possibly have gotten," this statement is situated between two statements about how useful writing with emotion was for him, how it helped create text that was more powerful. His more emotionally charged reflection (a self-assessment) provided Zach with a way to work through the differences in the assessment borderland that had frustrated him earlier in the semester. Even though he doesn't explain how things made sense to him, he sees a lesson and less frustration. He sees the usefulness of difference, of conflict, and even of his own earlier frustration. Zach finds answers in emotion and passion, not reason and logic, and he articulates these conclusions in somewhat ambiguous terms by saying, "sometimes wish I could write in such a manor or emulate this in other texts." In his final self-assessment letter in the course, he shows just how self-aware he is of all these issues, which I'll discuss in more detail in the next section.

Finally, it is significant that Zach focuses on emotion and passion, and that he wishes he could "write in such a manor" in other places. I want to read this as Zach tapping into the ontological aspects of writing as labor, as an act of being that Yagelski (2011) discusses. It seems to me that what Zach is finding out in this final reflection letter is that writing can be deeply enjoyable and engaging. It can be emotional and passion-filled. It can be a way of being that is good and helpful and insightful. And in these ways, it poses different problems for Zach to ponder, raises a different kind of critical consciousness for him, one that is connected to the sensual, to the bodily, to the material, to feeling.

Der engaged in different kinds of assessment labor than Zach, but with some similar results. At first glance, Der (a third year, Hmong student, majoring in business) appeared to have more difficulty migrating our assessment processes to her drafting processes, but she too migrates the processes of assessment to her drafting and texts. For draft 1 of Project 2, Der's group decided to change the ecological part that their stop and write method produced. They decided to offer bulleted lists that addressed the questions in the original stop and write method instructions. Unlike Zach's group's narrative form (paragraphs that talked to the writer) that accompanied annotated texts, Der's group's ecological part, their assessment documents, were only lists, usually asking questions to the writer. Refocusing their assessment labor practices on making fragmentary lists that did not try to explain their statements or reactions (the group felt they could explain in their group discussions) made migrating assessment practices, such as those Zach migrated, more difficult, but not impossible.

While the form of their assessment documents made it difficult to know exactly how useful their assessment processes were to assessors and writers, Der's assessment lists do illustrate what she as a reader cogitatively had to do during her reading and feedback processes. Der's assessment document of Gloria's draft 1 was typical of her labors:

> Gloria: Is It a Good Time to Come Out of the Shadows Yet?
> - What are the bills / laws that would make one hesitant?
> - Who would be against the Dream Act?
>   o What professions? – Why would they be?
> - Would you be including people who have done it and what they say about it?
> - What would you want us as readers to do? (Rubric)
> - What are the opinions of non-immigrants / citizens?
>   o Why would they react the way that would?

Her group members had similar lists, so Der was typical in the scope and depth of her questions. All of her items are questions to Gloria, and they likely are organized by where in the draft Der came up with the questions during her reading. For instance, the first two pages of Gloria's draft discusses the Deferred Action for Childhood Arrivals (DACA) federal memorandum, passed in June of 2012, while the rest of the draft draws out a history of laws that affect individuals taking advantage of DACA in California. Der's first two questions seem to belong with those first two pages, while the others relate to items Gloria had put into her draft later. Der's questions are good ones, helpful I think, even if under-explained. She makes reference to our project rubric when she asks Gloria to consider "what would you want us as readers to do?" Der is referring to the rubric dimension, "Use Rhetorical Methods, Purposes, and Strategies." We recorded several features by which one could translate this dimension, two being, "attempt to provoke a purposeful response in readers," and "use and discuss appropriate examples that help illustrate and/or complicate the ideas of the project." Der seems to use the idea of provoking a response in a reader to frame her question. In effect, she's asking Gloria, what is the purpose of this paper?

My own reading produced this same question since this early draft is mostly a list of summaries. Der appears to have figured out as a reader how to consider purpose and the use of various perspectives in order to complicate ideas in an academic discussion, something she'll attempt in her own drafting. What is less clear from Der's assessment document is what assessment processes she can migrate to her other writing, and whether a list of questions will provide her the ability to problematize any existential situation (assessment or otherwise), as Zach's narrative-based assessment documents appeared to offer him and Cristina.

Could Der's group's listing process for assessment documents be as successful as Zach's group's more elaborate processes? Like most groups, Der's was very talkative. Recall that Jane, one of Der's group members, mentioned in her reflections during our contract renegotiations that our writing assessment ecology allowed her to "enjoy" her "group discussion the most," "always [leaving] class in a great mood," and found that reading her colleagues' papers helped her in her own writing. So likely, the question listing method they employed was not meant to stand on its own. It was a method to allow them to have discussions in the ecological place of their group, not in the parts of their assessment documents. It was a method that accentuated their group's material conditions around feedback.

But did Der's assessment processes lead to successful drafting processes and textual parts in her projects? And did they lead to a rising critical consciousness? In her final portfolio, Der decided to include just her Project 1, which had gotten the more elaborate and lengthy stop and write method assessments earlier in the semester. It seems significant that after the experiment with the stop and write listing method that Der's group attempted, Der decided to leave out Project 2 from her final portfolio, a fascinating inquiry into the representations of Asian females in contemporary popular media. Der's Project 1 was personal, and she seemed more invested in it. Her research question asked: "how has being Hmong influenced my reading and writing?" She uses several kinds of evidence to explore this question, researched studies of Hmong students and their literacy practices, her own personal experiences with her family, and an extended interview with her older sister, who was also a college student, majoring in business accountancy.

Her paper developed in a cumulative way, starting with the literature review, then adding the interview, placing it in the second half of the paper. While Der's paper offers no rationale for the two-part structure or its order, concludes abruptly with one sentence, and doesn't quite come back to answering directly her question, she does indirectly explore the question in fascinating ways and could arguably be said to offer a counter-hegemonic discourse to the dominant one the rubric re-presented. At the paragraph and section levels, Der makes some sophisticated moves, some of the most sophisticated of the class. After opening the paper with her question and a brief overview of who the Hmong people are and where they came from, she discusses research, then implicitly applies those findings to her own life experiences:

> In the work of Katherine Fennelly's and Nicole Palasz's, "English Language Proficiency of Immigrants and Refugees in the Twin Cities Metropolitan Area," a study was done on how well the understudied Hmong, as well as, Russians, Somalis, and Mexicans were able to pick up the English language. Fennelly is a professor at the University of Minnesota whose expertise is in immigration and public policy; diversity and cross-cultural relations; as well as health and public policy. Palasz is a K – 16 Outreach Coordinator for the Institute of World Affairs in the Center for International Education at the University of Wisconsin, Milwaukee. Compared to all of those researched on, Hmong people had the least amount of people over the age of fourteen that knew English well. Only thirty four percent of the sampled Hmong in the research, which was conducted in 2003, had a high school diploma. The conclusion to why this is the reason is because Hmong people lived in a secluded environment from other people prior to their movement to the United States. Even when being compared to just other Asian refugees in the United States, "Hmong are at a significant socio – economic and educational disadvantage." (120).

Growing up within the Hmong community, we were taught to keep to our own kind. We were not supposed to mingle with others, well at least outside of school. When in school, we were to be an ideal student, but as soon as we go home we are supposed to forget all the "American ways" and be the ideal Hmong daughter or son. In my early years of elementary school, my family which included most of my father's extended side all lived in the same apartment complex. During this time it was hard, as well as wrong, to ignore the Hmong heritage in me as well as around me. I believe that I chose not to question the Hmong culture because even before I was aware of how taboo it was that my mother was a single parent, in both the Hmong and the American worlds, I did not want to

let my mother down. She could not stress enough the importance of keeping our culture going. In the Hmong culture,
once you are married you are part of the husband's side now.
If the husband dies, then the wife is supposed to marry one of
his brothers, primarily the youngest one. The reason for this is
because without the husband as the connection to the family,
the wife as well as the children would be basically disowned
from the whole. My mom chose not to marry any one of my
uncles. This is because she highly respected my aunts and
because of the move to the Americas changed a lot of feelings
about disowning family. Another reason could be that the old-
est of my siblings is my brother who is almost a decade older
than me. With him around my family would be able to say
we are of our father's. My father's side also figured it would
not be necessary because we all needed to stick together to be
able to fend off the American ways. The American impact was
of course inevitable. In some ways it hit them right in the face
of our parents' generation.

Unlike the stereotype of the multilingual writer, Der integrates her sources more
conventionally than Zach (a monolingual writer), and in many places above uses
our local SEAE more fluently than Zach's draft did, although her language does
break down periodically. More interesting, Der's family experiences substantiate
and subtly complicate the findings of Fennelly and Palasz. It appears Der, much
like Zach, still produced a project draft that was clearly attempting the things we
asked of each other in the project rubric. But it could be argued that Der was doing more complex things by including an interview and her own experiences as a
way to make sense of the research she draws on, which Zach had been asked by
his colleagues to include in his writing but choose not to. While Der's local place
in the writing assessment ecology didn't produce as interesting or provocative
assessment documents as Zach's place did, Der still ends up producing effective
drafts and appears to be equally cognizant of her learning. In fact, Der's draft
is a kind of problematizing of her own existential language situation in school.

Der's draft, unlike most others in the class, tacitly complicates her sources
and topic question, in large part because she includes the personal in ways that
problematize her own existential situation as a multilingual Hmong woman in
Fresno. And it is also, I argue, a closer rendition of what I was asking students to
do in their assessment processes. I wanted assessors to explain their judgments to
writers, to reveal how they came to judgments about drafts, not simply support
judgments with textual or other evidence. In her draft, Der doesn't truncate the

three parts of the stop and write method of assessing that Zach does in his drafts, and it ends up making her draft more complex, even more critically conscious of how her own language history and practices are racialized and cultural.

In the above passage, Der explains who Fennelly and Palasz are, providing her reader with their ethos (why we should listen to them), summarizes their study, then quotes them on Hmong's "significant socio-economic and educational disadvantage." Her second paragraph moves to her experience with her family and quickly nuances Fennelly and Palasz (the very move she was urging Gloria to do in her paper on DACA). Der's disadvantage at learning English in school wasn't simply due to socio-economic or educational disadvantages, instead it was a number of things that pulled against each other: Der's complex family demands to do well in school; the demand for her to come home and "forget the 'American ways' and be the ideal Hmong daughter"; her mother's urgings to "keep their culture going"; her mother's complicated and contradictory position as a single Hmong mother in the U.S. who elects not to follow Hmong traditions and not marry one of Der's uncles; her own sense of duty to her mother and not wanting "to let my mother down."

Der sees and attempts to represent in this passage the complex ways that Hmong girls/women must negotiate the demands and expectations of family, siblings, and children. It's not simply about language use in the home being different from the English expected at school. It's not simply about Hmong verses U.S. cultural ways. It is also about Der's specific cultural and material conditions in her family, a family who lacked a father, one whose older male siblings were not around much, one in which Der had to take on the duties of translating public documents for her mother and younger siblings because her mother didn't speak or read English well enough (she mentions this earlier in the draft).

Der also suggests a portrait of her mother as a complex figure who is perhaps more precariously balancing an American and Hmong *habitus*. She doesn't re-marry one of her uncles, as is Hmong tradition because she respects her aunts, and her son is there to take over as patriarch. I think it significant that despite the family's acceptance of her mother not remarrying, finding a rationale that fits the Hmong cultural traditions and that serves their needs to safeguard their family from American ways, Der articulates this key moment as her mother's choice: "My mom chose not to marry any one of my uncles." In a culture in which Der describes women as second-class citizens, ones mostly without agency, her mother takes control of her own life, and the implication is that this was a good use of American ways, but that this "American impact was of course inevitable," hitting her parents' generation "right in the face." So while Der's mother wants her to keep Hmong cultural ways, she herself cannot help but be influenced by those same American values, gaining agency in a cultural hybridity filled with tension that Der seems quite aware of. Her question about her Hmong heritage affecting her reading and writing practices clearly is a complex matter of material circumstances, language use, gendered expectations at school and home, the preserving and loosing of cultural customs and ways of living, family relations, and a respect and honoring of her mother's contradictory wishes.

If we read Der's draft as subtly exploring her research question, "how has being Hmong influenced my reading and writing?" then Der's answer is complex, even counter-hegemonic, working against her sources and beyond the convenient binaries readily available. It is a coming to critical consciousness, a problematizing of her own existential situation as a Hmong-American, multilingual English speaker and writer. For Der, the question about her Hmong heritage's influence on her use of English is not simply a binary choice, like the one that Richard Rodriquez (1982) offers in his famous account of his education: either Der accepts her Hmong heritage or she takes on American ways with language. It is contingency in material action. It is hybridity in practices. This complexity likely could not have occurred so clearly without her practicing the assessing processes of her writing group, and her willingness to let contentious and conflicting ideas sit next to each other in her draft, which springs from her use of the personal to nuance the research she reports on.

In more conventional peer review activities, students are asked to focus their attention only on ecological parts, drafts, rubrics. These parts are decontextualized from student labors and processes that created those parts. This doesn't allow students to consider the material conditions that create such drafts and rubrics. In our ecology, Der's focus was on the processes of reading, making judgments, then understanding those judgments as produced from material processes. This simple rhetorical pattern, seen in Der's draft repeatedly, is the stop and write method. Zach used it to help integrate and explain his sources, while Der used the method to complicate her sources by juxtaposing her family experiences. Process becomes part. Part becomes place. Thus, ecological elements flux into one another easily, and our ecology appears to allow students to take advantage of this and notice it. Noticing, in fact, provides more critical perspective.

It could be argued that Der was less self-aware than I'm giving her credit for, that she did not see such nuances in her discussion of Project 1, or more important, that she did not migrate her assessment processes to her drafting processes. But consider her final self-assessment of the course. In it, Der focuses mainly on the utility of her assessing processes, as well as the ecological place of her group as its context. She explains:

> In my past college English courses, I always felt as though I had to make my paper be as good as it can be on my own.

> I never really had a professor who showed helpful processes
> of brainstorming as you did. Some of these things would
> include the construction of the project rubric, article models,
> and the annotated bibliographies. For the longest of time, I
> always hated the thought of having to brainstorm for essays.
> I always felt the need to start my 'final' draft and just turn it
> in as such. I do not remember any helpful constructive ways
> my previous English professors has helped me to develop my
> portfolio. Even though some professors have done similar
> things, I never felt like I grasped it until now in this class.

In this final assessment of her learning in the class, she identifies the assessment processes, which she calls, "processes of brainstorming," that is processes of invention, and links them to her drafting of the projects. Der identifies the rubric-creation processes, the reading processes with model articles, an inductive activity that produced ideas for what made for good literature reviews, and the annotated bibliography processes that came just before the exploratory drafts, as important pre-drafting or invention processes. In each case, the processes that Der refers to had the same three components: (1) reading a text or set of texts, (2) marking or annotating those texts, and (3) producing a document that demonstrates the reader's reading process to others (i.e., explaining the reader's assumptions and reasons for making judgments). Der is quite aware of what she's been doing in the class and how that labor is situated within her group's place. Assessment processes, as such, were key to Der's writing practices.

A bit later in her final self-assessment, Der explains the importance of her group in the above processes:

> My group members helped me in more ways than I can ever
> explain. I have never really taken the advice of classmates
> before, but from this class, I learned to not rely on just the
> feedback from you as the professor, but from those who are
> in the same boat as me. The trust of colleagues and their
> advice / opinions on topics has me feel more secure in the
> fact that criticism can actually be helpful considering the
> fact that those opinions would be voiced by others as well.
> Being within the same group every class session helped me
> feel a role of consistency in the classroom. Each of group
> member has shown me new method of thinking for reading
> and writing.

Der finds the ecological place of her group to be most valuable to her learning and to the "consistency" of the course. She defines the importance of this place and the people in it as ones opposed to me, the teacher: "I learned to not rely on just the feedback from you as the professor, but from those who are in the same boat as me." Even in her metaphor, she visualizes her group as one isolated and different from me, and perhaps others in the same class, and these differences are important for her to see "new method[s] of thinking for reading and writing." Much like I described Lyna's group, Der associates her group with a locally diverse place, filled with diverse people who need their differences to help each other for judging processes. And this help concerns not just the pedestrian help with drafts, but help with thinking, with the meta-activities that our assessment processes were designed to encourage.

What I hope is clear is how students migrated assessment processes to their drafting processes, and how that was the typical flow of practices from one location (assessing essays) to another location (drafting essays), from ecological process to part to product, or from process to place to product. In both cases, a different kind of critical consciousness surfaced, each problematizing the student's existential situation in different ways. For Zach, it was his own white racial *habitus* in the assessment processes of Cristina's research on the media's role in racializing criminals and victims. Zach's assessment processes pushed him to implicate himself in her paper, then upon reflection, our assessment processes of the class helped him also find emotion and passion as critical feelings that aid him as a writer. For Der, it was her process of drafting that she migrated from our stop and write assessment method, a method that allowed her to problematize her own existential language situation through a discussion of studies on Hmong students and an historicizing of her family. Der's project, not her assessment documents, is the place where she finds critical practices, yet they flow from her assessment processes and group.

The flux of ecological elements shows also how consubstantial they all are. When we talk about the place of a writing group in an assessment ecology as a collection of students, as people, we are simultaneously talking about the way they are also the processes, parts, and products in the ecology. In most cases, students self-consciously used assessment processes in their drafting processes, which became parts and products, and students were able to talk about these elements cogently and in ways that tended to situate them in the specific places that their groups cultivated in the ecology. However seeing assessments and drafts as ecological places tends to be a better way to form critical stances toward language and judgments, ones that have the best opportunity to critique the *habitus* involved in judging writing. Students' near universal migration of assessment practices to drafting practices was designed into the assessment ecology by making assessment the central activity and defining it as processes. Assessment was introduced to them in their entrance into the ecology by way of our grading contract negotiation processes; it was reinforced through our rubric-creation processes; it was practiced weekly in their groups; it was reflected upon multiple times; and it was reconsidered one last time in their exit from the assessment ecology.

EXITING THE ECOLOGY

I wanted my students in some way to be aware of the way they were exiting and taking learning products with them. Instead of asking students to assess their colleagues' portfolios, which would have asked them to look mostly at the past by focusing on ecological parts but not necessarily on themselves as learners, I asked them to assess each other as on-going learners in a final assessment letter addressed to me and their colleagues. Each student had to write a letter that assessed each group member, and one that assessed themselves. All letters were written to the person being assessed and me. In our final conferences during finals week, each student and I read together her colleagues' final assessments of her, her own self-assessment, and mine. Just like all of the other assessment processes in the ecology, these readings constructed a landscape of judgments, a final borderland-place. These letters addressed three evaluative questions, asking for evidence of each: (1) how would you describe your colleague as a learner and writer? (2) What did you learn from your colleague during this semester? (3) What do you think your colleague can still work on, learn, or continue to develop? I asked students to spend at least 30-45 minutes writing each letter, and in their self-assessments, they could write just about items 1 and 3.

The final conference is always my favorite moment in every semester. I get a chance to see my students individually in my office one last time. Sometimes, I admit, I'm a little tearful. I cannot help being attached to my students, their success, and their writing. I've watched them do so much in many cases. At this culminating moment, a moment in which I help them all out of the ecology, I get to tell them in writing and in person the kind of learner they were in my eyes, what I learned from them, and my hopes for them in the future, which is usually a positive and warm conversation, even when some students do not always meet my expectations. Most of all, I get to hear their versions of themselves as learners and their hopes as writers and learners for the future, which often is surprising, humbling, illuminating, and wonderful.

I'm always surprised by a few students, ones I thought didn't buy into the class, or seemed too distant most of the semester, or those whom I thought I'd lost somewhere along the way, or who were enticed by what I consider the wrong product to focus on, a grade. Then final conferences happen, and sometimes, those students surprise me with beautiful articulations of lessons learned and questions lingering. Of course, there are also those students who from the beginning of the course clearly bought into the grading contract, took to every assignment in the spirit that it was asked, and moved through the writing assessment ecology in the ways I'd hoped all students would. Zach was one of those students. His journey wasn't free from danger or problems, but in his attitude and willingness to labor for its own sake, he was ideal.

Zach's end of semester self-assessment letter reveals him to be self-aware of much of the assessment ecology and its intended products. He picks up on all the themes I've discussed in his reflections on the grading contract, the rubric building process, his own drafting processes, his reflections on assessments, and the assessments made on his own writing. Many of the lessons he learns come from his dwelling in the borderland created by his conflicting assessments on his writing, encapsulated in his earlier question, "how I can be so close, but way off at the same time," which I believe amounted to his own coming to critical consciousness about his writing and its judgment as a complex network of people, texts, and *habitus*. Zach opens his final self-assessment document by discussing his initial feelings about the course, and how the contract's focus on labor laid the foundation for his learning:

> On that first day as I walked into the class I never felt so uncomfortable and insecure, growing up writing has never been my strongest attribute. By knowing this about myself I would be lying if I couldn't say that I was nervous about what might be expected of me throughout this course. I wasn't sure if I was going to be able to achieve the writing level that would be expected and therefore providing me that insecurity. Latter as we begin to discuss the contract which stated that I will receive no lower than a B if I provide the labor being asked. This was a very foreign and new idea because like most of us we always just earned our grades through the quality of the work completed. Now by having to not worry as much about writing to please the professor this contract provided me with a whole new outlook on writing. And simply provided me the confidence I have always wanted throughout my educational career. The reason why the contract provided me with the confidence is mostly due to the fact that I can just write and try my best without having to worry about a grade.

In one way, I hear Zach saying he writes with ease by not having to write to please. The contract did that for him. For Zach and most of the other monolingual and multilingual writers in the class, the grading contract opened the writing assessment ecology to them because it changed the way grades operated in the ecology. Even when grades are thought of as a reward, there is still the threat of punishment when one doesn't get the grade. Zach knows this, and it amounts to always "writing to please the professor." For Zach, our contract ecology provided "confidence," a confidence he "always wanted" but could not have because grades were always present in past ecologies, which is significant given the research on self-efficacy and its positive association with students' success in writing courses (McCarthy, Meier, & Rinderer, 1985; Reynolds, 2003; Shell, Murphy, & Bruning, 1989). Also interesting because many have discussed the negative association between grades and student performance in writing classes (Bernard-Donals, 1998; Bleich, 1997; Elbow, 1993, 1997). And this final statement of his (the self-assessment letter) occurs after Zach knows what his grade in the course is, so he has nothing to gain by telling me what he thinks I want to hear (he's not trying to please, but he is at ease). In fact, I made a point in class to tell them this, telling them that as long as they showed up for their conference with their assessments written and posted, as usual, it didn't matter what they said. They still met the contract's obligations. I wanted them to be honest and at ease.

When discussing the things he took away from the class, he immediately goes to his assessment practices, which he rearticulates as reading practices:

> One major aspect that has helped me grow in my writing is learning how to properly annotate sources. I never did this before and would often find myself rereading sources again and again until I had it almost memorized .... I was able to have a better understanding of the information at hand by using the stop and write method provided by this class. Overall I feel that this aspect alone has helped me in so many ways as a writer, and also has taught me how truly important it is to progress in reading before trying to progress in writing.

Without me saying anything, Zach figures it out and explains the benefit of our assessment processes, the stop and write method, which is not simply an assessment method but a method to read and annotated academic texts, a practice he struggled with in the past. Zach sees as he exits our ecology that the stop and write method wasn't just a way to provide feedback to his peers, but was a reading process, which then became a writing process for him, and now it is learning product. During the semester, I didn't talk to Zach about this method or him using it to write his papers. These lessons he came to on his own organically, yet in a determined way (i.e., I limited the options and pressed him toward their use and repurposing). Like all writing assessment ecologies, the ecological processes and places determines the ecological products, even though students have choices, arguably more in our assessment ecology. I expected some students to migrate their assessment processes to their drafting processes in some fashion, and most did in a variety of ways, as Der also shows in her practices. Finally, Zach also figures out an important academic behavior: read first, find your position on things, then write.

Near the end of his self-assessment letter, Zach closes the narrative loop that he began by discussing his initial reaction to the class and the contract. This time, his reflecting is framed in terms of what he has come to understand about himself as a writer and communicator in other ecologies. His conclusions are personal and nuanced, in some ways learning the lessons his colleagues had asked of him in Project 2 about considering the personal in his writing:

> project one was extremely personal to me do to the fact that it made me look at how I became the person and writer I am today. By grasping a better understanding of my family and my upbringing I was able to make some real connections to why and how I have such weak communication skills. As stated in project one I discovered that the lack of communication between my father and grandfather, and then me has truly rendered me with a far weaker ability to argue and write in this manner [academic manner]. As a result I learned that I must be the one to break this bad habit and not allow my future generation to carry this unfortunate family tradition.

How did he come to this very personal statement about his family and his own ways of communicating? Was it his access to the emotional and passionate ontological aspects of writing he found in our course? Was it his assessment processes that led him to problematize his own existential situation in the writing of others in his group? Is this a statement that suggests Zach is coming to critical consciousness about his own *habitus*, one inherited from his father and grandfather? Regardless of the answers to these questions, our writing assessment ecology provided Zach with a way to see his own history of communication, a way to come to personal insights on his own—not be told of them by some authority. He sees that his own language and ways with words are not simply due to his personality or interests, not arbitrary, but also due to long family histories that are gendered and difficult to break, determined. He sees how language is social and how particular groups, discourse communities, form communication practices, even how they embody them—his grandfather, father, and he are their discourses. And he takes a stance against the dominant practices of his family, a stance of difference, a counterhegemonic one. I'm not sure I could hope for anything more critical from a student than these kinds of learning products.

In his final self-assessment letter, Barry, a third-year African-American student, who was always a cautious but willing participant in the class, offers an unequivocal positive assessment of our grading contract, but discusses it as an ecology that had people involved in flexible decisions:

> The idea of flexibility in this class is something I will re-member and attempt to adapt to my lifestyle in the near future. To start off the class was a metaphor for change in my estimation. It was completely different from any sort of class I've ever been involved in. First the students got to pick the requirements for the grading of the course. In my opinion this was great. The teacher was not a tyrant and we actually got to participate in the blueprints for the class, this not only made the students engage in the class but it made us want to engage in the class. I find myself loving this idea. By using this idea, we became a lot more creative as a group, everyone's opinions were heard, everyone felt involved and there wasn't a lot of stress on one person. In the future if I'm ever given the responsibility to have some sort of control over people, I hope to use my power as gracefully as our professor did. I hope to be flexible. This means being open to suggestions like our teacher was. Or being willing to forgive or change codes of agreement. When I note forgiveness, I am specifically thinking about the instance where we decided as a class to give those who were late on assignments a few more free late assignments. From this I learned to not be so rigid. At this moment in my life I can't explain why this was good, but it seems as if forgiveness on some occasions may be an asset.

When students take control of the ecology, or at least their place in the ecology, as Barry and his group (Jane, Gloria, Gideon, and Der) did, they often come to their own lessons. They had, as Barry emphasizes above, power and control of things. They negotiated the terms of their work and its assessment, which encouraged them to "want to engage in the class." The lessons Barry learns I could not have anticipated as well as I did Zach's. Barry describes the class as a "metaphor for change," which I find intriguing, even though I'm not sure what he means by it, but I know it means something to him. He says that "everyone's opinions were heard, everyone felt involved and there wasn't a lot of stress on one person." Perhaps the change is in the way the ecology felt to him, the way it felt more engaging, or gave him more stake in more of the decisions being made. But his most intriguing lessons for me have to do with non-writing products, about his own bourgeoning *habitus*, the lessons I couldn't have anticipated. They are about the kind of leader he wants to be, one who isn't a "tyrant," but one who uses his power "gracefully." If there is one thing that assessment does in classrooms and other places in schools, it is manage power. Barry has figured this out and articulated it well.

And then, there is his lessons on forgiving. He isn't, I think, saying that forgiveness is needed when leading others, but "forgiveness on some occasions," which is more contingent and nuanced—it seems more rhetorical, more Sophistic-cated. These lessons, unlike Zach's, are less about Barry's writing or reading and more about Barry's stance in the world as a person, his *habitus*, about how power works, and how forgiveness is needed to exercise power ethically. He reminds me that forgiveness is power enacted. Remember, Barry found that our labors around the rubric made "better adults." I did not, could not, plan for such products to be produced for Barry in our ecology, but they are good ones, needed ones in our world, ones that also could be argued reveal writing assessment as an ontological act of compassion through the "graceful" use of power and forgiveness.

As mentioned earlier, Ashe often was ambivalent about the class and what she could get from it. She was always a respectful and good student, doing the labors asked of her, but in her reflections and self-assessments, she was also honest about what she learned and what she didn't understand. In her final self-assessment letter, Ashe again provides similar ambiguous conclusions about her learning journey in the class. As many students did, her letter's opening begins with a discussion of our grading contract:

> I remember reading the class contract for the first time and I noticed how different the grading contract was from other courses I have taken. One aspect of the contract that appealed to me was the fact that we were able to negotiate the grading contract with you as a class. Honestly speaking, I've seen my shares of professors who run their class as if students don't have a life to live other than focusing on academics or how they shouldn't have taken the course if one unexpected issue occurred in their life. Having this aspect in the contract gave me extra stepping stones if I happen to fall short along the way.

One of the class activity that I found interesting was getting

feedbacks from my colleagues. It was an interesting process
because of the different ideas and analysis my colleagues made
to help me better understand what they didn't understand
or what they felt was missing. Getting feedback from our
professor was also interesting. This was one of the confusing
feedbacks I received this semester. I've come to think that it's
really hard to satisfy anyone with my writing, anything really,
because of how critical people are with how they want writing
to be delivered. In any case, I hope to continue to write and
not get too focused on other's expectations, but just write.

Despite her more measured tone, Ashe noticed similar aspects in our grading contract as Barry and others did. Students "were able to negotiate" it, and like Barry's "forgivingness," she sees our assessment ecology as one that offers her "extra stepping stones" on the terrain, just in case she "f[e]ll short along the way." But the lessons she learns from our assessment processes are more ambiguous than most of her peers. This ambiguity stems from the "confusing feedbacks" that she received from me, which I'm assuming was because my assessments seemed so different from her colleagues (they had the binary judgments on them). What she learns, however, is that "it's really hard to satisfy anyone with my writing, anything really, because of how critical people are with how they want writing to be delivered." Yes, a good lesson about audiences and writing, I think. Likely, in her mind, I am the most critical person in the ecology. She seems to be talking directly to me in a gentle and respectful way, perhaps asking me, "why must you be so critical?" She ends on hope, a hope to keep writing, not to "get too focused on other's expectations, but just write." I'd like to read this as a counter-hegemonic hope to disregard future readers like me in her efforts to "just write." But I'd also like to think that Ashe's concerns, similar to Zach's question about his conflicting assessments, his borderland, is Ashe's first steps toward a critical consciousness through a similar struggle in a borderland of assessments on her writing.

Later in her letter, she comes back to her confusion and on-going concerns about her learning in the class:

This journey that we took together was quite a ride; the confusion and frustration that we shared, the exchange of ideas
that we commuted, the time we spent listening to each other's
advice, and the time and efforts that we dedicated to read
each other's work was time consuming, but it has brought us
all to understand each other more than an average classmate
would. All in all, my colleagues were the first individuals I am

able to see around campus and beckon a hello to, especially as a first time student at Fresno State.

I still think that I don't really understand rhetoric. I understand what it is, but not to the point where I know where to apply it. Sometimes I think that some professors are so critical with how they grade my papers that they ignore the reasoning and purpose that I may have intentionally made that sentence that way or why I put that comma there even if they don't think it is necessary.... I don't know whether my writing is meaningful to others, but it is meaningful to me, that's why I am writing. ...writing down what I feel or think at that moment and those who read this will do whatever they please with it.. take whatever it is that you think is meaningful to you ....you may find something meaningful to you along the way of thinking it as unimportant.

It seems significant to me that Ashe, a shy, introverted, multilingual (Hmong), "first time student at Fresno State," would find through the "time consuming" labors and "confusion and frustration" of the ecology friends she could talk to outside of class. It seems significant for Ashe that she could say, "my colleagues were the first individuals I am able to see around campus and beckon a hello to," and that she would say this in a letter of self-assessment, describing herself as a learner. These, to me, are important products of our writing assessment ecology, and not ones that everyone could or should get when they leave it. They certainly are not part of the formal learning outcomes of the course, but definitely make for warm, inviting, and educative environments.

Equally significant is her return to the frustration of "professors" who are "so critical," which could be another reference to me, but maybe not since she links these readers of her writing to graders. I was clearly not a grader. Ashe's focus on her closing paragraph above is on these readers' lack of empathy for her intentions when she writes: "I may have intentionally made that sentence that way or why I put that comma there even if they don't think it is necessary." This is such a good lesson for any teacher to remember about his students, especially his multilingual students, a lesson that reminds me of Min-Zhan Lu's (Horner & Lu, 1999, pp. 175-177) wonderful example and pedagogy that asked her students to map the contact zones in student writing that initially looked like error, but quickly revealed in deeper discussions possible writer intentions. Perhaps, I did not do this enough in this class when responding to Ashe's writing, a lesson I need to heed more often.

Yet Ashe isn't finished. She shows herself as a stronger woman than her shy,

271

introverted persona suggests. She concludes strongly about herself as a writer in an elegant and bold fashion, reminiscent of Hellenic Sophistic rhetorical thought: "I don't know whether my writing is meaningful to others, but it is meaningful to me, that's why I am writing....writing down what I feel or think at that moment and those who read this will do whatever they please with it." This isn't despair, at least not as I read it. It seems to come from a sense that writing is an ontological act, an act of being in the world. I see Ashe in this final, passionate passage finding her own way as a writer, determined to keep writing, no matter what others think. The ellipses are hers, and they appear to be places she pauses for emphasis, or asks her reader to pause and think. Despite her own sense that she doesn't understand how to apply rhetoric, I also hear a nascent Sophistic rhetorical philosophy of language in her final words, one akin to Protagoras' human-measure fragment. This is significant since Protagoras' fragment is one about judgment (Inoue, 2007, pp. 45-46). How her writing is assessed by readers, how it is read, is intimately connected to her sense of herself as a writer. I believe our ecology revealed this to her and could be one way to see her problematizing of her existential writing assessment situation. Despite the stumbles and falls in the ecology, Ashe had some stones to step on, ones she knew would be there, and they may have saved her in order that she might keep on writing.

Susan, on the other hand, was less enthusiastic about the writing assessment ecology in her final self-assessment letter, preferring one that offers "structure," and "the ability to write a comprehendible sentence," so that "even a brilliant idea is [not] lost." Susan, I should mention, was a consummate student. She was white, older than most, and had a full-time job and a daughter in college as well. Susan did her work thoroughly, and was always present for her group members. Her assessments were detailed and helpful. Her drafts were clear and exhibited the markers of our local SEAE. Despite her semester-long concern about the way our class was structured, she accepted my invitation to have some faith in our processes, to do the labors asked of her in the spirit asked. I think her willingness to have some faith in our contract and processes helped her see the good products she took from our environment. Susan explains near the end of her letter:

> Being older than most of my classmates, I think I unconsciously assume that I have nothing to learn from them and am frequently pleasantly surprised to learn how wrong I am. The feedback I received from my group members was helpful in keeping me on track and motivated. I struggled a lot this semester with motivation and this class, although the source of MUCH stress helped me get back on track. It is refreshing

to spend time with young minds that have goals and opinions and purpose. It gives me hope for the future and keeps me grounded. Thank you for the opportunity to learn something new. Although not a 100% fan of the structure of this class, I can see the benefit of the approach. Personally, it made this particular journey more difficult but it also gave me the opportunity to push myself and learn something about myself in the process.

Susan wasn't converted "100%" by the end of the semester, but because she labored so diligently, cultivated a place with her group members, she still found products worth taking with her as she left the ecology. She learned to listen to her younger student-peers, and through that listening she gained some "hope for the future." Additionally while her journey through our ecology was "more difficult" for her than perhaps a more conventional assessment ecology would have been, ours still offered her "the opportunity to push myself and learn something about myself in the process." While I wanted so much more for Susan—I wanted fireworks and dancing elves, spectacular insights about writing and assessment at her exit—because she gave her colleagues so much, it is not always clear at the end of a semester to anyone what products a student may eventually gain from any writing assessment ecology. Perhaps, Susan (or I) will find in years to come other products from her journey in the course. For now, I must be satisfied that Susan accepted her agency in our ecology, acted upon it, and while more difficult than it could have been for her, she pushed herself and learn something about her herself that she wouldn't have otherwise. And these products were revealed most noticeably for her in the ecological place of her writing group.

In contrast, Gideon comes to very specific insights about the products of the ecology, some expected, others unexpected. When discussing the writing and assessing processes in the class, he makes a distinction between different kinds of discourse in his life now:

> I learned the value of looking at the related work by academics whose work normally is scrutinized enough to be mostly objective valuable analysis.

> This was not natural for me and it was something of a milestone to find that there isn't as much bias and spin in academic writing as I previously thought. I found that the same holds true with academic papers as is true with news reporting. The stuff that is easiest to get to is usually the worst, but with diligence you find great information. What good academic re-

> sources have that good news reporting doesn't have is a more
> clear explanation of the questions that lead to certain infor-
> mation being presented which then leads to more questions.
> This sticks with me because until about half way through the
> semester I watched a lot of network news. My research of the
> healthcare legislation got me to see popular media for what
> it is. By and large they are selling conflict, not information. I
> haven't watched network news since.

In his usual fashion, Gideon coins a nice phrase, "selling conflict," which is a
conclusion that comes from another product about rhetoric that he takes from
our ecology. He explains that the information which is "easiest to get to is usually the worst," like all the network news he has watched. Additionally, these
insights come to him by his seeing how laborious good academic work is, and
how that hard labor corresponds to better writing of his own. It is through "dil-
igence" that one finds "great information." Gideon shows a coming to critical
consciousness about language in his world, how it is used around him and on
him, and how he has understood it next to how he understands it now. And this
product for him is another version of assessing, assessing news or the rhetoric in
the world around him.

I have to believe that it wasn't just his research and thinking on his project
that led him to this stance, but also his assessment labors in the course. All
of those labors were ones focused on this kind of discrimination, on asking
questions, on seeing questions in texts as important to academic inquiry and
important to understanding things in our world. Gideon sees the importance
of questions, saying that academic discourse offers "more clear explanation of
the questions that lead to certain information being presented which then leads
to more questions." For Gideon, good writing practices appear to be hard labor
that focuses on asking good questions that lead to more questions. Questions
were at the heart of our assessment practices, so in this very practical way, again,
the ecology set up writing assessment labors so that they flowed into other elements in the ecology, which ultimately manifested as ecological products.

Gideon continues his reflection by turning to non-writing or indirect writing products, but quickly returns to the theme of questions:

> This was one of those courses where it was impossible to
> blame the instructor for anything. That includes not having
> a substantial background in the subject at hand. This isn't
> always the case. When this isn't the case there is almost a
> built in excuse, or motivation, to put in a certain amount of
> effort. In either case what you get out is more closely tied to

what you put in. I think I ought to have made more the good fortune of your presence. I also learned to fight becoming jaded in my education experience through the grading rubric discussions and through being asked questions you and my peers more often than I was told to accept answers.

I learned that the rhetoric in messages can hold more information that what's being communicated. While the value of considering rhetoric isn't limited to this the messenger's rhetoric can hint at what values or questions drive them or what they are assuming about you and how to get a message to stick in your head or heart. What answers you think you may have found in that will lead to a wonderful endless stream of questions about the messenger and the message.

Most importantly I learned questions are more important than answers. A good question is hard to answer and what I learned from sharpening a good question to using better sources to attempt to explore my questions rather than find a finish line will serve me well in life.

He learned to "fight becoming jaded" about education "through the grading rubric discussions and through being asked questions." This sounds like something that may have been a fortunate by-product of the engagement and stake in the assessment ecology that Barry mentioned, who was one of Gideon's group members. And recall, it was Gideon and Der's group that attempted the question-listing method for assessing. Questions perhaps mostly obviously embodied assessment for Gideon's group. But as I argued already, these kinds of products, ones about building student agency and engaging students with questions about grading and judging, which for Gideon were questions that led him away from being jaded by his educational experiences in the past, were determined by how I designed the ecological elements of our writing assessment ecology. Gideon, through his focus on questions as his most enduring product, demonstrates the effectiveness of that design. If there is another way to describe our rubric processes, the rubric itself, and our assessment processes, it is that they all at their core are methods for posing questions, problematizing. To me, this simple but powerful stance is Gideon's coming to a critical consciousness about language and his own stance as a citizen, his own problematizing.

What I have attempted to reveal in Zach's, Barry's, Ashe's, Susan's, and Gideon's exits from our classroom writing assessment ecology is the variety of ecological products possible in an assessment ecology that focuses mostly on assessing but uses no grades during the semester as products. Some products are determined, like student agency and the lessons learned from that agency and the deeper engagement in the ecology. Zach and Barry are good examples of such products that students recognized upon their exits. Some products are unexpected, such as Ashe's finding friends to talk to on campus or Susan's seeing value in younger voices. And some products are not so clearly positive, such as Susan's less than "100%" approval of the course, or Ashe's uncertainty about meeting audience's expectations in her writing.

Most students' final self-assessment letters were positive in nature, similar to Zach's and Gideon's. In this closing section, I tried to use final self-assessment letters that were the most representative of the class, while also attempting to close the stories of some of the students I had opened earlier in the chapter. Perhaps the only truly atypical self-assessment letter was Susan's, since it was not fully supportive of our assessment ecology, but this is not a requirement of the course, or these final self-assessments, or even of exiting the ecology with worthwhile products in hand. I am arguing that most students left with a fledgling critical consciousness, a problematizing attitude that came from the central labor of assessing. All the insights, all the ecological products each student discusses, come from our labors as assessors, aided by constant reflections on assessment, the rubrics, and our labors themselves. For my students, the ecology was visible, and this made a difference.

To close, I turn to Jessica's self-assessment letter. Jessica, a monolingual, Latina, who was a third year psychology major and budding musician, was perhaps the most complete in her appreciation of the grading contract, group work, and the writing assessment ecology as a whole. She was a very good student, always seated near the front, always ready for discussions, always prepared. In many ways, I didn't worry much about Jessica during the semester. In part, because she was extraverted enough to ask questions when she had them in class, or after class. She also produced a lot of writing, much like Der, Zach, Jane, and Susan. She had, like most in the class, some difficulties with the dominant academic discourse promoted in the course, but through revision she always improved her drafts. Jessica seemed always to be doing fine. However, I end with Jessica because in some ways, like Zach, she represented the sweet-spot of the class and their exit from the ecology. Jessica's comments represent what most said about themselves as learners and about the products they took away from our ecology, only Jessica's letter personalizes the lessons at every turn, which to me highlights the local diversity of our classroom and shows how any writing assessment ecology always produces locally diverse products from locally diverse people in them that we cannot anticipate.

In Jessica's final self-assessment letter, she begins in typical fashion, discussing the contract. Her first paragraph, however, moves quickly from the abstraction of grades to herself and her relations in the ecology:

> First and foremost I would like to thank you for incorporating this new grading method in my writing, it was something very new to me and I will admit at first I was a bit hesitant but I think it definitely grew on me. I don't know if you remember but the first day that we went around and discussed what we were hoping to take from this class and the grade we wanted etc., I said all I cared about was getting an A, after that you went on to discuss how that was not important and I thought "psh an A not important, right!" but now I see it the way you do. I mean do not get me wrong, I love getting A's and if it is possible I will get it, but I do not look at it the way I did at the beginning of this semester. I think your method gave me a lot more freedom to write, which is something that I want and need when I write. It made me feel secure that my writing was not going to simply be given a letter grade after it was read only once, I had the chance to work on it until I made it into something better than the last, and I got feedback, and I felt very secure. I think it is because I did not have to stress about making it so amazing the first time so that I could get a decent grade, I was comfortable and I knew I was going to get another chance to work on it again. I do not know how to explain it, but to make this short I definitely see what you meant that first day now.

The sense of writing with ease, freedom, and comfort—feeling secure. These were common sentiments in most self-assessment letters. I hear her saying a version of Zach's sentiment: I wrote with ease, not to please. These sentiments embrace writing and assessing as ontological acts, as ways we are in classrooms. Most, like Jessica, link these sentiments to the contract and the larger classroom writing assessment ecology that gave them power. I do not take lightly sentiments like, "it made me feel secure," which Jessica makes twice, as well as saying, "I was comfortable." Feeling secure, while not my number one priority in class, surely for students is vital and necessary for writing. Security came from a lack of grades on drafts—or rather, not punishing drafts. Not only does Jessica figure out why grades are so harmful, why they are an ineffective product in a writing assessment ecology, she also explains the value of our assessment ecology in terms of a "method," a process, which led her to have "more freedom to write," a common comment on the grading contract at Fresno State in first-year writing courses, only it typically occurs in Hmong student formations (Inoue, 2012a, p. 89).

What I find encouraging about this self-assessment is Jessica's focus on her and her group members' labors of writing, reading, and assessing. It is these labors, not the approvals or positive comments from a teacher, not a grade or even a positive validation from me, that matters most to her. This is more powerful, and I think more productive, than any set of teacher comments on her writing or grades could have been. What matters most is her labor that is focused in a direction that she determines and controls, which in some ways is very similar to Ashe's determined hope to keep writing. In a different way not so like Ashe's, Jessica writes because of the ecology, because of the feedback she got, not in spite of it.

Jessica continues with method and process by describing the way the ecology, through our processes, changed her own processes and relations with others:

> This class as a whole changed not only my mindset but also
> the way I write, and the way I work with others. I hated
> group work before this class, I felt it was a waste of my time
> and I dreaded being stuck with people who were irresponsible
> and did not get the job done in time, and then I'd have to
> deal with lecturing them and then them end up hating me be-
> cause I do not know how to keep my mouth shut. But in this
> class I was able to work great with my group, we got the job
> done all the time, and sometimes we even talked about stuff
> that had nothing to do with the class (pretty bad, I know) but
> I think because we got to know each other that way as well, it
> helped our understanding of each other, the way we approach
> things, what is important to us, we learned to respect each
> other because of that. I cannot say I will enjoy working in a
> group as I did in this class in another class, but this changed
> the way I look at group work at least for now. I believe that
> is the biggest milestone that I was able to accomplish, along
> with as I stated before in my letter of reflection, the whole
> idea of me actually taking the time to read someone else's
> work and give helpful feedback.

The place cultivated by the locally diverse members of her group was important to the success of the assessment processes in the class. And perhaps most interesting, Jessica makes a good argument for the importance of the personal in academe, at least for students writing and reading each other's work: "because we got to know each other that way as well, it helped our understanding of each other, the way we approach things, what is important to us, we learned to respect each other because of that." Respect through the personal, through getting to know the locally diverse people around you, knowing their *habitus*, this seems an important learning product to take away, one only determined by the processes of assessing in the course. But of course, Jessica doesn't connect our group work with all group work. Like Barry's lesson about forgivingness, Jessica's lessons about group work are contingent and qualified. It may not work out so well in the next class.

Finally, Jessica's following paragraph moves to her dispositions as a writer. I don't think it is typical of most in the class, but my hope is that there is a degree of her enthusiasm for writing before and after the class that could be a product of our writing assessment ecology for more students. That is, I hope that through focusing on the labors of writing, reading, and judging, students not like Jessica, or not like Ashe, who are both determined to keep writing, but students more like Zach or Der who could produce text but may not call themselves writers at heart, or like Dwight, Gloria, and Kyler, who had various struggles with writing, could find a space in which they liked to write, could problematize the judgment of their writing. If writers like them could feel more like Jessica, they may experience writing and reading as ontological acts of judgment that can and should be problematized for their own good. I'm not sure how I could encourage this ecological product, but it seems important to strive for, and it's surely connected to antiracist writing assessment ecologies that feel safe and secure. Jessica reflects:

> As a learner I came in to this class thinking I knew what it was going to be about. I thought it would be all about just writing papers, reading stuff and writing a paper on that, grammar, essay structure, boring stuff like that, but it was not like that at all, and I really loved that! I feel that I grew as a learner as well. As where before I hated writing such long papers for a class, this class was different, I was able to choose my own topics, approach it in the way that I wanted to approach it and everything just made me feel so comfortable. I love writing, but I only love writing outside of school, I like to go in depth with things and discuss what is important to me, show empathy, create different scenarios, take the time to let my mind let everything out onto a piece of paper, everything important to me that is, I like to speak to the paper as if it were an actual person listening to me, and in this class I was able to do that. I cannot say I did it in my first project but I definitely did it in my second project. I was able to talk about something that is important to me, which is music. I listen to it, I sing it, I write it, I read it, I breathe it, it has been a part of my life for so long. There are musicians in my family as well, so it is kind

of easier to see that writing about music was important to me
and it was easier. I was able to take country music and turn it
into something not so personal, which I had no idea I would
be able to do, and I still do not think I did such a great job in
that area, but definitely better than I thought.

What a profound statement to make: "I love writing, but I only love writing outside of school." I've heard versions of this sentiment from many students in the past. And it's frustrating, not the student's statement, but the conditions I know that create such a response by a student, conditions I'm sure are similar if not the same as those that created Gideon's frustration and jadedness, or Ashe's ambiguity, or Der's and Zach's insecurities. These conditions are created by writing assessment ecologies that are not comfortable or secure, even harmful, and likely racist, despite their intended purposes. They don't let writing be an act of ease because they are too focused on it being an act to please.

One of the most memorable examples of this sentiment was from an African-American female student, a fifth year student graduating that semester (at a different university), who told me in her reflections how she'd loved keeping a journal, writing poetry and stories in high school, then took a timed writing exam for placement in college, and "failed it," placing her in study skills courses and not the first year writing course. This experience, as I imagine so many other similar writing assessment ecologies do, quickly and efficiently killed her love for writing—that is what she told. It killed it, clipped it from the vine while it was still blooming. She stop writing immediately, didn't begin again until five years later in my class. It's heartbreaking at times to know that this fundamental aspect of the college experience, writing assessment, fucks up so many young students who stop using writing for their own ontological purposes because the assessment ecologies they enter are unfriendly, caustic, uncomfortable, and unsafe. In my past student's case, it was because that placement ecology was racist. I know this because the first-year writing exemption exam at the same university, one based on the placement exam, never exempted an African-American student writer in its entire time of use.

But for Jessica, what she means by writing is something quite cerebral, creative, organic, and explorative. Writing for Jessica, as I would hope it could be for more of my students, is a labor that allows her to "take the time to let my mind let everything out onto a piece of paper, everything important to me that is, I like to speak to the paper as if it were an actual person listening to me," which our ecology allowed her to do and rewarded her for it. But she also demonstrates why writing assessment ecologies kill students' organic love for or enjoyment of the act of writing. As she puts it, "I listen to it, I sing it, I write it, I read it, I breathe it, it has been a part of my life for so long." This is a similar description of how my past student who was so destroyed by her placement exam described herself as a writer, a writer who wrote daily in a diary, wrote poems and stories, then took an exam and stopped writing completely. If writing and its assessment are ontological acts, then the words they produce, the labor they expend, and the products they create are *of them*, which means that the writing assessment ecologies that simply rank, rate, grade, or push students around, that give them very little power or agency, that do not allow them to cultivate their own ecological purposes, that do not acknowledge students' labors as valuable—central even to the ecology—will destroy students' interest, engagement, and love of writing. This is the real academic tragedy of most writing assessment ecologies. They kill most students' love of writing and willingness to have others read and discuss it.

There is much to like and say about Jessica's letter. For this discussion, I'll conclude by saying that it is a good demonstration of the way locally diverse writing assessment ecologies always transform the intended products of our pedagogies and learning outcomes. Zach, Susan, Ashe, Barry, Gideon, and Jessica demonstrate the ways locally diverse students transform broader determined consequences, and do so because the ecology is visible to them. Locally diverse ecological products are a result of the contingent nature of what and how we teach writing, as much as they are of the locally diverse students and teachers who inhabit and construct the assessment ecology. Chris Gallagher (2012), in fact, argues a very similar point when arguing for writing programs to focus on assessing for "consequences" or "aims," not for outcomes (p. 47), because "consequences direct our attention to singularity and potentiality" (p. 48). This, I believe, is one of the strengths of using an ecological theory of writing assessment. It assumes the inherent diverse nature of students, their languages, their evolving purposes, their reading and writing processes, their parts or artifacts, the degrees and kind of power exercised (or not), the places on the landscape they construct in order to survive, and the products with which they leave our classes. It also makes visible and dramatizes the interconnected nature of all these elements.

Finally, what I hope I've shown through my discussion of my classroom as a writing assessment ecology is, among other things, the ways that every writing classroom is first and foremost a writing assessment ecology that is either racist or antiracist. To be antiracist, it first must be visible to everyone as an ecology. I believe that making more obvious to ourselves and students our own classroom writing assessment ecology as such, even when a teacher has not taken advantage of key opportunities, can still provide ways to offer students the seeds of critical consciousness, ways to problematize their own existential writing assessment situations, ways to become antiracist in their languaging. And as teachers and WPAs, we should be inquiring about these elements when we design, revise, and assess our pedagogies, and especially when we assess our assessment ecologies (when we validate them). If we do not, it may appear that our students are not learning, or not learning enough, when likely, they are learning what they want to learn, or can learn, or what's important to them, or some hybrid, code-meshed, translingual version of products we (teachers and writing administrators) think our students need or want. In other ways, they may be learning things we, their teachers, cannot possible learn. Ultimately though, to understand any of the learning in our writing classrooms, and how to assess such learning, we must understand our writing assessment ecologies as borderland-places where local diversities, dominant discourses, and hegemonic structures of norming and racing clash and shock/*choque* one another, flux and move, creating expected and unexpected ecological places, people, and products.

CHAPTER 5: DESIGNING ANTIRACIST WRITING ASSESSMENT ECOLOGIES

In this final chapter, I offer a heuristic for building antiracist classroom writing assessment ecologies. I assume that when designing any writing course, a teacher must think very carefully about the ways that writing will be assessed in the course, from rubric activities, feedback, and peer responses on drafts to assessing in-class impromptu writing, and grading. This thinking through one's assessments comes before (or at least simultaneously with) thinking through one's pedagogy and curriculum. In fact, as I hope my example in Chapter 4 illustrates, it may be most productive to think about one's classroom writing assessment ecology as one's pedagogy. Writing assessment in its fullest sense as an ecology, is pedagogy.

Thus a large part of designing a writing course is considering how the assessment of writing creates the ecology of the classroom in which students and teacher interact and learn together. An assessment ecology is the heart of any Freirean problem-posing pedagogy, which I've articulated in this book as the central practice in antiracist writing assessment ecologies. Learning in writing courses is driven by assessment if that learning is understood as a product of the ecology. In one sense, the assessment of writing completes the cycle that drafting begins. It forms the audience, their purposes for reading, and that audience's responses to writing, which provide information to the writer. But writing assessment as ecology is more than reading and providing feedback, it's also thinking privately and publically about expectations for writing, about the nature of judgment, about the nature of discourse itself, about one's own existential writing assessment situation, one's relation to the dominant discourse expected in the classroom or academy, and one's own *habitus* that informs one's judgments of texts. Thus a writing classroom that purports to "teach" writing cannot fully do so without interrogating the nature of judging and valuing language, the nature of dominant discourses (e.g., local SEAEs or white racial *habitus*), and the students' relations to these phenomena.

Antiracist writing assessment ecologies explicitly pay close attention to relationships that make up the ecology, relationships among people, discourses, judgments, artifacts created and circulated. They ask students to reflect upon them, negotiate them, and construct them. Antiracist writing assessment ecologies also self-consciously (re)produce power arrangements in order to examine and perhaps change them. When designing an antiracist writing assessment ecology, a teacher can focus students' attention on a few of the ecological elements discussed in Chapter 3, which inter-are. This means addressing and negotiating one element, say the part of a rubric, means you are addressing others, such as power relations and the ecological places where students problematize their existential writing assessment situations.

When designing the foundations for an antiracist writing assessment ecology, I offer the following heuristic, a set of questions that can be used to guide a teacher's thinking and planning. I have reordered the elements in a way that makes sense to me when designing a course from scratch, but I see no reason why a teacher couldn't begin in the heuristic where she wishes. I begin with purposes and processes, thinking about them together, because my own orientation as a teacher is to think first about what I want my students to do, what I envision they will be doing each week, and why they might want or need to do that labor. The heuristic is not meant to be exhaustive, but generative. There are surely other ways to ask the questions below or consider each element in an ecology. The heuristic is aimed at helping teachers begin to think about the ways their classrooms are antiracist writing assessment ecologies, and ways to invent such ecologies. Furthermore, these questions may offer ways to prompt students to investigate and negotiate each element as well.

- **Purposes**. *What various purposes for learning are made explicit about the assessment of students' writing, and how well do they articulate a problematizing of the students' existential writing situations?* Why are you or your students reading or judging any particular piece of writing or a draft in the way you are? Does each assessment process have its own unique purpose? How do you ensure that students are not penalized because they are not white and middle class, yet still guarantee that they develop as readers and writers in meaningful and productive ways? In what ways are you asking students to problematize their existential writing assessment situations, or asking them to see their own *habitus* next to ideal ones that assignments imagine or other readers imagine? How are students' various relations to the dominant discourse expected in the course, which is usually based on a white racial *habitus* and a local SEAE, accounted for in the purposes of assessment in the course? How are the purposes for assessing writing helping students critique the white racial *habitus* and local SEAE that they may still have to approximate?
- *Course/Teacher Purposes*. Is there a larger antiracist purpose for the assessment of writing in general in the course? Is that larger purpose made clear to students and is it consistently maintained across all the

activities in the course? Is there a formal moment when students can reflect upon this larger purpose, and connect it to their own practices and experiences?

- *Student Purposes.* How involved are students in constructing and articulating the purposes for each assessment process? Do they have opportunities to create and act upon their own purposes for individual assessment activities? How are those individual purposes accounted for in the assessment processes and parts in the ecology?

- **Processes**. *What processes, work, or labor will students do each day or week that contribute to, feed into, or create the parts, products, or places of the ecology?* What processes do you plan for or anticipate students doing in order to read, make judgments, then articulate and disseminate those judgments to writers? What processes occur because of or after those articulations (e.g., discussions, revisions/rethinking, reflections)? How are processes or labor accounted for in the calculation of course grades?

- *Rubric-Building.* How are the codes and expectations for writing (the rubric) constructed, articulated to students, and justified to them as appropriate expectations of the course? Can your rubric(s) be an articulation of something other than standards, such as a set of dimensions worth exploring and questioning, a starting point, not end point? What role do students play in the creation or revision of the rubric and writing assignments? How does the rubric address, identify, or name the dispositions it promotes as a part of a white racial *habitus*? How are students' *habitus* made apparent and used as a critical comparative lens to critique the rubric? Is the rubric (or the course's writing expectations) set up as static or do they change during the course of the semester? Are there processes in place that help encourage and discuss those changes? Are students a part of those processes?

- *Feedback.* How do students create feedback for peers' writing? What do students do with feedback or assessments? How is difference and conflicting judgments created or manufactured in feedback processes? How do students confront difference and conflict, particularly in the judgments on their writing? How are the goals of that confrontation in processes expressed (are they about finding agreement or understanding difference and perspectives)? Do students dialogue or revise their original judgments and feedback after discussing them face to face? How do the processes of reading and judgment help students to articulate a white racial *habitus* as an arbitrary set of expectations for making meaning and communicating? How are they led to understand, then articulate their own *habitus* used to judge writing?

- *Reflection.* Are there on-going reflective processes that ask students to make sense of peer reviews, rubric building activities, or your feedback? How do the processes of reflecting help students toward a problematizing of their existential writing assessment situations? How do these reflection processes show them a way to consider their own *habitus* in reading and writing as a *habitus*, as a set of historically determined dispositions that they don't have complete control over, and that are not inherently better or worse than the dominant *habitus* of the academy or western society?

- *Labor monitoring.* Are there ways students can keep track of their labor, its duration, frequency, and intensity? How might students reflect upon their labor practices in order to interrogate them as a part of their *habitus*? What patterns might students look for in their labor practices that might tell them something about their language practices, or their reading practices, or what they can (or are able to) read and value in texts? Are there ways to compare students' labor practices, not find ideal practices, but notice the diverse ways students attend to the course processes?

- **Places.** *What ecological places (figurative or real) are created through the judgment of writing or the assessment processes students enact?* What attention is paid to the places created in the ecology and can students reflect on the conditions and effects of those places? Where do students inhabit or dwell in the ecology and what are the effects or consequences of dwelling in those places? What places are created by judgments of writing and how do students engage in conflict in those places? Are there ways in which the places your ecology creates become places that unconsciously or unreflectively norm students to some universal standard, such as a white racial *habitus*? Are there places in your ecology that are constructed by the presence of mostly students of color, places where mostly multilingual students inhabit, where Blacks or Latinos/as inhabit? How much control do students have in creating or changing the places created by the ecology, for naming them, critiquing them, resisting them, establishing the processes or labor that constitute them, or identifying what they get from those places? How is that control formally designed into the ecology and how much attention is paid to the ways those places are controlled?

- *Writing groups.* Do students work in consistent writing groups, or different ones each week? How many students make up those places? How are those places composed or designed? Do you hand-pick in order to ensure diverse writing groups? Do students have a say in their creation, or in their on-going cultivation? How much reflection is done on the dynamics of their writing groups, and what happens with those reflections afterwards? How is trust and respect built into the writing group dynamics?

- *Failure and Success.* How is failure constructed as a place in the ecology? How often can students fail at writing (either publically or privately)? How is success constructed and how often are students positioned in the place of success? Is success public or private? Are there grades? If so, how do your grading practices construct places in which students are positioned, and then become inherent to that place? Do you offer any formal moments in the course to ask students about how failure and success are created in the class, in their writing, in their labors, or how the nature of success and failure have changed for them?

- *Texts.* How are the places of texts, particularly those used as examples for discussion (either published or student texts), constructed relative to the expectations of the course, which often are a product of a white racial *habitus*? Are published texts used as model places only? How are those same textual places compared to (set against, set next to) the locally diverse *habitus* of students that organically occur in the classroom and in student writing? Is race made present in the writing and authors of published examples or "models"? Are there ways that white textual places and textual places of color might be juxtaposed so that students might problematize those places and their writer's *ethos*?

- **Parts.** *What ecological parts (i.e., the codes, texts, documents, and artifacts that comprise writing assessment processes) are present, developed, exchanged, and manipulated?* How is each part generated and agreed upon by students and teacher? How do the ecological parts and students' reflections on them help students consider the course's expectations as participating in a white racial *habitus* that may be different from their own? How might students compare non-hierarchically their own writing dispositions (their own various *habitus*) next to the dominant white racial *habitus*, not to see themselves as inferior but to see the diversity of languaging and making meaning, and perhaps to critique the hegemonic? How might those insights be incorporated into the purposes, processes, and products of the ecology?

- *Rubrics.* How are the expectations of writing (e.g., assignment instructions, assignment processes, and rubrics) created and revised? Do students have a say in their creation or revisions? What does the artifact that embodies expectations in writing look like? What do students do with it? What does the teacher do with it? How is the articulation of the rubric such that it calls attention to its own participation in a white racial *habitus*, or others?

- *Discourse of Assessment and Judgment.* How do you ensure student participation in developing the codes of assessment and judgment, the ways that writing is talked about, reflected upon, made sense of, and theorized in the class? In what formal ways do students reflect upon the codes and artifacts of assessment, not their drafts, but the discourse around their drafts, feedback, dialogue, rubrics, etc.? How is that reflecting informed by any pertinent literature on whiteness and race, feedback to writing, or composition theory? How is their reflecting used to help students problematize their existential writing assessment situations?

- *Texts.* What student-generated texts are expected? How are students involved in creating the general expectations for their texts? What are those texts expected to look like? What are readers expected to do with them, or how do students read in order to make judgments? What assessment texts (or texts that articulate judgments of peers' writing) are students expected to produce and what do they look like? How are they produced? Will the teacher produce the same kind of assessment texts? What do students do with their assessment texts? How do they function in writing groups or in class discussions? How much freedom do students have in deviating in form, format, or content of the texts they are asked to produce? Are there discussions that set up those conversations if and when students do deviate from expected forms, formats, or content?

- **Power.** *What power relations are produced in the ecology and what are the most effective or preferable ones for students' individual learning goals and the course's overall learning goals?* How much control and decision-making do students have in the creation and implementation of all assessment processes and parts? How are vulnerable students (e.g., quiet students, introverted students, students of color, multilingual students, students with disabilities, etc.) respectfully and conscientiously encouraged to participate in the creation, monitoring, and revision of the assessment ecology?

- *Monitoring.* How might the teacher and students monitor power and its movements in the class in ways that can help make sense of judgments, processes, and parts? How might observations be made about the way particular *habitus* carry with them or assume more power in communication contexts, say in past writing classes or in the present one? How is that power embodied? Are there racial aspects to it? Are there trends that seem racialized?

- *Student Participation.* How are students involved in the assessment ecology generally? Do students get to create or control any aspects of the ecology? Do they have any say in what is assessed, how that writing is assessed, who assesses it, and what those assessments mean to the calculation of their course grades? Do students get to negotiate the way their grades or any evaluations of their writing is done?

- *Difference (from the white racial norm).* How will power relations be affected by various students who come with different *habitus* from the dominant white racial *habitus* that informs the expectations of the classroom? How will students interactions with you or with each other be mediated so that power relations can be explicitly discussed with students and equalized (realizing they are never made equal)? How do you plan to discuss and get students to listen to each other, to listen for difference in productive ways, to engage in what Trimbur (1989) calls "dissensus," or what Ratcliffe (2005) calls "rhetorical listening"?

- *Teacher Power.* How do you mediate your own power as the teacher in the ecology? How do you plan to get students to avoid seeing your position in the ecology as someone who will tell them what to do or fix in their writing? What control of the ecology does the teacher have that she might reasonably and explicitly give up or share with students?

- **People**. *How are the various people involved in writing assessment (students, teacher, outside readers or experts) defined in the ecology and what are their roles?* How are their various literacy histories and dispositions with English acknowledged, reflected upon, and used to help judge writing and think about writing as (counter)hegemonic?

- *Interconnection.* How are the people of the ecology (i.e., students, teacher) interconnected in explicit ways? How is any individual's success or failure in any activity connected explicitly to his peers' success or failure? How are students encouraged to see or explore the ways assessment is a diverse ecology that is about cultivating a livable and sustainable place together for everyone?

- *Local Diversity.* How are the locally diverse students and teacher in the ecology used to understand the local white racial *habitus*? In what ways might the local diversity help construct difference in writing as more than the expectations, and help link that value added to writers and readers? What methods or processes are in place to help students understand their own *habitus* and ways of judging and valuing writing,

reflect upon those *habitus,* and discuss them as a part of the dispositions used in the assessment processes of the course?

- *Inter-being as Problem-Posing.* How do various people participate in the
assessment processes and the construction of the ecological parts, purposes, and products? How might the ecology help students experience
the interconnected nature of all the elements in the ecology so that the
lessons learned are ones about one's own existential writing assessment
situation in a socially structured and hegemonic historic bloc? In other
words, how do you help students see that lessons about what a rubric
(a part) means are also lessons about their own individual reading and
writing practices, lessons about choices and degrees of consent to larger structural forces, to the hegemonic? How do you help students see
their own ways of judging language as determined (both constrained
and pressured) in particular directions?

- **Products**. *What products or consequences do you reasonably foresee the
ecology producing?* What direct products are there? Will there be a
course grade, or even individual grades on drafts? Will there be decisions about proficiency, placement, learning, development, or passing
that must be made at the end of the course? What indirect products
might there be and how might these products change given different
locally diverse students? In what ways are those products fair and
unfair to produce?

- *Discussion.* How is the subject position of the writer discussed in or
around student texts? How is learning and development discussed?
How is that learning or development compared to formal expectations of the course? Are those expectations explicitly associated with
a white racial *habitus* as such? In feedback activities (with the teacher
or among students) what responses to feedback might student-writers
reasonably have? What opportunities do writers have to respond back
to readers or assessors of their writing? How are those responses fed
into students' articulations of learning?

- *Products of Other Ecological Elements.* What effects or consequences
might the kind of ecological part used to articulate judgments on
students' writing have on various locally diverse writers, or in writing
groups that may discuss them? How might those ecological parts or
processes have historically racialized consequences for your students,
patterns that students intuitively have accepted or not questioned?
Could some racial formations in your classroom have different
experiences than what you reasonably hope for or expect, and thus
learn something very different from the same ecology? How might

the class monitor these differences? How can this alternative learning be acknowledged? How would you measure these unintended consequences (learning) or observe them? How might students be involved in measuring or observing them (e.g., reflections that ask about their learning and its relation to their past ways of learning)?

In the above heuristic, I move between a macro sense of the course as a large ecology that is most characterized by the way a writing assessment ecology creates the course and the experiences of students moving through the course to micro ecologies that are characterized by individual activities, assignments, and processes, which ultimately make up the larger classroom writing assessment ecology. When designing beforehand, a teacher should think in terms of the macro ecology of the course that evolves throughout the semester, an ecology in which every element inter-is the others. This will help maintain consistency and reduce contradictory processes, parts, or other elements.

An antiracist classroom writing assessment ecology, then, is interconnected at all levels. All elements inter-are. And so, in each category above, I blend elements, prompting teachers for instance to consider issues of power when considering processes. This means that one could think about a rubric as an articulation of expectations (part) which is used in the processes of feedback, a set of activities and labor that constructs evolving expectations (process), or an articulation of learning, of what students have been getting out of the ecology (product). This inter-being is intentional. While we can talk about ecological elements as distinct and separate entities, when we design them into a course we must keep in mind the way they exist in the material world as interconnected and dynamic elements.

This interconnectedness of the elements makes designing antiracist assessment ecologies complex. When you consider a part, you should consider the ways it becomes a place or a product at some point or for some reason. A feedback activity with peers feeds into, informs, inter-is with the larger classroom writing assessment ecology that produces a course grade (product). A rubric (part) inter-is the people that designed it, or the place of the writing classroom or group that uses it. It may even be an on-going process that gives power to students, which in turn provides indirect learning products. This interconnectedness of ecological elements shows why a teacher designing an assessment ecology can begin anywhere in the system, begin with the element that seems most important or salient to her. They all lead to each other. In fact, much like Burke's (1969) dramatistic Pentad, the key to making the ecology critical is seeing the interconnected nature of the elements, seeing their consubstantiality. Burke discusses this by thinking about ratios in the pentad. In a similar way, I'm suggesting that a teacher begin where she feels most comfortable thinking about writing assessment in her course, then discover (perhaps with her students) the ways that ecological element inter-is the others.

However, there is a caveat to this method. The ecological element you begin designing, say processes, will likely be more primary than what those processes become. In my ecologies, I'm usually thinking first about process, since my larger purposes for most activities are the same, so each week's activities often are a variation on the same purpose. So the process, the labor, that students engage in is where we spend most of our time making decisions and discussing, not on the parts. For instance, the rubric building processes in my class discussed in Chapter 4 do produce a part, a rubric, but the experience of students tends to be a process, to be the laboring they do. I doubt many remember the items on our rubric after the course is over, but it is clear from their end of semester reflections and assessments that the labor and processes of building the rubric, testing it, revising it, reflecting upon it, using it in reading peers' drafts had a lasting impression. The rubric process inter-was a part (the rubric) as much as it inter-was a set of learning products (lessons about writing), but primarily it was a set of processes (labors). And this was a big part of my larger purpose in the ecology. I cared more about students laboring with words and judgment in meaningful ways than forming them in particular ways in ideal products. This is due to the fact that the other half of my larger purpose was to have students confront their own existential writing assessment situations, and the only way they could do that is over time, through laboring, writing, reflecting, assessing, and being conscious of these processes as processes structured by their *habitus* and the white racial *habitus* that informed our rubric.

Additionally, my larger antiracist purpose is threaded into the above heuristic. In one sense, I'm suggesting that it be a part of any antiracist writing assessment ecology. Consider again my rubric-building activity, where students inductively created a rubric they used to judge each other's drafts by finding models in their research then distilling from those models a set of expectations they all wished to develop in their drafts. If the processes of reading, discussion, agreement-building, and articulation of the rubric are pointed back toward the student as an element in the ecology, which I tried to do, then the student can see the interconnection between the rubric as a part and herself as a person in the same ecology. This illustrates how they inter-are for the student. This could be done in reflections that ask the student to consider the rubric as a set of dominant dispositions (a *habitus*) that the class agrees upon that is similar and different from her own dispositions to judge and write. Or she might reflect upon the challenges she thinks she'll have when she writes from the rubric, or when she reads and uses it to judge her peers' papers. Or she might reflect after using the rubric in a reading process, discussing the problems she had with making it work, or agreeing with it, or its inadequacies, or the way it could not account for important or valuable aspects of her peers' papers and why.

Let me reiterate for emphasis. My tendency is to have a larger ecological purpose-product established in the ecology, one that fits my antiracist agenda. In order to confront any racism, students should experience a problematizing of their existential writing assessment situations as racialized situations (at least in part). I begin this through rubric-building processes. The problem posed, then, is one that must ask students to consider carefully a white racial *habitus*, say in a rubric, and the local SEAE we may be promoting in the course, say in models or published writing discussed in class. This means we need some additional theory or information that helps us think in productive ways about our own racialized subject positions in language next to the social, disciplinary, and racial structures that form expectations of English language communication in college, in the world, in our families, in churches, in other affinity groups.

My class didn't provide this literature. I should have offered some of the readings I list in Chapter 3. This also means that my references to race (in the heuristic and in my classroom) are really references to power, references to particular groups' relations to power, to the hegemonic, to whiteness, to a white racial *habitus*. And the language of power (or lack of it) is often how I begin in some classes that seem resistant to discussing race. However, an antiracist writing assessment ecology would encourage students to confront race in language in ways connected to the personal, the *habitus* of the individual student as a person who participates in larger racial formations in society. Frankie Condon's (2013), Catherine Myser's (2002), Maurice Berger's (1999), and Victor Villanueva's (1993) discussions seems most accessible as a way into such discussions with students.

In many ways, what I've been attempting in this book is an extension of what I've tried to do my entire life, first as a boy, then a student in schools, then as a teacher. So I end this book with a few perhaps self-indulgent, personal stories about me as a writer and assessor, stories that illustrate the problems that classroom writing assessment ecologies reveal to me when I see them as antiracist projects, good problems that should not be ignored, but racial problems that go beyond the classroom and words on the page. I should warn you. My stories of writing assessment ecologies in my childhood and early adulthood are not school stories, not really, which should suggest things about the problems that writing classrooms have with creating healthy, sustainable, engaging ecologies for students of color or multilingual students. Creating healthier, fairer, more sustainable assessment ecologies in classrooms is not always about the classroom.

FINAL STORIES OF WRITING ASSESSMENT ECOLOGIES

When I was eleven or twelve years old, my identical twin brother and I would often type stories to one another on my mom's old manual typewriter, a Signature 440T Montgomery Ward's model that typed in black and red ink. We lived in Las Vegas and attended year-around schools, so there were significant periods of time in elementary and junior high in which we were "latchkey" kids, confined to inside our apartment, curtains drawn, doors locked. "Don't answer the door for anyone," my mom would say, "and be quiet—no one can know you're here." So typing stories to my brother was a silent escape in which we could go anywhere, be anyone, and do almost anything. I can still feel the plastic of the keys that felt almost like cold bone, feel their tension when pressed, and the snap of the type bars when they hit the old-fashioned typing paper. The paper was crisp, like a thin skin of dried onion, but more durable. Typing on it and holding the paper in my hands made my words feel real, feel important. I found joy and engagement in both writing to my brother and discussing with him my stories. The discussions always ended up as collaborative sessions in which by the end it was hard to tell who was the writer and who the reader.

Now, my brother and I were always very rhetorically savvy, good with words on the block, quick-witted, fast with a snappy comeback. Our momma was well-defended. But writing in school was always a difficult task because I was never rewarded for it, and no one really took my ideas seriously, at least not as seriously as my errors. In fact, I was in remedial reading classes until about the eighth grade, yet I won reading contests—you know the ones: how many books can you read in a semester? But for some reason, despite my interests in language and books, I didn't like writing for school, or rather, I didn't like turning in my writing to a teacher. The feedback I got on all my writing in school was lots of marks, often on every sentence I wrote. Writing for school was usually about finding out how bad or wrong I was in putting sentences together. It was about being measured, not communicating or dialoguing with someone else. It was always about submission, submitting to power, losing power, being measured, graded. And it was always, always, without fail, a submission to a white racial authority figure. What I experienced in school, even into college, were writing experiences that separated, and often ignored, three important aspects of any meaningful writing activity to me: (1) the importance of my labor in writing, (2) the importance of the material conditions in which I labored to read and write and that allowed me to read and write the way I did, and (3) the importance of the way all my writing participated in an ecology of assessment, which meant that what I wrote inter-was who I was. My words were me. A teacher never was just reading my paper. That paper inter-was me, my labor, my context for writing at home or in the classroom. No matter what they said, my teachers were always grading me, not simply my papers.

Let me explain the third aspect, the one I'm guessing is the most confusing to readers, a sense that all my early joyful and engaging writing participated in ecologies of assessment. I wouldn't have voiced things this way back then. My typing experiences with my brother were ecologies themselves, organically produced by one of us simply saying, "let's write stories. You can read mine and tell me what you think, and I'll read yours and tell you what I think." We certainly knew the paradigm of correction and grading from school, but our ecology didn't mimic that. We were not in school. We were on break, trapped in a trailer, unable to go outside. It was just us, a typewriter, and paper. Those school ecologies, those grading and correcting ecologies, didn't seem appropriate because we weren't looking to be corrected or meet some idealized standard. That wasn't our purpose at all. We were looking for an experience of writing with each other. We wanted to labor in particular ways because it was enjoyable to do so. We constructed our ecology by first thinking about the two people, the writers who would also be readers, and what they wanted to experience and do alone in a trailer in Las Vegas.

And now that I think about it, our stories, the parts created, inter-were us. My story was me, and that is how my brother talked about it, responded to it, and talked to me about it. The two of us sitting cross-legged on our bed (one we shared) in front of the typewriter was the ecological place created by our labor of writing, and the typewriter, and us, and the discourse we created over those stories. It didn't matter that we were poor. It didn't matter that our language wasn't the standard expected in school. It didn't matter that we had few friends, or that our neighbor would yell racist slurs at us as we walked past his house almost every day. It didn't matter what anyone else thought or did. It only mattered that we did this thing together, that we played with words together. Our purpose was simple, even simpler than to communicate to an audience. It was to create words and share those words with the only person in the world who was as consubstantial to oneself as another can be, an identical twin brother.

Power in this situation flowed from our control over everything, the purpose, process, the writing as an artifact, the responses (the products), the typewriter and material conditions (place), and our time, our laboring in time. There were no teachers or adults to tell us what to do, or how well we did it. I don't even think anyone knew we wrote those stories. We embodied power in all that it could be, and we did so equally. Being a twin can be the most democratic and equal relationship one can possibly experience, more so than a partner or spouse.

As a twin, you feel your inter-being with your sibling most acutely. For me, my interconnectedness to my twin brother defined me growing up.

This inter-being, this sameness, is not only something a twin can feel but something that is placed onto you as a twin by everyone around you. My mom always made sure that everything was equal, that what I got my brother also got, from clothes to toys to food to space in the bedroom. She made a point to say so: "you get what your brother gets," "you both will get the same," "you are both equally special and wonderful." And being identical, you confront on a daily basis how much the same you are to your twin, how equal you are and are perceived to be by others around you every day. People constantly compare you. "Look how similar they are." "Do you think the same things?" "Can you read each other's minds?" "Wow, you two look exactly alike." "You sound exactly like your brother. You talk just like him."

The discourse and practices of inter-being around us as identical twins constructed an equal power relationship, even to this day. Thus there were no power plays in our language games as kids. My language could be interrogated and judged by my brother, and I could take those judgments as they were, not as rule or law, but as my brother telling me his perspective of my text, as me interrogating myself. It was as pure as any judgment and dialogue could be.

> "I don't understand this. Why is he jumping into the water here? It would be better if he ...."
>
> "He's jumping because he wants to get over to the island. He wants to get to her."
>
> "I know but he could take the boat."
>
> "How is that exciting?"
>
> "Maybe he takes the boat, maybe he gets into trouble on the way, maybe ...."
>
> "Maybe the boat has a leak, and ...."
>
> "Yeah, maybe there are sharks in the water?"
>
> "And he has to paddle faster and faster."

Our discussions, as I remember them, always were like this. We were one organism. His ideas inter-were my ideas. Our unique power relations allowed us to engage in a collaborative process that was both judgment and drafting, that was assessing and writing. That's literally what I remember about our exchanges, not a lot of details, just emotions and feelings, just images of the typewriter, of the onion paper and its feel between my fingers, of the feeling of creating words and seeing them on the page—a clean text on paper—of talking to my brother about his words and mine, of the excitement of creating and recreating together, of playing with words with myself who was my brother, of feeling like a real writer who writes, of writing and judging text as joy. In short, what I recall most is the ecology of writing assessment as an embodiment of inter-being, yet more than that, more than just stories, more than just talk about words, more than just an escape from the racist conditions of our lives.

Part of what made this private ecology with my brother so special is that it could escape all the problems that plagued us outside the trailer, on the block and in school. And these problems were dictated by our racial subject position next to our white, working-class neighbors, who all—just about to the very last one—disliked us. In short, my private twin ecology escaped racism in the only way one can escape racism today. The people in it, my brother and I, were not diverse. We were the same, linguistically, racially, culturally, age-wise, all of it. This isn't the answer to racism in the classroom. I point this out because it seems clear to me now that I needed this democratic, monolingual ecology in order to find joy and love for the written word since there were few places outside this ecology that offered joy or love in language to me, and that joy and love was a direct consequence, a product, of the private twin ecology of assessment. I need-ed to write to myself, a raced body, and not to a white teacher.

But outside this ecology were other ecologies that were more complicated, less equal, more hurtful to me as a person of color in mostly white, working-class schools. During this period, we lived in Pecos Trailer Park. It seemed a step up from the last place we lived, a government subsidized apartment on Stats Street in the Black ghetto, North Las Vegas. It was a strange transition for a brown boy like me. I was the lightest skinned kid on Stats, but at Pecos, I was the darkest. And it mattered to everyone, recall the letter written to my family threatening our eviction. I was loud and boisterous on Stats but at Pecos I was quiet, espe-cially around adults, all of whom didn't want me near their children. For most of my childhood in order to play with anyone my age, I had to sneak around parents, hide behind trailers, waiting for friends to sneak out and play. None of the kids in the trailer park, not one, were allowed to be around us or play with us. If they were caught being seen with my brother or me, they would get grounded, punished.

And the ironies of my situation didn't escape me. One of our neighbors, whose daughter I liked quite a bit (her name was Heather), was adamant about how "bad" my brother and I were. He was vocal to me about my negative influ-ence on his daughter. I was a troublemaker. I can still see him standing on his porch, looking down at me, glaring at me with eyes that said, "Get away from my daughter, you dirty spic." He banned his daughter and son from associating with my brother and me. It hurt. But within a year after they moved into the park, he was arrested and sent to a federal prison. The family wouldn't say what happened, except that he'd done some bad things at work in Arizona, where they had most recently lived, perhaps some embezzling or skimming. Even then, I remember thinking to myself, "And I'm the bad influence?"

Another neighbor kid was arrested for stealing in a department store. Her sister smoked weed, starting in junior high (and their father was a police officer). Another kid on my street, the park manger's grandson, was constantly in trouble for destroying property and fighting. Another kid, the assistant manager's son, was a bully in school and out, fought all the time, got bad grades, flunked out and was held back one year. All these kids were white, and clearly possessed the privilege of whiteness. None were banned for being "bad kids" or "bad influences" on anyone else. None were given a warning of eviction. I saw the irony in this every day, and I saw it connected to my perceived racial subjectivity. And I wrote in this context, from this *habitus*.

Flash forward. I moved to Oregon my senior year of high school. While expected of me by my family, college didn't seem realistic in my mind. I wasn't good enough. I didn't read the right things. I didn't have any money, nor did my mom. My writing wasn't very good. I wasn't smart enough. I was still that troublemaker, somehow. I could still feel my poverty in my skin. I could feel the judgments on me from my past. I was the dirty spic. Forget that by high school I was almost a straight-A student. The A's ceased to matter. It was the real judgments of me that mattered by people around me. It was the looks, the comments, the racial slurs. It was a general assessment that no matter what I did, what I said—no matter what—I wasn't good enough.

The army seemed a good delay. When I enlisted into the army national guard and spent nine months training in New Jersey and Missouri, I turned again to writing. Writing was a kind of escape for me, and it proved deeply enjoyable, mostly because of the way response and assessment were a natural part of the labor of writing. You see, it was the first time I was away from family and friends, alone with strangers, doing something I was not that thrilled about, but had made a commitment. I was eighteen. And while we never agreed to do it, never made any plans up front, my brother and I wrote each other letters every day I was gone, every day for the entire nine months. Not a day went by that I wasn't deeply engaged in reading my brother's words, hand-written for me so far away in Oregon. And I never let a day go by in which I didn't write and reply back to him. The reading and writing of letters to my brother that I did each night in my bunk in an army barracks far from home was the most meaningful literacy experience of my life. It felt like it saved my life, saved me from feeling isolated and alone, reminded me that my twin brother was out there, far away, thinking about me and only me, writing to me, showing me that our life, friends, college, were all still going on. One could say my brother and his letters gave me freedom to write, freedom to reflect upon my choices, and freedom to see myself as a twin far from his brother, far from his real self. And all this freedom came from words and their affirmations, my brother's responses to them.

This long-distance ecology we created, much like our more intimate typing of stories on the Signature typewriter, was ironically an embodiment of freedom in a place and time I felt the least free in my life. The letters created a figurative place that was free, free from my obligations to the army, free from the daily labors of training, free from the company of strangers, free from the green of army uniforms, free from marching and marching and marching, free from weapons ranges and classrooms. The ecology of letters was an ecology of freedom to be me with me, with my brother.

Freedom, though, is a tricky word. It is a powerful word. It is yoked closely to race in U.S. history. In the U.S. whites have always been free in most aspects of their lives, so much so that freedom of choice and doing and being are often taken for granted. We call it white privilege. This isn't the case for Blacks, or Japanese, for instance, especially before the end of WWII. It isn't true for Latinos/as who are always suspected to some degree of being "illegal aliens" in public, especially if they speak with an accent or speak Spanish (a language that reminds me of their history of colonization). And it isn't true for Native Americans, who live with the legacy of the slaughter and genocide of their ancestors, customs, and their languages.

Freedom is also a theme that many Fresno State Hmong students voice in reflections and exit survey responses in the FYW program each year (Inoue, 2012a). They are the only racial formation that articulates this theme. When I read such reflections by Hmong students, I cannot help but think of the well know book of testimonies by Hmong refugees, *Hmong Means Free*, published in 1994 by Sucheng Chan, which recounts several families fleeing Laos from oppression and massacre, emmigrating to the U.S. around 1976. Or John Duffy's (2007) historical account in *Writing from These Roots* of Hmong literacy practices and school experiences, which were filled with "loneliness, racism, and physical abuse" (p. 139). Or the powerful memoir by Kao Kalia Yang, *The Latehomecomer* (2008). The lack of freedom in the lives of Hmong punctuate their migrations: they flee from the Yellow River Valley to the jungles of China, then to Indochina, then to northern Laos. After the war, they are hunted and slaughtered by the North Vietnamese. Even when they escape, they're herded into refugee camps with armed guards. Several groups have attempted to colonize them, the Chinese, the French, the Japanese. It appears that freedom to do anything, to live and prosper, let alone to write or read, is crucial to many Hmong's sense of well-being, learning, progress, and development. Freedom appears often to be a racial condition.

Furthermore, what makes a sense of freedom important to writing assessment ecologies, what makes it important to antiracist ones, is the way in which it signifies a sense of racial equality, or liberation. Freedom has usually been the purpose, the goal for most racial movements. The feeling that one is free, free to choose, free to speak, free to act, free to labor in the ways one is most accustomed, free to be, inter-is agency. I know this is too simple of an equation for agency. It seems to erase the degrees of choice in agency, the complications, particularly those I've pointed out around the hegemonic and Marxian determination. But I'm only talking about a feeling of freedom in the writing classroom, not actual freedom. I wonder how many writing assessment ecologies possess the character of freedom in students' experiences, and if that character is evenly distributed across the various racial formations that exist within the ecology? I wonder what freedom feels like to various racialized students in a writing assessment ecology that promotes blindly or uncritically a white racial *habitus*?

My mom used to say that my twin brother and I spoke a special language only to each other for the first few years of our speaking lives. I only vaguely recall the language, but do remember using it. And perhaps the writing assessment ecologies I recall were us trying to escape the confines of our lives, to be free in language, free from racism, to reinvent our lost twin language, a pure and organic, non-judgmental language of consubstantiality, a twin language of inter-being.

I think over the years as a teacher and scholar of writing, I have tried unconsciously to understand and recreate my writing experiences with my brother in my classes for my students, tried to find ways to cultivate ecologies that conceive of the inevitable and scary assessment of writing *as* writing and the writing of "primary texts," essays and such, *as* feedback or dialogue, as the student's own urge to communicate and identify with others. Reading and writing are just other ways to say assess, judge. I have tried to construct ecologies that work as sustainable, livable, fair ecologies that address racism by not avoiding it in the language we write or speak. Perhaps mostly though, my stories I hope demonstrate that even a remedial student like me from the ghettos of North Las Vegas, from a poor, single-parent home, can find freedom and power through writing assessment ecologies, but to do so means one must confront racism himself in his own language, in school, on the block, and in the nature of judgments on him and from him.

NOTES

1. In this book, I use the term Standardized Edited American English (SEAE) to denote the kind of discourses typically promoted and valued in academic settings in the way that Greenfield (2011) and other linguists use the term. My use of this term, SEAE, highlights the superficial and typographical features of text, which often are characterized by particular conventions of grammar and punctuation. I realize SEAE is not singular but varied and multiple, slightly different at each site and classroom. Additionally, I use "standardized" and not "Standard" to emphasize, like Greenfield, the local brand of English valued in a writing assessment as not inherently the correct version of English, but one actively made standard. There is no single preferred or correct version. There are only versions promoted and made standard by their use in writing assessments. Thus I often use the term local SEAE.

2. Throughout this book, I make a distinction between a local SEAE and a local dominant discourse promoted in a writing classroom. Beyond conventions of grammar and punctuation, a dominant discourse, which is the broader term, also includes particular rhetorical moves that are typically judged as acceptable within the community that uses the discourse. The discourse of summary and engaging in academic conversations that Graff and Birkenstein (2014) offer in their popular text, *They Say/I Say*, is a good example of a text that focuses on explaining and showing the rhetorical moves that make up part of a dominant discourse. Conventions within local SEAEs certainly intersect within this dominant discourse, and their text may even influence such SEAEs.

3. Catherine Prendergast (1998) makes a similar argument about composition studies generally.

4. I thank Tom Fox for bringing this important point to my attention.

5. Omi and Winant (1994) define racial projects as projects in society that create or maintain racial groups, identities, or categories in some way. They link racial projects to the function of hegemony (pp. 55-56, 68). Racial projects could be racist (those that contribute to racial hierarchies and subordination) or work against such categorizing by race.

6. According to today's U.S. common sense, for a language practice to be efficient and effective, it would need concision, which SEAE doesn't always have. Take the use of articles and plural endings that cause many L2 speakers difficulty. Oftentimes, they simply are not needed to communicate an idea. For instance, "I walked the dog around the block three times" (nine words, 36 characters)

conforms to most local SEAEs, but a more concise and still communicative way to say this could be, "I walked dog around block three time" (seven words, 30 characters).

7. For a fuller discussion of remediation and its institutional construction and reification, see Soliday (2002) and Stanley (2009). For a related summary of the field of basic writing, see Otte and Mlynarczyk (2010). For an important complication and rethinking of who the basic writer is, see Horner and Lu's (1999) important collection, which also prefigures their work on translingual approaches (Horner & Trimbur, 2002; Horner et al., 2011) that they advocate. All these scholars reveal associations between the concept of remediation with the body of color.

8. While the Asian-American population is mostly Hmong, I realize that the figures shown also include other Asian-American formations, but this is how California State University reports EPT results. When I've looked more closely at just the Hmong formation, the remediation rates are even higher. According to Fresno State's Office of Institutional Effectiveness, the average remediation rate for all Hmong students at Fresno State between 2007-2012 was 77% of the population.

9. The famous motto originated during Chavez' 25 day fast in Phoenix, Arizona in 1972. He and Dolores Huerta coined the phrase (Rodriquez, 1998).

10. For a discussion of the way race is an historically changing concept, see Hannaford (1996); for a discussion of an instance of a racial formation that changes, see Ignatiev's (1995) discussion in *How the Irish Became White*; and for a discussion of the way race is an historically changing construct that produces racial hierarchies and categories, see Omi and Winant (1994).

11. I realize that Bonilla-Silva's sociological work on racial frames comes from frame analysis, a methodology created by Erving Goffman (1974). Goffman's methodology attempts to explain the way people organize experience into conceptual frames, like a picture frame. A frame in Goffman's terms is a set of conceptual terms (concepts) and theoretical perspectives that then structure and influence actions. To be clear, I'm simply cherry-picking from Bonilla-Silva's frames, and because he speaks in terms of the language used that articulate racial attitudes, his frames amount to rhetorical tropes, rhetoric. Villanueva (2006) also identifies such "new racist" language through the use of four kinds of tropes that come from Burke (i.e., metaphor, metonymy, synecdoche, and irony), which amount to Bonilla-Silva's racial frames (Villanueva even references Bonilla-Silva).

12. For key discussions on whiteness, see Lipsitz' (1998) discussion on the way whiteness is connected to and supports a whole range of social projects, such as immigration, labor, white desire, and identity politics; see Roediger (1991)

for the ways whiteness is connected historically to wage labor in the U.S.; see Munro (2004) for a summary of scholarship on whiteness that connects it to antiracist Marxism and Black antiracist traditions; and see Myser (2003) on the ways whiteness affects bioethics research and classrooms.

13. Brookhiser (1997) identifies the following traits as those of the WASP: a Protestant conscience that often functions from seeing truth (optically) and guilt if truth is ignored (p. 16-17); civic-mindedness that prioritizes society as a whole, and demonizes groups or special interests (p. 18-19); an anti-sensuality that constructs sensual pleasures or enjoyment as bad or wrong (p. 21); a focus on industry that places a value on doing work, which is often connected to capitalism (p. 17); a valuing of use, which says that everything and everyone must be useful for something (p. 19); and success, or the "outward and visible signs of grace" (p. 18).

14. The directed self-placement at Fresno State was designed after the one at Grand Valley State University and discussed by Royer and Gilles (1998; 2003).

15. To see a study of grading practices in the Fresno State writing program, see Inoue (2012a); to see the validation study of the DSP along racial formations in the program, see Inoue (2009a); to see a fuller discussion of the failure rate changes after changing course writing assessments (grading systems), see Inoue (2014b). All show one thing: how various racial formations' are constructed through writing assessments as racial projects.

16. The National Poverty Center (2014) at the University of Michigan explains that the threshold for poverty in the U.S. for a two adult household with one child is $17,552, two children is $22,113, and three is $26,023. For a single parent household with one child the threshold is $15,030, and for two children it is $17,568.

17. It is worth noting that the Kingdom of Thailand is the only nation in Southeast Asia not to have been colonized by either France or Great Brittan. So to U.S. Americans' eyes of the 1950s, the Siam of the 1860s is an ideal place to imagine white-Asian racial relations.

18. I find the title of the film *The King and I* to be particularly telling, as it reveals clearly the primary subject(ivity) of the film. It isn't the king, nor his children, but the white female teacher, sent to educate, who is the subject of the film. It is her story. And this seems analogous to our writing classrooms and their assessments. The dominant subject(ivity) of the assessment ecology, the central *habitus*, is a white one, perhaps a white female one. The vast majority of writing teachers at Fresno State are white females, and this has been the case at every college and university at which I've taught (three other state universities and one

community college).

19. The 18 clans represented at Fresno State are: Cha, Chue, Cheng, Fang, Hang, Her/Herr/Hue, Khang, Kong, Kue, Lee/Le/Ly/Lyfoung, Lor/Lo, Moua/Mouanatoua, Pha,Thao/Thor, Vang, Vue/Vu, Xiong, Yang.

20. These are the terms the NCES uses.

21. Validity refers to a judgment that explains the adequacy of an assessment's decision. Samuel Messick (1989) provides perhaps the most definitive treatment of the concept and its procedures (validation), and defines validity as: "an integrated evaluative judgment of the degree to which empirical evidence and theoretical rationales support the *adequacy* and *appropriateness* of *inferences* and *actions* based on test scores or other modes of assessment" (p. 13, his emphasis). As one can see, validity is an argument, as several have argued already (Cronbach, 1988; Kane, 1992; Shepard, 1993), and so it is a rhetorical process (Inoue, 2007).

22. CSU's Division of Analytic Studies separates the category of "Asian-American" from "Pacific Islander" and Filipino, thus these students are certainly mostly Hmong students. As a comparison, the remediation rate for whites entering Fresno State in Fall 2011 was only 25.3%, Mexican Americans was 58.5%, and African-Americans was 58.9%.

23. I am mindful of one concern of assessment ecologies that define course grades by labor. Students who work and go to school, or who have complex family obligations that take up much of their time may be at a disadvantage. But as those in travel and mobility studies (a field that looks at the processes, structures, and consequences of people's movement across time and geography) remind us, people may do all kinds of labor and work as they move from bus to park, to job, or from home to school to wherever. I thank Tom Fox for this reminder.

24. I realize that many students work outside of school, take care of family members, and have other constraints on their time, so not all students have the same amount of free time. These limitations can be negotiated with each class since they will be different for each class.

25. I realize the there is no indication that Lindsey is white, but the whiteness I reference here is not a white skin privilege, rather a white *habitus* associated with her dispositions in language.

26. Lester Faigley (1989) offers a concise way to think about Althusser's interpellation that is helpful here:

> discourses interpellate human beings by offering them an
> array of subject positions that people recognize, just as when
> a person turns when someone shouts "hey, you." The term

subject contains a pun. People are subjected to dominant ideologies, but because they recognize themselves in the subject positions that discourses provide, they believe they are subjects of their own actions. The recognition, therefore, is a misrecognition because people fail to see that the subject positions they occupy are historically produced, and they imagine that they are freely choosing for themselves. (p. 403)

27. I realize we are not talking about liberation in the same ways as Freire may have, but I believe that providing students ways to problematize their existential writing assessment situations is a form of liberation from the hegemonic in the assessment of their writing.

28. In the places I cite from the prison notebooks, Gramsci provides historical analyses by invoking Lenin's *Theses on Feuerbach* and Marx and Engel's *The Eighteenth Brumaire of Louis Bonaparte*, *The Civil War of France*, and *Revolution and Counter-Revolution in Germany*. He makes his own analysis in section VIII (2000, pp. 249-274).

29. It should be noted that through the dialectical term base, Gramsci extends the traditional concept of economic base to include the moral, ethical, and cultural aspects and practices of civil society (2000, pp. 194-195), which he describes as "ethico-political," a term from the Italian idealist philosopher Benedetto Croce.

30. In *The Interpretation of Dreams*, Freud (1913) explains overdetermination as a confluence of "dream thoughts," in which "[e]very element of the dream content turns out to be over-determined—that is, it enjoys a manifold representation in the dream thoughts" (par. 13). Later in the same chapter, he discusses the term by considering the dream of the neurotic character: "Hence emotions in the dream appear as though formed by the confluence of several tributaries, and as though over-determined in reference to the material of the dream thoughts; sources of affect which can furnish the same affect join each other in the dream activity in order to produce it" (par. 266). Contrast this with Marxian determination that has both constraints and pressure toward some hegemonic end. The hegemonic appears not to be a part of Freudian overdetermination.

31. Black, Daiker, Sommers, and Stygall (1994) found that white female student reflections tended to be judged more highly in portfolios at Miami University. At Fresno State, Hmong female student reflections also were rated by judges more highly than their male counterparts (Inoue & Richmond, in press).

32. The average EPT scores for Hmong students during 2007-12 was 134

for males, and 135 for females. The cut score that determined remediation is 147.

33. I discuss the contract's focus on labor in detail in Inoue (2014a) and in Chapter 4 for my own classroom. I also discuss the labor model next to quality models of failure from empirical data from the Fresno State program in Inoue (2014b).

34. The study was conducted by nine graduate students (Meredith Bulinski, Jocelyn Stott, Megan McKnight, Sharla Seidel, Andy Dominguez, and Maryam Jamali, Holly Riding, Adena Joseph, and Patrice Isom) and myself in a graduate seminar of mine in the spring of 2008, then presented at CCCC in 2009. The session was titled, "'Shit-plus,' 'AWK,' 'Frag,' and 'Huh?': An Empirical Look at a Writing Program's Commenting Practices" and the study was presented by Meredith Bulinski, Jocelyn Stott, Megan McKnight, Sharla Seidel, Andy Dominguez, and Maryam Jamali. The video they produced for that conference session can be found at: https://www.youtube.com/watch?v=-LA6nBFkNb8.

35. All EPT scores discussed here are taken from CSU's Analytic Studies Website (CSU, Division of Analytic Studies, 2013).

36. I use subaltern as a term to identify individuals of a particular social formation (not class) that is subordinate to other formations, realizing that in much critical and post-colonial theory, the subaltern is often defined as one who is outside the hegemonic, excluded; however, one who is subordinate is inside the hegemonic power structures, since subordination is a relative concept. I use the term more closely to its original reference in the British military, which identified officers of lower rank, relative to a higher ranking officer. This appears to be in line with Gramsci's own use of the term. Morton (2007) explains that in *Prison Notebooks*, Gramsci uses the term to "denote subordinate groups such as the rural peasantry in Southern Italy, whose achievement of social and political consciousness was limited and their political unity weak." As a subaltern, the rural peasantry had not become conscious of their "collective economic and social oppression as a class," not like the industrial proletariat of Italy had (Morton, 2007, p. 96). Thus subaltern is not referencing a class but rather a more loose-knit social formation, like students, or even Hmong students at Fresno State. Additionally, one is not simply subaltern or not. There are degrees of subalternity.

37. For instance, the first edition of Blumenbach's *On The Natural Varieties of Mankind* (1775) contained only four racial categories by geography: people from (1) Europe; (2) Asia, the Ganges river, and parts of North America; (3) Africa; and (4) North America. The second edition (1781) contained five categories by geography: people from (1) Europe, including North India, North Africa, North America; (2) Asia and beyond the Ganges river; (3) Africa, except for North Africa; (4) America, and (5) the southern world, such as the Philip-

pines. And the third edition (1795) contained five refined, abstract categories: (1) Caucasians; (2) Mongolians; (3) Ethiopians; (4) Americans; and (5) Malays.

38. It should be noted that technically, Blumenbach's Caucasians are geographically located in Asia (Middle East) around Armenia, Azerbaijan, Georgia, and Russia, not Europe, which indicates Blumenbach's and others' need to locate the norm in a white European center.

39. I use the racial codes and terms used by Fresno State and its Office of Institutional Effectiveness when citing their findings or information, otherwise I use my own. For instance Fresno State tends to use "Hispanic," while I prefer "Latino/a," which by in large refers to Chicano or Mexican-American.

40. Twitter has been helpful in other ways. For example, it's helpful in understanding the general labor patterns of the class, when students do work for our class most often, and who has more trouble with the labor than others. Knowing these patterns has helped me think about what assignments will be more productive, helpful, and doable than others. It does make some students feel a bit vulnerable, since it can make their labors more present, more noticeable to everyone. I try hard to let students know that when they do labor for our class is not important to me, but that they do it, how long they do it, and the spirit in which they do it (are they trying to engage and learn?) are more important. Additionally, as discussed in Chapter 3, I've found asking students to quantify both the duration of their labor sessions each week and the level of engagement in sessions (usually with a simply rating) in simple spreadsheets can help us reflect more carefully in our journals.

41. I discuss elsewhere (Inoue, 2004) one version of the way inductively built rubrics can be done and can function. The difference in the present class is that I built two rubrics: one based on expectations for the project's artifact, and one on the labor expectations of those artifacts.

42. I discuss these three questions as central to my ideal course in another place (Inoue, 2014a).

43. Recently, I have considered adding an "incomplete" category that tabulates assignments done and turned in on time (so not late) but not done according to the assignment guidelines. The initial contract might begin with a "B" grade having two or fewer "incomplete" assignments. However, in this class a few students initially, as usual, turned in assignments that were incomplete. If it was in the first two weeks of the semester, particularly if it was the first instance of a certain kind of assignment, then I didn't count the assignment as late, but did talk with the student about expectations and meeting guidelines.

44. Ironically, yes, A's do mean less (are meaningless) as indicators of prog-

ress and quality, as most of the research on grades in writing classes demonstrate.

45. While Spidell and Thelin do not discuss their findings in terms of white racial student formations, I analyze their methods and show how one might reasonably see their conclusions concerning mostly white, Midwestern students from Ohio (Inoue, 2012b).

46. When quoting students' writing, I have preserved all spellings and punctuation, not correcting things, except in the most obvious cases where there is clearly a typo. When getting permission to use each student's work for this book, I asked them to look at their quoted material and make sure I have not misrepresented them, or corrected a typo that shouldn't be.

47. While Kyler, like Zach, participates in a white racial formation, both did not always demonstrate in their writing a white racial *habitus* that the writing program expected. This may be why both had misgivings about their past experiences with grades in their writing courses. They mostly deviated in their uses of the local SEAE, while most of their other dispositions were close to a white racial *habitus*.

48. For a fuller, more detailed account of grade distributions by college, Fresno State's Office of Institutional Effectiveness provides reports on them at their Website (http://www.fresnostate.edu/academics/oie/index.html).

49. Ashe is a pseudonym, which the student chose.

50. Assuming one, unified audience, with a singular *habitus* makes sense given the conventional ways that writing has been evaluated and graded in schools. There is usually only one teacher, and she is the only reader and evaluator of student writing, therefore, no matter what an assignment sets up as its audience(s), students know that there is really only one, singular audience, the teacher. No other *habitus* (or set of dispositions) for reading and evaluating their writing matters.

51. Interestingly, Lyna's use of cooking problematizes Plato's own description of the rhetoric of the Sophists as "cookery" (a "knack" or "flattery," containing no substance) in Gorgias.

52. I had only one multilingual male student, a student who was Southeast Asian from India. He entered the course late, missing the first two weeks of class, and participated minimally in the course. His work schedule often got in the way of class and his labor, so he struggled to even complete mundane, daily labor. Thus I cannot make many observations about his orientation to the assessment ecology, except that it was not articulated very clearly or abundantly.

53. Gideon claims white as his racial identity, but has a middle name that is

historically Filipino.

54. I conducted this survey for a writing across the curriculum program project in which I first met with the Hmong Student Association on campus, explained the survey and project on Hmong writing practices, then conducted the anonymous survey through an online service. The project culminated in a 2013 CCCC presentation, "The Construction of Hmong Masculinity in Fresno State University's Writing (and Other) Classrooms." That presentation was first vetted by several members of the Hmong Student Association, and in Fall 2013, I presented it and the full survey results to the Hmong Student Association.

55. In the course, I introduced stasis theory early so that we had that language. I used excerpts from Crowley and Hawhee's textbook, *Ancient Rhetorics for Contemporary Students* (2008), in which they define four stases: questions of conjecture, definition, quality, and policy (p. 86). For simplicity I collapsed the first two, conjecture and definition into questions or claims of "fact." This made sense to my students.

56. Pageen Richert Powell (2013) makes this very argument from the literature on retention, first arguing that most first-year writing students will not need to learn academic discourse (half leave the university and most of the other half take careers outside academia), then offering a "kairotic pedagogy" that teaches students writing they can use now in their lives (p. 118).

57. In retrospect, I should have helped them critique this subject position of mine. I was a remedial reading student, in many ways less capable than many of them in the room. I was a poor student of color from North Las Vegas, the ghetto. I had told them about my educational past already, so these facts wouldn't have been new, but don't they matter to me as a reader and judge of texts?

REFERENCES

Allison, L., Bryant, L., & Hourigan, M. (Eds.). *Grading in the post-process classroom: From theory to practice*. Portsmouth, NH: Boynton/Cook.

Althusser, L. (1971). *Lenin and philosophy and other essays* (B. Brewster, Trans.). London: New Left Books.

Ancheta, A. (1998). *Race, rights, and the Asian American experience*. New Brunswick, NJ: Rutgers University Press.

Andrade, H. G. (2000). Using rubrics to promote thinking and learning. *Educational Leadership, 57*, 13-18.

Andrade, H. G., Wang, X., Du, Y., & Akawi, R. L. (2009). Rubric-referenced self-assessment and self-efficacy for writing. *The Journal of Educational Research, 102*, 287-301.

Anson, C. M. (2000). Response and the social construction of error. *Assessing Writing, 7*(1), 5-21.

Anzaldúa, G. (1999). *Borderlands/la frontera: The new Mestiza* (2nd ed.). San Francisco: Aunt Lute Books.

Arter, J., & Chappuis, J. (2007). *Creating and recognizing quality rubrics*. Upper Saddle River, NJ: Pearson Education, Inc.

Arum, R., & Roska, J. (2011). *Academically adrift: Limited learning on college campuses*. Chicago/London: University of Chicago Press.

Asian American Center for Advancing Justice. (2013). *A community of contrasts: Asian Americans, native Hawaiians and Pacific islanders in California*. Retrieved from http://advancingjustice-la.org/media-and-publications/publications/community-contrasts-asian-americans-native-hawaiians-and-pacific-islande-0

Associated Press. (2007, April 10). Immigration activities call for May 1 boycott. *NBC News.com*. Retrieved from http://www.nbcnews.com/id/18040460/ns/politics/t/immigration-activists-call-may-boycott/#.U8A-f_mzHB0

Baker, L. (1998). *From savage to negro: Anthropology and the construction of race, 1896-1954*. Berkeley, CA: University of California Press.

Ball, A. F. (1997). Expanding the dialogue on culture as a critical component when assessing writing. *Assessing Writing, 4*(2), 169-202.

Ball, A. F., & Lardner, T. (2005). *African American literacy unleashed: Vernacular English and the composition classroom*. Carbondale, IL: Southern Illinois University Press.

Banton, M. (1998). *Racial theories* (2nd ed.). Cambridge, UK: Cambridge University Press.

Barbezat, D. P., & Bush, M. (2014). *Contemplative practices in higher education: Powerful methods to transform teaching and learning.* San Francisco: Jossey-Bass.

Barnett, T. (2000). Reading "whiteness" in English studies. *College English, 63*(1), 9-37.

Bartholomae, D. (1985). Inventing the university. In M. Rose (Ed.), *When a writer can't write: Studies in writer's block and other composing-process problems* (pp. 134-166). New York: Guilford Press.

Beach, Richard. (1976). Self-evaluation strategies of extensive revisers and non-revisers. *College Composition and Communication, 27*(2), 160-164.

Belanoff, P. (1991). The myths of assessment. *Journal of Basic Writing, 10*(1), 54-66.

Belanoff, P., & M. Dickson (Eds.). (1991). *Portfolios: Process and product.* Portsmouth, NH: Boynton/Cook and Heinemann.

Bell, D. (2004). *Silent covenants: Brown v. board of education and the unfulfilled hopes for racial reform.* Oxford, UK: Oxford University Press.

Berger, M. (1999). *White lies: Race and the myths of whiteness.* New York: Farrar, Straus, and Giroux.

Berlin, J. (1987). *Rhetoric and reality: Writing instruction in American colleges, 1900-1985.* Carbondale, IL: Southern Illinois University Press.

Bernard-Donals, M. (1998). Peter Elbow and the cynical subject. In F. Zak & C. C. Weaver (Eds.), *The theory and practice of grading writing: Problems and possibilities* (pp. 53-65). Albany, NY: SU NY Press.

Bhopal, R. (2007). The beautiful skull and Blumenbach's errors. *British Medical Journal, 335*(22-29), 1308-1309. Retrieved from http://www.bmj.com/cgi/content/full/335/7633/1308

Bireda, S., & Chait, R. (2011). *Increasing teacher diversity: Strategies to improve the teacher workforce.* Center for American Progress. Retrieved from http://cdn.americanprogress.org/wp-content/uploads/issues/2011/11/pdf/chait_diversity.pdf

Black, L., Daiker, D., Sommers, J, & Stygall, G. (Eds.). (1994). *New directions in portfolio assessment: Reflective practice, critical theory, and large-scale scoring.* Portsmouth, NH: Boynton/Cook.

Black, L., Daiker, D., Sommers, J., & Stygall, G. (1994). Writing like a woman and being rewarded for it: Gender, assessment, and reflective letters from Miami University's student portfolios. In L. Black, D. Daiker, J. Sommers, & G. Stygall ("Eds.), *New directions in portfolio assessment: Reflective practice, critical theory, and large-scale scoring* (pp. 235-247). Portsmouth, NH: Heinemann.

Bleich, D. (1997). What can be done about grading? In L. Allison, L. Bryant, & M. Hourigan (Eds.), *Grading in the post-process classroom: From theory to practice* (pp. 15-35). Portsmouth, NJ: Boynton/Cook.

Blumenbach, J. F. (1775/2000). *On the natural varieties of mankind* (T. Bendyshe, Trans.). In R. Bernasconi & T. L. Lott (Eds.), *The idea of race* (pp. 27-37). Indianapolis, IN/Cambridge, UK: Hackett Publishing.

Bonetto, S. (2006). Race and racism in Hegel—An analysis. *Minerva: An Internet Journal of Philosophy, 10.* Retrieved from http://www.minerva.mic.ul.ie//vol10/Hegel.html

Bonilla-Silva, E. (1997). Rethinking racism: Toward a structural interpretation. *American Sociological Review, 62*(3), 465-480.

Bonilla-Silva, E. (2001). *White supremacy and racism in the post-civil rights era.* Boulder, CO: Lynne Rienner Publishers.

Bonilla-Silva, E. (2003a). "New racism," color-blind racism, and the future of whiteness in America. In A. W. Doane & E. Bonilla-Silva (Eds.), *White out: The continuing significance of racism* (pp. 271-284). New York/ London: Routledge.

Bonilla-Silva, E. (2003b). *Racism without racists: Color-Blind racism and the persistence of racial inequality in the United States.* Lanham, MD/Boulder, CO/ New York/Oxford, UK: Rowman & Littlefield.

Booth, W. C. (1963). The rhetorical stance. *College Composition and Communication, 14,* 139-145.

Boulle, P. H. (2003). François Bernier and the origins of the modern concept of race. In S. Peabody & T. Stovall (Eds.), *The color or liberty: The histories of race in France* (pp. 11-27). Durham, NC: Duke University Press.

Bourdieu, P. (1977). *Outline of a theory of practice* (R. Nice, Trans.). Cambridge, UK: Cambridge University Press.

Bowman, J. P. (1973). Problems of the grading differential. *The Journal of Business Communication, 11*(1), 22-30.

Brannon, L., & Knoblauch, C. H. (1982). On students' rights to their own texts: A model of teacher response. *College Composition and Communication,* 33(2), 157-166.

Breland, H., Kubota, M., Nickerson, K., Trapani, C., & Walker, M. (2004). *New SAT writing prompt study: Analyses of group impact and reliability.* New York: College Board Examination Board.

Broad, B. (2003). *What we really value: Beyond rubrics in teaching and assessing writing.* Logan, UT: Utah State University Press.

Broad, B., Adler-Kassner, L., Alford, B., Detweiler, J., Estrem, H., Harrington, S., ... Weeden, S. (2009). *Organic writing assessment: Dynamic criteria mapping in action.* Logan, UT: Utah State University Press.

Brookfield, S. D. (1995). *Becoming a critically reflective teacher.* San Francisco: Josey-Bass.

Brookhiser, R. (1997). The way of the WASP. In R. Delgado & Stefancic, J.

(Eds.), *Critical white studies: Looking behind the mirror* (pp. 16-23). Philadelphia: Temple University Press.

Bruffee, K. (1984). Collaborative learning and the "conversation of mankind." *College English, 46*(7), 635-653.

Burke, K. (1966). *Language as symbolic action: Essays on life, literature, and method*. Berkeley, CA/Los Angeles/ London: University of California Press.

Burke, K. (1950/1969). *A grammar of motives*. Berkeley, CA/Los Angeles/London: University of California Press.

Butler, J. (1990/ 1999). *Gender trouble: Feminism and subversion of identity*. New York: Routledge.

California State University. (2006). Home page. Retrieved from http://www.calstate.edu/

California State University. (2011). CSU early start course listing. Retrieved from http://earlystart.csusuccess.org/

California State University. (2013). Early start Initiative. Retrieved from http://www.calstate.edu/acadaff/EarlyStart/

California State University, Division of Analytic Studies. (2013). Proficiency Reports of Students Entering the CSU System. Retrieved from http://www.asd.calstate.edu/performance/proficiency.shtml

California State University Analytic Studies. (2014). Proficiency reports of students entering the CSU System. Retrieved from http://www.asd.calstate.edu/performance/proficiency.shtml

California State University, Fresno. (n.d.). Office of Institutional Effectiveness. Retrieved from http://www.fresnostate.edu/academics/oie/data/student.html

Canagarajah, S. (2006). The place of world Englishes in composition: Pluralization continued. *College Composition and Communication, 57*(4), 586-619.

Canagarajah, S. (2013). Negotiating translingual literacy: An enactment. *Research in the Teaching of English, 48*(1), 40-67.

Carr, A. (2013). In support of failure. *Composition Forum, 27*(Spring). Retrieved from compositionforum.com/issue/27/

Carr, J. (1997). *Aristotle's use of "genus" in logic, philosophy, and science*. (Dissertation, University of Edinburgh). Retrieved from http://www.era.lib.ed.ac.uk/bitstream/1842/1794/1/Jeffrey%20Carr_1997.pdf

CCCC. (1974). Students' right to their own language. Retrieved from http://www.ncte.org/library/NCTEFiles/Groups/CCCC/NewSRTOL.pdf

CCCC. (2009). Writing assessment: A position statement. Retrieved from http://www.ncte.org/cccc/resources/positions/writingassessment

Centers for Disease Control and Prevention. (2007). Emergency preparedness and response. Retrieved from http://emergency.cdc.gov/snaps/data/06/06019_lang.htm

Chambers, R. (1997). The unexamined. In M. Hill (Ed.), *Whiteness: A critical reader* (pp. 187-203). New York: New York University Press.

Chan, S. (1994). *Hmong means free: Life in Laos and America.* Philadelphia: Temple University Press.

Charnley, M. V. (1978). Grading standards vary considerably, experiment shows. *Journalism Educator*, (October), 49-50.

Chödron, P. (2013). *How to meditate: A practical guide to making friends with your mind.* Boulder, CO: Sounds True.

Coe, R. (1975). Eco-Logic for the composition classroom. *College Composition and Communication, 26*(3), 232-237.

Coles, W. E., Jr., & Vopat, J. (1985). *What makes writing good.* Lexington: Heath.

Condon, F. (2013). *I hope I join the band: Narrative, affiliation, and antiracist rhetoric.* Logan, UT: Utah State University Press.

Conlee, J. (Ed.). (2004). Poems comic, satiric, and parodic. KalamazooMI: Medieval Institute Publications. Retrieved from http://www.lib.rochester.edu/camelot/teams/duntxt4.htm#P77Connors, R. (1997). *Composition-rhetoric: Backgrounds, theory, and pedagogy.* Pittsburgh: University of Pittsburgh Press.

Conway, G. (1994). Portfolio cover letters, students' self-presentation, and teachers' ethics. In L. Black, D. A. Daiker, J. Sommers, & G. Stygall (Eds.), *New directions in portfolio assessment: Reflective practice, critical theory, and large-scale scoring* (pp. 83-92). Portsmouth, NH: Boynton/Cook.

Cooper, M. M. (1986). The ecology of writing. *College English, 48*(4), 364-375.

Cooper, M. M. (2011). Rhetorical agency as emergent and enacted. *College Composition and Communication, 62*(3), 420-449.

Covington, M., & Beery, R. (1976). *Self-Worth and school learning.* New York: Holt Rinehart & Winston.

Cowan, R. S. (1997). *A social history of American technology.* Oxford, UK: Oxford University Press.

Cornell College. (2011). *Cornell eReport, 35*(1). Retrieved from http://www.cornellcollege.edu/cornell-report/issues/2011-fall/article1/sidebar-armstrong.shtml

Council of Writing Program Administers. (2011). *Framework for success in postsecondary writing.* Creative Commons. Retrieved from http://wpacouncil.org/framework

Couture, B. (1998). *Toward a phenomenological rhetoric: Writing, profession, and altruism.* Carbondale, IL: Southern Illinois University Press.

Crenshaw, K. W. (1991). Mapping the margins: Intersectionality, identity politics, and violence against women of color. *Stanford Law Review, 43*, 1241-1299.

Cronbach, L. J. (1988). Five perspectives on validity argument. In H. Wainer (Ed.), *Test validity* (pp. 3-17). Hillsdale, NJ: Erlbaum.

Crowley, S. (1998). *Composition in the university: Historical and polemical essays.* Pittsburgh: University of Pittsburgh Press.

Crowley, S., & Hawhee, D. (2009). *Ancient rhetorics for contemporary students* (4th ed.). New York: Pearson/Longman.

Danielewicz, J., & Elbow, P. (2009). A unilateral grading contract to improve learning and teaching. *College Composition and Communication, 61*(2), 244–268.

Dao, Y. (1981). Why did the Hmong leave Laos? (S. Downing, Trans.). In B. T. Downing & D. P. Olney (Eds.), *The Hmong in the West: Observations and reports.* Minneapolis: Center for Urban and Regional Affairs.

De Certeau, M. (1984). *The practice of everyday life.* Berkeley, CA: University of California Press.

De Kock, L. (1992). Interview with Gayatri Chakravorty Spivak: New nation writers conference in South Africa. *ARIEL: A Review of International English Literature, 23*(3), 29-47.

Delgado, R., & Stefancic, J. (Eds.). (1997). *Critical white studies: Looking behind the mirror.* Philadelphia: Temple University Press.

Delpit, L. (2002). Introduction. In L. Delpit & J. Kilgour, J. (Eds.), *The skin that we speak: Thoughts on language and culture in the classroom.* New York: New Press.

Dewey, J. (1910). *How we think* (2nd ed.). Boston, MA: D. C. Heath.

Diederich, P. B. (1974). *Measuring growth in English.* Urbana, IL: National Council of Teachers of English.

Dobrin, S. I. (2012). *Postcomposition.* Carbondale/ Edwardsville, IL: Southern Illinois University Press.

Dobrin, S. I., & Weisser, C. R. (2002). Breaking ground in ecocomposition: Exploring relationships between discourse and environment. *College English, 64*(5), 566-589.

Dressman, M., Wilder, P., & Connor, J. J. (2005). Theories of failure and the failure of theories: A cognitive/sociocultural/macrostructural study of eight struggling students. *Research in the Teaching of English, 40*(1), 8-61.

Duffy, J. (2007). *Writing from these roots: Literacy in a Hmong-American community.* Honolulu, HI: University of Hawai'i Press.

Dulaney, J. (2013, August 20). Survey: Most high school graduates not ready for college. *Los Angeles Daily News.* Retrieved from http://www.dailynews.com/social-affairs/20130821/survey-most-high-school-graduates-not-ready-for-college

Dulek, R., & Shelby, A. (1981). Varying evaluative criteria: A factor in differential grading. *The Journal of Business Communication, 18*(2), 41-50.

ecology, n. (2015). *OED Online*. Oxford University Press. Retrieved from http://www.oed.com.offcampus.lib.washington.edu/

Ede, L., & Lunsford, A. (1984). Audience addressed/audience invoked: The role of audience in composition theory and pedagogy. *College Composition and Communication, 35*(2), 155-171.

Edgington, Tony. (2005). What are you thinking?: Understanding teacher reading and response through a protocol analysis study. *Journal of Writing Assessment, 2*(2), 125-148.

Elbow, P. (1973). *Writing without teachers*. New York: Oxford University Press.

Elbow, P. (1993). Ranking, evaluating, and liking: Sorting out three forms of judgment. *College English, 55*(2), 187-206.

Elbow, P. (1996). Writing assessment in the 21st century: A utopian view. In L. Bloom, D. Daiker, & E. White (Eds.), *Composition in the twenty-first century: Crisis and change* (pp. 83-100). Carbondale/Edwardsville, IL: Southern Illinois University Press.

Elbow, P. (1997). Taking time out from grading and evaluating while working in a conventional system. *Assessing Writing, 4*(1), 5-27.

Elbow, P. (2012). Good enough evaluation: When is it feasible and when is evaluation not worth having? In N. Elliot & L. Perelman (Eds.), *Writing Assessment in the 21st century: Essays in honor of Edward M. White* (pp. 303-325). New York: Hampton Press.

Faigley, L. (1989). Judging writers, judging selves. *College Composition and Communication, 40*, 395-412.

Faigley, L. (1992). *Fragments of rationality: Postmodernity and the subject of composition*. Pittsburgh: University of Pittsburgh Press.

Feenberg, A. (1991). *Critical theory of technology*. New York/ Oxford, UK: Oxford University Press.

Ferrante, J. W., & Brown, P. (Eds.). (1998). *The social construction of race in America*. New York: Longman.

Finkelstein, I. E. (1913). The marking system in theory and practice. *Educational Psychology Monographs, No. 10*. Baltimore, MD: Warwick & York, Inc.

Flynn, E. (1989). Learning to read student papers from a feminine perspective, I. In B. Lawson (Ed.), *Encountering student texts: Interpretive issues in reading student writing* (pp. 49-58). Urbana, IL: NCTE.

Foucault, M. (1977). *Discipline and punish: The birth of the prison*. (A. Sheridan, Trans.). New York: Vintage.

Foucault, M. (1980). Truth and power. In Gordon, C. (Ed.) (C. Gordon, L. Marshall, J. Mipham, & K. Soper, Trans.), *Power/knowledge* (pp. 109-133). New York: Pantheon Books.

Foucault, M. (1982). The subject and power. In H. Dreyfus, & P. Rabinow

(Eds.), *Michel Foucault: Beyond structuralism and hermeneutics* (pp. 208-228). Chicago: University of Chicago Press.

Foucault, M., & Miskowiec, J. (1986). Of other spaces. *Diacritics, 16*(1), 22-27.

Fowler, J., & Ochsner, R. (2012). Evaluating essays across institutional boundaries: Teacher attitudes toward dialect, race, and writing. In A. B. Inoue & M. Poe (Eds.), *Race and Writing Assessment* (pp. 111-126). New York: Lang Publishers.

Fox, T. (1993). Standards and access. *Journal of Basic Writing, 12*(1), 37-45.

Fox, T. (1999). *Defending Access: A critique of standards in higher education.* Portsmouth, NH: Boynton/Cook.

Frankenberg, R. (1993). *White women, race matters: The social construction of whiteness.* Minneapolis: University of Minnesota Press.

Freire, P. (1970). *Pedagogy of the oppressed* (M. B. Ramos, Trans.). New York, NY: Continuum. (reprinted 2005).

Freire, P., & Macedo, D. (1987). *Literacy: Reading the word & the world.* South Hadley, MA: Bergin & Garvey Publishers.

Freud, S. (1913). Chapter VI. The dream-work. (A. A. Brill, Trans.). In *The Interpretation of Dreams* (3rd ed.). New York, NY: Macmillan Company. Retrieved from http://www.bartleby.com/285/

Gallagher, C. (2010). Assess locally, validate globally: Heuristics for validating local writing assessments. *Journal of the Council of Writing Program Administrators, 34*(1), 10-32.

Gallagher, C. (2012). The Trouble with outcomes: Pragmatic inquiry and educational aims. *College English, 75*(1), 42-60.

Gerald, D., & Haycock, K. (2006). *Engines of inequality: Diminishing equity in the nation's premier public universities.* Washington, DC: The Education Trust.

Gilyard, K. (1991). *Voices of the self: A study of language competence.* Detroit: Wayne State University Press.

Glaister, D., & MacAskill, E. (2006, May 01). US counts cost of day without immigrants. *The Guardian*, Retrieved from http://www.theguardian.com/world/2006/may/02/usa.topstories3

Goffman, E. (1974). *Frame analysis: An essay on the organization of experience.* Cambridge, MA: Harvard University Press.

Goldberg, D. T. (1993). *Racist culture: Philosophy and the politics of meaning.* Malden, MA: Blackwell.

Goldberg, D. T. (2002). *The racial state.* Malden, MA: Blackwell.

Gorman, A., Miller, M., & Landberg, M. (2006, May 02). Marchers fill L.A.'s streets. *Los Angeles Times*, Retrieved from http://www.latimes.com/news/la-me-march2may02-story.html#page=1

Gossett, T. (1963). *Race: The history of an idea in America.* New York: Schocken.

Gould, S. J. (1981). *The mismeasure of man*. New York/London: W. W. Norton.

Graff, G., & Birkenstein, C. (2014). *They say/I say: The moves that matter in academic writing* (3rd ed.). New York: W. W. Norton and Company.

Gramsci, A. (1971/2000). *The Gramsci reader: Selected writings 1916-1935*. Forgacs, D. (Ed.). (Q. Hoare & G. Nowell-Smith, Trans.). New York: New York University Press.

Greenfield, L. (2011). The "standard English" fairy tale: A rhetorical analysis of racist pedagogies and commonplace assumptions about language diversity. In L. Greenfield & K. Rowan (Eds.), *Writing centers and the new racism: A call for sustainable dialogue and change*. Logan, UT: Utah State University Press.

Guba, E., & Lincoln, Y. (1989). *Fourth generation evaluation*. Newbury Park, CA: Sage.

Gutherie, W. K. C. (1971). *The sophists*. London/New York: Cambridge University Press.

Hairston, M. (1982). The winds of change: Thomas Kuhn and the revolution in the teaching of writing. *College Composition and Communication, 33*(1), 76-88.

Hamp-Lyons, L, & Condon, W. (2000). *Assessing the portfolio: Principles for practice, theory, and research*. Cresskill, NJ: Hampton Press.

Hanh, T. N. (1987). *Being peace*. Berkeley, CA: Parallax Press.

Hanh, T. N. (1991). *Peace is every step: The path of mindfulness in everyday life*. New York: Bantam.

Hannaford, I. (1996). *Race: The history of an idea in the west*. Baltimore, MD: Johns Hopkins University Press.

Hanson, F. A. (1993). *Testing testing: Social consequences of the examined life*. Berkeley: University of California Press.

Hanson, F. A. (2000). How tests create what they are intended to measure. In A. Filer (Ed.), *Assessment: Social practice and social product* (pp. 67-81). London/New York: Routledge/Falmer.

Harris, J. (1989). The idea of community in the study of writing. *College Composition and Communication, 40*(1), 11-22.

Harris, J. (2012). *A teaching subject: Composition since 1966*. New Edition. Logan, UT: Utah State University Press.

Haswell, R. (1998a). Multiple inquiry in the validation of writing tests. *Assessing Writing, 5*(1), 89-109.

Haswell, R. (1998b). Rubrics, prototypes, and exemplars: Categorization theory and systems of writing placement. *Assessing Writing, 5*(2), 231-268.

Haswell, R. (Ed.). (2001). *Beyond outcomes: Assessment and instruction within a university writing program*. Westport, CT: Ablex.

Haswell, R. (2013). Writing assessment and race studies sub specie aeternitatis: A response to race and writing assessment. *Journal of Writing Assessment*.

Retrieved from http://jwareadinglist.blogspot.com/2013/01/writing-assessment-and-race-studies-sub_4.html

Hayes, J. R. (2012). Modeling and remodeling writing. *Written Communication, 29*(3), 369-388.

Hong, W. P., & Youngs, P. (2008). Does high-stakes testing increase cultural capital among low-income and racial minority students? *Education Policy Analysis Archives, 16*(6). Retrieved from http://epaa.asu.edu/epaa/v16n6

hooks, b. (1994). *Teaching to transgress: Education as the practice of freedom.* New York: Routledge.

Horner, B. (1992). Rethinking the "sociality" of error: Teaching editing as negotiation. *Rhetoric Review, 11*(1), 172-199.

Horner, B., & Lu, M. (1999). *Representing the "other": Basic writers and the teaching of basic writing.* Urbana, IL: NCTE.

Horner, B., Lu, M., Royster, J. J., & Trimbur, J. (2011). Language difference in writing: Toward a translingual approach. *College English, 73*(3), 303-321.

Horner, B., & Trimbur, J. (2002). English only and U.S. college composition. *College Composition and Communication, 53*(4), 594-630.

Hull, G., & Rose, M. (1989). Rethinking remediation: Toward a social-cognitive understanding of problematic reading and writing. *Written Communication, 6*(2), 139-154.

Huot, B. (2002). *(Re)Articulating writing assessment for teaching and learning.* Logan, UT: Utah State University Press.

Hurlbert, C. (2012). *National healing: Race, state, and the teaching of composition.* Logan, UT: Utah State University Press.

Ignatiev, N. (1995). *How the Irish became white.* New York/ London: Routledge.

Inda, J. X. (2000). Performativity, materiality, and the racial body. *Latino Studies Journal, 11*(3), 74-99.

Inoue, A. B. (2004). Community-based assessment pedagogy. *Assessing Writing, 9*(3), 208-238.

Inoue, A. B. (2007). Articulating sophistic rhetoric as a validity heuristic for writing assessment. *The Journal of Writing Assessment, 3*(1), 31-54.

Inoue, A. B. (2009a). *Program assessment and dsp validation study: First-year writing program and its pilot DSP.* Retrieved from http://www.csufresno.edu/english/programs/first_writing/ProgramAssessment.shtml

Inoue, A. B. (2009b). Self-Assessment as programmatic center: The first year writing program and its assessment at California State University, Fresno. *Composition Forum, 20*(Spring). Retrieved from http://compositionforum.com/

Inoue, A. B. (2009c). The technology of writing assessment and racial validity. In C. S. Schreiner (Ed.), *Handbook of research on assessment technologies, methods, and applications in higher education* (pp. 97-120). Hershey, PA: IGI Global.

Inoue, A. B. (2010). Teaching the rhetoric of assessment. In J. Harris, J. D. Miles, & C. Paine (Eds.), *Teaching with students texts* (pp. 46-57). Logan, UT: Utah State University Press.

Inoue, A. B. (2012a). Grading contracts: Assessing their effectiveness on differential racial formations. In A. B. Inoue & M. Poe (Eds.), *Race and writing assessment* (pp. 79-94). New York: Peter Lang.

Inoue, A. B. (2012b). Racial methodologies for composition studies: Reflecting on theories of race in writing assessment research. In L. Nickoson & M. P. Sheridan (Eds.), *Writing studies research in practice: Methods and methodologies* (pp. 125-139). Carbondale/Edwardsville, IL: Southern Illinois University Press.

Inoue, A. B. (2014a). A grade-less writing course that focuses on labor and assessing. In D. Teague & R. Lunsford (Eds.), *First-year composition: From theory to practice* (pp. 71-110). West Lafayette, IN: Parlor Press.

Inoue, A. B. (2014b). Theorizing failure in writing assessments. *Research in the Teaching of English, 48*(3), 329-351.

Inoue, A. B., & Poe, M. (Eds.). (2012a). *Race and writing assessment.* New York: Peter Lang.

Inoue, A. B., & Poe, M. (2012b). Racial formations in two writing assessments: Revisiting White and Thomas' findings on the English placement test after 30 years. In N. Elliot & L. Perelman (Eds.), *Writing assessment in the 21st century: Essays in honor of Edward M. White* (pp. 343-361). New York: Hampton Press.

Inoue, A. B., & Richmond, T. (in press). Theorizing the reflection practices of female Hmong college students: Is "reflection" a racialized discourse? In K. B. Yancey (Ed.), *A rhetoric of reflection.* Logan, UT: Utah State University Press.

Irmscher, W. F. (1979). *Teaching expository writing.* New York: Holt Rinehart & Winston.

Isocrates. (1929/2000). *Loeb classical library: Isocrates, volume II.* (G. Norlin, Trans). Cambridge/London: Harvard University Press.

Jencks, C., & Phillips, M. (1998). *The black-white test score gap.* Washington, DC: Brookings Institute.

Jensen, A. R. (1976). Test bias and construct validity. *Phi Delta Kappan, 58*, 340-346.

Jordan, J. (2012). *Redesigning composition for multilingual realities.* Studies in Writing and Rhetoric Series. Urbana, IL: CCCC, and NCTE.

Kane, M. T. (1992). An argument-based approach to validity. *Psychological Bulletin, 112*(3), 527-535.

Kastman Breuch, L. M. (2011). Post-process "pedagogy": A philosophical exercise. In V. Villanueva & K. L. Arola (Eds.), *Cross-Talk in comp theory: A reader* (3rd ed.) (pp. 97-125). Urbana, IL: National Council of Teachers of English. (Reprinted from *JAC, 22*(1), pp. 119-150).

Keating, A. (1995). Interrogating "whiteness," (de)constructing "race." *College English, 57*(8), 901-918.

Kerschbaum, S. L. (2014). *Toward a new rhetoric of difference.* Urbana, IL: NCTE.

Klein, C. (2003). *Cold war orientalism: Asia in the middlebrow imagination, 1945-1961.* Berkeley, CA: University of California Press.

Kohn, A. (1993). *Punished by rewards: The trouble with gold stars, incentive plans, a's, praise, and other bribes.* Boston/New York: Houghton Mifflin.

Kroll, B. M. (1984). Writing for readers: Three perspectives on audience. *College Composition and Communication, 35*(2), 172-185.

Kroll, B. M. (2013). *The open hand: Arguing as an art of peace.* Logan, UT: Utah State University Press.

Kubota, R., & Ward, L. (2000). Exploring linguistic diversity through world Englishes. *The English Journal, 89*(6), 80-86.

Kuper, A. (2000). *Culture: The anthropologists' account.* Cambridge, MA: Harvard University Press.

Kynard, C. (2013). *Vernacular insurrections: Race, black protest, and the new century in composition-literacies studies.* Albany, NY: State University of New York Press.

Lee, R. (1999). *Orientals: Asian Americans in popular culture.* Philadelphia: Temple University Press.

Lieb, E. (1996). *The Hmong migration to Fresno: From Laos to California's central valley.* (Unpublished masters thesis). California State University, Fresno.

Lippi-Green, R. (1997). *English with an accent: Language, ideology, and discrimination in the United States.* London: Routledge.

Lipsitz, G. (1998). *The possessive investment in whiteness: How white people profit from identity politics.* Philadelphia: Temple University Press.

Lu, M. (1991). Redefining the legacy of Mina Shaughnessy: A critique of the politics of linguistic innocence. *Journal of Basic Writing, 10*(1), 26-40.

Lu, M. (1992). Conflict and struggle: The enemies or preconditions of basic writing? *College English, 54*(8), 887-913.

Lu, M. (1994). Professing multiculturalism: The politics of style in the contact zone. *College Composition and Communication, 45*(4), 442-58.

Lynne, P. (2004). *Coming to terms: Theorizing writing assessment in composition studies.* Logan, UT: Utah State University Press.

Madaus, G. (1990). *Testing as a social technology: The inaugural Boisi lecture in education and public policy.* Boston: Center for the Study of Testing Evaluation and Educational Policy, Boston College.

Madaus, G. (1993). A national testing system: Manna from above?: An historical/technological perspective. *Educational measurement, 1*(1), 9-26.

Madaus, G. (1994). A technological and historical consideration of equity issues associated with proposals to change the nation's testing policy. *Harvard Educational Review, 64*(1), 76-95.

Madaus, G., & Clarke, M. (2001). The adverse impact of high-stakes testing on minority students: Evidence from one hundred years of test data. In G. Orfield & M. L. Kornhaber (Eds.), *Raising standards or raising barriers? Inequality and high-stakes testing in public education* (pp. 85-106). New York: Century Foundation.

Madaus, G., & Horn C. (2000). *Testing technology: The need for oversight.* In Filer, A. (Ed.), *Assessment: Social practice and social product* (pp. 47-66). London/ New York: Routledge/Falmer.

Marable, M. (2002). The political and theoretical contexts of the changing racial terrain. *Souls, 4*(3), 1-16.

Marcuse, H. (1998). *Technology, war and fascism: Collected papers of Herbert Marcuse* (Vol. 1). D. Kellner (Ed.). London/ New York: Routledge.

Mastroianni, D. (2012). Hegemony in Gramsci. Retrieved from http://postcolonialstudies.emory.edu/hegemony-in-gramsci/

Matsuda, P. K. (2006). The myth of linguistic homogeniety in U.S. college composition. *College Engish, 68*(6), 637-651.

McCarthy, P., Meier, S., & Rinderer, R. (1985). Self-Efficacy and writing: A different view of self-evaluation. *College Composition and Communication, 36*(4), 465-471.

Merleau-Ponty, M. (1945/2002). *The phenomenology of perception.* (C. Smith, Trans.). New York: Routledge.

Messick, S. (1989). Validity. In R. L. Linn (Ed.), *Educational measurement,* 13-103. New York: American Council on Education, Macmillan.

Miller, S. (1991). *Textual carnivals: The politics of composition.* Carbondale, IL: Southern Illinois University Press.

Mills, C. (1997). *The racial contract.* Ithaca, NY/ London: Cornell University.

Morrison, T. (1992). *Playing in the dark: Whiteness and the literary imagination.* Cambridge: Harvard University Press.

Morton, S. (2007). *Gayatri Spivak: Ethics, subalternity and the critique of postcolonial reason.* Malden, MA: Polity Press.

Moss, P. A., Girard, B. J., & Greeno, J. G. (2008). Sociocultural implications for assessment II: Professional learning, evaluation, and accountability. In P. A. Moss, D. C. Pullin, J. P. Gee, E. Haertel, & L. J. Young (Eds.), *Assessment, equity, and opportunity to learn.* New York: Cambridge University Press.

Murray, D. (2011). Teach writing as a process not product. In V. Villanueva & K. L. Arola (Eds.), *Cross-talk in comp theory: A reader* (3rd ed.) (pp. 3-6). Urbana, IL: National Council of Teachers of English. (Reprinted from *The Leaflet,* November 1972).

Murphy, S. (2007). Culture and consequences: The canaries in the coal mine. *Research in the Teaching of English, 42*(2), 228-244.

Myers, G. (1986). Reality, consensus, and reform in the rhetoric of composition teaching. *College English, 48*(2), 154-174.

Myser, C. (2003). Differences from somewhere: The normativity of whiteness in bioethics in the United States. *The American Journal of Bioethics, 3*(2), 1-11.

National Center for Law and Economic Justice. (n.d.). Poverty in the United States: A snapshot. Retrieved from http://www.nclej.org/poverty-in-the-us.php

National Poverty Center. (2014). Poverty in the United States. Retrieved from http://www.npc.umich.edu/poverty/

NCTE & WPA, (n.d.). White paper on writing assessment in colleges and universities. Retrieved from http://wpacouncil.org/whitepaper

O'Hagan, L. K. (1997). It's broken —Fix it! In S. Tchudi (Ed.), *Alternatives to grading student writing* (pp. 3-13). Urbana, IL: NCTE.

Ohmann, R. (1996). *English in America: A radical view of the profession.* Hanover,NH/London: Wesleyan University Press.

Omi, M., & Winant, H. (1994). *Racial formation in the United States: From the 1960s to the 1990s.* (2nd ed). New York: Routledge.

Omi, M., & Winant, H. (2015). *Racial formation in the United States: From the 1960s to the 1990s.* (3rd. ed). New York: Routledge.

O'Neill, P., Moore, C., & Huot, B. (2009). *A Guide to College Writing Assessment.* Logan, UT: Utah State University Press.

Ong, W. J. (1975). The writer's audience is always a fiction. *PMLA, 90*(1), 9-21.

O'Reilley, M. R. (1998). *Radical presence: Teaching as contemplative practice.* Portsmouth, NH: Boynton/Cook Publishers.

Orfield, G., & Kornhaber, M. (Eds.). (2001). *Raising standards or raising barriers? Inequality and high-stakes testing in public education.* New York: Century Foundation.

Otte, G., & Mlynarczyk, R. W. (2010). *Basic writing.* West Lafayette, IN: Parlor Press & The WAC Clearinghouse.

Painter, N. I. (2010). *The History of white people.* London: W.W. Norton & Company.

Pianko, S. (1979). Reflection: A critical component of the composing process. *College Composition and Communication, 30*(3), 275-278.

Plata, M. (1995). Success of Hispanic college students on a writing examination. *The Journal of Educational Issue of Language Minority Students.* Retrieved from http://www.ncela.gwu.edu/files/rcd/BE021059/Success_of_Hispanic.pdf

Poe, M., Elliot, N., Cogan, J.A., & Nurudeen, T. G. (2014). The legal and the local: Using disparate impact analysis to understand the consequences of writing assessment. *College Composition and Communication, 65*(4), 588-611.

Powell, P. R. (2013). *Retention and resistance: Writing instruction and students who leave*. Logan, UT: Utah State University Press.

Prashad, V. (2000). *The karma of brown folk*. Minneapolis, MN: University of Minnesota Press.

Pratt, M. L. (1991). Arts of the contact zone. *Professions, 91*, 33-40.

Prendergast, C. (1998). "Race: The absent presence in composition studies." *College Composition and Communication, 50*(1), 36-53.

Prendergast, C. (2003). *Literacy and racial justice: The politics of learning after Brown v. board of education*. Carbondale, IL: University of Illinois Press.

Pulfrey, C., Buchs, C., & Butera, F. (2011). Why grades engender performance-avoidance goals: The mediating role of autonomous motivation. *Journal of Educational Psychology, 103*(3), 683-700.

"race" *Oxford Dictionary of Word Origins*. by Julia Cresswell. *Oxford Reference Online*. Oxford University Press. Retrieved from http://www.oxfordreference.com/views/ENTRY.html?subview=Main&entry=t292.e4038

Ratcliffe, K. (2005). *Rhetorical listening: Identification, gender, and whiteness*. Carbondale, IL: Southern Illinois University Press.

Reichert, N. (2003). Practice makes perfect: Contracting quantity *and* quality. *Teaching English in Two-Year Colleges*, (September), 60-68.

Reither, J. A. (1985). Writing and knowing: Toward redefining the writing process. *College English, 47*(6), 620-628.

Reynolds, C. R. (1982a). Methods for detecting construct and predictive bias. In R. A. Berk (Ed.), *Handbook of methods for detecting test bias* (pp. 199-227). Baltimore, MD/London: Johns Hopkins University Press.

Reynolds, C. R. (1982b). The problem of bias in psychological assessment. In C. R. Reynolds & T. B. Gutkin (Eds.), *The handbook of school psychology* (pp. 178-208). New York: Wiley.

Reynolds, E. (2004). The role of self-efficacy in writing and directed self-placement. In D. J. Royer & R. Gilles (Eds.), *Directed self-placement: Principles and practices* (pp. 73-103). Cresskill, NJ: Hampton Press.

Reynolds, N. (2004). *Geographies of writing: Inhabiting places and encountering difference*. Carbondale, IL: Southern Illinois University Press.

Ritter, K. (2009). *Before Shaughnessy: Basic writing at Yale and Harvard, 1920-1960*. Carbondale, IL: Southern Illinois University Press.

Rodriquez, A. S. (1998, March 31). Statement from Arturo S. Rodriquez, President United Farm Workers of America, AFL-CIO. *Press Release*. Retrieved from http://www.ufw.org/_board.php?mode=view&b_code=news_press&b_no=185&page=16&field=&key=&n=53

Rodriguez, R. (1982). *Hunger of memory: The education of Richard Rodriquez*. Boston: David R.Godine.

Roediger, D. (1999). *The wages of whiteness: Race and the making of the American working class.* (Revised ed.). London/New York: Verso.

Royer, D. J., & Gilles, R. (1998). Directed self-placement: An attitude of orientation. *College Composition and Communication, 50*(1), 54-70.

Royer, D. J., & Gilles, R. (Eds.). (2003). *Directed self-placement: Principles and practices.* Cresskill, NJ: Hampton Press.

Ruth, L., & Murphy, S. (1988). *Designing writing tasks for the assessment of writing.* Norwood, NJ: Ablex.

Ryan, C. (2013). Language use in the United States: 2011. *American Community Survey Reports (ACS-22).* Retrieved from http://www.census.gov/prod/2013pubs/acs-22.pdf

Said, E. (1979). *Orientalism.* New York: Vintage.

Salih, S. (2002). *Judith Butler.* New York: Routledge.

San Juan, E. (2002). *Racism and cultural studies: Critiques of multiculturalist ideology and the politics of difference.* Durham, NC: Duke University Press.

Satzewich, V. (1998). Race, racism, and racialization: Contested concepts. In V. Satzewich (Ed.), *Racism and social inequality in Canada: Concepts, controversies, and strategies of resistance* (pp. 25-46). Toronto: Thompson Educational Publishers.

Schon, D. (1987). *Educating the reflective practitioner.* San Francisco: Josey-Bass.

Scott, T. (2005). Creating the subject of portfolios: Reflective writing and the conveyance of institutional prerogatives. *Written Communication, 22*(1), 3-35.

Scott, T. (2009). *Dangerous writing: Understanding the political economy of composition.* Logan, UT: Utah State University Press.

Schroeder, C. (2011). *Diverse by design: Literacy education within multicultural institutions.* Logan, UT: Utah State University Press.

Shaughnessy, M. (1977). *Errors and expectations: A guide for the teacher of basic writing.* New York: Oxford University Press.

Shakespeare, W. (1600/ ??) *The merchant of Venice.* [publication info, edition?].

Shell, D., Murphy, C., & Bruning, R. (1989). Self-efficacy and outcome expectancy mechanisms in reading and writing achievement. *Journal of Educational Psychology, 81*(1), 91-100.

Shepard, L. A. (1993). Evaluating test validity. In L. Darling-Hammond (Ed.), *Review of Research in Education,* (Vol. 19, pp. 405-450). Washington DC: American Educational Research Association.

Shor, I. (2009). Critical pedagogy is too big to fail. *Journal of Basic Writing, 28*(2), 6-27.

Soliday, M. (2002). *The politics of remediation: Institutional and student needs in higher education.* Pittsburgh: University of Pittsburgh Press.

Soares, J. A. (2007). *The power of privilege: Yale and America's elite colleges*. Stanford, CA: Stanford University Press.

Sommers, N. (1980). Revision strategies of student writers and experienced adult writers. *College Composition and Communication, 31*(4), 378-88.

Sommers, N. (1982). Responding to student writing. *College Composition and Communication, 33*(2), 148-156.

Spidell, C., & Thelin, W. H. (2006). Not ready to let go: a study of resistance to grading contracts. *Composition Studies, 34*(1), 35-68.

Stanley, J. (2009). *The rhetoric of remediation: Negotiating entitlement and access to higher education*. Pittsburgh: University of Pittsburgh Press.

Starch, D., & Elliott, E. C. (1912). Reliability of the grading of high-school work in English. *The School Review, 20*(7), 442-457.

Sternglass, M. (1997). *Time to know them: A longitudinal study of writing and learning at the college level*. Mahwah, NJ: Erlbaum.

Stigmata, n. (2015). *OED Online*. Oxford University Press, March 2015. Retrieved from http://www.oed.com.offcampus.lib.washington.edu/

Stoddard, L. (1922). *The rising tide of color against white world-supremacy*. New York: Scribner's Sons.

Straub, R. (1996a). The concept of control in teacher response: Defining the varieties of "directive" and "facilitative" commentary. *College Composition and Communication, 47*(2), 223-251.

Straub, R. (1996b). Teacher response as conversation: More than casual talk, an exploration. *Rhetoric Review, 14*(2), 374-399.

Straub, R. (1997). Students' reactions to teachers' comments: An exploratory study. *Research in the Teaching of English, 31*, 91-120.

Straub, R. (2000). The student, the test, and the classroom context: A case study of teacher response. *Assessing Writing, 7*, 23-56.

Strand, S. (2010). Do some schools narrow the gap? Differential school effectiveness by ethnicity, gender, poverty, and prior achievement. *School Effectiveness and School Improvement, 21*(3), 289-314.

Takaki, R. (2000). *Iron cages: Race and culture in 19th-century America*. (Revised ed.). New York/ Oxford, UK: Oxford University Press.

Tchudi, S. (Ed.). (1997). *Alternatives to grading student writing*. Urbana, IL: NCTE.

Thorndike, R. M. (1971). Concepts of culture-fairness. *Journal of Educational Measurement, 8*(2), 63-70.

Total Military Recruits: Army, Navy, Air Force (per capita) by state. (2004). *National Priorities Project Database*. Retrieved from http://www.StateMaster.com/graph/mil_tot_mil_rec_arm_nav_air_for_percap-navy-air-force-per-capita

Trachsel, M. (1992). *Institutionalizing literacy: The historical role of college entrance examinations in English.* Carbondale/Edwardsville, IL: Southern Illinois University Press.

Trimbur, J. (1989). Consensus and difference in collaborative learning. *College English, 51*(6), 602-616.

Trimbur, J. (1996). Response: Why do we test writing? In E. White, W. Lutz, & S. Kamusikiri (Eds.). *Assessment of writing: Politics, policies, and practices* (pp. 45-48). New York: MLA.

Tuan, Y. (1977). *Space and place: The perspective of experience.* Minneapolis, MN: University of Minnesota Press.

U.S. Census Bureau. (2011). American Community Survey. Retrieved from http://factfinder2.census.gov/faces/tableservices/jsf/pages/productview.xhtml?pid=ACS_11_1YR_S1601&prodType=table

U.S. Department of Education & National Center for Education Statistics. (2011). Higher Education General Information Survey (HEGIS), Fall Enrollment Survey (IPEDS-EF:90). Retrieved from http://nces.ed.gov/programs/digest/d11/tables/dt11_237.asp

van den Berghe, P. L. (1967). *Race and racism: A comparative perspective.* New York: Wiley.

Villanueva, V. (1993). *Bootstraps: From an American academic of color.* Urbana: NCTE.

Villanueva, V. (1997). Maybe a colony: And still another critique of the comp community. *JAC: A Journal of Composition Theory, 17*(2), 183-190.

Villanueva, V. (2006). Blind: Talking about the new racism. *The Writing Center Journal, 26*(1), 3-19.

Villanueva, V. (2012). The rhetorics of racism: A historical sketch. In L. Greenfield & K. Rowan (Eds.), *Writing centers and the new racism: A call for sustainable dialogue and change* (pp. 17-32). Logan, UT: Utah State University Press.

Voloshinov, V. (1929/1986). *Marxism and the philosophy of language.* (L. Matejka & I. Titunik Trans.). Cambridge, MA: Harvard University Press.

Wardle, E., & Roozen, K. (2012). Addressing the complexity of writing development: Toward an ecological model of assessment. *Assessing Writing, 17*(2), 106-119.

Watkins, J. R., Jr. (2009). *A taste for language: Literacy, class, and English studies.* Carbondale, IL: Studies in Writing and Rhetoric & Southern Illinois University Press.

Weaver, R. (1953). *The ethics of rhetoric.* South Bend, IN: Henry Regenery.

Wednesday, M. (2007, May 02). The Great American Boycott II. *Los Angeles Indymedia: Activist News.* Retrieved from http://la.indymedia.org/news/2007/05/197741.php

Weiser, I. (1997). Revising our practices: How portfolios help teachers learn. In K. B. Yancey & I. Weiser (Eds.), *Situating portfolios: Four perspectives* (pp. 293-301). Logan, UT: Utah State University Press.

White, E. M. (1994). *Teaching and assessing writing: Recent advances in understanding, evaluating, and improving student performance.* San Francisco: Jossey-Bass.

White, E. M. (1996). Power and agenda setting in writing assessment. In E. M. White, W. D. Lutz, & S. Kamusikiri (Eds.), *Assessment of writing: Politics, policies, practices* (pp. 9-24). New York: MLA.

White, E. M. (2001). The opening of the modern era of writing assessment: A narrative. *College English, 63*(3), 306-320.

White, E. M. (2007). *Assigning, responding, evaluating: A writing teacher's guide.* New York: St. Martin's Press.

White, E. M., Lutz, W. D., & Kamusikiri, S., (1996). *Assessment of writing: Politics, policies, practices.* New York: MLA.

White, E. M., & Thomas, L. L. (1981). Racial minorities and writing skills assessment in the California State University and colleges. *College English, 43*(3), 276-283.

Williams, J. (1981). The phenomenology of error. *College Composition and Communication, 32*(2), 152-168.

Williams, R. (1977). *Marxism and literature.* Oxford, UK/ New York: Oxford University Press.

Williams, R. (1985). *Keywords: A vocabulary of culture and society.* (Revised ed.). New York: Oxford University Press.

WPA outcomes statement for first-year composition. *WPA: Writing Program Administration, 23*(1-2), 59-70.

Xiong, Y. S. (2012). Hmong Americans' educational attainment: Recent changes and remaining challenges. *Hmong Studies Journal, 13*(2), 1-18.

Yagelski, R. P. (2011). *Writing as a way of being: Writing instruction, nonduality, and the crisis of sustainability.* New York: Hampton Press.

Yancey, K. B. (1998). *Reflection in the writing classroom.* Logan, UT: Utah State University Press.

Yancey, K. B. (1999). Looking back as we look forward: Historicizing writing assessment. *College Composition and Communication, 50*(3), 483-503.

Yancey, K. B., & Weiser, I. (Eds.). (1997). *Situation portfolios: Four perspectives.* Logan, UT: Utah State University Press.

Yang, K. (2009). The experiences of Hmong Americans: Three decades in retrospective review. In G. Y. Lee (Ed.), *The impact of globalization and transnationalism on the Hmong* (pp. 79-99). St. Paul, MN: Concordia University, Center for Hmong Studies Press.

Young, V. A. (2004). Your average nigga. *College Composition and Communication*, 55(4), 693-715.

Young, V. A.. (2007). *Your average nigga: Performing race, literacy, and masculinity*. Detroit: Wayne State University Press.

Young, V. A.. (2011). "Nah, we straight": An argument against code switching, *JAC* 29(1-2), 49-76.

Young, V. A., & Martinez, A. Y. (Eds.). (2011). *Code-Meshing as world English: Pedagogy, policy, performance*. Urbana, IL: NCTE.

APPENDIX A: ENGLISH 160W'S GRADING CONTRACT

OUR GRADING CONTRACT FOR ENGL 160W-24

(Adapted from Peter Elbow's contract; see Elbow, 1997; Danielewicz & Elbow, 2009.)

ASAO B. INOUE

Dear Class:

In most learning situations in life outside of school, grades are never given. The learning that occurs in Kung Fu dojos, or cooking, dance, or yoga studios do not use any grading. Why? In these "studio" cases, it seems meaningless to give students grades, and yet without any grades, those students get better at yoga, dance, and cooking. These studio learning situations should prompt us to ask some questions: Why are grades meaningless in those settings but seem so important in a school setting? How do grades affect learning in classrooms? What social dynamics does the presence of grades create? In both situations, instructors provide students/participants with evaluative feedback from time to time, pointing out where, say, they've done well and where the instructor suggests improvement. In the studio situation, many students would help each other, even rely on each other for feedback.

Using conventional grading structures to compute course grades often lead students to think more about their grade than about their writing or learning; to worry more about pleasing a teacher or fooling one than about figuring out what they really want to learn, or how they want to communicate something to someone for some purpose. Additionally, conventional grading may cause you to be reluctant to take risks with your writing or ideas. It doesn't allow you to fail at writing, which many suggest is a primary way in which people learn from their practices. Sometimes grades even lead to the feeling that you are working *against* your teacher, or that you cannot make a mistake, or that you have to hide part of yourself from your teacher and peers. And the psychological research in education, over thirty years of it, has shown over and over that grades not only do not help students learn but they actually harm your learning, keep you from learning. For these reasons, I am incorporating a contract for grading in our class, which avoids the uses of grades and numbers.

I offer this first draft of a contract that focuses on the responsibilities we'll assume, not the things to which someone else (usually the teacher) will hold you accountable. The pedagogical shift I'm suggesting is in part a cultural one. Therefore, we will try to *approximate* the evaluative conditions of a home studio course. That is, we will try to create a culture of support, or rather a *community of compassion*, a group of people who genuinely care about the wellbeing of each other—and part of that caring, that compassion, is acting, doing things for each other. It turns out, this also helps you learn. The best way to learn is to teach others. So we will function as collaborators, allies, as fellow-travelers with various skills, abilities, experiences, and talents that we offer the group, rather than adversaries working against each other for grades or approval by teachers.

So if you're looking to game the system, and do the least amount of work to get the highest possible course grade, this is NOT the class for you. You'll only be frustrated, even angry. Things will seem unfair at times. But if you wish to learn and improve yourself as a writer and reader, are willing to do a lot of work to reach those goals, accept the idea that your labor will be rewarded and not the quality of your work (although we will discuss quality and it is important to your success, but not important to your course grade), then this is the class for you.

Finally, taking grades out of the class, I hope will allow you freedom to take risks and really work hard. Do not be afraid to take risks in your writing and work. Failing or miss the mark is healthy for learners. Good, deep, important learning often happens because of failure—so it's really not failure at all. Failure really only happens in our class when you do not do the work, or do not labor in the ways we ask of you. Most importantly, what looks like failure in writing can show us our weaknesses, misunderstandings, and opportunities for growing and changing. Furthermore, since I won't grade anything, this allows you the chance to rely more authentically on your colleagues and your own assessment and revision advice. This will help you build strategies of self-assessment that function apart from a teacher's approval. I want you to learn to listen carefully to colleagues' differing judgments, assess the worth of those judgments for your work and its purposes, express why one idea is more workable and better than others, and most importantly, make informed, careful decisions in your writing that you can explain to others.

The default grade, then, for the course is a "B." In a nutshell, if you do all that is asked of you in the manner and spirit it is asked, if you work through the processes we establish and the work we assign ourselves during the semester, then you'll get a "B." If you miss class, turn in assignments late, or forget to do assignments, etc., your grade will be lower.

"B" Grades

You are guaranteed a course grade of "B" if you meet all of the following conditions. Please note that in each item below, there are questions that I cannot decide alone, particularly questions of definition. The results/conclusions of our discussions will be put into this contract in the places below.

1. **Attendance/Participation**. You agree to attend and fully participate in at least 87.5% of our scheduled class sessions and their activities and assignments, which means **you may miss (for whatever reason) 4 class sessions**. For our class, attendance should equate to participation, so we need to figure out together what "participation" means and when does someone not get credit for it?

NOTE: Assignments not turned in because of an absence, either ones assigned on the schedule or ones assigned on earlier days in class, will be late, missed, or ignored (depending on when you turn it in finally, see the guidelines #4, #5, and #6 below).

Any absence due to a university-sponsored group activity (e.g., sporting event, band, etc.) will not count against you, as stipulated by university policy, as long as the student has FIRST provided written documentation in the first two weeks of the semester of all absences. This same policy applies to students who have mandatory military-related absences (e.g., deployment, work, duty, etc.). Again, the student must provide written documentation, stating the days he/she will be absent. This will allow us to determine how he/she will meet assignments and our contract, despite being absent.

---

2. **Lateness**. You each agree to come on time or early to class. Five minutes past our start time is considered late. Walking into class late a few times in a semester is understandable, but when does lateness become a problem (for the class as a whole and/or for the individual)? As a rule of thumb, **coming in late 4 or more times in a semester will constitute an absence**.

3. **Sharing and Collaboration**. You agree to work cooperatively and collegially in groups. This may be the easiest of all our course expectations to figure out, but we should have some discussions on what we expect from each other.

4. **Late Assignments**. You will turn in properly and on time all essays, assessments, evaluations, portfolio evaluations, reflections, and other assignments. Because your colleagues in class depend on you to get your work done on time so that they can do theirs on time, all late assignments are just as bad as missed assignments. However, depending on what we agree to in the first week or two of the semester, you may turn in a late assignment or two (see the "Breakdown" table below). In order for an assignment to be considered a **"late assignment," it STILL must be turned in, at least two days (48 hours) after its initial due date, and it should be complete and meet all the assignment's requirements** (e.g., if an essay was due on Friday,

Sept 20 at noon, a late essay must be turned in by noon on Sunday, Sept 22). Please note that a late assignment may be due on a day when our class is not scheduled to meet.

5. **Missed Assignments.** A missed assignment is NOT one not turned in; it is one that has missed the guidelines for a late assignment somehow but is still complete and turned in at some point in the semester (e.g., after the 48 hours). Most missed assignments are those turned in after the 48-hour late turn-in period (see #4 above). **In order to meet our contract for a "B" grade, you cannot have any "missed assignments."** Please note that assignments *not turned in at all* are considered "Ignored Assignments" (see #6 below). A missed assignment is usually one turned in after the 48 hour "late" assignment deadline.

6. **Ignored Assignments.** Any assignments not done period, or "ignored," for whatever reasons, are put in this category. One of these in the grade book means an automatic "D." Two acquired gives you an "F." Additionally, if any of the essays or portfolios become ignored assignments, it constitutes an automatic failure of the course.

7. **All Work and writing** needs to meet the following conditions:
   - *Complete and On Time*. You agree to turn in on time and in the appropriate manner complete essays, writing, or assessments that meet all of our agreed upon expectations. (See #4 above for details on late assignments). This means that assignments are not just done but done in the spirit and manner asked. They must meet the expectations given in class or on handouts.
   - *Revisions*. When the job is to revise your thinking and work, you will reshape, extend, complicate, or substantially clarify your ideas—or relate your ideas to new things. You won't just correct, edit, or touch up. Revisions must somehow respond to or consider seriously your colleagues' (or teacher's) assessments in order to be revisions.
   - *Copy Editing*. When the job is for the final publication of a draft, your work must be well copy edited—that is, free from most mistakes in spelling and grammar. It's fine to get help in copy editing. (Copy editing doesn't count on drafts before the final draft or portfolio.)

"A" Grades

All grades in this course depend upon how much *labor* you do. If you do all that is asked of you in the manner and spirit asked, and meet the guidelines in this contract, specifically the "Break-Down" section at the end of this contract, then you get a "B" course grade. Grades of "A," however, depend on doing advanced projects for both Project 1 and 2, which equates to about twice the work or length of the final project documents. Thus you earn a B if you put in good time and effort, do all the work, and do both projects in an acceptable fashion. But you earn an "A" if you do more work in the two projects—that is, do more in-depth projects (described on the Project handout and in the Syllabus).

While you do not have to worry about anyone's judgments or standards of excellence to meet the grading contract, you are obligated to listen carefully to and address your colleagues' and my concerns in all your work of the class. This means that when you receive feedback you'll use that feedback to help you continually improve your writing. So while others' judgments of your work is not important to your course grade, it is important to your learning and development.

Grades Lower Than B

I hope no one will aim for lower grades. The quickest way to slide to a "C," "D," or "F" is to miss classes, not turn in things on time, turn in sloppy or rushed work, or show up without assignments. This much is nonnegotiable: you are not eligible for a grade of "B" unless you have attended at least 86% of the class sessions (see also #1 above), and meet the guidelines above. And you can't just turn in all the late work at the end of the semester. If you are missing classes and get behind in work, please stay in touch with me about your chances of passing the course.

Break-Down

Below is a table that shows the main components that affect your successful compliance with our contract.

Table 1. The break-down of labor that calculates your final course grade

	# of Absences	# of Late Assigns.	# of Missed Assigns.	# of Ignored Assigns.
A	4 or less	5*	0	0
B	4 or less	5*	0	0
C	5	6	1	0
D	6	7	2	1
F	7	8 or more	2	2 or more

*For those who were able to meet the contract's original guidelines (i.e., three or fewer late assignments) will receive extra consideration during the final conferences. This means a student who has three or fewer late assignments and has met the contract in all other ways may get the benefit of the doubt should his/her portfolio not fully meet the requirements for an "A" contract.

Plea. I (Asao), as the administrator of our contract, will decide in consultation with the student whether a plea is warranted in any case. The student must come to the teacher (Asao Inoue) as soon as possible, usually before the student is unable to meet the contract (before breaching the contract), in order that he/she and the teacher can make fair and equitable arrangements, ones that will be fair and equitable to all in the class and still meet the university's regulations on attendance, conduct, and workload in classes. **You may use a plea for any reason, but only once in the semester**. Please keep in mind that the contract is a public, social contract, one agreed upon through group discussion and negotiation, so my job is to make sure that whatever agreement we come to about a plea will not be unfair to others in class. The plea is NOT an "out clause" for anyone who happens to not fulfill the contract in some way; it is for rare and unusual circumstances out of the control of the student.

By staying in this course and attending class, you accept this contract and agree to abide by it. I also agree to abide by the contract, and administer it fairly and equitably (Asao).

APPENDIX B: EXAMPLE PROBLEM POSING LABOR PROCESS

REFLECTION LETTER: PROBLEMATIZING OUR EXISTENTIAL WRITING ASSESSMENT SITUATIONS [TO BE DONE AFTER OUR ASSESSMENT DISCUSSIONS IN CLASS ON FEB 26]

The final step in this process is to reflect in writing on the problems posed by the process of assessing your colleagues' drafts in a letter to me. Like last time, here are the questions that can help you think about what you might say in your reflection letter to me:

- What problems about your own judgment of writing, of language, might you pose to yourself at this point?
- What contradictions were there in judgments or assumptions (explanations) about language, ideas, or sentences?
- What perspectives did you notice others reading from that shaped very different observations and judgments than yours?

These are the sources of the problems posed by your judgments of writing. Point out one or two problems in your reflection. Show me their sources in your colleagues' assessment letters and your assessment letters. Quote from one or two colleagues' letters (you have them available on G'drive). Quote from the drafts in question. Be precise with the language, since it is the problems of judging language that I'm asking you to reflect upon. In your reflection, try to come to an articulation of the problem as a question. Most important, think of your discussion in the letter not as one in which you figure out which judgment is correct, but as one in which you see them both (or all) as reasonable, as a paradox (a puzzle with multiple ways of approaching it and solving it). You don't have to have answers, but you may have some hypotheses that show tensions. To do this labor, do the following:

1. Find a quiet spot where you can do your work in peace and be completely there for yourself and me.
2. Using our methods from class, spend **five minutes** practicing mindful breathing. As you breathe out slowly, say in your mind, "I am here," then as you breathe out again, say in your mind, "I give my time to myself to problem pose." Repeat these two statements during the entire five min-

utes.

3. Take just **three minutes** and review our handout on deep reading, so that you can do some deep reading of these assessment letters.

4. Spend **at least 20 minutes** looking through your assessment letters and those of your colleagues, looking for the problems you might pose about your judgment of writing or language.

5. Next, reflect in writing for **at least 25 minutes** on the above questions. Your job: problematize your existential writing assessment situation, in other words, pose problems about your judging of writing, think them through, consider the paradoxes (i.e., unresolvable conflicts). The final product should be between **300-400 words**. Place this G'doc in your named folder—this will make it easier for me to get to it. Name it: your name—problem posing 3, so an example of the file name would be: Jen - problem posing 3. These are due by Mon, Mar 02 at 11:59 pm.

NOTE: Typically, this assignment is done after each assessment labor on major drafts (usually around three times in a quarter or four to five times in a semester). Because I now use Google Drive and Google Docs, I can quickly respond to these letters in writing, tweeting students when I'm done. This means most students get at least one revision in before the first due date of the letter. Most of my responses ask students to revise or respond with more discussion, more thinking about the emerging problems they are trying to pose. My responses usually ask about their *habitus* (Where did this idea come from in your life? How do these sources help you understand this text in the way you do?) or to be more specific about the judgment of language (What did your colleagues say exactly about this sentence?). It takes one or two times of doing this assignment for most students to figure out what I'm asking them to do.

The reference to mindful breathing comes from my own contemplative practices that I incorporate into classrooms and invite students to do with me. I do not suggest a teacher use such practices unless, (1) she has a contemplative practice of her own that she feels comfortable with, and (2) that she supports such uses of meditation or mindfulness with some readings and practices in the classroom, which my classes do. If you are interested in such practices, I suggest Daniel Barbezat and Mirabi Bush's (2014) excellent book *Contemplative Practices in Higher Education: Powerful Methods to Transform Teaching and Learning*, which offers a range of contemplative practices and some theorizing of them. Much of the book can be read with students. For a good reflective discussion of how contemplative practice helps a teacher think about her teaching and the learning in her classroom, Mary Rose O'Reilley's (1998) *Radical Presence: Teaching as Contemplative Practice* is excellent, as well as beautifully written and accessible to students. Additionally, I've used excerpts from Thich Nhat Hanh's

(1991) *Peace is Every Step*, Pema Chodron's (1991) *How to Meditate* (2013), and numerous online selections and videos to help students understand mindful breathing and the research on it that shows its effectiveness in lowering stress and increasing focus and attention.

Finally, the deep reading handout referenced is an extension of the assessment and mindfulness activities done in my classrooms. It is a labor practice that helps us do problem posing. Students and I build a list of behaviors and actions that we feel create a mindful and compassionate reading practice that we can use in all of our reading labors. To help us with our thinking, my students have read excerpts from Barbezat and Bush (2014), O'Reilley (1998), Ratcliffe (2005), and Elbow (1993). All offer explicit discussions on listening mindfully, reading rhetorically, and reading to like in compassionate yet critical ways.

CPSIA information can be obtained
at www.ICGtesting.com
Printed in the USA
FSHW011648131219
64858FS